FIXED INCOME RELATIVE VALUE ANALYSIS

Since 1996, Bloomberg Press has published books for financial professionals on investing, economics, and policy affecting investors. Titles are written by leading practitioners and authorities, and have been translated into more than 20 languages.

The Bloomberg Financial Series provides both core reference knowledge and actionable information for financial professionals. The books are written by experts familiar with the work flows, challenges, and demands of investment professionals who trade the markets, manage money, and analyze investments in their capacity of growing and protecting wealth, hedging risk, and generating revenue.

For a list of available titles, please visit our web site at www.wiley.com/go/bloombergpress.

FIXED INCOME RELATIVE VALUE ANALYSIS

A Practitioner's Guide to the
Theory, Tools, and Trades

**Doug Huggins and
Christian Schaller**

WILEY | **Bloomberg**
PRESS

© 2013 John Wiley & Sons, Inc.

Registered office
John Wiley & Sons Ltd, The Atrium, Southern Gate, Chichester, West Sussex, PO19 8SQ,
United Kingdom

For details of our global editorial offices, for customer services and for information about how to apply for
permission to reuse the copyright material in this book please see our website at www.wiley.com.

Wiley publishes in a variety of print and electronic formats and by print-on-demand. Some material
included with standard print versions of this book may not be included in e-books or in print-on-demand.
If this book refers to media such as a CD or DVD that is not included in the version you purchased, you
may download this material at http://booksupport.wiley.com. For more information about Wiley
products, visit www.wiley.com.

Designations used by companies to distinguish their products are often claimed as trademarks. All brand
names and product names used in this book are trade names, service marks, trademarks or registered
trademarks of their respective owners. The publisher is not associated with any product or vendor
mentioned in this book.

Limit of Liability/Disclaimer of Warranty: While the publisher and author have used their best efforts in
preparing this book, they make no representations or warranties with respect to the accuracy or
completeness of the contents of this book and specifically disclaim any implied warranties of
merchantability or fitness for a particular purpose. It is sold on the understanding that the publisher is not
engaged in rendering professional services and neither the publisher nor the author shall be liable for
damages arising herefrom. If professional advice or other expert assistance is required, the services of
a competent professional should be sought.

Library of Congress Cataloging-in-Publication Data

Huggins, Doug, 1965–
    Fixed income relative value analysis : a practitioner's guide to the theory, tools, and trades / Doug
Huggins and Christian Schaller.
        1 online resource.
    Includes bibliographical references and index.
    Description based on print version record and CIP data provided by publisher; resource not viewed.
    ISBN 978-1-118-47720-5 (hbk) — ISBN 978-1-118-47721-2 (ebk)
    ISBN 978-1-118-47722-9 (ebk) — ISBN 978-1-118-47719-9 (ebk)
        1. Fixed-income securities.   2. Securities—Valuation.   I. Schaller, Christian, 1971–   II. Title.
HG4650
332.63'2044–dc23

                                                                                2013009914

A catalogue record for this book is available from the British Library.

ISBN 978-1-118-47719-9 (hbk) ISBN 978-1-118-47720-5 (ebk) ISBN 978-1-118-74197-9 (ebk)
ISBN 978-1-118-47722-9 (ebk) ISBN 978-1-118-47721-2 (ebk)

Set in 11/13pt AdobeGaramond by MPS Limited, Chennai, India

Printed in the UK

Contents

Relative Value: a Practitioner's Guide

I remember very clearly the beginnings of the Relative Value Group at Deutsche Bank. The year was 1995. I was one of a small group of Research and Sales professionals who had recently arrived at Deutsche Bank. We became convinced that significant opportunities existed to apply relative value concepts to fixed income instruments in a way that was highly interesting for sophisticated clients. We realized that by analyzing separately the opportunities and risks of certain fixed income products, we could help our clients achieve the performance they aimed for while mitigating credit, market and liquidity risk. Our goal was simple: to help our clients achieve the best possible risk–reward equation.

We soon realized that we could apply these principles more widely across our client base in fixed income. For example, some of our clients held clear beliefs on areas of value in the market, but were seeking new ways to invest which reflected those beliefs. These were clients who provided important liquidity to the markets in which they operated, and this provided us with another important insight: as relative value addressed irrational differences between the prices of related instruments, we saw markets become more transparent, more liquid, and more efficient. Unquestionably, the science of relative value, and the transparency it brings to relationships between the prices of different instruments, has contributed to the growth of derivatives and other financial products which reduce market risk.

These were years in which Deutsche Bank was building up a world-leading markets platform, and as a comparable new entrant in many areas, we needed to innovate to prosper. Relative value disciplines formed a core part of our intellectual capital. Relative value provided us with a way to reduce risk and spot opportunities between different instruments, both within and across asset classes, and thus to help our clients perform better for their investors. Relative value gave us a systematic way to address the fundamental question: what's expensive and what's cheap? That discipline contributed greatly as we advised clients on asset allocation in their portfolios, and gave us valuable insights about how to deploy our own resources: capital, technology and people. Already, relative value at Deutsche Bank had evolved far beyond its origins as a method of identifying pricing inefficiencies in fixed income instruments. It gave us a framework for a much wider range of portfolio and business decisions.

The financial crisis of 2008 and early 2009 was a defining period in the development of relative value analysis. Under conditions of extreme market stress and acute shortages of liquidity, we saw the 'conventional' relationships between the prices of related securities break down. Put simply: the normal rules ceased to apply. The risk of sovereign default, suddenly much more apparent, profoundly impacted the prices of government debt and the derivatives related to it. This posed a major challenge for our clients and for the sound functioning of financial markets on which the global economy depends. But this extremely difficult period also brought us fundamental insights. Our experience with Long-Term Capital Management, and the Russian and Asian crises, warned us that at times of significant market stress, the conventional 'rules' governing relationships between assets cease to function and for us, this was a clear signal to reduce our balance sheet and risk exposures. Perhaps most significantly of all: as market conditions stabilized and liquidity returned, well-funded investors were able to invest in good-quality assets at very favorable prices. Relative value analysis was able to guide us toward many opportunities for us to create value for our clients.

In retrospect, the relative value perspective was invaluable to us throughout the most difficult months of 2008 and 2009. This perspective helped us protect ourselves better during the crisis, and take advantage of opportunities faster as stability returned. For Deutsche Bank in 2009, the ability to identify pricing anomalies enabled us to spot investment opportunities for our clients right across the fixed income spectrum. Relative value brings clarity to complex products, and helps us understand market behavior. We know now how important that is. There is no doubt that a deeper understanding and use of relative value disciplines across the world's markets would have helped the financial industry navigate through the financial crisis and contribute to the stabilization of financial markets which was the first step toward global economic recovery.

It's therefore no surprise that relative value has become increasingly important in post-crisis markets. It has evolved into a way of comparing prices and valuing the different risk elements across a broad range of asset classes. It gives market participants a method for arriving at a deeper understanding of new instruments as they appear. This added visibility contributes to market transparency, which in turn gives investors confidence. This encourages liquidity across a wide range of market areas, and makes pricing more efficient – which benefits issuers and investors alike. In emerging or immature markets, relative value disciplines can contribute to a 'virtuous circle' of improved transparency, liquidity and pricing efficiency. This lays the ground for healthy and sustainable growth in a wide diversity of markets – from the funding of governments and large corporations, to the pricing of a wide range of essential commodities. In other words, relative value disciplines make a host of real-world decisions clearer and easier to make. Deep, diverse, well-functioning and well-trusted markets have never been more important for the real economy than they are today.

Relative value thinking has played a significant role in my professional life. At its outset a way to serve sophisticated clients in fixed income markets, relative value gave me a methodology for identifying investment opportunities across a wide range of asset classes and added to my understanding of how markets behave. We can turn that knowledge to the advantage of our clients, and help financial markets do their job for the wider economy. At Deutsche Bank, relative value disciplines have contributed significantly to the development of our markets platform, as we allocate resources, mitigate risks, and find new ways of helping our clients perform. In my career, I have witnessed the evolution of relative value from a specialist methodology to an essential part of the market practitioner's toolbox. This *Practitioner's Guide* is both timely and relevant.

Enjoy the book.

Henry Ritchotte,
Chief Operating Officer and member
of the management board, Deutsche Bank

CHAPTER 1

Relative Value

The Concept of Relative Value

Relative value is a quantitative analytical approach toward financial markets based on two fundamental notions of modern financial economics.

Proposition 1: If two securities have identical payoffs in every future state of the world, then they should have identical prices today.

Violation of this principle would result in the existence of an arbitrage opportunity, which is inconsistent with equilibrium in financial markets.

This proposition seems relatively straightforward now, but this wasn't always the case. In fact, Kenneth Arrow and Gérard Debreu won Nobel prizes in economics in 1972 and 1983 in part for their work establishing this result. And Myron Scholes and Robert Merton later won Nobel prizes in economics in 1997 for applying this proposition to the valuation of options. In particular, along with Fischer Black, they identified a self-financing portfolio that could dynamically replicate the payoff of an option, and they were able to determine the value of this underlying option by valuing this replicating portfolio.

Most of the financial models discussed in this book are based on the application of this proposition in various contexts.

Proposition 2: If two securities present investors with identical risks, they should offer identical expected returns.

1

This result may appear intuitive, but it's somewhat more difficult to establish than the first result. Of particular interest for our purposes is that the result can be established via the *Arbitrage Pricing Theory*, which assumes the existence of unobservable, linear factors that drive returns.

In this case, it's possible to combine securities into portfolios that expose investors to any one of the risk factors without involving exposure to any of the other risk factors. In the limit, as the number of securities in the portfolio increases, the security-specific risks can be diversified away. And in this case, any security-specific risk that offered a non-zero expected return would present investors with an arbitrage opportunity, at least in the limit, as the remaining risk factors could be immunized by creating an appropriate portfolio of tradable securities.

For our purposes, this is a powerful result, as it allows us to analyze historical data for the existence of linear factors and to construct portfolios that expose us either to these specific factors or to security-specific risks, at our discretion. In fact, *principal component analysis* (PCA) can be applied directly in this framework, and we'll rely heavily on PCA as one of the two main statistical models we discuss in this book.

The Sources of Relative Value Opportunities

From these two propositions, it's clear that the absence of arbitrage is the assumption that drives many of the models we use as relative value analysts. This should come as no surprise, since one of the main roles of a relative value analyst is to search for arbitrage opportunities.

But for some people, this state of affairs presents a bit of a paradox. *If our modeling assumptions are correct about the absence of free lunches, why do analysts and traders search so hard for them?*

This apparent paradox can be resolved with two observations. The first is the recognition that arbitrage opportunities are rare precisely because hard-working analysts invest considerable effort trying to find them. If these opportunities could never be found, or if they never generated any profits for those who found them, analysts would stop searching for them. But in this case, opportunities would reappear, and analysts would renew their search for them as reports of their existence circulated.

The second observation that helps resolve this paradox is that even seemingly riskless arbitrage opportunities carry some risk when pursued in practice. For example, one of the simpler arbitrages in fixed income markets is the relation between bond prices, repo rates, and bond futures prices. If a bond futures contract is too rich, a trader can sell the futures contract, buy the bond, and borrow the purchase price of the bond in the repo market, with the bond being used as collateral for the loan. At the expiration of the contract, the bond will be returned to the trader by his repo counterparty, and the trader can deliver the bond into the futures contract. In theory, this would allow the trader to make a riskless arbitrage profit. But in practice, there are risks to this strategy.

For example, the repo counterparty may fail to deliver the bonds to the trader promptly at the end of the repo transaction, in which case the trader may have difficulty delivering the bonds into the futures contract. Failure to deliver carries significant penalties in some cases, and the risk of incurring these penalties needs to be incorporated into the evaluation of this seemingly riskless arbitrage opportunity.

These perspectives help us reconcile the existence of arbitrage opportunities in practice with the theoretical assumptions behind the valuation models we use. But they don't explain the sources of these arbitrage or relative value opportunities, and we'll discuss a few of the more important sources here.

Demand for Immediacy

In many cases, relative value opportunities will appear when some trader experiences an unusually urgent need to transact, particularly in large size. Such a trader will transact his initial business at a price that reflects typical liquidity in the market. But if the trader then needs to transact additional trades in the same security, he may have to entice other market participants to provide the necessary liquidity by agreeing to transact at a more attractive price. For example, he may have to agree to sell at a lower price or to buy at a higher price than would be typical for that security. In so doing, this trader is signaling a demand for immediacy in trading, and he's offering a premium to other traders who can satisfy this demand.

The relative value trader searches for opportunities in which he can be paid attractive premiums for satisfying these demands for immediacy. He uses his capital to satisfy these demands, warehousing the securities until he can liquidate them at more typical prices, being careful to hedge the risks of the transactions in a cost-effective and prudent manner.

Because these markets are so competitive, the premiums paid for immediacy are often small relative to the sizes of the positions. As a result, the typical relative value fund will be run with leverage that is higher than the leverage of, say, a global macro fund. Consequently, it's important to pay attention to small details and to hedge risks carefully.

Misspecified Models

It sometimes happens that market participants overlook relevant issues when modeling security prices, and the use of misspecified models can result in attractive relative value opportunities for those who spot these errors early.

For example, until the mid-1990s, most analysts failed to incorporate the convexity bias when assessing the relative valuations of Eurodollar futures contracts and forward rate agreements. As market participants came to realize the importance of this adjustment, the relative valuations of these two instruments changed over time, resulting in attractive profits for those who identified this issue relatively early.

As another example, until the late 1990s, most academics and market participants believed vanilla swap rates exceeded the yields of default-free government bonds as a result of the credit risk of the two swap counter-parties. Due in part to our work in this area, this paradigm has been shown to be flawed. In particular, the difference over time between LIBOR and repo rates now is considered to be a more important factor in the relative valuations between swaps and government bonds.

In recent years, as credit concerns have increased for many governments, it has become increasingly important to reflect sovereign credit risk as an explicit factor in swap spread valuation models, and we discuss this issue in considerable detail in this book.

Regulatory Arbitrage

The fixed income markets are populated by market participants of many types across many different regulatory jurisdictions, and the regulatory differences between them can produce relative value opportunities for some.

For example, when thinking about the relative valuations of unsecured short-term loans and loans secured by government bonds in the repo market, traders at European banks will consider the fact that the unsecured loan will attract a greater regulatory charge under the Basel accords. On the other hand, traders working for money market funds in the US won't be subject to the Basel accords and are likely to focus instead on the relative credit risks of the two short-term deposits. The difference in regulatory treatment may result in relative valuations that leave the European bank indifferent between the two alternatives but that present a relative value opportunity for the US money market fund.

The Insights from Relative Value Analysis

In some sense, relative value analysis can be defined as the process of gaining insights into the relationships between different market instruments and the external forces driving their pricing. These insights facilitate arbitrage trading, but they also allow us more generally to develop an understanding of the market mechanisms that drive valuations and of the ways seemingly different markets are interconnected.

As a consequence, relative value analysis, which originated in arbitrage trading, has a much broader scope of applications. It can reveal the origins of certain market relations, the reasons a security is priced a certain way, and the relative value of this pricing in relation to the prices of other securities. And in the event that a security is found to be misvalued, relative value analysis suggests ways in which the mispricing can be exploited through specific trading positions. In brief, relative value analysis is a prism through which we view the machinery driving market pricing amidst a multitude of changing market prices.

As an example, consider the divergence of swap spreads for German Bunds and US Treasuries in recent quarters, which might appear inextricable without considering the effects of cross-currency basis swaps (CCBS), intra-currency basis swaps (ICBS), and credit default swaps (CDS).

In this case, CCBS spreads widened as a result of the difficulties that European banks experienced in raising USD liabilities against their USD assets. On the other hand, arbitrage between Bunds, swapped into USD, and Treasuries prevented an excessive cheapening of Bunds versus USD LIBOR. As a consequence, Bunds richened significantly against EURIBOR (see Chapter 14 for more details).

However, given the relationship between European banks and sovereigns, the difficulties of European banks were also reflected in a widening of European sovereign CDS levels. Hence, Bunds richened versus EURIBOR at the same time as German CDS levels increased.

An analyst who fails to consider these interconnected valuation relations may find the combination of richening Bunds and increasing German CDS opaque and puzzling. But a well-equipped relative value analyst can disentangle these valuation relations explicitly to identify the factors that are driving valuations in these markets. And armed with this knowledge, the analyst can apply these insights to other instruments, potentially uncovering additional relative value opportunities.

The Applications of Relative Value Analysis

Relative value analysis has a number of applications.

Trading

One of the most important applications of relative value analysis is relative value trading, in which various securities are bought and others sold with the goal of enhancing the risk-adjusted expected return of a trading book.

Identifying relatively rich and relatively cheap securities is an important skill for a relative value trader, but additional skills are required to be successful as a relative value trader. For example, rich securities can and often do become richer, while cheap securities can and often do become cheaper. A successful relative value trader needs to be able to identify some of the reasons that securities are rich or cheap in order to form realistic expectations about the likelihood of future richening or cheapening. We discuss this and other important skills throughout this book.

Hedging and Immunization

Relative value analysis is also an important consideration when hedging or otherwise immunizing positions against various risks. For example, consider a flow trader who is sold a position in ten-year (10Y) French government bonds by a customer. This trader faces a number of alternatives for hedging this risk.

He could try to sell the French bond to another client or to an interdealer broker. He could sell another French bond with a similar maturity. He could sell Bund futures contracts or German Bunds with similar maturities. He could pay fixed in a plain vanilla interest rate swap or perhaps a euro overnight index average (EONIA) swap. He could buy payer swaptions or sell receiver swaptions with various strikes. He could sell liquid supranational or agency bonds issued by entities such as the European Investment Bank. Depending on his expectations, he might even sell bonds denominated in other currencies, such as US Treasuries or UK Gilts. Or he might choose to implement a combination of these hedging strategies.

In devising a hedging strategy, a skilled trader will consider the relative valuations of the various securities that can be used as hedging instruments.

If he expects Bunds to cheapen relative to the alternatives, he may choose to sell German Bunds as a hedge. And if he believes Bund futures are likely to cheapen relative to cash Bunds, he may choose to implement this hedge via futures contracts rather than in the cash market.

By considering the relative value implications of these hedging alternatives, a skilled flow trader can enhance the risk-adjusted expected return of his book. In this way, the value of the book reflects not only the franchise value of the customer flow but also the relative value opportunities in the market and the analytical skills of the trader managing the book.

Given the increasing competitiveness of running a fixed income flow business, firms that incorporate relative value analysis as part of their business can expect to increase their marginal revenues, allowing them to generate higher profits and/or to offer liquidity to customers at more competitive rates.

Security Selection

In many respects, a long-only investment manager faces many of the same issues as the flow trader in the previous example. Just as a flow trader can expect to enhance the risk-adjusted performance of his book by incorporating relative value analysis into his hedging choices, a long-only investment manager can expect to enhance the risk-adjusted performance of his portfolio by incorporating relative value analysis into his security selection process.

For example, an investment manager who wants to increase his exposure to the 10Y sector of the EUR debt market could buy government bonds issued by France, Germany, Italy, Spain, the Netherlands, or any of the other EMU member states. Or he could buy Bund futures or receive fixed in a EURIBOR or EONIA interest rate swap. Or he might buy a US Treasury in conjunction with a cross-currency basis swap, thereby synthetically creating a US government bond denominated in euros.

An investment manager who incorporates relative value analysis as part of his investment process is likely to increase his alpha and therefore over time to outperform an otherwise similar manager with the same beta who doesn't incorporate relative value analysis.

The Craft of Relative Value Analysis

Relative value analysis is neither a science nor an art. Rather, it's a craft, with elements of both science and art. For a practitioner to complete the journey from apprentice to master craftsman, he needs to learn to use the tools of the trade, and in this book we introduce these tools along with their foundations in the mathematical science of statistics and in the social science of financial economics.

We also do our best to explain the practical benefits and potential pitfalls of applying these tools in practice. In the development of an apprentice, there is no substitute for repeated use of the tools of the trade in the presence of a master craftsman. But we make every effort in this book to convey the benefit of our experience over many years of applying these tools.

Since financial and statistical models are the tools of the trade for a relative value analyst, it's important that the analyst choose these tools carefully, with an eye toward usefulness, analytical scope, and parsimony.

Usefulness

In our view, models are neither right nor wrong. Pure mathematicians may be impressed by truth and beauty, but the craftsman is concerned with usefulness. To us, various models have varying degrees of usefulness, depending on the context in which they're applied.

As Milton Friedman reminds us in his 1966 essay "The Methodology of Positive Economics", models are appropriately judged by their implications. The usefulness of a particular model is not a function of the realism of its assumptions but rather of the quality of its predictions.

For relative value analysts, models are useful if they allow us to identify relative misvaluations between and among securities, and if they improve the quality of the predictions we make about the future richening and cheapening of these securities.

For example, we agree with critics who note that the Black–Scholes model is *wrong*, in the sense that it makes predictions about option prices that are in some ways systematically inconsistent with the prices of options as repeatedly observed in various markets. However, we've found the Black–Scholes model to be useful in many contexts, as have a large number of analysts and traders. It's important to be familiar with its problems and pitfalls, and like most tools it can do damage if used improperly. But we recommend it as a tool of the trade that is quite useful in a number of contexts.

Analytical Scope (Applicability)

For our purposes, it's also useful for a model to have a broad scope, with applicability to a wide range of situations. For example, principal component analysis (PCA) has proven to be useful in a large number of applications, including interest rates, swap spreads, implied volatilities, and the prices of equities, grains, metals, energy, and other commodities. As with any powerful model, there is a cost to implementing PCA, but the applicability of the model once it has been built means that the benefits of the implementation tend to be well worth the costs.

Other statistical models with broad applicability are those that characterize the mean-reverting properties of various financial variables. Over considerable periods of time, persistent mean reversion has been observed in quite a large number of financial variables, including interest rates, curve slopes, butterfly spreads, term premiums, and implied volatilities. And in the commodity markets, mean reversion has been found in quite a number of spreads, such as those between gold and silver, corn and wheat, crack spreads in the energy complexes, and crush spreads in the soybean complex.

The ubiquity of mean-reverting behavior in financial markets means that mean reversion models have a tremendous applicability. As a result, we consider them some of the more useful tools of a well-equipped relative value analyst, and we discuss them in some detail in this book.

Parsimony

From our perspective, it's also useful for a model to be parsimonious. As Einstein articulated in his 1933 lecture "On the Method of Theoretical Physics", "It can scarcely be denied that the supreme goal of all theory is to make irreducible basic elements as simple and as few as possible without having to surrender the adequate representation of a single datum of experience".

In our context, it's important to note the relative nature of the word "adequate". In most circumstances, there is an inevitable trade-off between the parsimony of a model and its ability to represent experience. The goal of people developing models is to improve this tradeoff in various contexts. The goal of people using models is to select those models that offer the best tradeoff between costs and benefits in specific applications. And it's in that sense that we characterize the models in this book as being useful in the context of relative value analysis.

Summary of Contents

Relative value analysis models can be divided into two categories: statistical and financial. Statistical models require no specific knowledge about the instrument that is being modeled and are hence universally applicable. For example, a mean reversion model only needs to know the time series, not whether the time series represents yields, swap spreads, or volatilities, nor what drives that time series.

Financial models, on the other hand, give insight into the specific driving forces and relationships of a particular instrument (and are therefore different for each instrument). For example, the specific knowledge that swap spreads are a function of the cost of equity of LIBOR panel banks can explain why their time series exhibits a certain statistical behavior.

While we present the models in two separate categories, comprehensive relative value analysis combines both. The successful relative value trader described above might first use statistical models to identify which instruments are rich and cheap relative to each other, and then apply financial models in order to gain insights into the reasons for that richness and cheapness, on which basis he can assess the likelihood for the richness and cheapness to correct. If he sees a sufficient probability for the spread position to be an attractive trade, he can then use statistical models again to calculate, among others, the appropriate hedge ratios and the expected holding horizon.

Statistical Models

The two types of statistical models presented here are designed to capture two of the most useful statistical properties frequently observed in the fixed income markets: the tendency for many spreads to revert toward their longer-run means over time and the tendency for many variables to increase and decrease together. Chapter 2 and Chapter 3 are largely independent and therefore do not need to be read sequentially. However, Chapter 3 does refer to the application of mean-reverting models to the estimated factors and to specific residuals, so a reader with no preference would do well to read the chapter on mean reversion first.

Mean Reversion

Many financial spreads exhibit a persistent tendency to revert toward their means, providing a potential source of return predictability. In this chapter, we discuss stochastic processes that are useful in modeling this mean reversion, and we present ways in which data can be used to estimate the parameters of these processes. Once the parameters have been estimated, we can calculate the half-life of a process and make probabilistic statements about the value of the spread at various points in the future.

We also present the concept of a first passage time and show ways to calculate probabilities for first passage times. Once we have these first passage time densities, we can provide probabilistic answers to some of the more perplexing questions that are typical on a trading desk. *Over what time period should I expect this trade to perform? What sort of return target is reasonable over the next month? How likely am I to hit a stop-loss if placed at this level?* First passage time densities can provide probabilistic answers to these questions, and we discuss practical ways in which they can be implemented in a trading environment.

Principal Component Analysis

Many large data sets in finance appear to be driven by a smaller number of factors, and the ability to reduce the dimensionality of these data sets by projecting them onto these factors is a very useful method for analyzing and identifying relative value opportunities. In this chapter we discuss PCA in some detail. We address not only the mathematics of the approach but also the practicalities involved in applying PCA in real-world applications, including trading the underlying factors and hedging the factor risk when trading specific securities.

Financial Models

The financial models in this section are relative value models in that they value one security in relation to one or more other securities. To some extent, the chapters build on one another, with the material for one chapter serving as a starting point for the material in another chapter. For example, the chapter comparing risky bonds denominated in multiple currencies synthesizes the material on OIS–repo spreads, ICBS, cross-currency basis swaps, swap spreads, and CDS. Not every chapter needs to be read sequentially, but readers should be alert to the dependencies that exist between the various chapters, which we do our best to highlight in the subsequent previews.

Some Comments on Yield, Duration, and Convexity

A working knowledge of bond and interest rate mathematics is a prerequisite for this book. But we believe some of the basic bond math taught to practitioners is simply wrong, or at the very least misleading. For example, the *basis point value* of a bond is fundamentally a different concept from the *value of a basis point* for a swap, yet many practitioners are unclear about this difference. As another example, the Macaulay duration of a bond is often referred to as the weighted average time to maturity of a bond, but this is only true when all the zero-coupon bonds that constitute the coupon-paying bond have the same yield, a condition that is almost never observed in practice. We also discuss the frequent misuse of bond convexity and suggest a more practical interpretation of the concept.

Bond Futures Contracts

A simple no-arbitrage relation applies to the relative values of a cash bond, the repo rate for the bond, and the forward price of the bond. But government bond futures contracts typically contain embedded delivery options, which complicate the analysis. We present a multi-factor model for valuing the embedded delivery option, which can be implemented in a spreadsheet using basic stochastic simulation.

LIBOR, OIS Rates, and Repo Rates

Overnight index swaps (OIS) are based on unsecured overnight lending rates, whereas repo transactions are secured with collateral. In addition to the difference in credit risks, the two transactions will be subject to different treatment with regard to regulatory capital. We present a simple model for OIS rates that incorporates repo rates, the default probability, the presumed recovery rate, the risk-weighting of the transaction, the amount of regulatory capital required for the transaction, and the cost of the regulatory capital.

Intra-currency Basis Swaps

For this purpose, an ICBS is one in which the legs of the swap reference floating rates are in the same currency but with different maturities. For example, one party might agree to pay three-month EURIBOR for five years in exchange for receiving six-month EURIBOR less a spread for five years. We present a simple model for valuing these swaps based on the concepts presented in the OIS–repo model of the preceding section.

Theoretical Determinants of Swap Spreads

Up until the mid-1990s, it was widely believed that swap rates tended to be greater than government bond yields because of the credit risk of the two swap counterparties. Now, swap spreads are seen to be a function of the spreads between the LIBOR and repo rates over the life of the bond being swapped. We present this model in detail, incorporating the results of the OIS–repo model and the ICBS model of the preceding sections.

Swap Spreads from an Empirical Perspective

While it's critical to consider the theoretical determinants of swap spreads, it's also important to consider swap spreads from an empirical perspective. In particular, we examine the crucial link between swap spreads and LIBOR–repo spreads and find considerable empirical support for our conceptual framework. We also consider the role of credit quality in the valuation of sovereign debt relative to swaps in the aftermath of the subprime and European debt crises of recent years.

Swap Spreads as Relative Value Indicators for Government Bonds

Swap spreads often have been used to assess the relative valuations between different bonds along an issuer's yield curve. We discuss the different ways this can be done and chronicle the numerous pitfalls that accompany these approaches. We conclude that none of these approaches is particularly good for assessing relative valuations among bonds, and we suggest using fitted bond curves as an alternative approach.

Fitted Bond Curves

There are many functional forms that are candidates for fitting yield curves, discount curves, and forward curves. In our experience, the particular functional form chosen is less important than the careful selection of the bonds used to fit the curve and the weighting methods used in the calibrations. In this chapter, we use a basic but widely used functional form to illustrate the important considerations that should apply when fitting bond curves. We then discuss the way in which the results can be used to identify relatively rich and cheap bonds within particular sectors.

A Brief Comment on Interpolated Swap Spreads

The most popular structure for trading bonds against swaps is the interpolated swap spread, with the end date of the swap set equal to the maturity date of the bond. While this structure has advantages relative to alternative structures, it can subject a trader to curve steepening or flattening positions, an issue we discuss in the context of an example.

Cross-Currency Basis Swaps

For our purposes, a CCBS is one in which the two legs are floating rates denominated in different currencies. For example, one party might agree to pay three-month EURIBOR for five years in exchange for receiving three-month USD LIBOR plus a spread for five years. If the tenor of the swap is less than one year, we typically refer to this as an FX swap, and there are no intermediate interest payments. Because the counterparties exchange principal at the beginning and end of the swap, these swaps have been in considerable demand in recent years. We discuss the valuation issues in this chapter.

Relative Values of Bonds Denominated in Different Currencies

A fundamental proposition of international financial economics is that in open and integrated capital markets securities should have the same risk-adjusted expected real return regardless of the currency of denomination. One implication of this is that two otherwise identical bonds, denominated in different currencies, should have identical yields once one is combined with the relevant interest rate swap and relevant basis swaps. We apply this notion in the context of global asset selection, by incorporating CCBS in the techniques for fitting bond curves.

Credit Default Swaps

The time has long since passed that we could assume the existence of default-free sovereign debt. CDS can play a role in assessing and adjusting for these credit implications, and in this chapter we review the salient features of these instruments.

USD Asset Swap Spreads versus Credit Default Swaps

The swap spread model developed in the preceding section assumed the sovereign bond had no default risk. That assumption has become increasingly less tenable in the current environment, and we discuss ways in which CDS can be used to reflect the default risk of specific issuers.

Options

We address the analysis and trading of options in a relative value context by discussing three broad categories of option trades. In the first, the trader simply buys or sells an option with a view that the underlying will finish in-the-money or out-of-the-money, with no dynamic trading. In the second, the trader attempts to capitalize on the difference between the implied volatility of the option and the actual volatility that the trader anticipates for the underlying instrument, by trading the option against a dynamic position in the underlying. In the third, the trader positions for a change in the implied volatility of the option, irrespective of the actual volatility of the underlying instrument.

Relative Value in a Broader Perspective

We conclude our sometimes rather technical description of relative value analysis by taking a broader perspective on its macroeconomic functions. At a time when professionals in the financial services industry increasingly need to justify their role in society, we present a few thoughts about the benefits of arbitrage for society.

Throughout the book, we offer pieces of general advice – words of wisdom that we've gleaned over time. We've been mentored by some of the best in the business over the years, with particular thanks to our managers and colleagues in Anshu Jain's Global Relative Value Group at Deutsche Morgan Grenfell, and especially to David Knott, Pam Moulton, and Henry Ritchotte. They were good enough to impart their wisdom to us, and we're happy to pass along this treasure trove of useful advice, hopefully with a few additional pearls of insight and experience that we've been able to add over the years.[1]

Please visit the website accompanying this book to gain access to additional material www.wiley.com/go/fixedincome

---

[1] When reviewing this book, Christian Carrillo, Martin Hohensee, Antti Ilmanen and Kaare Simonsen have provided valuable feedback, enhancing our product.

PART I

Statistical Models

CHAPTER 2

Mean Reversion

What Is Mean Reversion and How Does It Help Us?

Mean reversion is one of the most fundamental concepts underpinning relative value analysis. But while mean reversion is widely understood at an intuitive level, surprisingly few analysts are familiar with the specific tools available for characterizing mean-reverting processes.

In this chapter, we discuss some of the key characteristics of mean-reverting processes and the mean reversion tools that can be used to identify attractive trading opportunities. In particular, we address:

- model selection;
- model estimation;
- calculating conditional expectations and probabilities;
- calculating ex ante risk-adjusted returns, particularly Sharpe ratios;
- calculating first passage times, also known as stopping times.

For each concept, we start with a verbal and intuitive description of the concept, followed by a mathematical definition of the concept, and finish with an example application of the concept to market data.

A variable is said to exhibit mean reversion if it shows a tendency to return to its long-term average over time. Mathematicians will object that this definition is simply an exercise in replacing the words "exhibit", "mean", and "reversion" with the synonyms "shows", "long-term average", and "return". To address such objections, we'll provide a more mathematical definition shortly. But first we'll attempt to establish some further intuition about mean-reverting processes. To some extent, Justice Stewart's famous maxim on pornography, "I know it when I see it", applies to mean reversion.

With that in mind, let's take a look at some processes that exhibit mean reversion and a few that don't.

Figure 2.1 and Figure 2.2 show two simulated time series. Both have an initial value of zero, and both have identical volatilities. But one is constructed to be a simple random walk, with zero drift, while the other is

FIGURE 2.1 Simulated random walk.

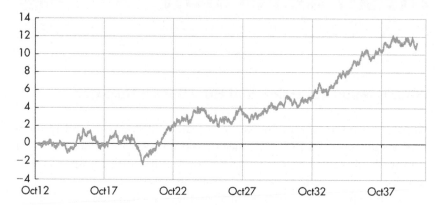

Source: Authors.

FIGURE 2.2 Simulated mean-reverting process.

Source: Authors.

constructed to have a tendency to return toward its long-run mean, constructed to be zero in this example. In fact, the two series were constructed with identical normal random variates. In the case of the random walk, the mean of each observation was the value of the previous observation, so that the process was a martingale. In the case of the mean-reverting process, the mean of each observation was set to reflect the tendency for the process to return to the mean. At this point, we'd hope most readers would identify Figure 2.2 as the one with the mean-reverting variable. If we observe both figures closely, we can see that the mean-reverting process is in some sense a transformation of the random walk in Figure 2.1.

The speed with which a variable tends to revert toward its mean can vary. For example, Figure 2.3 and Figure 2.4 show time series that were simulated using the same random normal variates that generated the mean-reverting variable in Figure 2.2 but with an important difference. The variable in Figure 2.3 was constructed to have a faster speed of mean reversion than the variable in Figure 2.2, while the variable in Figure 2.4 was constructed to have a still faster speed of mean reversion.

While it's well and good to consider variables simulated via known equations by a computer, traders and analysts have to make judgments about real-world data, which are almost always messier in some respects than simulated data. So it's also useful to consider a few real-world examples.

FIGURE 2.3 Simulated mean-reverting process: Faster mean reversion.

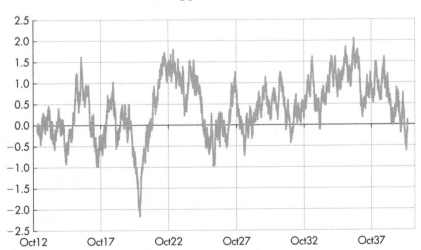

Source: Authors.

FIGURE 2.4 Simulated mean-reverting process: Even faster mean reversion.

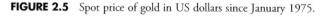

Source: Authors.

FIGURE 2.5 Spot price of gold in US dollars since January 1975.

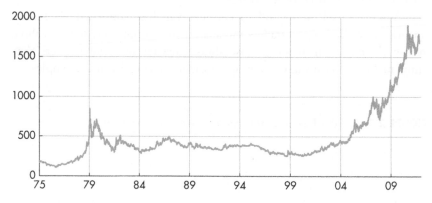

Source: Bloomberg.

Figure 2.5 shows the spot price of gold in US dollars since January 1975. In our view, the strong upward drift exhibited in this series makes it a poor candidate to be modeled by a mean-reverting process.

Figure 2.6 shows the realized volatility of the ten-year (10Y) US Treasury yield since January 1962. Given that this series has repeatedly returned to a long-run mean in the past, it appears to be a relatively good candidate for modeling with a mean-reverting process.

As another example, Figure 2.7 shows the 2Y/5Y/10Y butterfly spread along the USD swap curve since 1998. Given the number of times during the

FIGURE 2.6 Realized volatility of 10Y US Treasury bond yield (bp/year).

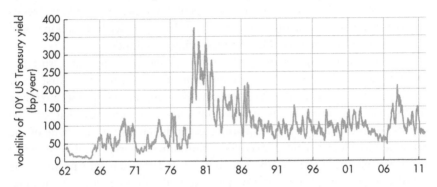

Source: Bloomberg.

FIGURE 2.7 2/5/10 butterfly spread along USD swap curve since 1988.

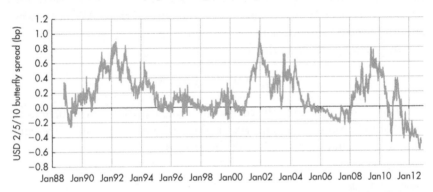

Source: Bloomberg.

sample that this spread returns to its long-run mean, we consider it another good candidate for modeling with a mean-reverting process.

Mathematical Definitions

Having provided verbal and graphical intuition regarding mean reversion, it's time to attempt to provide a few useful mathematical definitions.

Stochastic Differential Equation

First, we'll provide a brief definition of a *stochastic differential equation* (SDE). In practice, this term is fairly simple to define, as most of the definition is contained within the name. In other words, it's an equation that characterizes the random behavior of a variable over an infinitesimal period of time. As a result, it gives us the data-generating mechanism for the variable. For example, the equation would allow us to simulate the variable over time using a computer.

For example, $dx_t = k(\mu - x_t)dt + \sigma dW_t$ is the SDE for an Ornstein–Uhlenbeck (OU) process, the continuous-time limit of a first-order autoregressive process. The OU process is a popular SDE for modeling mean-reverting variables, as it has moments and densities that can be expressed analytically. In this equation, dx_t is the change in the value of the random variable x at time t, over the infinitesimal interval dt. The speed of mean reversion is given by the parameter k and the long-run mean of the variable is given by μ. The instantaneous volatility of the variable is given by σ, and the term dW_t is the change in the value of W_t over the instantaneous time interval dt. In fact, W_t is ultimately the source of randomness that drives the process in this equation. In particular, W_t is a pure random walk, often referred to as Gaussian white noise. W_t is also referred to as a Wiener process, after the American mathematician Norbert Wiener.

In general, SDEs take the form

$$dx_t = f(x_t)dt + g(x_t)dW_t$$

The term $f(x_t)$ is the drift coefficient of the equation, and it defines the mean of the process. The term $g(x_t)$ is the diffusion coefficient of the equation, and it defines the volatility of the process.

Conditional Density

Next, we'll define the *conditional density* of a process, also referred to as a *transition density*. In particular, the conditional density gives us the probability density for the future value of a random variable conditional on knowing some other information about the variable. In the case of a time series process, the conditioning information is usually some earlier value of the variable. For example, in the case of the OU process, the transition density of $x_{t+\tau}$ for $\tau > 0$ is a normal density with mean given by $\mu + (x_t - \mu)e^{-k\tau}$ and with a variance given by $\frac{\sigma^2[1 - e^{-2k\tau}]}{2k}$.

Unconditional Density

The unconditional density of a process is the probability density for the future value of a random variable without being able to condition the density on any additional information. You could think of the unconditional density as the histogram that would result from simulating the process over an infinitely long period. More precisely, it's the limit of the conditional density $p(x_{t+\tau})$ as τ goes to infinity. So in the case of the OU process, the unconditional density is a normal density with mean given by μ and with variance given by $\frac{\sigma^2}{2k}$.

Stationary Densities and Mean-Reverting Processes

In some cases, a variable will have a conditional density, but it won't have an unconditional density. In other words, the limit of the conditional density $p(x_t)$ won't converge to a limiting density.

A simple example of this would be a random walk with drift, given by the SDE $dx_t = \rho dt + \sigma dW_t$. The transition density or unconditional density for this process is normal with mean $x_t + \rho\tau$ and variance given by $\sigma^2\tau$. In this case, neither the mean nor the variance has a limit as $\tau \to \infty$, and the limit of the conditional density doesn't exist.

Even in the case of a random walk with no drift, given by the SDE $dx_t = \sigma dW_t$, there is no unconditional density. In this case, the mean for all future transition densities is simply the current value of the variable x_t, but since there is no limit to the variance of the process, there is no limit to the conditional density, and the unconditional density doesn't exist.

However, in many cases the limit of the conditional density will exist, and the random variable is said to be mean reverting. We also say that stationary density exists and that the process is stationary.

Return Predictability and Alpha

Having provided some intuition and some mathematical definitions of mean-reverting processes, it's helpful to take a step back and consider the usefulness of mean-reverting models for investors and traders.

Return predictability is a necessary, though not sufficient, condition for generating alpha, defined here as an atypically high, risk-adjusted return. If we identify a financial variable that exhibits return predictability, then either the risks of that variable are predictable or the risk-adjusted returns are predictable.

Mean reversion is a form of return predictability. If a financial variable exhibits mean reversion, then we can use that information to improve our predictions for the future value of the variable. In our view, more often than not, mean reversion in a financial variable is an indication that risk-adjusted returns of the variable are predictable. Of course, in some cases, some or all of the mean reversion in a variable will be the result of risks that exhibit mean reversion rather than the result of mean reversion in the risk-adjusted returns. But in our view, the more typical result is that the risk-adjusted returns are predictable. In this case, mean reversion can be used to generate alpha for traders and investors.

Diagnostics for Model Selection

The key for modeling any mean reversion in the variable x is to select a functional form for the drift coefficient, $f(x)$, that is useful in depicting the tendency of x to decline toward its long-run mean when it's above the mean and to increase toward its long-run mean when it's below the mean. So at a minimum, we need a function $f(x)$ that satisfies three conditions:

- The value of $f(x)$ is negative when x is above the long-run mean.
- The value of $f(x)$ is positive when x is below the long-run mean.
- The value of $f(x)$ is zero when x is equal to the long-run mean.

Of course, one simple function that satisfies these properties is a line, in which $f(x)$ could be parameterized as $f(x) = k(\mu - x)$. In this case, μ is the long-run mean of the process and k is the strength with which the variable x is "pulled" toward the long-run mean. An equivalent parameterization of $f(x)$ is $f(x) = a + bx$, in which case $a = k\mu$, and $b = k$.

As it happens, the simplicity of this linear parameterization simplifies the estimation of parameters from historical data, as the likelihood function will often have a closed-form representation in this case, depending on the specification of the diffusion coefficient, $g(x)$. The linear specification for $f(x)$ also simplifies the calculation of transition densities and first passage time densities for x.

But of course a line is not the only function that could be used to represent the mean-reverting tendencies of x, and we may be willing to sacrifice some simplicity in exchange for a functional form for the drift coefficient that is more useful in capturing the actual mean-reverting tendencies exhibited in the data.

For example, a more flexible functional form that has been used in a variety of applications is $f(x) = a + bx + cx^2 + dx^3$, a third-order polynomial in x. In particular, this nonlinear specification allows for the variable x to exhibit increasingly strong mean reversion as it moves further away from the long-run mean. A similar function form that has been used successfully in a variety of applications is $f(x) = \frac{a}{x} + bx + cx^2 + dx^3$, as the $\frac{1}{x}$ term allows for the drift coefficient to become increasingly strong as x approaches zero, allowing zero to act as a reflecting barrier for the process. Examples of these three functional forms appear in Figure 2.8.

In this case, we want to restrict the value of d to be non-positive, to avoid the drift coefficient going to infinity as x increases, in which case x would be an explosive process rather than a stationary, mean-reverting process. For a similar reason, we'd like to restrict the value of a to be non-negative.

Strictly speaking, the drift coefficient, $f(x)$ also needs to satisfy other, rather technical, mathematical conditions in order to ensure that this SDE has a solution. In practice, we tend to assume that these conditions are satisfied (perhaps more often than we should), as the processes typically studied in financial applications tend to be well behaved.

At this point, we should stress that the drift coefficient, $f(x)$, can assume an unlimited variety of functional forms, including nonparametric forms, and the particular form used in practical applications must be specified by the analyst.

If the analyst is open to sacrificing some analytical tractability in an attempt to more usefully model certain aspects of the process, he would

FIGURE 2.8 Examples of drift coefficients.

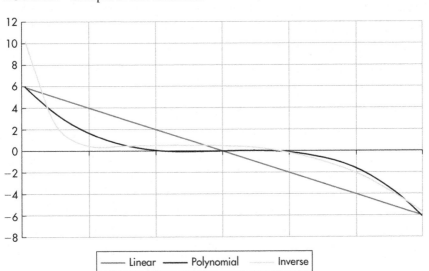

Source: Authors.

benefit from some diagnostic guidance as to the functional forms for $f(x)$ that are likely to be most useful.

To our knowledge, the most useful diagnostic is one suggested by Richard Stanton in a Stanford research paper in the mid-1990s. The basic idea behind this diagnostic tool is to create a nonparametric, empirical approximation of the drift coefficient using historical data. An illustration of this is provided in Figure 2.9.

Each point in the graph represents the estimated strength of mean reversion when the variable assumes values in the neighborhood of that point. Perhaps the most expedient way to explain this concept is to start by listing the steps involved in creating the graph.

(1) Group the observations into "buckets", with the number of buckets determined by the analyst.
(2) For each bucket, calculate the average subsequent change of each observation in the bucket.
(3) For each bucket, plot a point with a horizontal coordinate equal to the midpoint of the observations in the bucket and with a vertical coordinate equal to the average subsequent change of the observations in the bucket.

For example, let's imagine that we have 1,000 observations in our data series and that we want to group these into 20 buckets of equal width, with equally

FIGURE 2.9   Diagnostic tool for drift coefficient.

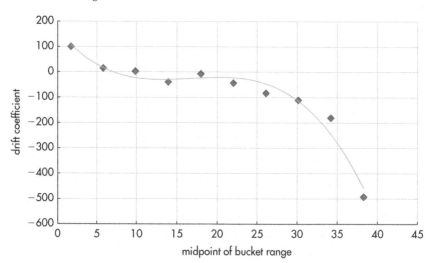

Source: Authors.

spaced midpoints. We can separate the range (high–low) into 20 segments of equal length and then place each of our 1,000 observations into one of these 20 buckets. Some buckets may have many observations, while some buckets may have relatively few observations. As a general rule, if a bucket has very few observations, it would be wise to decrease the number of buckets, which should increase the number of observations in most buckets, in an attempt to reduce the estimation error of the average change within that bucket.

Once each observation has been placed into a bucket, calculate the subsequent change of each observation in the bucket. For example, if the 400th data point in the series has been placed into the sixth bucket, the subsequent change associated with the 400th observation would be the 401st observation less the 400th observation, even if the 401st observation is itself within a different bucket.

In other words, we're calculating the average change of observations whose starting values are within the same bucket, and then we repeat the calculation for each of the remaining buckets.

In this example, once we're done with the calculations in each of these 20 buckets, we'll have 20 points to plot on our diagnostic graph. The horizontal coordinate of each point will be the midpoint of the bucket, and the vertical coordinate of each point will be the average change of the observations in that bucket.

As an illustration, let's specify a nonlinear functional form for $f(x)$ and a constant value for the drift coefficient, $g(x)$. In particular, let's use the functional form illustrated in Figure 2.10.

Then let's simulate some data from the SDE we've specified and create our diagnostic graph using the method described above.

Figure 2.11 shows the resulting diagnostic graph. We see that this diagnostic graph is useful in that it helps identify a specification for $f(x)$ consistent with the mean reversion actually exhibited by the data.

The intention when creating this diagnostic graph is to identify the properties that are likely to be useful to the analyst trying to model the mean-reverting tendency in the data. The most straightforward way to do this is to select a functional form for $f(x)$ that has the ability to match the general shape traced out by the points in this diagnostic graph.

Of course, the same diagnostic graph can be created for the diffusion coefficient, $g(x)$. In this case, the standard deviation of the subsequent changes in each bucket would replace the average of the subsequent changes. The analyst then can specify a functional representation for $g(x)$ that most usefully captures the key properties of the diffusion coefficient, $g(x)$, as a function of x.

FIGURE 2.10   Target drift coefficient.

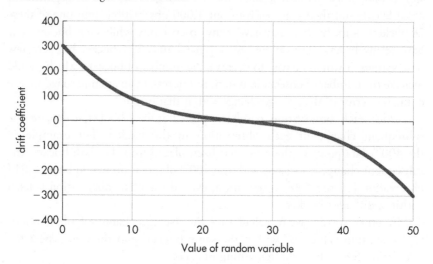

Source: Authors.

FIGURE 2.11   Diagnostic graph for drift coefficient.

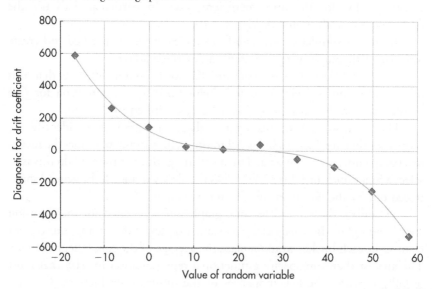

Source: Authors.

As with the drift coefficient, $f(x)$, there are some technical conditions that must be satisfied for $g(x)$ in order to ensure that the SDE has a solution. In practice, we simply tend to make sure that $g(x)$ has some commonsense restrictions. For example, we'd like to restrict $g(x)$ to assuming only positive values, as a negative value for the diffusion coefficient would be equivalent to allowing time to run backward for our process.

Model Estimation

Once functional forms have been specified for the drift coefficient, $f(x)$, and for the diffusion coefficient, $g(x)$, the analyst must specify precise values for the functions $f(x)$ and $g(x)$ within the class of functions having the specified forms. For example, if the drift and diffusion coefficients have been specified with parametric representations, the analyst must choose specific, numeric values for these parameters. If nonparametric representations have been specified, the analyst still must assign specific values to the functions $f(x)$ and $g(x)$ over the relevant domain.

Most analysts will choose to specify numeric values for $f(x)$ and $g(x)$ to "most closely match" a set of historical data. For example, we can specify $f(x)$ and $g(x)$ so that the resulting SDE is the one from which the data are most likely to have been generated. This is the principle behind maximum likelihood estimation.

However, some analysts may prefer a different approach to specifying the drift and diffusion coefficients. For example, some analysts may want to specify $f(x)$ and $g(x)$ so that the moments of the resulting transition densities most closely match the empirical moments of the historical data. For example, some analysts will specify drift and diffusion coefficients so that their SDE has a conditional mean and a conditional variance that matches the conditional means and variances of their historical data. More generally, we could match the theoretical and empirical expected values for a variety of functions of the data. Indeed, this is the general approach behind the method of moments. In some cases, using the method of moments will produce results that are precisely identical to the results obtained via maximum likelihood, though in general this need not be the case.

In some cases, an analyst may prefer to specify part or all of the SDE so that the theoretical moments of the process match some other data. For example, when the variable we're modeling is the price of a security that serves as the underlying instrument for one or more derivative securities, the analyst may wish to specify the SDE so that the theoretical volatility of the process following the SDE is the same as the volatility implied by the prices of the derivative securities.

The important point to note is that different criteria can be used when specifying precise, numeric values for the drift coefficient, $f(x)$, and the diffusion coefficient, $g(x)$. The particular criteria used in any given application should be chosen in accordance with the goal of the analysis.

In some cases, an analyst may wish to conduct the analysis twice using different criteria in each instance, to see whether the results of the analysis are robust to the choice of criteria. For example, if the ex ante Sharpe ratios of a trade are very different depending on whether the SDE is specified via maximum likelihood estimation or by matching the implied volatilities in the options markets, this difference is likely to be useful information for the analyst.

If an analyst elects to specify $f(x)$ and $g(x)$ via estimation using historical data, he needs to keep in mind that some estimation approaches can be problematic, conceptually and practically. For example, for some functional specifications of $f(x)$ and $g(x)$ (e.g. $f(x)$ is a line and $g(x)$ is a constant), the transition densities that comprise the likelihood function will have closed-form expressions. But for general choices of $f(x)$ and $g(x)$, there will be no closed-form representations of the likelihood function. In theory, the analyst could proceed in this case by calculating the likelihood function using numerical methods, such as simulations or by solving the partial differential equations for each transition density numerically, using finite difference grids. In practice, such methods are so numerically cumbersome as to be intractable (or at least impractical).

This problem also affects the method of moments in cases for which there are no closed-form representations of the moments of the process.

When no closed-form expressions exist for the likelihood function, analysts sometimes approximate the likelihood functions. When the likelihood function is approximated, we refer to the approach as pseudo-maximum likelihood estimation (PMLE) or quasi-maximum likelihood estimation (QMLE).

In the case of PMLE, the approximations are based on the fact that the transition densities for the process are increasingly well approximated by normal densities when the time period between observations decreases. In other words, for small time intervals, the transition densities appear "locally normal".

One problem with PMLE is that the estimators obtained by maximizing the pseudo likelihood function are generally not consistent, meaning the estimate can't be guaranteed to converge to the true parameter value as more data become available. In addition, we typically don't know the distribution of the estimator, even asymptotically, complicating the process of making inferences and testing hypotheses from the data.

At times, the lack of consistency and asymptotic normality will be an acceptable price to pay in order to work with an estimation procedure that is tractable in practice. In particular, this will be the case when the drift and diffusion are relatively "smooth" and particularly when the time between successive observations is small. Note that both of these conditions increase the extent to which the transition densities appear "locally normal".

In our experience working with a large variety of financial variables over many years, the results obtained by using PMLE with daily data are virtually indistinguishable from the results one gets from using the exact likelihood function. In other words, the cost of using PMLE rather than exact MLE tends to be small. Given that PMLE is much more tractable than most other methods in these cases, we recommend without any hesitation using PMLE when dealing with daily data.

While the scope of this book doesn't include the basics of maximum likelihood estimation (which we assume most analysts know), we can provide a sketch of the process.

Typically, a multivariate, nonlinear, numerical optimizer will choose parameter values so as to maximize the likelihood function, which is a function of both the historical data and the parameter values. The likelihood function is the product of the transition densities governing all the observations (i.e. the density of each observation conditional on the preceding observation). Clearly, each transition density is a function of two adjacent observations and of the historical data. From a purely computational perspective, working with the sum of functions often is easier than working with the product of functions. (For example, a product of many functions all of which are less than one may result in a value that is small relative to the precision of the machine performing the calculations.)

As it happens, the logarithm of a function achieves its maximum at the same point as the original function. And since the log of a product of functions is equivalent to the sum of the logarithms of the individual functions, this log likelihood function typically is very straightforward to calculate. As a result, it's often easier to maximize the logarithm of the likelihood function.

Once the log of the likelihood function has been specified, the analyst finds the set of parameter values that maximizes the value of this function, subject, possibly, to any constraints imposed by the analyst.

There are a variety of numerical algorithms for performing this nonlinear, numerical (possibly constrained) optimization. We won't discuss different algorithms in this book, except to note that gradient methods of one sort or another are almost always preferred by experienced analysts, as they tend to find local optima fairly quickly.

It's useful to note that these optima may be local rather than global, so it's good practice to start the optimization algorithm from a variety of starting points, to see whether the optimum obtained is robust to the choice of starting point. In our experience, most likelihood functions appear to be fairly well behaved, in the sense that we observe robust convergence to the global optimum. But this isn't always the case, and it's usually worth testing this proposition informally, to enhance our confidence in the results.

Once the drift and diffusion functions have been estimated, it's typically useful to plot the estimates, for a couple of reasons. First, plotting the coefficients can sometimes reveal nonsensical results, such as a drift coefficient that is negative over a portion of its range. Second, our intuition about the behavior of a financial variable will be a function of the overall drift and diffusion functions rather than a particular parameter that appears in the drift or diffusion coefficient. Unless you're a savant, you're likely to gain intuition via graphical consideration of the coefficients that you wouldn't obtain by simple inspection of the parameter values.

In the theory of estimation, hypothesis testing is often an important topic. However, it's beyond the scope of this book. For our purposes, we'll simply mention that it's useful to have a sense for precision of our estimates of the drift and diffusion coefficients. As is often the case, a larger amount of data allows us to estimate the coefficients with greater precision than we can with a smaller amount of data. When it's important to gain some qualitative sense for the precision of our estimate, simulation often can be a useful exercise, for two reasons. First, in many cases, the asymptotic distributions of the estimators aren't known. And second, even when we know the asymptotic distribution of an estimator, we don't know whether our particular data set is large enough for the asymptotic results to be relevant.

To simulate the distributions of the drift and diffusion coefficients, under the hypothesis that these coefficients have known values, we can simulate the process so as to generate a simulated sample equal in size to our actual sample. Then we can estimate the drift and diffusion coefficients using the simulated sample as our historical observations. If we repeat this procedure, say, 10,000 times, we'll obtain 10,000 individual estimates of the drift and diffusion coefficients, which we could use to quantify the estimation error of our estimators or for the purpose of making inferences and/or testing hypotheses, under the hypotheses that the data were generated from the SDE used to generate our simulated data.

As it happens, this approach to quantifying estimator error, making inferences, and/or testing hypotheses tends to produce better results than relying upon the asymptotic results in cases where they're known, since in this case we don't rely on the assumption that our data are of sufficient length for the results to approach an asymptotic limit.

Calculating Conditional Expectations and Probability Densities

In the previous section, on estimation, we discussed the notion that transition densities tend to appear locally normal as the time between successive observations decreases, even for rather general diffusion processes. And we used this result to motivate our discussion of PMLE as an approach toward estimation of the drift coefficient, $f(x)$, and the diffusion coefficient, $g(x)$. But when we're assessing the merits of a trade over a horizon of more than, say, one week, we can rely less on the local normality of our transition densities. In these cases, we need to be able to calculate transition densities and their properties using other approaches.

As we mentioned previously, it is possible to solve for transition densities by solving the underlying partial differential equations that they must satisfy. One approach to doing this is to use finite difference grids. While this approach is straightforward at a conceptual level, it tends to be cumbersome in practice.

A more useful approach is to compute the transition densities and their moments numerically via stochastic simulations. The basic idea is simple. For any SDE, we simply simulate paths between the desired starting time and starting point until the desired ending time. By simulating more paths, we can compute these densities and their moments with as much accuracy as we'd like.

If we'd like to know the mean of a transition density, we can simulate sample paths and calculate the sample average of the terminal values. If we'd like to know the standard deviation of a transition density, we can simulate sample paths and calculate the sample standard deviation of the terminal values.

Similarly, if we'd like to consider the transition density in its entirety, we can simulate sample paths and produce a histogram of the resulting terminal values. An example of this is given in Figure 2.12.

One way to increase the smoothness of the depicted transition density is to simulate an increasing number of sample paths. However, another way is to impose some smoothness conditions on the results directly. For example,

FIGURE 2.12 Histogram of simulated values.

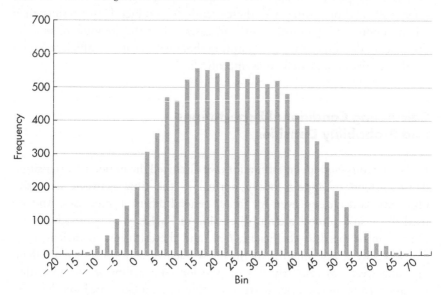

Source: Authors.

we can produce a smooth, continuous, and differentiable function representing a transition density nonparametrically by applying a kernel density to the data.

For example, one form of kernel density is the Gaussian kernel density, which uses the Gaussian function (i.e. a normal density) as its kernel. The functional form of the Gaussian kernel density, Q, is given by:

$$Q(x; h) = \sum_{i=1}^{N} K_i(x; h)$$

$$K_i(x; h) = \frac{1}{h\sqrt{2\pi}} e^{\frac{-(x-y_i)^2}{2h^2}}$$

where x is the argument of the kernel density, Q; K is our Gaussian kernel; N is the number of data points, y_i, used to estimate the nonparametric density; and h is the bandwidth parameter, which determines the smoothness of the Gaussian kernel density.

An analogy to a histogram might be helpful. Recall that a histogram sums the number of observations that fall into a particular bin or bucket. If an observation falls into a bucket, it increases the frequency of that bucket by one, and it doesn't change the frequency of any other buckets.

In contrast, when evaluating the kernel density for any particular argument, every data point makes some contribution to the value of the kernel density evaluated at that argument. If a data point is close to the argument, it makes a relatively large contribution, and if the data point is far from the argument, it makes a relatively small contribution.

The relative sizes of the contributions of each data point are determined in part by the bandwidth parameter, h, which acts like the standard deviation of the Gaussian kernel. When h is small, the standard deviation of each Gaussian kernel is small. In that case, data points that are close to the argument make particularly large contributions to the Gaussian kernel, and data points that are far from the argument make particularly small contributions to the Gaussian kernel, since the standard deviation causes the Gaussian density to be especially peaked around its mean. When h is small, the standard deviation of the Gaussian kernel is large, and there is relatively less difference between the contribution to the kernel density made by data points that are close to the argument and those that are far from the argument. In this sense, the bandwidth parameter, h, plays a key role in determining the tradeoff between the smoothness and the granularity in the Gaussian kernel density.

The bandwidth parameter, h, is specified by the analyst. There are a number of optimal criteria that have been developed for this bandwidth parameter under various assumptions. But in our experience, it's fine simply to use the "eyeball metric" in which the choice is made to produce a non-parametric density that appears most useful from simple visual inspection. To illustrate, Figure 2.13 shows nonparametric densities corresponding to the simulated data of Figure 2.12 for three different choices for the bandwidth parameter: $h = 2$, $h = 6$, and $h = 15$.

In our view, $h = 2$ produces a density that is insufficiently smooth, while $h = 15$ produces a kernel density that may have been smoothed too much.

Figure 2.14 shows the kernel density corresponding to bandwidth parameter $h = 6$, along with the histogram from Figure 2.12.

In our view, this choice for the bandwidth parameter produces the nonparametric density with the most useful tradeoff between smoothness and granularity.

FIGURE 2.13 Nonparametric kernel densities with different bandwidths.

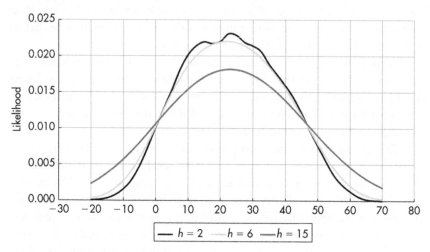

Source: Authors.

FIGURE 2.14 Nonparametric kernel density and histogram.

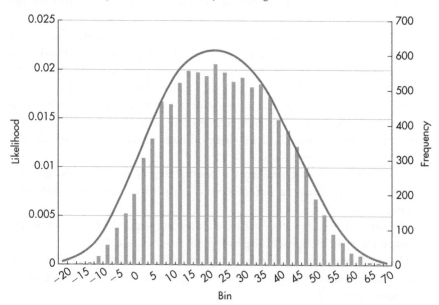

Source: Authors.

Calculating Conditional, Ex Ante Risk-Adjusted Returns

Sharpe Ratio as One Measure of Risk-Adjusted Return

Traders and investors tend to use a wide variety of measures to quantify risk, including value at risk, probability of threshold loss, and expected maximum drawdown. Each of these has merit, and we recommend viewing risk from multiple perspectives whenever possible. So we encourage using all these measures, and others, to gain an understanding of risks.

But for the purpose of this chapter, we'll focus our discussion of risk on a single measure, standard deviation. In choosing this risk measure, we don't mean to imply that standard deviation is somehow superior to other measures of risk. But it is relatively simple to calculate, and most people have at least a rudimentary intuition about standard deviations, whereas this isn't always the case when dealing with other risk measures.

One of the fundamental results of financial economics is that investors face tradeoffs between the risks to which they expose their portfolios and the returns that they reasonably can expect to earn. As a result, in any ex ante evaluation of a trade or portfolio, or in any ex post performance attribution exercise, one should consider risks and returns simultaneously.

There are a variety of ways in which analysts can compare risks and returns. The one we focus on in this chapter is to calculate risk-adjusted returns, that is we adjust returns for the risks incurred in the pursuit of those returns.

There are a number of sophisticated ways in which analysts could try to adjust returns to reflect risks, many of which rely on multi-factor pricing models. Again, we encourage analysts to avail themselves of these models and to perform these risk-adjustment exercises whenever possible.

But for the purpose of this chapter, we'll focus on one of the simplest approaches possible: we'll simply calculate the return per unit of risk, where risk is taken to be the standard deviation. In other words, we'll divide the return by the risk.

In this chapter, we refer to this measure as the Sharpe ratio. Strictly speaking, the Sharpe ratio is the ratio of excess return to standard deviation, where excess return is defined as the difference between the return of the asset and the risk-free rate over the same period. In this chapter, we take liberties by referring to the ratio of return to risk with the term Sharpe ratio. In most of our analysis, trades already are financed at a rate equal to (or very close to) the risk-free rate. So the returns we experience already are net of the risk-free rate. So we actually are dealing with Sharpe ratios, properly defined. However, we appreciate that this won't be the case for everyone, and we encourage people to be sure to use excess returns rather than unadjusted returns when calculating Sharpe ratios.

Once we have specified an SDE to model the mean reversion of a trade, and once we have calibrated the parameters of the model (most likely, but not necessarily, estimating these via historical data), we can calculate the conditional expected value and the conditional standard deviation of the return distribution.

In the case of simple models, such as the OU process, the transition densities are normal, and the expected values and the standard deviations of the transition densities can be calculated analytically via closed-form expressions.

In the case of more complex models, we face a number of choices, as mentioned above, including numerical solutions to partial differential equations or series approximations to the actual densities.

In our experience, these methods are relatively difficult to implement in practice, and we prefer simply to calculate these conditional moments via simulation.

Once the conditional expected value and the conditional standard deviation of the return has been calculated, the conditional Sharpe ratio can be calculated simply by dividing the conditional expected return by the conditional standard deviation.

Conditional Sharpe ratios can be calculated for each individual trade in a portfolio, but we remind readers that the relevant consideration is the effect that inclusion of a trade has on the conditional risk-adjusted return of the entire portfolio. In other words, when evaluating the attractiveness of a trade, the important consideration is not the risk-adjusted return of the trade on a stand-alone basis but rather the extent to which adding a position can improve the risk-adjusted return of the overall portfolio.[1]

First Passage Times

Consider a swap spread trading currently at 40 basis points (bp). Let's imagine that we start a stopwatch with the spread at 40 bp, and then we stop the stopwatch when the spread first reaches a level of 50 bp. The first passage time from 40 bp to 50 bp is the amount of time recorded by the stopwatch when it reaches this 50 bp level. In this case, it's the amount of time it takes for the spread to hit 50 bp, given that it's currently trading at 40 bp. For this

---

[1] In most relative value analysis of fixed income markets, we tend to model swap rates and bond yields rather than swap net present values and bond prices. As these tend to be interest-bearing instruments, one needs to consider not only the change in the interest rate over time but also the fact that these instruments pay interest, may involve financing, and experience "pull-to-par" effects over time – a collection of features often referenced under the broad rubric of "carry". Spread trades with positive carry are particularly attractive in that they provide an additional positive bias to a trade, and these considerations should be included when calculating ex ante Sharpe ratios as well.

reason, the first passage time also is referred to as the *hitting time*, and we'll use these two terms interchangeably.

The first thing to note about the first passage time is that it is specified by two values: a starting value and an ending value. In our example, the starting value was 40 bp, and the ending value was 50 bp. But we just as easily could have specified that the ending value would be 35 bp, or 20 bp. But of course, if we had specified a different stopping value, we would be considering a different hitting time.

The second thing to note about these first passage times is that they're random variables. We don't know the amount of time that will pass before our swap spread hits 50 bp. It could take 10 minutes, or it could take 10 weeks. It could even take 10 months or 10 years.

As random variables, we can calculate moments and other expectations of functions of hitting times. In other words, we can calculate means, standard deviations, skewness, kurtosis, densities, distributions, etc. for first passage times.

As an illustration, imagine that the SDE followed by the swap spread in our example was $dx = k\ (\mu - x)dt + v\ dw$, with $k = 0.30$, $\mu = 20$ and $v = 20$. In this case, we can generate, say, 10,000 simulated paths, all starting at 40 bp and then calculate the first passage times to a level of 50 bp along these sample paths. We'll have a simulated sample of 10,000 hitting times, which we can use to make a histogram, generate a nonparametric density, calculate an average hitting time, etc. In particular, Figure 2.15 illustrates a histogram and a nonparametric density resulting from this exercise.

FIGURE 2.15 Nonparametric kernel density and histogram.

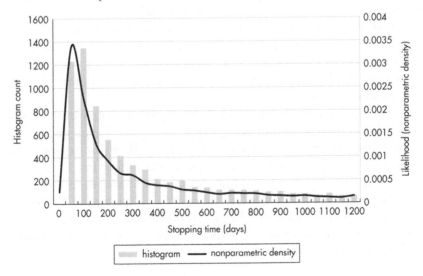

The hitting times have a number of practical applications, in that they allow us to answer a number of very useful questions. For example, consider a few useful questions in the context of trading:

- What is the likelihood of stopping out of a trade during the next two weeks if I set my stop at 55 bp?
- At what level should I set my stop if I want the probability of hitting my stop within the next month to be 20%?
- What is the likelihood of hitting my profit target during the next two months if I set it at 35 bp?
- How much time should I expect to pass before this spread next reaches its long-term mean?
- What is a 70% symmetric confidence interval for the amount of time that will pass before this spread next reaches its long-run mean?

Note that these last two questions can't be answered simply by considering the transition densities for the process used to model the spread. For example, let's consider a case in which we have used a linear specification for the drift coefficient in the SDE used to model our variable. In that case, the expected value of our variable as a function of time will be exponential, approaching the long-run mean asymptotically but never actually reaching the long-run mean.

In this case, we might ask a different question that gives a false impression of being similar, namely, "How far into the future is the expected value of my variable equal to the long-run mean?"

In this case, the answer is that there is no point in the future at which the expected value of the process is equal to the long-run mean, as the expected value approaches the long-run mean asymptotically. In this case, therefore, we might erroneously conclude that expected first passage time to the long-run mean is infinite.

We can see intuitively that this is the wrong answer simply by thinking of a simulation exercise. If we start the process at the current value of our variable and simulate it over a long period, it's very likely that the process will cross back and forth over the long-run mean quite a few times.

The key for anyone who finds the relation between these two questions paradoxical is to appreciate that they're two different questions. One question refers to the path of expected values as a function of time, whereas the other question refers to the expected values of the times taken to travel a certain distance along a sample path.

A Practical Example Incorporating all the Ideas

The Difference between EUR and GBP 5Y5Y Swaption Volatilities

As an example, let's consider the difference between implied volatilities, expressed in bp/year, between 5Y (five-year) options on 5Y swaps denominated in EUR and GBP from 25-May-05 until 4-Jul-12.

The two series are shown in Figure 2.16 below.

The main point to note from Figure 2.16 is the strong correlation between the two series over time. In particular, the correlation over the period shown in the graph was 0.87.

Figure 2.17 shows the EUR 5Y5Y swaption volatility less the GBP 5Y5Y swaption volatility over the same period.

There are two points worth noting in this figure.

- The difference between the EUR and GBP swaption volatilities does appear to have been mean reverting over the period.
- The difference appears to be more volatile during the second portion of the data sample than it does during the first portion.

To illustrate this aspect of the data more clearly, Figure 2.18 shows the daily changes in the series displayed in Figure 2.17.

Figure 2.18 supports our intuition from Figure 2.17 that the volatility of the difference has increased during our sample. There are approaches for dealing with changes in parameter values over time, but these are beyond the

FIGURE 2.16 EUR and GBP 5Y5Y implied swaption volatilities.

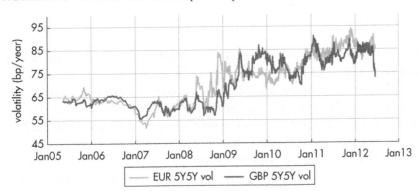

Source: Bloomberg.

FIGURE 2.17 Swaption volatility difference: EUR 5Y5Y – GBP 5Y5Y.

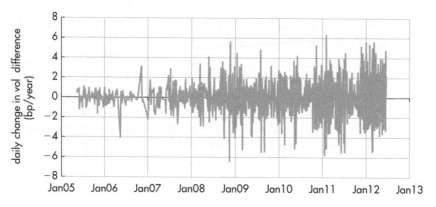

Source: Bloomberg.

FIGURE 2.18 Daily change in swaption volatility difference series.

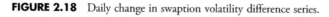

Source: Bloomberg.

scope of this book. For our purposes, we'll simply note this feature of the data and keep it in mind as we draw inferences from our analysis.

The next step in the analysis is to consider the diagnostic graphs discussed above. In particular, the first-order nonparametric estimates of the drift and diffusion coefficients are shown in Figure 2.19 and Figure 2.20.

As one would hope when dealing with a mean-reverting process, the average change is negative for values above the mean, and the average change is positive for values below the mean. Otherwise, there are no obvious strong nonlinearities apparent that might cause us to consider using a nonlinear specification for the drift coefficient.

FIGURE 2.19 First-order nonparametric estimate of drift coefficient.

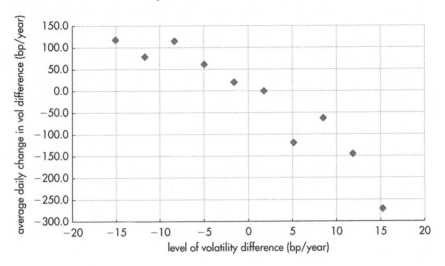

Source: Bloomberg.

FIGURE 2.20 First-order nonparametric estimate of diffusion coefficient.

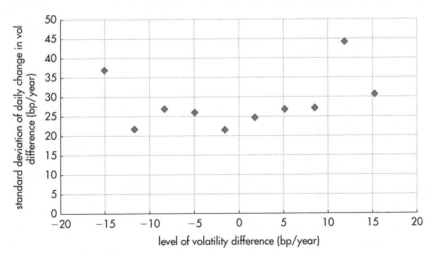

Source: Bloomberg.

In this case, we may wish to investigate further the benefits of a nonlinear specification for the diffusion coefficient, given that a bucket at either end of the data range seems to have exhibited greater volatility than have the other buckets. In particular, we would want to see how many observations were in each of the buckets showing elevated volatility. If each bucket contains relatively few observations, the volatility information from each bucket may not be so informative. For now, we'll use a constant to model the diffusion coefficient, but we'll note the possibility of nonlinearity when making inferences about the process.

Given the two diagnostic graphs in Figure 2.19 and Figure 2.20, we'll choose to model the volatility spread with the OU process described above. In this case, we'll need to estimate three parameters: the long-run mean, the speed of mean reversion, and the instantaneous volatility of the spread.

As the OU process has a transition density that can be represented analytically, we'll use maximum likelihood estimation to estimate the parameters of the specified process given our data.

In this case, the estimate is for a long-run mean of 1.0, for an instantaneous volatility of 28.25, and for a speed of mean reversion of 16.5.

As seen from the equation above giving the conditional mean of the OU process, the expected value of the process decays exponentially, approaching the long-run mean asymptotically.

In this case, it's also useful to express the speed of mean reversion in terms of the half-life of the process, the amount of time by which the expected value of the process is halfway between the current value and the long-run mean. In our example, the half-life of the process is 15.4 calendar days, meaning we can expect the spread to close half the remaining distance toward its long-run mean every 15.4 calendar days.

Figure 2.21 shows the unconditional density (or stationary density) for the process along with the transition densities for a variety of time horizons. The current value of the spread, 12.35, is denoted by a grey vertical line.

From this figure, we see the way in which the transition densities shift their means and standard deviations over time as they approach their limit, the unconditional density for the process.

Note also that the probability of the spread being greater in the future than it is now decreases over time. For example, the probability on a one-week horizon is 18%, but the probability on a one-month horizon is only 4%. At a horizon of three months, the probability that the spread is greater than its current value of 12.35 is less than 1%, according to this model.

Another way to quantify the behavior of this volatility spread is to calculate the risk-adjusted return over various horizons. We do this by dividing the

FIGURE 2.21 Unconditional and conditional densities for the volatility spread.

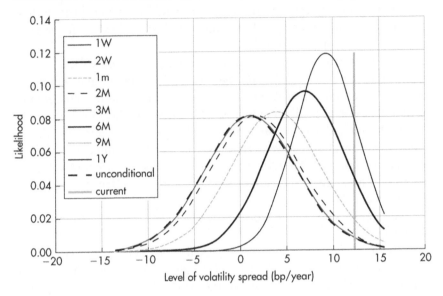

Source: Bloomberg.

expected value of the change over the horizon by the standard deviation of the change over the same horizon. As this measure resembles the well-known Sharpe ratio, we'll refer to it by this name in the remainder of this chapter. The Sharpe ratio on a one-week horizon is already 0.91, and this increases to 1.78 on a one-month horizon. By three months, the ratio has increased to 2.26.

However, to compare Sharpe ratios for different horizons, we should normalize all the calculations to the same time interval, since the expected values of random variables are additive, while the standard deviations increase at the rate $\sqrt{N}$, where N is the number of times the opportunity is taken. (In other words, to compare an investment with a one-year horizon to an investment with a one-month horizon, we need to consider repeating the one-month opportunity for 12 successive occasions.)

In this case, the annualized Sharpe ratio for the one-week investment horizon is 6.56, while the annualized Sharpe ratio for a one-month investment horizon is 6.12. The annualized Sharpe ratio on a three-month horizon is 4.5.

The fact that the annualized Sharpe ratios decline over time tells us that the best risk-adjusted opportunity is at short horizons. In other words, most of the performance in the trade is expected to come in the early days.

The implication is that if we had repeated opportunities to commit to trades with similar risk-adjusted return profiles, it would be better for us to hold these positions for short periods of time and then reallocate our capital to other short-term opportunities.

Another way to analyze the risk and return profile of this volatility spread opportunity is to consider first passage times. As we discussed earlier in this chapter, first passage times are random variables corresponding to the amount of time that elapses until a random variable hits a specified level.

As an example, let's say we're interested in positioning for our volatility spread to narrow, but that we're concerned about the possibility that it might widen further instead. To start, let's calculate the first passage time density to a level of, say, 7, given the current level of 12.35. This density is shown in Figure 2.22.

The modal value for this density is seven days, and the mean value is 14.9 days.

Note that the target value we've picked, 7, is slightly less than half the distance between the current value of 12.35 and the mean of 1.046. So perhaps it should be no surprise that the expected value of our first passage time density is slightly below the half-life of 15.4 days.

In general, there is no need for the half-life to correspond to the mean of the first passage time density, in part because each first passage time density is

FIGURE 2.22 First passage time density of volatility spread from 12.35 to 7.

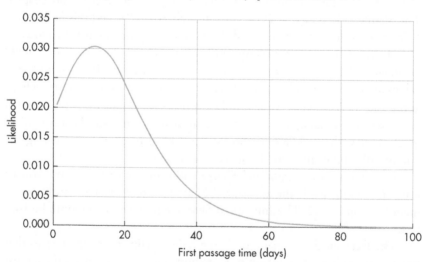

Source: Bloomberg.

defined by a different target. For example, let's consider the first passage time density corresponding to the mean of the process, in this case 1.046. This density is shown in Figure 2.23.

In this case, the modal value is 26 days, and the average value is 38.25 days. In comparison, the expected value of the volatility spread in the future, according to our model, is *never* precisely equal to its mean, since the expected value approaches the mean asymptotically from its current value. Of course, saying that an infinite amount of time must pass before the expected value equals the long-run mean isn't the same as saying that we expect an infinite amount of time to pass before the volatility spread next reaches its long-run mean.

First passage time densities are useful for a variety of reasons. For example, we can use them to make probabilistic statements about profit targets or stop levels.

As an example, let's say we're interested in setting a target of 7, with the current level at 12.35. The first passage time density for this scenario is shown in Figure 2.22. We saw earlier that the average hitting time was 14.9 days, but we can make additional probabilistic statements using this density. For example, the probability of hitting our target of 7 within five days is 13.1%, and the probability of hitting the target within 10 days is 45.1%. For 15 days, the probability is 66.5%. From these statements, we also can calculate that the probability of hitting the target between five and 10 days is 32.0%.

FIGURE 2.23 First passage time density of volatility spread from 12.35 to 1.046.

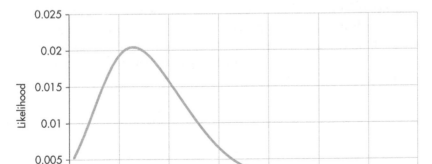

Source: Bloomberg.

As another example, let's say we're considering placing a stop at 16.35, four volatility points above the current level of 12.35. By calculating the first passage time density to 16.35, we can calculate that the probability of hitting our stop within 10 days is 5.2%. The probability of hitting this stop within 20 days is 8.8%. For 30 days, the probability of hitting this stop is 9.5%. It's 10.5% for 40 days, and 11.1% for 50 days. If we're uncomfortable with those probabilities for any reason, we can calculate a new set of probabilities that correspond to another stop level.

Of course, in some of these cases, our stop would have been hit after we had taken profits on the trade, and we could use simulations to calculate multiple scenarios, such as "hitting 16.35 before hitting 8.35".

Conclusion

Mean-reverting processes provide a rich set of tools for modeling financial time series exhibiting mean-reverting behavior. But care needs to be shown in choosing the appropriate tool for the job and in drawing inferences from the results.

For example, the decision to employ a nonlinear specification for the drift and/or the diffusion coefficient should be made carefully. In general, the nonlinear specification allows the model to capture a richer set of dynamics in the process, but it also allows a great opportunity to capture spurious aspects of the data that may result from nothing more than sampling error.

There are no clear rules for making these sorts of determinations, and our best advice is for the analyst to benefit from experience. We've attempted to provide the benefit of our experience in this chapter and throughout the book. But in the end, multiple repeated applications of the approach discussed in this chapter are likely to be of greatest use to the relative value analyst over time.

CHAPTER 3

Principal Component Analysis

Introduction: Goal and Method

The market presents itself to the observer through a surface of incommensurably many data and movements. The links between those data and movements, for example the tendency of two-year (2Y) and 10Y interest rates to rise and fall together, point toward a more or less systematic mechanism hidden in the core of the market. Our goal is to see through the surface of the market and into its structural core.

To do so, we face the problem of finding the right (degree of) formal assumptions about the structure of a market. As an extreme position, if we made no formal assumptions at all, we would remain stuck to the surface of incommensurable market data, unable to understand anything about their structural core. So, in order to reach our goal we will need to use structural terms (i.e. mathematical formalism) and hence to impose some assumptions on the market. However, we shall use those assumptions which have turned out to fit the structure of the real market well and otherwise keep them as minimal as possible, thereby leaving enough space for the market to express its own mechanisms in our form.

Principal component analysis (PCA) has only one (main) assumption: that the market is driven by a set of uncorrelated linear factors. This is not only a relatively weak assumption (allowing the market to fill in the remaining structural information, in particular about the shape and strength of each factor) but also a very useful one both for relative value (RV) analysis and hedging. It satisfies the condition of asset pricing theory (see Chapter 1) and allows us to construct portfolios that are exposed to or hedged against any factor, just as specified by the investor. For the purpose of RV analysis,[1] PCA therefore appears to be a useful tool.

A main goal of this chapter is the empirical illustration of the way PCA leads us through the surface of the market into its core, where we can see its inner driving forces, gaining meaningful and deep insights in market mechanisms. After developing the mathematics, we shall spend a large part of this chapter exploring the application of PCA to actual market mechanisms, thereby illustrating the way the structure of real markets reveals itself through PCA.

On one hand, the relationship between market and mathematical form can involve problematic assumptions. On the other hand, however, it also connects the real world to its mathematical representation. PCA is therefore a link between the economy and mathematics, generating economically relevant statistics. In the example of 2Y and 10Y rates from above, a PCA could identify one factor behind moves of both rates in the same direction, and another, uncorrelated factor behind moves of both rates in opposite directions. Interpreting the identities of those factors (perhaps linked to economic data, like inflation) gives a deep understanding of the driving forces of the yield curve. In the next step, an investor who has a view on those factors (e.g. inflation) could construct through PCA the best trading position and hedge it against factors on which he has no view.

With PCA linking statistics to fundamentals, it also links the first to the second part of the book. While the focus in the preceding section was on statistics, it now shifts to statistics linked to economic insights. Correspondingly, the present goal is not an optimization of Sharpe ratios but to gain insights into the fundamental mechanisms. This will complement statistical optimality with the confidence of understanding the real economic driving forces behind a trade.

An Intuitive Approach toward PCA

An assumption-free start to market analysis could be to simply plot data observations into a scatter chart. Figure 3.1 shows an example for 2Y versus 10Y Bund yields (from 1996 to mid-2012). Then, one can try to distinguish structural relationships. In the current example, there seems to be a strong relationship driving both yields up and down together, which has been in force more or less over the whole time period. Moreover, that relationship seems to be rather linear and can thus be approximated quite well by a straight line. In addition, there seems to be a second mechanism driving both yields in

---

[1] Other purposes may require other tools.

FIGURE 3.1 Structure of point cloud of 2Y and 10Y Bund yields.

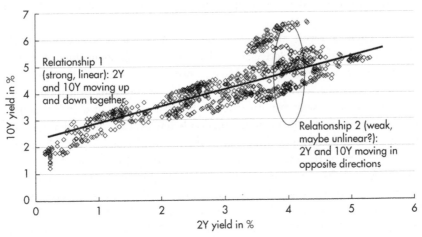

Sources: data – Bloomberg; chart – Authors.
Data period: 1 Jan 1996 to 4 Jun 2012, weekly data.

opposite directions. Compared to the first relationship, however, it appears to be weaker than the first one over the whole time period and with an impact that varies significantly over time, being quite strong when 2Y yields were around 4% and less so in other sectors. Furthermore, it is not clear whether this relationship can be reasonably assumed to be linear as well.[2]

Broadly speaking, PCA assumes the relationships to be linear and uncorrelated[3] and provides a *quantification* of the intuitive approach from above, telling us in mathematical form:

- *which* (linear) relationships exist in a given set of market data (i.e. what the *shape* of market mechanisms looks like). In the current example, this would correspond to quantifying the impact of the relationship 1 and 2 (short and long Bund yields moving up and down together or in opposite directions) on 2Y and 10Y yields.

---

[2] One could also remark a systemic divergence from the line for very low yield levels. The discussion following Figure 3.24 will reveal the background of that deviation.

[3] The absence of correlation is a result of the linear algebra behind a PCA. It is also a very convenient feature for the usual purposes of relative value analysis, as it allows decomposing a market into uncorrelated factors, which is the basis for analyzing them individually. However, it is also conceivable to construct a factor model with correlated factors. For example, in order to obtain a particular analytical goal it might be useful to model a market as a function of two macroeconomic variables, even if they are correlated.

- *how strong* the relationships are relative to each other, that is how much of market action (yield curve variation) is explained by a particular mechanism.

In mathematical terms, the shape of market mechanisms corresponds to the eigenvectors and their relative strength to the (scaled) eigenvalues of a PCA.

Before moving on, we would like to note that a chart like the one above can serve as a check on the suitability of the assumptions of a model for a particular market segment. In case of the assumptions of a PCA (such as linearity) seeming to violate actual market behavior, caution is advisable, and the diagnostic techniques discussed in the previous chapter could be used.

Furthermore, this intuitive approach to PCA may give the wrong impression that PCA works like a regression, with relationship 1 being the regression line and relationship 2 representing the residuals. However, the mathematics is different, and so (usually) are the results (i.e. the relationships calculated via a PCA will in most cases differ from the regression line). We shall discuss the reasons for the difference in the section about appropriate hedging, which will also show the superiority of using PCA-based relationships for calculating hedge ratios.

Factor Models: General Structure and Definitions

We shall now repeat the discussion from above in formal terms, thereby constructing PCA. The goal of understanding the few key mechanisms behind all market moves can be mathematically addressed by extracting the most relevant information from a given set of market data. Expressing this a bit more formally, it means reducing the dimensionality, with the remaining dimensions containing most of the information. Thus, the result of this exercise will reveal the number, strength, and shape of the market mechanisms.

We observe a number n of market data (e.g. yields) y_i^t $(i = 1, \ldots, n)$ at time t. The general form of a k-factor linear model is given by:

$$\begin{pmatrix} y_1^t \\ \vdots \\ y_n^t \end{pmatrix} = \sum_{i=1}^{k} \alpha_i^t \cdot \begin{pmatrix} f_{i1} \\ \vdots \\ f_{in} \end{pmatrix} + \begin{pmatrix} \varepsilon_1^t \\ \vdots \\ \varepsilon_n^t \end{pmatrix}$$

where α_i^t (a number which changes over time) is called the i-th factor (at time t), $\begin{pmatrix} f_{i1} \\ \vdots \\ f_{in} \end{pmatrix}$ (a vector which does not change over time) is called the i-th factor loading and

$$\begin{pmatrix} \varepsilon_1^t \\ \vdots \\ \varepsilon_n^t \end{pmatrix}$$ (a vector which changes over time) is called the k-factor-residual

(at time t), that is the portion unexplained by the factors.

The factor loadings, which do not change over time, can be considered as containing the market mechanisms, while the factors show how much of a specific market mechanism is active at a certain point in time. As an intuitive comparison, consider a sound mixer: the (invariable) individual sounds correspond to the factor loadings, while their (variable) strengths at a certain point in time (as adjusted by the volume regulator on the mixer board) correspond to the factors. The other way around, we can decompose the overall sound we hear into its individual components by looking at the regulators and labels on the mixer. Likewise, we are able to decompose the overall market action we observe into its individual driving forces by looking at the factors and factor loadings of a PCA.

Example: Imagine we decide to model the yield curve from one to 10 years

$(n = 10)$ by $\begin{pmatrix} y_1^t \\ \vdots \\ y_{10}^t \end{pmatrix} = \alpha_1^t \cdot \begin{pmatrix} 1 \\ \vdots \\ 1 \end{pmatrix}$ (a one-factor model). This particular factor

loading allows only parallel shifts. This is an example for a very strong assumption from our side, which limits our perceptive ability to observing parallel shifts only. The reality of the market would protest against our imposed form by exhibiting large residuals.

So far, we have only assumed that market mechanisms are linear factors. The question is how much more we should assume. The answer to that question classifies factor models into two categories.

In the first category, the analyst determines the factor loadings himself. The Nelson–Siegel (NS) model is a prominent example of this approach,

assuming a priori that the first factor loading is the vector $\begin{pmatrix} 1 \\ \vdots \\ 1 \end{pmatrix}$ and the

second a vector whose entries follow the discount factor curve. Thus, it expands the simple one-factor model from our example above (parallel shifts) with a second factor accounting for curve steepening and flattening.

The advantage of that approach is that by choosing the factor loadings appropriately one can ensure that the model exhibits the desired properties (e.g. is arbitrage-free). This is probably the main reason academic market analysis often prefers factor models falling into the first category.

The disadvantage is that the model results may reflect the assumptions of the analyst rather than the true market mechanisms. In the case of the NS model, for example, curve steepening and flattening moves that do not follow the shape of the assumed discount factor curve cannot be explained and will appear as residuals. Hence, the steepening mechanism of the real market will be ignored in the factor loadings (overwritten by an arbitrary a priori assumption) and pushed into the residuals unexplained by the factors of the model.

In the second category, the factor loadings are extracted from the market: rather than making his own a priori assumptions about the factor loadings (i.e. market mechanisms), the analyst lets the market reveal its own dynamics and *then* a posteriori *interprets* the factor loadings. For our goal of seeing into the core of the actual market (rather than imposing our hypotheses on it), the second category is thus the right place to look.

PCA is the main representative of the second category: it forces the market to reveal its mechanisms under the form of uncorrelated linear factors but usually leaves enough freedom for the market to reveal its real dynamics within that formal framework. For example, the steepening mechanism (net of direction) of the market will show up in the second factor loading just as it is, revealing the actual market dynamics rather than overwriting them with a priori assumptions of the analyst. Consequently, market mechanisms will be visible in the factor loadings rather than pushed into the residuals.

PCA: Mathematics

Since PCA is a tool from linear algebra, we first need to represent the market in the form of a matrix. The straightforward approach is therefore to express the structural information contained in the market under consideration in the form of a covariance matrix.[4]

---

[4] Obviously, we lose some statistical information in this step, in particular above the second order. However, in practice this is seldom of relevance for the goals of relative value analysis.

Technical points

- Market data should be of sufficient length to allow the parameters of the model to be estimated with sufficient accuracy.
- Depending on the goal of the analysis, either level or change data can be used as inputs.
- It is important to use the *covariance* rather than *correlation* matrix since the difference in volatility (sensitivity) is a key element of the analysis and must not be netted out by using correlations.

Now that we have the market information in the form of a covariance *matrix*, we can extract information by applying the powerful tools of linear algebra, transforming the covariance matrix into the orthonormal basis of its eigenvectors.

Definition: If $Ax = \lambda x$ $(x \neq 0)$, for a matrix A, then the vector x is called an eigenvector of A and the number λ is the associated eigenvalue of A.

Hence, an eigenvector does not change its direction, only its length, when the matrix is applied to it. For example, if A represents the rotation of a globe by 90 degrees, then the rotation axis through the two poles is an eigenvector with an associated eigenvalue of one. Another example: if one holds a ball with both hands and squeezes it, the line connecting both hands contains eigenvectors, whose associated eigenvalue is less than one.

Theorem: For every covariance matrix[5] Cov, it is true that

$$Cov = B^{-1} \begin{pmatrix} \lambda_1 & 0 & 0 \\ 0 & \ddots & 0 \\ 0 & 0 & \lambda_n \end{pmatrix} B,$$ where λ_i are the eigenvalues of Cov and the

columns of B consist of the eigenvectors of Cov.

---

[5] In fact, this theorem is true for every matrix which is symmetric and positive semi-definite.

Intuitive interpretation: The matrix B acts like a transformation of the coordinate system and allows us to consider the covariance matrix from the perspective of the orthonormal basis given by its eigenvectors. Since these eigenvectors are orthogonal, they decompose the covariance matrix into uncorrelated relationships. Moreover, the eigenvector associated with the greatest absolute eigenvalue points into the direction of the highest variation, that is it represents the most important structural relationship in the market.

Example: $Cov = \begin{pmatrix} 7 & 3 \\ 3 & 2 \end{pmatrix}$ has the eigenvalues 8.4 and 0.6 with eigenvectors (e.g.) $\begin{pmatrix} 0.91 \\ 0.42 \end{pmatrix}$ and $\begin{pmatrix} -0.42 \\ 0.91 \end{pmatrix}$. Figure 3.2 shows the image of the unit circle under Cov and illustrates that most variation occurs along the direction of the first eigenvector.

FIGURE 3.2   *Cov* and examples for its two eigenvectors.

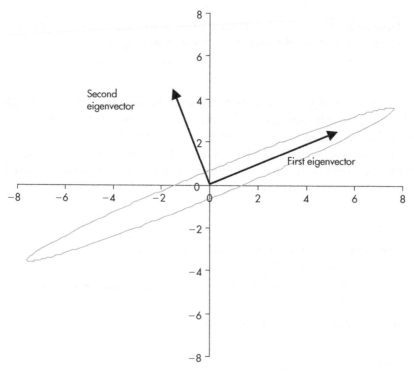

Technical point: Numerical issues involved in eigenvalue calculation

Eigenvalue calculation is famous for its numerical challenges. The main problem is to distinguish between two different eigenvalues and two slightly different numerical representations of the same eigenvalue. Since some of the eigenvalues tend to get very small when their number increases, this distinguishing becomes quite difficult for large covariance matrices and requires numerical representations with many digits and very high accuracy.

When an in-house PCA tool is required, the following hints could be useful:

- Scale the covariance matrix appropriately.
- Use a combination of numerical methods. In particular, since the largest eigenvalue is of crucial importance for the application of PCA to markets, confirm it through the Lanczos algorithm.
- Use as starting points for a Newton algorithm on the characteristic polynomial of the covariance matrix after a Householder transformation the following set of numbers: $a + 2 \cdot b \cdot \cos\left(i \cdot \dfrac{\pi}{n+1}\right)$ for $i = 1, \ldots, n$,

  with $a = \dfrac{1}{n}\sum_{i=1}^{n} a_i$, $b = \dfrac{1}{n-1}\sum_{i=2}^{n} b_i$ and with $\begin{pmatrix} a_1 & b_2 & 0 & 0 \\ b_2 & a_2 & \ddots & 0 \\ 0 & \ddots & \ddots & b_n \\ 0 & 0 & b_n & a_n \end{pmatrix}$ being

  the Householder transformation of the covariance matrix.
- Additionally, run a systematic search for eigenvalues, whereby the largest eigenvalue found via the Lanczos algorithm determines the width of steps and range of starting points for the Newton algorithm.
- Run checks, whether the computed eigenvectors are really eigenvectors (i.e. fulfill $Ax = \lambda x$) and orthogonal to each other.

The PCA sheet on the website accompanying this book implements these tricks. However, also due to numerical restrictions of Excel, it reaches its limitations rather soon and should not be expected to work for larger covariance matrices.

PCA as Factor Model

PCA becomes a factor model by using the eigenvectors e_{ij} of the covariance matrix as factor loadings, that is by defining $f_{ij} := e_{ij}$, with the factor model being thus:

$$\begin{pmatrix} y_1^t \\ \vdots \\ y_n^t \end{pmatrix} = \sum_{i=1}^{n} \alpha_i^t \cdot \begin{pmatrix} e_{i1} \\ \vdots \\ e_{in} \end{pmatrix}$$

where $\begin{pmatrix} e_{i1} \\ \vdots \\ e_{in} \end{pmatrix}$ is the i-th eigenvector.

We sort the eigenvalues (and associated eigenvectors) by the percentage of total variation explained, that is

$$|\lambda_1| \geq |\lambda_2| \geq \cdots \geq |\lambda_n|$$

Hence, the first factor explains most of the market variation, the second explains most of the market variation not explained by the first factor, and so on. Correspondingly, the first factor loading, that is the first eigenvector, reveals the structure of the most important market mechanism, the second eigenvector the structure of the second most important, and so on. The importance of a market mechanism, that is the strength of its impact on the overall market variation, is quantified by the eigenvalues.

Technical point

If x is an eigenvector of Cov, then for every $a \neq 0$, ax is also an eigenvector of Cov. Thus, for every eigenvalue, there exist infinitely many eigenvectors, pointing in the same direction (or, if $a < 0$, in the opposite direction), but of different length. Any one of those can be chosen as a factor loading, and there is no reason to prefer one over the other.

In the end, one needs to arbitrarily decide the length of a particular eigenvector. For example, eigenvectors often are scaled to have unit length. However, there still exist two eigenvectors, x and y, with length one, with $x = -y$. Again, there is no criterion to decide for one or the other and one has to arbitrarily choose one. However, it is therefore important for the analyst to conduct the analysis and interpret the results with the particular choices of eigenvectors in mind. For example, if rates are an increasing function of factor 1 when x is chosen as the eigenvector, then rates will be a decreasing function of factor 1 when $y = -x$ is chosen as the eigenvector. Many analysts have fallen into this trap, which can be avoided only by constantly remembering the eigenvectors. As in this example, factors are only meaningful when analyzed in conjunction with the factor loadings.

Insight into Market Mechanisms through Interpretation of the Eigenvectors

So far, we have developed the mathematical framework for PCA. For the rest of the chapter, we will see how PCA reveals the inner structural relationships of the market and how it can be applied to trading.

For the following example, we use weekly data from 4 Jan 2010 to 3 Oct 2011 for generic Bund yields (yield level, not change) for two, five, seven and 10 years. The input data and the PCA can be seen in the PCA sheet accompanying this book. In the first step, the covariance matrix is calculated and depicted in Figure 3.3. While this is not a necessary step in the analytical process based on PCA, displaying and examining the covariance matrix (i.e. the input into a PCA) can already give an intuition about the market mechanisms (i.e. the output of a PCA). In Figure 3.3, we can observe an area of maximal covariance in the medium part of the yield curve.

Then, the information about the market (as represented in the covariance matrix) is extracted through a PCA. As with any factor model, the eigenvectors of the covariance matrix represent the structural relations and

FIGURE 3.3 Covariance across the Bund yield curve.

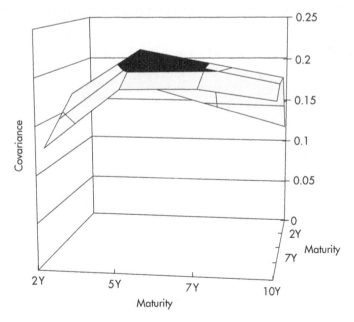

Sources: data – Bloomberg; chart – Authors.
Data period: 4 Jan 2010 to 3 Oct 2011, weekly data.

mechanisms between the data series, while the eigenvalues show the relative significance of these factors in explaining the behavior of the data.

A typical situation for the relative strength of the factors, as quantified by the relative size of their eigenvalues, is depicted in Figure 3.4. As can be seen in that figure in the case of the Bund yield curve, the first factor explains more than 90% of the yield curve variation; and the first three factors together, almost everything. This means that basically the whole information the Bund market provides can be reduced to, captured, and expressed in three numbers (the first three factors), with the factor loadings translating the information between the full Bund market and the three factors (numbers) back and forth.

The next step to extract information about market mechanisms from a PCA is to examine the shape of the eigenvectors. The interpretation of the structural information contained in the eigenvectors can be done by applying the following scheme: if the i-th factor (α_i) increases by one, what happens to the rate curve? The answer to this question translates the market mechanisms from the mathematical language of eigenvectors of the covariance matrix into everyday terms.

In the following, we provide this interpretation for the first three eigenvectors of a PCA on the Bund curve, which are depicted in Figure 3.5. In this example, we find that a unit increase in the first factor corresponds to an increase in every point along the yield curve, since every entry in the first

FIGURE 3.4   Scaled eigenvalues of a PCA on the Bund yield curve.

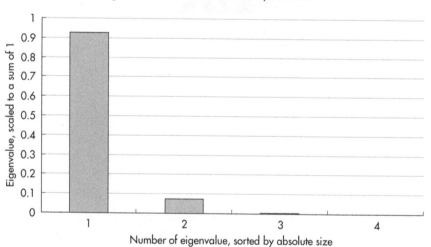

Sources: data – Bloomberg; chart – Authors.
Data period: 4 Jan 2010 to 3 Oct 2011, weekly data.

FIGURE 3.5 First three eigenvectors of a PCA on the Bund curve.

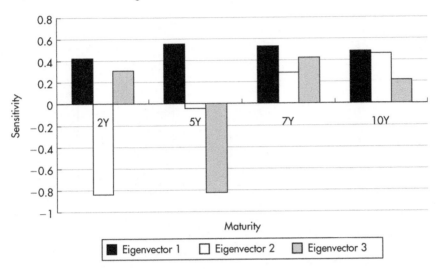

Sources: data – Bloomberg; chart – Authors.
Data period: 4 Jan 2010 to 3 Oct 2011, weekly data.

eigenvector has the same sign. Hence, we can interpret the first factor as representing the directional dynamics of the yield curve.

Moreover, the *shape* of the first eigenvector in Figure 3.5 represents the *shape* of directional moves: if α_1 increases by one, all yields increase, but medium yields (five-year, or 5Y) increase more than both short (2Y) and long (10Y) yields. This can be translated into everyday terms by saying that the pivotal point of directional moves of the yield curve is the 5Y area. We note that the output (eigenvector) of a PCA corresponds to the input (covariance matrix), with the shape of the first eigenvector reflecting the maximal covariance in the medium part of the yield curve we observed in Figure 3.3.

Now, let's compare this with the first eigenvector of a PCA on the Bund curve with data from 1993 to 1997, which is depicted in Figure 3.6. While for 5Y, 7Y, and 10Y the sensitivity is almost identical to the current situation, back in the 1990s, the sensitivity of 2Y yields was as high as that of 5Y yields (i.e. the market exhibited a bull-steepening/bear-flattening pattern). This is typical for a market with an active central bank driving the yield curve up and down, which corresponds to a higher sensitivity of shorter yields to directional moves, hence a higher entry in the first eigenvector. Thus, the decreasing activity of the central bank from the 1990s until now (partly a function of rates approaching zero) is reflected by the decreasing sensitivity of 2Y yields to the first factor. Note how the mathematics (entry in eigenvector) corresponds to

FIGURE 3.6   First eigenvector of a PCA on the Bund curve with data from 1993 to 1997.

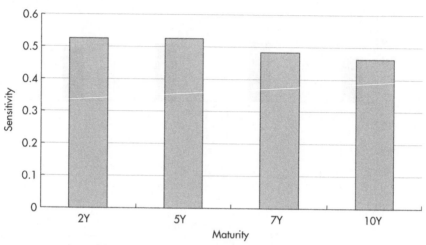

Sources: data – Bloomberg; chart – Authors.
Data period: 1 Jan 1993 to 31 Dec 1997, weekly data.

real economic mechanisms. Even if we did not know anything about central bank history, one look at the PCA results would reveal both the structural shift in market mechanisms (pivotal point of directional moves shifting from the short end to the medium curve sector) and its likely source. Also note the stability displayed by the eigenvector over the past 20 years (apart from the short end), which we shall analyze in more detail later in this chapter.

Furthermore, note the difference to the approach of a factor model in the first category, like the NS model: rather than *assuming* a priori that direction is the strongest market dynamic, the market reveals that this is the case for this particular market segment. And contrary to the a priori assumption of parallel shifts in the NS model, it shows that the real directional market mechanism follows a 2Y-5Y bear-steepening/5Y-10Y bear-flattening shape.

Also, together with the information about the eigenvalues shown in Figure 3.4, we have found (rather than assumed) that directional market mechanisms have indeed the strongest impact on the yield curve and can quantify their strength relative to other factors. Moreover, we could compare the strength of directional mechanisms in different markets and how it evolves over time by following the evolution of the scaled first eigenvalue. Interestingly, we found that the development of markets is characterized by a decreasing scaled first eigenvalue. In undeveloped markets, almost 100% of the action is explained by one single variable (direction), while increasing sophistication results in other mechanisms gaining strength. For example, while 10 years ago the Indian domestic bond market had a scaled first eigenvalue of virtually one, it has now decreased to levels more in line with Western government bond markets, reflecting its increasing development. The Indian MIFOR–MIBOR basis swap market, on the other hand, has always been similar to the Bund market depicted in Figure 3.4. This could be interpreted as evidence that the basis swap market has induced the development of the domestic Indian bond market. In a sense, the scaled first eigenvalue is a universal (reverse) indicator of the sophistication of a market, allowing comparisons over space and time.

Moving on with the interpretation to the second eigenvector, if α_2 increases by one, short yields decrease and long yields increase. Thus, the second factor represents the slope element of the curve that is not explained by the first factor (i.e. by directional impacts on the slope). This is due to the entries in the second eigenvector crossing the x-axis once. Again, the shape of the second eigenvector reveals and quantifies the shape of steepening moves.

And if α_3 increases by one, short yields increase, medium yields decrease, and long yields increase, which we interpret as the curvature dynamics of the curve (not explained by the first and second factors). This corresponds to the entries in the third eigenvector crossing the x-axis twice.

These results are typical, with the i-th eigenvector crossing the x-axis $i - 1$ times.[6] However, it is not always the case, as in a particular market steepening moves could explain more of the overall yield curve variation than directional moves. Sometimes, no reasonable interpretation is possible at all, which could indicate that modeling this particular market through PCA is not useful. An advantage of PCA versus factor models falling into the first category is that it reveals these issues as they are, including cautioning against its own use when appropriate.

Applying Eigenvector Interpretation in Different Markets

Statistical models like PCA require no specific knowledge about the instrument that is being modeled and are hence universally applicable. PCA only needs to know the time series, not whether the time series represents yields, swap spreads, or volatilities, or what drives that time series. Thus, the range of its possible applications is far larger than the yield curve example we have been using so far. In fact, interpretation of eigenvectors may become less predictable and straightforward, hence more interesting and revealing, when

---

[6] One can back up this statement theoretically by linking PCA to a Fourier analysis.

PCA is applied to other markets. Here, we illustrate the use of PCA in a number of different contexts, starting with volatility data as input variables.

The two-dimensional surface of at-the-money-forward (ATMF) volatilities (or, if skew is considered as well, the three-dimensional volatility cube) must first be transformed into a one-dimensional vector. After the PCA is conducted, the outcome in vector form can be displayed again in a two-dimensional format. The complete results are discussed in detail in Chapter 17, from which we pick the chart of the second eigenvector as a typical result in Figure 3.7.

Usually, the first factor represents the overall level of volatility, the second factor differentiates across expiry, and the third one across underlying swap maturity of the options. However, the second and third factors sometimes change place (i.e. the differentiation across underlying maturity explains more of the overall variation of the volatility surface than the differentiation across expiry). Thus, PCA decomposes the volatility surface into its two dimensions (expiry and underlying swap maturity), with the first factor affecting both dimensions and the second and third factor reflecting the dimension-specific information.

FIGURE 3.7   Second eigenvector of a PCA of the vega sector of the JPY implied volatility surface.

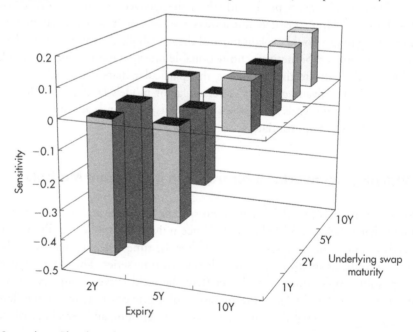

Sources: data – Bloomberg; chart – Authors.
Data period: 5 Jan 2009 to 19 Sep 2011, weekly data.

FIGURE 3.8 Example for a cluster analysis of the whole JPY volatility surface.[7]

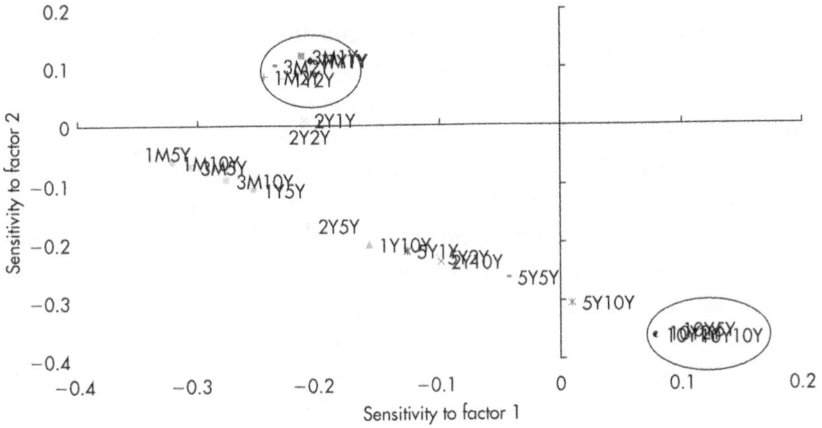

Sources: data – Bloomberg; chart – Authors.
Data period: 5 Jan 2009 to 19 Sep 2011, weekly data.

When the number of instruments in the data set increases, as in the case of volatility analysis, the ability of PCA to reduce the dimensionality of the data becomes increasingly important. One can use that ability to detect relationships in large data sets. One tool supporting this process is cluster analysis, which depicts each instrument as a function of its sensitivity to various factors (typically the first and second, as in Figure 3.8). If the first and second eigenvalues are large relative to the others, then the behavior of an instrument will be largely determined by its sensitivity to the first and second factors. Thus, if two instruments have similar sensitivities to the first and second factors (i.e. they are close to each other in Figure 3.8), they can be expected to behave similarly (i.e. to form a "cluster"). In the example in Figure 3.8, we can observe two clusters: one containing all options with both short expiries and short underlying swap maturities and the other containing all options with both long expiries and long underlying swap maturities. We therefore conclude that volatilities at both ends of the diagonal of the volatility surface usually move closely together, while further away from those two corners of the volatility surface, options behave more individually. The same sort of analysis can be applied to other combinations and numbers

---

[7] Note that the input data for Figure 3.8 consist of the whole volatility surface, while for Figure 3.7 only options with an expiry of at least 2Y are used. The reason for this is explained in Chapter 17. As there are two different PCAs behind the two charts, the sensitivities to factor 2 displayed in Figure 3.7 and Figure 3.8 are also different.

of factors as well, for example by forming three-dimensional clusters of the first three sensitivities.

In Chapter 15, we shall use PCA to gain insights into the structure of various credit default swap (CDS) markets. Picking one result as an example, Figure 3.9 shows the first three eigenvectors of a PCA with the 5Y CDS quotes of sovereign issuers in the core Eurozone as input. The first eigenvector (in which all entries are positive) represents the overall level of Eurozone CDS quotes, with the sensitivities measuring the impact a general widening of Eurozone CDS quotes has on individual countries: it affects France more than Austria, Austria more than the Netherlands, and the Netherlands more than Germany. The second eigenvector groups together Germany and France (negative sensitivities) versus the Netherlands and Austria (positive sensitivities). Thus, if factor 2 increases, the CDS of the small core countries widen relative to the CDS of the big core countries. Therefore, factor 2 can be interpreted as differentiating between the big and small countries in the core Eurozone. This means that the size of the bond market is the second-most-important determining factor of core Eurozone countries' CDS levels (after the overall CDS level as measured by factor 1).

FIGURE 3.9   First three eigenvectors of a PCA on 5Y CDS for core Eurozone sovereign issuers.

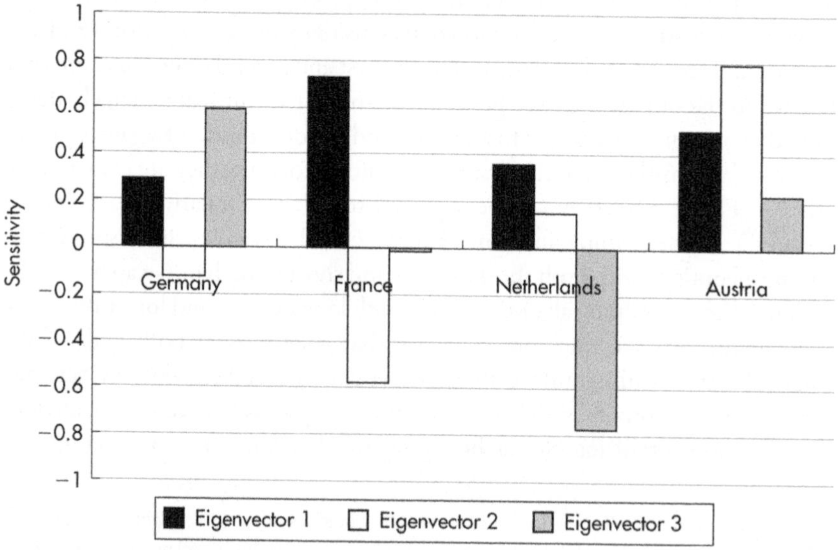

Sources: data – Bloomberg; chart – Authors.
Data period: 6 May 2009 to 26 Sep 2012, weekly data.

For an example from the commodity market we have run a PCA on weekly data for the front month contract on the three soy-related series (soybeans, soybean meal, and soybean oil) from 2000 onward. The scaled eigenvalues shown in Figure 3.10 indicate that almost everything is explained by factor 1, with factor 2 having only 0.2% of explanatory power and factor 3 virtually nothing. This indicates that differentiation across the three soy products is limited relative to the variability of the overall price changes in the three commodities.

Figure 3.11 displays the eigenvectors. Note that the difference in sensitivities to the first factor is a function of the difference in the size of the input numbers (e.g. 1,600 for soybeans versus 51 for soybean meal). This could be avoided by creating synthetic time series with similar numbers, for example all starting with a value of one. It turns out that the overwhelming factor 1 affects all soy products in the same way (i.e. all rise and fall together). The (little) differentiation between different soy products which is measured by factor 2 shows that soybeans and soybean oil move together versus soybean meal.

Finally, a look at the evolution of the PCA factors over time (Figure 3.12) reflects the increasing demand for soy products over the last decade in a rise of factor 1, which has led to all three products richening. Factor 2, on the other hand, has not exhibited a clear trend, which means that the price differentiation between soybeans and soybean oil on the one hand and soybean meal

FIGURE 3.10 Scaled eigenvalues of a PCA on the soy market.

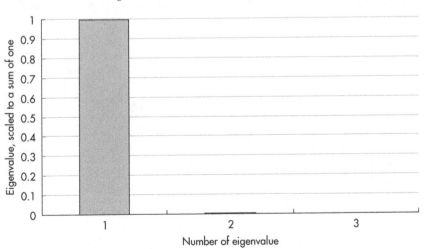

Sources: data – Bloomberg; chart – Authors.
Data period: 3 Jan 2000 to 6 Aug 2012, weekly data.

FIGURE 3.11 Eigenvectors of a PCA on the soy market.

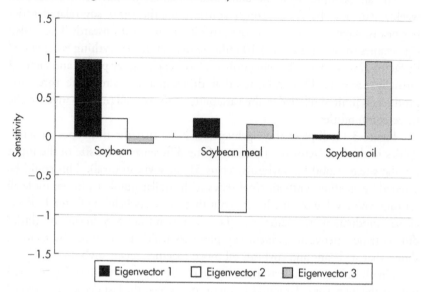

Sources: data – Bloomberg; chart – Authors.
Data period: 3 Jan 2000 to 6 Aug 2012, weekly data.

FIGURE 3.12 Historical evolution of the first and second factor of a PCA on the soy market.

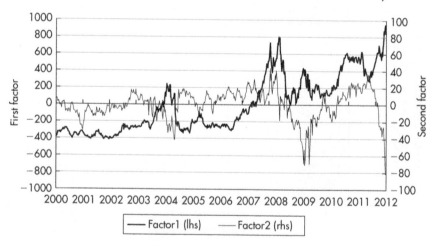

Sources: data – Bloomberg; chart – Authors.
Data period: 3 Jan 2000 to 6 Aug 2012, weekly data.

on the other tends to be temporary (i.e. factor 2 tends to be mean reverting). From this historical perspective, the current unprecedented deviation of factor 2 from its mean could be seen as a good trading opportunity. Factor 2 being too low (historically) translates through the sensitivities to eigenvector 2 in soybean meal being too expensive versus soybeans and soybean oil. Hence, a low factor 2 reflects the relative richness of soybean meal versus other soy products.

Up until this point, the analysis has been purely statistical, revealing the driving forces of historical and current pricing. This provides a good basis for a trading decision, which needs to incorporate elements besides statistical properties as well. For example, is the current deviation of factor 2 an outlier that can be expected to revert to mean as quickly as it did in the past? Or is there a potential for the current drought to cause a permanent regime shift in the soy markets? While this assessment is beyond the reach of statistics, PCA both enables us to detect and formulate these trading decisions and indicates that any cause for a permanent regime shift would need to be extraordinarily strong – stronger than anything that has happened over the past decade. Thus, PCA shows that arguing for a regime change (i.e. for no reversion of factor 2 to the longstanding mean) would require very good reasons.

An investor believing in the current drought not to be such an extraordinary regime-changing event and thus in factor 2 continuing its decade-long behavior and returning to its mean may therefore want to consider selling soybean meal versus either soybeans or soybean oil. Which of the two is better? And precisely how much should be bought for one short soybean meal futures contract? The answer to these questions is again within the realm of statistics. Given the much stronger impact of factor 1 on the soy market, there is actually a high risk that a position that intends to exploit the current mismatch in factor 2 could end up being driven mainly by factor 1 and not 2 (i.e. overall direction of soy, not the spreads between different soy products), if hedge ratios are not calculated properly. Subsequently, we shall develop PCA into tools that answer these questions.

These examples could serve to give an impression of the analytical strength of PCA, thereby empirically proving our claim that PCA is a very useful tool for the relative value craftsman to dig out and clarify the key market mechanisms hidden below a muddy surface of incommensurable market actions.

So far, we have used PCA to gain insights into the structural core of markets. From now on, we shall focus on applying these insights to find, analyze, and construct trading ideas. This will take place in the framework of PCA and thus show the way PCA supports the translation of its insights into practical trading positions.

Decomposing Markets into Uncorrelated Factors

As the eigenvectors are orthogonal, the factors are uncorrelated by construction. Hence, one can decompose a complex market into individual, uncorrelated, and simple relationships. This ability is the key to a variety of analyses.

Technical points

- Factors are uncorrelated, not necessarily independent. This issue has led to the development of independent component analysis recently, though we have not seen a convincing application to market analysis yet.
- While factors are uncorrelated over the whole sample period, there can occur significant measured correlation within subperiods. Thus, the rolling correlation of factors should be investigated before relying on the model. This is a key point, which we shall discuss in detail toward the end of this chapter.

The decomposition into uncorrelated factors isolates a particular relationship from others. This makes it possible to analyze and trade individual market mechanisms, such as yield curve steepness, without being influenced by other effects, such as direction.[8] The most important application of this ability is the exclusion of directional effects (typically associated with the factor with the greatest explanatory power). If relative value trades are defined as offering return opportunities that are uncorrelated to market direction, then the ability of PCA to produce and analyze time series uncorrelated with market direction is a key aspect of the analysis.[9] In other words, if the first factor represents the market direction (beta), then alpha (P&L uncorrelated to the market direction) can be found in the other factors.

Using the example of the Bund yield curve from Figure 3.5, the second factor has been interpreted as explaining the steepness not explained by the first, directional factor (i.e. representing the *non-directional steepness*). Note that also

---

[8] This requires the assumption that the future curve dynamic will be the same as the current curve dynamic expressed in PCA eigenvectors. Toward the end of this chapter we shall investigate the validity of this assumption.

[9] Likewise, one could use the same techniques to analyze and execute trading positions, which are uncorrelated to, for example, non-directional steepness (represented here by the second factor). However, in practice most of the time the main concern will be to prevent the all-pervasive directional effects from influencing relative value positions, in other words to create alpha.

the first factor has a steepness component (i.e. direction impacts steepness). If yields increase, the 5Y-10Y yield curve tends to flatten. The second factor is uncorrelated to direction *and to directional impacts on the steepness* and therefore shows the steepness of the curve *net* of directional impacts.

To repeat this key point: given the current yield level, the curve should have a certain steepness, given by the first eigenvector. The second factor shows the steepness of the curve that remains after taking into account the steepness already explained by the direction. There were many instances in which the 5Y-10Y yield curve has been steep but in which the steepness was due entirely to the low yield level, while on a non-directional basis the curve was actually too flat. In this case, one could argue for a non-directional steepening trade hedged against directional impacts, despite the steepness of the 5Y-10Y curve.

This example illustrates the importance of factor decomposition for RV analysis:

- Given the all-pervasive directional effects (e.g. on curve steepness, curvature, swap spreads, volatility) the indispensable prerequisite for any RV analysis is a measure for steepness or curvature *unaffected* by directional effects. The second and third factors provide that measure and thus the *starting point* for any RV analysis.
- As the first eigenvector shows the way yield levels affect slope, we can hedge against these effects, thereby formulating RV trades with no directional exposure.
- PCA is thus a direct way to gain access to true RV trades and thereby to much more trading, sales, and research opportunities than straight directional positions. Simply put, by using a three-factor model, one obtains three uncorrelated time series and thus three times as many possibilities for trades.

Embedding PCA in Trade Ideas

So far, we have discovered two important features of PCA: its ability to decompose a market into uncorrelated factors and the possibility to interpret these factors economically (via examining the shape of the eigenvectors).[10]

---

[10] While the shape of the eigenvector always allows an economic interpretation of the factors such as "yield curve steepness", it may not always be possible to link each of the factors with an obvious and specific macroeconomic variable like "inflation". In fact, the latter relationship will be the subject of a heuristic regression below.

Together, PCA decomposes a market into uncorrelated factors with an economic meaning.

The process of taking a view on the market therefore can be achieved by taking a view on each of the factors. Hence, for each factor, the analyst can decide independently whether to take a view on that factor. His decision should reflect:

- statistical criteria like mean reversion
- fundamental and structural criteria
- flow and other concerns.

A key benefit of PCA is that it links all those criteria (separately for each of the separate factors). PCA factors are not only mean reverting but often also have a meaningful economic interpretation. Hence, they do not only fulfill desired statistical properties but also reveal (in fundamental terms) *why* they have those properties. For example, knowing that the first factor is linked to GDP growth explains its mean reversion by the business cycles and its slow speed of mean reversion by the length of those cycles.

Hence, PCA decomposes the market into uncorrelated mean-reverting factors, which often carry an economic meaning. In other words, PCA allows us to combine statistical analysis with economic analysis so as to associate statistical features of a trade with particular fundamental considerations. For example, the second factor may be negatively correlated to the EUR exchange rate. In this case, a statistically attractive steepening trade looks even more appealing to an investor if he expects the EUR to weaken for fundamental reasons.

While statistical analysis is by construction backward looking, linking it to fundamental variables enables traders to incorporate forward-looking (economic) expectations. This ability to incorporate potential future risks in the analysis is a key benefit of linking statistics to external driving forces. In the example above, a steepening trade may well look statistically attractive, but this could all be due to EUR strength. Thus, a further EUR strengthening, which may be caused by political decisions independent of any statistical properties, is a risk to the trade. The link of statistics through a PCA to these external driving forces can identify these risks. An analyst knowing that the statistically attractive steepness is due to EUR strength will refrain from the trade if he sees a significant risk for further EUR appreciation. As in this example, outside information about macroeconomic events can help with both explaining some observed statistical properties and incorporating forward-looking information into the analysis.

TABLE 3.1 Correlations of the First Three Factors of a PCA on the Bund Yield Curve versus Candidates for External Explaining Variables

	Factor 1	Factor 2	Factor 3
Factor 1 of a PCA on USD swaps	0.73	0.62	−0.10
Factor 2 of a PCA on USD swaps	0.89	0.40	−0.02
Factor 3 of a PCA on USD swaps	−0.21	−0.59	0.31
5Y Bund vol (6M rolling)	−0.52	−0.65	0.03
S&P500	0.60	−0.55	0.11
VIX	−0.72	0.01	−0.16
EUR FX rate	0.44	−0.63	−0.23
Oil	0.58	−0.63	0.08

The general form of this analysis is to investigate the following link, (e.g. via a regression):

$$\text{Factor} \sim \text{External explaining variable(s)}$$

While by construction this type of analysis is outside of the statistical reach of PCA, PCA both *enables* this analysis by generating the dependent variable and *facilitates* the search for relevant external explaining variables by revealing the meaning of its factors. One could investigate the link to external variables by heuristic methods, for example by trying all available financial time series in a regression table against all factors. Note that some financial time series could be trending and therefore not suitable for a regression.[11] The interpretation of the eigenvectors can facilitate the search for the "right" explanatory variables. As these relationships evolve, we recommend monitoring them over time, for example via rolling correlations. For the example of a PCA on the Bund yield curve, the correlations versus some candidates for external driving forces[12] are summarized in Table 3.1.

---

[11] Over the time period used for Table 3.1, the independent variables – including the S&P500, EUR, and Oil – did not exhibit a significant trend and are therefore included. Of course, this could be different over other time periods.

[12] Additionally, economic variables like inflation or GDP (growth) could be included. However, given the low frequency of these data (e.g. quarterly), it is statistically meaningful only for time series spanning several years, not in the current example, which has less than two years of data.

It can be seen that both factor 1 and 2 are significantly influenced by a number of macroeconomic variables. We note in particular the strong link to the US yield curve (as represented by the factors of a PCA) with the surprising fact that factor 1 of the Bund PCA is most correlated to factor 2 of the USD PCA and factor 2 of the Bund PCA to factor 1 of the USD PCA. This could be the starting point for a further investigation, which may reveal interesting differences in the driving forces of global bond markets and their interconnections. Furthermore, the link between factor 2 and currencies as well as commodities jumps out at you, indicating that further analysis may well yield valuable results. Factor 3, on the other hand, seems to be rather uncorrelated to external driving forces. This could indicate that factor 3 is a relatively "pure" relative value factor (i.e. with little correlation to macroeconomic events). This is a typical result, that is while the lower factors often exhibit a high correlation to macroeconomic variables (reflecting the high impact of economic events on markets), higher factors are usually less correlated. As a rule of thumb, the higher the factor, the more weight statistical analysis carries, while the examination of potential external economic risks and the incorporation of forward-looking analysis described above become less important.

As an alternative to the regression of PCA factors versus explaining variables, which is done outside of the PCA itself, one could also include the candidates for explaining variables in the PCA, for example by running a PCA on input data consisting of time series for Bund yields and USD swap rates simultaneously.

Furthermore, PCA may reveal how flows affect the pricing. For example, how much does the k-factor residual for 5Y rates move when a new 5Y bond is issued? Is this a stable pattern? Is the spike linearly dependent on the issuance size? This allows traders to incorporate more technical issues into the framework of a PCA.

Let's see how the ability of PCA to decompose the Bund yield curve into economically meaningful uncorrelated and statistically mean-reverting factors could support finding trade ideas in practice. Figure 3.13 shows the evolution of the first three factors of the Bund yield curve over time.

Using mean reversion models, we can assess for all factors the distance from their long-run means and the speed with which they are likely to return to these means. In our current example, we may conclude that factor 1 has insufficient speed of mean reversion and thus we take no view. Similarly, factor 2 is relatively close to its mean, so we take no view. Factor 3, however, seems to be considerably away from its mean and to have a high speed of mean reversion. Hence, we decide to investigate further for trade ideas based on factor 3 (i.e. butterflies hedged against factors 1 and 2).

FIGURE 3.13 History of the first three factors of a PCA on the Bund yield curve.

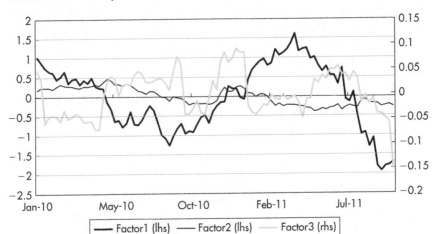

Sources: data – Bloomberg; chart – Authors.
Data period: 4 Jan 2010 to 3 Oct 2011, weekly data.

The statistical side of that investigation is done by a formal mean reversion model, which can calculate the expected return and risk attributes of various trades for specific time horizons.

Factor 3 has little exposure to economic variables and can thus be treated as a "pure" relative value play on mean reversion, with little risk of its statistical properties being thrown off track by macroeconomic events. In this case, the regression Table 3.1 above can serve as justification for restricting the analysis to statistics.

If we took a view on factor 1, on the other hand, we would need to consider the link of the time series of factor 1 and its statistical properties to its external driving forces. Since we found factor 1 to be positively correlated to USD rates and negatively to volatility, among others, the spike in the VIX on 3 Oct 2011 could help us understand the current statistical deviation from the mean. And if we thought that volatility was going to decrease again soon (e.g. because we expected the ECB to calm fears about the euro crisis), we would have both a statistical (mean reversion) and a fundamental reason to bet on an increase in factor 1. Conversely, the mean reversion of factor 1 (as given by statistics) certainly supports our fundamental expectation for volatility to decrease again (i.e. for the current point to be an outlier, i.e. a good entry opportunity). Additionally, one could run a regression between the VIX and factor 1 and decide via the current residual whether the fundamental expectation of decreasing volatility would be better expressed by a short option or a short Bund position.

As in this example, PCA guides the analyst through the process of taking informed views (or the informed absence of a view) on each of the uncorrelated factors: it reveals the statistical properties and economic meaning of each factor behind a position and gives thereby a good basis for a reasonable and substantiated decision, separately for each factor, whether or not to take a view on it.

Once the analyst has decided on which factors he wants to take a view, PCA does both jobs that are needed to execute that view via the most suitable position:

- PCA provides the hedge ratios to immunize against exposure to factors to which he does not want to be exposed.
- The $(n-1)$-factor residuals indicate those individual instruments that provide the best execution for his view on factor n. This can also be used to apply PCA for general asset selection purposes.

In the following, we will develop these features of PCA, before we integrate them back into the process of finding and analyzing trades.

Appropriate Hedging

PCA not only breaks down the driving forces of a trade (like a 5Y-10Y steepening position) into uncorrelated factors but also quantifies their impact and thereby allows us to hedge against specific factors. In order to create a 5Y-10Y steepening position which is not affected by the first factor (i.e. by direction and by directional impacts on the slope), we can simply see how changes in the first factor impact 5Y and 10Y yields and choose the hedge ratios in such a way that both net out. This leaves a position, which is hedged against changes in the first factor, that is a steepening trade which is only affected by the non-directional steepness (and higher factors like curvature), not by directional impacts on the curve and thus a source of P&L uncorrelated to market direction (alpha).

In the PCA framework, hedge ratios are calculated in order to immunize a portfolio against changes in factors. In order to execute the non-directional 5Y-10Y steepening position of the example above, we need to hedge against changes in the directional factor α_1, and the ratio of notionals for 5Y and 10Y is thus: $\dfrac{n_5}{n_{10}} = \dfrac{BPV_{10}}{BPV_5} \cdot \dfrac{e_{110}}{e_{15}}$.

In the formula above, the ratio $\dfrac{e_{110}}{e_{15}}$ represents the quotient of 10Y and 5Y sensitivities to changes in the first factor. This may sound similar to the "beta-adjustment" of basis point value (BPV) hedge ratios by the slope of the regression line of a regression between the two instruments involved. However, as a regression minimizes the *conditional* expected value of deviations, it is conceptually quite different from a PCA. This is reflected in the practical problem that, unless the correlation is 1 or -1, the hedge ratio determined by beta adjustment changes when the dependent and independent variable in the regression are exchanged. PCA works without conditional expected values and is hence free from this problem.

Hedge ratios against more factors are best calculated via matrix inversion. For example, the hedge ratio for a 2Y-5Y-10Y butterfly which is neutral to changes in the first and second factor can be calculated for a given notional n_5 for 5Y by:

$$\begin{pmatrix} n_2 \\ n_{10} \end{pmatrix} = \begin{pmatrix} BPV_2 \cdot e_{12} & BPV_{10} \cdot e_{110} \\ BPV_2 \cdot e_{22} & BPV_{10} \cdot e_{210} \end{pmatrix}^{-1} \cdot \begin{pmatrix} -n_5 \cdot BPV_5 \cdot e_{15} \\ -n_5 \cdot BPV_5 \cdot e_{25} \end{pmatrix}$$

We argue that hedge ratios should be based on PCA rather than on BPV neutrality. BPV neutrality corresponds to assuming arbitrarily that all entries in the first eigenvector are the same (which is in fact our very crude example for a factor model of the first category at the beginning of this chapter). The market tells us that they are not. In other words, directional shifts do affect different points on the yield curve in different ways. If the 5Y Bund yield increases by one basis point (bp), the 10Y yield is expected to increase by 0.87 bp. True neutrality with respect to the level of yields needs to take these impacts of the direction on the curve shape into account by using hedge ratios based on PCA eigenvectors. By contrast, BPV neutrality results in positions with directional exposure.

To illustrate our point, we have regressed a BPV-neutral weighted 2Y-5Y-7Y butterfly and a PCA-neutral weighted 2Y-5Y-7Y butterfly on the Bund curve against the first factor (representing directionality), the second factor (representing non-directional steepness), and the third factor (representing curvature net of the impacts of the first and second factor on curvature, i.e. net of the impacts of direction and of non-directional steepness on curvature[13]). The results are depicted in Figure 3.14. It turns out that the BPV-neutral butterfly is not only directional but also provides little exposure to the third factor. Hence, by choosing BPV-neutral weights for a 2Y-5Y-7Y butterfly, the investor ends up with a fuzzy exposure to direction, non-directional steepness, and just a bit of net curvature. Given the strength of directional impacts, virtually all of his performance will be driven by the market direction, thus transacting Bund futures

---

[13] These verbal monstrosities are the translation of mathematical factor decomposition into everyday terms.

FIGURE 3.14 Driving forces of a BPV-neutral and a PCA-neutral 2Y-5Y-7Y butterfly on the Bund curve.

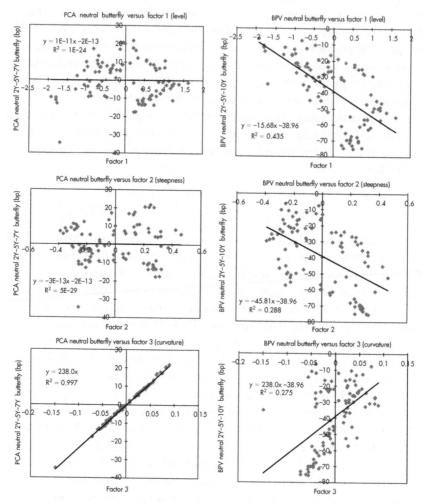

Sources: data – Bloomberg; chart – Authors.
Data period: 4 Jan 2010 to 3 Oct 2011, weekly data.

would have resulted in almost the same exposure (with fewer costs and a cleaner understanding of the risk profile). Presumably, he wanted to be exposed to factor 3 rather than a fuzzy combination of risks; however, by BPV-neutral weighting, he lost almost all net curvature exposure and ended up with a risk profile he probably did not even know of (because PCA is needed for the decomposition into factors) and is now heavily dependent on the market direction against which he thinks he is "hedged". Note that this example is still benign in the sense that at least the correlation of the BPV-neutral butterfly to the third factor is positive. However, this does not need to be the case and there are instances where BPV-neutral steepeners are actually non-directional *flatteners*. Thus, BPV-neutral "hedging" may give any exposure, by chance the right one, a completely different one (like in the butterfly example above, which is mainly dependent on factor 1 rather than 3), or even an exposure which is opposite to the intended one. Only PCA allows the decomposition of the exposure into its components – and hence also the calculation of the "right" hedge ratio (i.e. the one leaving only the desired exposure).

This is depicted in Figure 3.14 in the regression charts of the PCA-neutral butterfly, which is fully exposed to the net curvature (factor 3). Further, this is the only factor to which the PCA-neutral butterfly is exposed.[14] Hence, only the PCA hedge produces a position with a clean and clear exposure to precisely those factors, to which an exposure is intended.

Note the difference of goals in PCA-neutral hedging and hedge ratios, which are calculated in order to maximize Sharpe ratios. While hedge ratios determined by maximizing Sharpe ratios (or another desired feature) obviously have the best statistical properties, PCA-neutral positions give a clear picture, to which factors a trade is exposed. And since these factors often have a meaningful economic interpretation, the investor can assess and adjust his risk profile in economic terms. For example, he knows that the PCA-neutral butterfly is hedged against directional impacts on the yield curve. One cannot say that statistically optimized hedge ratios or PCA-neutral hedge ratios are "better", they just achieve different goals by construction: statistical optimality of a position or a position with a clear exposure to economically interpretable variables. In a manner of speaking, the investor choosing PCA-neutral hedge ratios rather than those optimizing Sharpe ratios gives up some statistical benefits in order to gain the confidence of knowing the exposure of his trade in economic terms, for example the confidence of knowing that it is immune from directional impacts.

Analyzing the Exposure of Trading Positions and Investment Portfolios

Just as in the example of Figure 3.14, any position can be regressed against the uncorrelated factors of a PCA. Thereby, its driving forces reveal

---

[14] In fact, it is also exposed to factors 4 and higher, but they have much less impact on the overall yield curve variation (and butterfly trade performance) than factor 3 does. The crucial point is to hedge against all factors of lower order than the one to which exposure is wanted.

themselves. This gives a clear picture of what really impacts the P&L of complex trades. For those investors using BPV-neutral hedging, the result can be quite surprising, as in the example above. Fortunately, if the actual exposure turns out to be different from the desired one, applying the appropriate PCA hedge ratios solves the problem.

For example, if a market maker has just transacted a BPV-neutral 2Y-5Y-7Y butterfly with an investor, he could run the regressions from above, find that he is now exposed 44% to factor 1, 29% to factor 2, and 28% to factor 3, see how this nets out with other positions in his portfolio and initiate the appropriate hedging (against those factors to which he does not want to be exposed).

Moreover, basing analysis on orthogonal eigenvectors "orthogonalizes" the mind of analysts. It helps us provide a clean and clear analysis. Which trade is exposed to which factors? Do I like that exposure or not? If not, how can I hedge against it? Do I recommend a butterfly due to its directionality or due to its curvature exposure? This breakdown of any trade into its uncorrelated driving forces prevents the all-too-common mix-up of arguments, for example an analyst arguing via curvature for a butterfly while it has, in fact, a purely directional exposure.

Market Reconstruction and Forecasting

Reversing the decomposition of a complex market into its uncorrelated components, factor models in general allow an approximate reconstruction of the larger market from a limited number of factors.

And among all factor models, PCA does the best job in that it provides the closest possible reconstruction to reality given limited information. This is the basis for a variety of applications, a couple of which we briefly highlight now.

Often, market participants are interested in knowing how a certain event would impact the overall market. For example, how would the yield curve be expected to react if CPI were to increase by 1%? Or what would it mean for the yield curve, if 2Y Bund yields increased by 25 bp? In mathematical terms, this corresponds to reconstructing the whole set of information (yield curve) from one single piece of information (short rates go up by 25 bp). The first eigenvector contains just this transformation, as it translates the movement of one point on the yield curve into the move of the whole curve. Using the sensitivities of Figure 3.5, an increase of 2Y yields by 25 bp would be associated with 5Y yields rising by 33 bp, 7Y by 24 bp, and 10Y by 23 bp on average. These numbers are given by multiplying 25 bp with the ratio of sensitivities to the first factor, just as in the calculation of PCA hedge ratios.

Since by construction, the first factor contains maximum information, the PCA reconstruction minimizes the residuals (i.e. provides the best possible picture of the overall market given the informational constraints).

If the reaction of the yield curve to external driving forces should be estimated, the change of an external variable can in a first step be translated via a regression into changes of factors and then the yield curve can be reconstructed from those factors. For example, a change in the EUR FX rate affects all three factors of a PCA on the Bund curve (see regression Table 3.1). Thus, the impact of a one-point change in the EUR FX rate on the whole Bund yield curve can be assessed by calculating its impact on the first three factors (via a regression) and then reconstructing the whole yield curve from those factors.

A similar method can be used to hedge and price trading books. Imagine that since the last close, Schatz, Bobl, and Bund futures have moved by 2, 3, and 2 bp respectively. Now, a client asks a trader to buy an illiquid 7Y Bund, in which no market action has occurred since the last close, from him. The best hedge the trader can achieve in that situation is to reconstruct the yield curve (or only the 7Y point) from the information about the 2Y, 5Y, and 10Y points via the first three factors of a PCA and hedge his position in an illiquid 7Y Bund via a combination of Schatz, Bobl, and Bund futures. The hedge ratios are calculated as described above in order to achieve neutrality against the first three factors. Again, given the constraints (just three liquid instruments), this is the best hedge possible (i.e. it has smallest residual to the actual moves of the 7Y Bund).

A Yield Curve Model Based on PCA

PCA is a deterministic linear algebra tool that simply transforms the basis of the covariance matrix without introducing any stochastic process. Correspondingly, if there are n input variables, PCA will return n factors ($k = n$), and the PCA model outlined above has no residual.

One can now *artificially* introduce a residual by redefining factors as residuals. With $\begin{pmatrix} \varepsilon_1^t \\ \vdots \\ \varepsilon_n^t \end{pmatrix} := \sum_{i=k+1}^{n} \alpha_i^t \cdot \begin{pmatrix} e_{i1} \\ \vdots \\ e_{in} \end{pmatrix}$, the PCA model $\begin{pmatrix} y_1^t \\ \vdots \\ y_n^t \end{pmatrix} =$

$\sum_{i=1}^{n} \alpha_i^t \cdot \begin{pmatrix} e_{i1} \\ \vdots \\ e_{in} \end{pmatrix}$ becomes $\begin{pmatrix} y_1^t \\ \vdots \\ y_n^t \end{pmatrix} = \sum_{i=1}^{k} \alpha_i^t \cdot \begin{pmatrix} e_{i1} \\ \vdots \\ e_{in} \end{pmatrix} + \begin{pmatrix} \varepsilon_1^t \\ \vdots \\ \varepsilon_n^t \end{pmatrix}$ and now

looks like a k-factor stochastic yield curve model.

This specific approach has two important consequences. First, the analyst can decide the number of factors to use for a PCA-based model. There is no argument that forces him to limit the factor decomposition to two, three, or seven factors. Hence, he can choose the number of factors freely in his model. He will typically base his choice on the goal of the analysis and the structure of the eigenvalues. In particular, external knowledge about market mechanisms can be introduced via the selection of the number of factors. If, for example, in the process of eigenvector interpretation it turns out that the yield curve is driven by the first three factors, then the analyst can conduct a three-factor decomposition and justifiably treat the remaining factors as stochastic residuals.

Second, and key for the following, the residuals will continue to exhibit a factor structure when the number of factors used in the model is lower than the number of factors exhibited by the data. In the example above, the two-factor residuals will consist of both the third factor and the three-factor residuals (which, in this example, are assumed to have no clear factor structure and are therefore indiscriminately treated as noise). In general, if the eigenvalues are decreasing quickly, it will hold true that

$$\begin{pmatrix} \varepsilon_1^t \\ \vdots \\ \varepsilon_n^t \end{pmatrix} \approx \alpha_{k+1}^t \cdot \begin{pmatrix} e_{k+1\,1} \\ \vdots \\ e_{k+1\,n} \end{pmatrix}, \text{ that is:}$$

k-factor residual $\approx (k + 1)$-th factor $\times (k + 1)$-th factor loading.

In particular, the shape of k-factor residuals will correspond to the shape of the (k+1)-th factor loading and the size of k-factor residuals to the size of the (k+1)-th factor. Thus, k-factor residuals are high if and only if factor $(k+1)$ is high (in absolute terms). And as high residuals indicate candidates for trading opportunities, the analyst only needs to follow a few factors in order to keep track of all potential trades. This obviously greatly simplifies the task of screening the market for trade ideas.

PCA as a Tool for Screening the Market for Trade Ideas

This factor structure means in practice that by following a few uncorrelated factors the analyst can monitor all relevant market developments in an easy and orderly manner. Outliers in the factors can be directly translated into candidates for trade ideas. By contrast, the set of all BPV-neutral butterflies, which may at first glance appear to offer more independent trading possibilities (through different combinations, like 1-2-3, 1-2-5, 2-5-7), do not contain *more* information than the three factors (and their residuals) but just represent the same information in different and meaningless *mixtures*. For example, a 1-3-5 butterfly may mix 70% of factor 1, 25% of factor 2, and 5% of factor 3. A 2-7-10 butterfly may mix 80% of factor 1, 10% of factor 2, and 10% of factor 3. All these mixtures are endless repetitions of the same information, which can be identified and expressed cleanly, clearly, and easily through a few uncorrelated PCA factors.

Therefore, the yield curve model based on PCA can be used to screen the market for statistically attractive trading opportunities.

Applying this theory to the example of the Bund yield curve, we see with one glance on Figure 3.13 that factor 2 is close to its mean and hence it makes no sense to look for non-directional steepness positions.[15] Factor 3, on the other hand, seems to be significantly away from its mean (and, unlike factor 1, exhibits a sufficient speed of mean reversion). Thus, we would focus our attention on butterfly positions (neutral against factor 1 and 2).

Note again that almost all the relevant information needed to assess the statistical features and attractiveness of yield curve trades is contained in the single Figure 3.13. A screenshot like this can therefore greatly simplify the efforts of an analyst and direct them toward the most promising targets. This is a direct exploitation of the mathematics of a PCA, which reduce almost all the information contained in the Bund curve to three numbers (factors). Correspondingly, the single Figure 3.13 contains all information about the historical evolution of the Bund market, in an orderly and clear way. This is the basis that enables in practical terms an easy and systematical screening of the whole Bund market for trades, missing none and counting no one twice. After getting used to it, one does not like to follow a market in a different form than a factor decomposition like Figure 3.13.

PCA as a Tool for Asset Selection

Having identified butterflies as candidates for curve trades, we can select the best maturities (from a statistical point of view) by looking at their two-factor residuals (i.e. the sum of the third factor times the third factor loadings and the three-factor residuals). In case of the eigenvalues decreasing quickly, this will almost equal the *shape* of the third factor loadings, and indeed the shape seen in Figure 3.15 is very similar to that of the third-factor loadings depicted in Figure 3.5 (mirrored by the x-axis since the third factor is currently

---

[15] This discussion is obviously restricted to *statistical* reasons for a trade. Of course, there can be other reasons, like fundamental views or anticipated flows, for or against a trade.

FIGURE 3.15 Two-factor residuals.

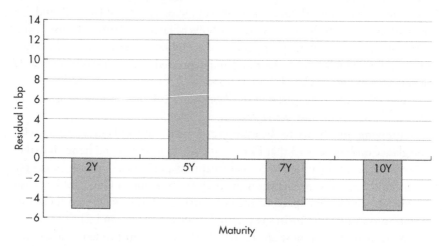

Maturity

Sources: data – Bloomberg; chart – Authors.
Data period: 4 Jan 2010 to 3 Oct 2011, weekly data; current residuals as of 3 Oct 2011.

negative). Consequently, a 2Y-5Y-10Y butterfly maximizes the potential profit from the current deviation of factor 3 from its mean.

Moreover, the third factor mainly determines the *size* of the two-factor residuals (i.e. the potential profit from mean reversion). Given that factor 3 is currently quite exceptionally far away from its mean (Figure 3.13), the residuals (Figure 3.15) are large by historical standards and hence the 2Y-5Y-10Y butterfly looks attractive also from a historical point of view. Note how favorably such a PCA-based top-down analysis compares to the bottom-up approach of screening all possible butterfly combinations.[16]

When analyzing swap curves, the selection of the best maturities can of course also be done by displaying a residual chart like Figure 3.15 for the swap rates of each maturity. Additionally or alternatively, one can use the consecutive one-year forward swap rates (i.e. the 1Y, 1Y forward 1Y, 2Y forward 1Y, 3Y forward 1Y etc. swap rate) as input in a PCA. This is like running the analysis on the consecutive building blocks of the yield curve rather than on the combinations of those building blocks into usual swap rates. Since there is less information overlap between the consecutive one-year forward swap rates than between usual swap rates (the 29Y and 30Y swap

---

[16] Actually, PCA was first applied in engineering with the aim to find the common behavior of a production series and to detect outliers, quite similar to our application in finance, where common behavior = market mechanisms and outliers = candidates for trading opportunities.

FIGURE 3.16 Two-factor residuals of a PCA on consecutive one-year forward EUR swap rates.

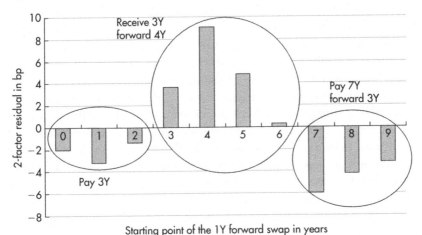

Sources: data – Bloomberg, authors; chart – Authors.

rates contain the same consecutive 29 one-year forward swap rates and differ just in the last one), usually the correlation between the consecutive one-year forward swap rates is lower, which may result in better statistical properties of the PCA. Furthermore, the output of that PCA will be a residual chart showing richness and cheapness *of the individual building blocks* of the yield curve. For the example of a factor 3 trade on the consecutive one-year forward swap rate curve, the picture of two-factor residuals could look like the one shown in Figure 3.16.

Then, the areas of richness and cheapness can be combined. In the example of Figure 3.16, the resulting butterfly trade would be pay 3Y (the combination of 1Y, 1Y forward 1Y, and 2Y forward 1Y), receive 3Y forward 4Y (the combination of 3Y forward 1Y, 4Y forward 1Y, 5Y forward 1Y, and 6Y forward 1Y), pay 7Y forward 3Y (the combination of 7Y forward 1Y, 8Y forward 1Y, and 9Y forward 1Y). Note that this approach allows a much sharper selection of rich and cheap areas than the usual swap rates. For example, the cheap 5Y swap rate contains the rich 2Y swap rate, while the 3Y forward 4Y rate does not. Thus, combining the building blocks of the rich and cheap rate curve areas together offers the maximal exploitation of the residuals. On the other hand, transaction costs are usually higher for awkward forward rate combinations than for plain vanilla swap rates. There is hence a tradeoff between the higher residuals and the higher transaction costs for trades on the consecutive forward rate curve. Altogether, using consecutive forward rates is particularly advisable in case the statistical properties of the PCA need to be improved and in case the profit from asset selection (residuals) is high.

In general terms, once an investor has defined the desired factor exposure of his portfolio, the PCA residuals to these factors will show the best way to get this exposure. And since the residuals are uncorrelated to the factors, this asset selection method offers a source of profit which is uncorrelated to the factors (i.e. to whether the view on factors turns out to be right or wrong).

For example, imagine an investor is bullish on Bunds in general and thus decides to buy a Bund[17] (i.e. to get exposure to factor 1). He can then look at the chart shown in Figure 3.17 of one-factor residuals (i.e. the difference between actual Bund yields and where they typically should be, given the overall yield level). (Note again how closely the shape of one-factor residuals follows the shape of the second eigenvector.) A residual of 17 bp for 2Y means that a 2Y Bund trades 17 bp too cheaply relative to the overall yield level (factor 1). These 17 bp are a source of profit uncorrelated to the direction (i.e. alpha), enhance the return in case of the bet on direction turning out to be right, and serve as a cushion in case of the bullish view turning out to be wrong.

Of course, it is also possible to trade only the residuals, without exposure to the factors. In the case of a three-factor model, this corresponds in our

FIGURE 3.17   One-factor residuals.

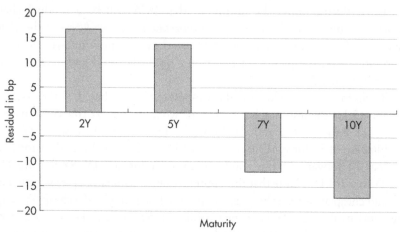

Sources: data – Bloomberg; chart – Authors.
Data period: 4 Jan 2010 to 3 Oct 2011, weekly data; current residuals as of 3 Oct 2011.

---

[17] Of course, he could also receive swaps instead, or buy futures, or calls on futures etc. We shall discuss asset selection among different classes of instruments in the following chapters.

framework to taking no view on any of the three factors, hence hedging against all of them (by using a combination of four instruments, what is sometimes called a *condor*), leaving exposure only to the residuals. As we have seen already, the influence of economic variables is typically concentrated on the lower factors; hedging against all factors and just exploiting the residuals (i.e. the combination of all higher "factors") usually leads to "pure" relative value trading with a focus on statistical properties.[18]

Example of a PCA-based Trade Idea

Let us now put together the elements developed above to illustrate the flow of analysis that could lead to a PCA-based trade recommendation. For the sake of simplicity, we present it in the form of a step-by-step guide (Box 3.1), but note that this cooking recipe is only a rough template that may need to be adjusted to different situations. Also, a reader wishing to get started with PCA would do well to set up an IT environment that was able to reproduce the charts used here. To facilitate this task, we have put the Excel sheet that produced these screenshots on the website accompanying the book, while referring to the disclaimer and warnings contained in it.

Box 3.1   Constructing trade ideas with PCA: A step-by-step guide

Step 1: Decide on the relevant input data for the PCA, depending on the goals of the analysis: time horizon, type and number of variables, change or level data. Usually, at least one year of data is advisable. In our example, we use weekly level data for 2Y, 5Y, 7Y, and 10Y Bund yields from 4 Jan 2010 to 3 Oct 2011.

For heuristic purposes (i.e. to find the best instruments), use a large number of variables (e.g. all yields from 1 to 30 years); if the instruments of the trade are already known, restrict the input to these. Actually, one can run the PCA twice, first with a large set of variables (like from 1 to 30 years), and after the best instruments have been found for a second time (e.g. just with 2Y, 5Y, and 7Y for a butterfly trade), in particular to calculate the hedge ratios.

---

[18] Any correlation a high factor (e.g. factor 7) might have to an external economic variable is likely to disappear in the combination of the high factors (e.g. factors 4–10) to a residual.

Step 2: Run the PCA. Check numerical stability and the results: are the calculated eigenvectors really eigenvectors and orthogonal to each other?

Step 3: Display the eigenvalues (Figure 3.4) and assess the factor structure of the market analyzed. In particular, does factorization makes sense at all (i.e. do the eigenvalues exhibit a clear factor structure)? A strong decrease of eigenvalues (i.e. $|\lambda_1| >> |\lambda_2| >> \cdots >> |\lambda_n|$) together with a high correlation within the data, corresponds to a clear factor structure and allows a meaningful reduction in the dimensionality of the data, of information into factors.

On the other hand, if correlation within the data is small, meaningful information reduction will be impossible. For example, if

$$Cov = \begin{pmatrix} 1 & 0 & 0 \\ 0 & \ddots & 0 \\ 0 & 0 & 1 \end{pmatrix}, \text{ then every point on the yield curve will have its}$$

own factor.

Step 4: Display the (relevant) eigenvectors (Figure 3.5) and interpret them.

Step 5: Display the time series of the (relevant) factors (Figure 3.13). This is a crucial result that serves as the basis for a number of subsequent actions, for example:

- Assess the statistical qualities of each factor; in particular, is it close to its mean or far away?
- Check the correlation between factors over subperiods. We discuss this issue in detail later.
- Use the time series of a factor as input into an Ornstein–Uhlenbeck (OU) process, for example to assess its speed of mean reversion.
- Use that time series as explaining variable in regressions, as in Figure 3.14, in order to check the exposure of a certain position. In particular, after a trade idea has been formulated, run those regressions in order to confirm that it really has the desired exposure (especially that an RV trade is really non-directional).
- Use that time series as dependent variable in regressions versus external (candidates for) explaining variables. This is the link of the statistical analysis to the fundamental and structural analysis, which allows complementing backward-looking statistics with forward-looking expectations about macroeconomic events and potential risks. For the current example, we have provided that analysis in Table 3.1.

Step 6: Based on statistical, fundamental/structural and flow/other considerations, decide on which factor you want to take a view. In the example above and restricting ourselves to statistical reasons only, we might conclude that factor 1 has too little speed of mean reversion, thus take no view. Factor 2 is close to its mean, thus we take no view. Factor 3, however, seems to be significantly away from its mean and to have a high speed of mean reversion. Hence, we decide to investigate further for trade ideas based on factor 3 (i.e. butterflies hedged against factors 1 and 2).

Step 7: In order to select the best points on the yield curve to express that view, display the relevant residual chart, in our example the two-factor residual chart (Figure 3.15). Decide on the instruments.[19] In our example, we may want to choose sell 2Y, buy 5Y, sell 7Y (10Y has a little more negative residual than 7Y, but we might decide that the additional 0.5 bp residual is not worth the risk of going out three years further on the yield curve).

Step 8: Calculate and display the time series of that specific residual butterfly (Figure 3.18). This represents the actual performance of the trade in the past and the future performance will depend on that series. Now, run the regressions from Figure 3.14 in order to check that the individual selection of instruments offers the desired factor exposure.[20]

FIGURE 3.18   2Y-5Y-7Y butterfly of two-factor residuals.

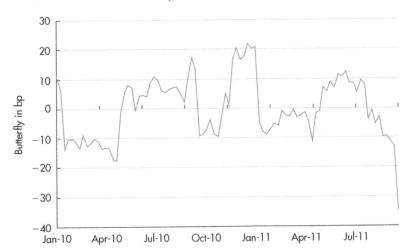

Sources: data – Bloomberg; chart – Authors.
Data period: 4 Jan 2010 to 3 Oct 2011, weekly data.

---

[19] Again, other considerations than statistics play a major role, too, in particular flow information and carry/roll-down concerns.

[20] It could happen, for example, that the sensitivities to factor 3 of all the specific instruments selected are zero and that therefore the performance of the specific butterfly is uncorrelated to factor 3 and rather a function of factor 4.

Step 9: Run the OU model for the time series of Figure 3.18 in order to assess the expected performance of the trade. As outlined in Chapter 2, calculate:

- the expected profit. In our example: 32 bp;[21]
- the expected downside risk. In the OU framework, the stop loss could be set at the two-sigma level (Figure 3.19), resulting in a stop loss level that moves over time. In our example this approach would result in a stop loss level at −42 bp (loss of 7 bp) after one week.

FIGURE 3.19   PCA-neutral 2Y-5Y-7Y Bund butterfly and its future path as modeled by an OU process.

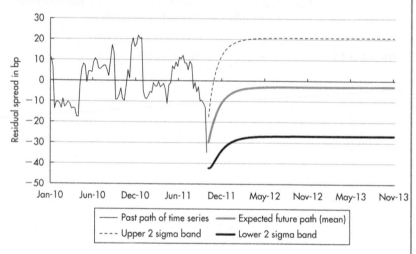

Sources: data – Bloomberg; chart – Authors.
Data period: 4 Jan 2010 to 3 Oct 2011, weekly data as input; forecast period as output from OU model.

---

[21] This chart has been generated by applying the general tool on the website, which *estimates* the mean. In the current case, the estimated mean of −3 bp is slightly different from the actual mean, which is 0 for any factor or residual time series from a PCA. If the actual mean is known, as in the current case, the estimation of the mean from the general tool on the website could be overwritten. Then, the expected profit would be 3 bp higher.

- The first passage time density and the expected time until mean reversion (Figure 3.20). In our example, the trade returns to its (estimated) mean (yields 32 bp profit) on average over 84 calendar days.

FIGURE 3.20 First passage time density for the PCA-neutral 2Y-5Y-7Y butterfly as modeled by an OU process.

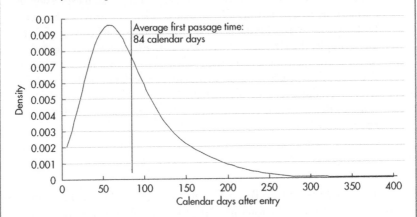

Sources: data – Bloomberg; chart – Authors.
Data period: 4 Jan 2010 to 3 Oct 2011, weekly data as input for the OU model.

Step 10: Calculate the hedge ratios. In our example, we achieve factor 1 and 2 neutrality (i.e. the exposure to the time series of Figure 3.18) by selling 80m 2Y, buying 100m 5Y, and selling 58m 7Y Bunds. This has been calculated by a matrix inversion as discussed above. The numbers worked out as follows: with a BPV for 2Y of 1.98, for 5Y of 4.86, and for 7Y of 6.62 and sensitivities of 0.42, 0.55, and 0.53 to the first and of -0.84, -0.04, and 0.29 to the second factor of 2Y, 5Y, and 7Y (these numbers are the entries of the eigenvectors, which can be taken from the sheet on the website), the matrix $\begin{pmatrix} BPV_2 \cdot e_{12} & BPV_7 \cdot e_{17} \\ BPV_2 \cdot e_{22} & BPV_7 \cdot e_{27} \end{pmatrix}$ is $\begin{pmatrix} 0.84 & 3.51 \\ -1.66 & 1.91 \end{pmatrix}$ and its inverse thus $\begin{pmatrix} 0.26 & -0.47 \\ 0.22 & 0.11 \end{pmatrix}$. Multiplying to that matrix the vector $\begin{pmatrix} -n_5 \cdot BPV_5 \cdot e_{15} \\ -n_5 \cdot BPV_5 \cdot e_{25} \end{pmatrix}$ (with n_5 to be assumed to be one), that is $\begin{pmatrix} -2.69 \\ 0.22 \end{pmatrix}$, gives the vector of weights for 2Y and 7Y: $\begin{pmatrix} -0.80 \\ -0.58 \end{pmatrix}$. Then, the relative weights can be scaled to the desired trade size, in the example above by multiplying with 100m.

Step 11: Based on the expected holding horizon (84 calendar days) of the OU process and the hedge ratios, calculate the carry. Note that in the absence of BPV neutrality carry cannot naturally be expressed in bp terms anymore. Therefore, calculate the carry in money terms (i.e. euros and cents), based on the PCA-neutral hedge ratios. In a PCA framework, it is natural to express carry in money terms; should expression in bp terms be required, it must be stated, to *which* maturity the bps refer (as PCA does away with the false assumption of parallel curve shifts). In our example, the 84 calendar day carry is EUR 70,000 positive,[22] thus rather negligible compared to the profit potential from mean reversion. If the carry had been significantly negative, calculating additionally the carry until the 90% quartile of Figure 3.20 could have helped assess whether the trade was still attractive in case it took unusually long to revert back to its mean.[23]

And how did the trade in Box 3.1 perform in reality? Figure 3.21 compares the actual evolution with the forecast of the OU model. It may be no surprise to the reader that we have picked an example that worked well. In the following we will discuss instances where PCA might not work that smoothly.

Problems and Pitfalls of PCA 1: Correlation between Factors during Subperiods

By construction, factors are uncorrelated over the whole sample period used as input data into a PCA, which allows one to construct a position hedged against certain factors. However, there could occur correlation between factors during subperiods. In such a case, the hedge could break down during

---

[22] As this is for illustration purposes only, we have used general collateral (GC) rates for the carry calculation.

[23] Imagine a trade with a 10 bp profit potential and a three-month negative carry also of 10 bp. If the OU model shows an expected holding horizon of just two weeks (over which the negative carry is, say, 2 bp), the negative carry might be acceptable. The confidence in this position could increase further if the OU process suggests a 90% chance of the 10 bp profit to materialize over one month. Alternatively, one could calculate the probability of the mean reversion taking longer than three months (i.e. the likelihood that the negative carry would exceed the profit from mean reversion).

FIGURE 3.21 Performance of Bund butterfly after entry compared to OU model forecast.

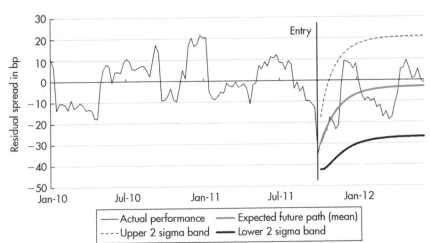

Sources: data – Bloomberg; chart – Authors.
Data period: 4 Jan 2010 to 11 Jun 2012, weekly data.

that subperiod. For example, a trade on factor 2 hedged against factor 1 would be exposed to factor 1 during a time period, in which ephemeral correlation between factor 1 and 2 occurred. In this case, the performance of what was intended to be a non-directional steepening position would be driven (ephemerally) by direction.

To see how the theoretical problem of correlation between factors during subperiods can affect trades, let's consider the example of a 2Y-10Y PCA-neutral steepening trade on the Bund curve. In October 2010 and October 2011, the time series shown in Figure 3.22 may well have looked too good to resist from entering the trade.

However, before hitting the target (reverting back to mean), a steepening position entered in October 2011 broke through the OU stop loss and subsequently underperformed further. The reason for this misbehavior can be seen in the graph in Figure 3.23, which regresses the residual spread (PCA-neutral steepening trade) against the first factor, just like in Figure 3.14.

It turns out that, while overall the correlation is zero, there has been a high correlation to the first factor on the left-hand side of the chart in Figure 3.23. Further investigation reveals that in the six months before entry the trade (a factor 2 position) followed factor 1 very closely. Thus, the reason for

FIGURE 3.22 PCA-neutral 2Y-10Y Bund steepening position.

Sources: data – Bloomberg; chart – Authors.
Data period: 7 Jan 2008 to 11 Jun 2012, weekly data.

FIGURE 3.23 PCA-neutral steepener versus factor 1.

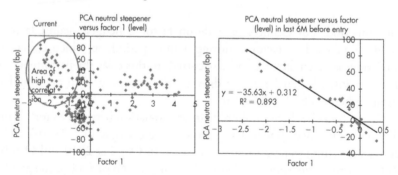

Sources: data – Bloomberg; chart – Authors.
Data period: 7 Jan 2008 to 22 Aug 2011, weekly data (left chart), 28 Feb 2011 to 22 Aug 2011, weekly data (right chart).

the underperformance of the PCA-neutral Bund steepening trade was that it was in fact a directional trade, and, since the direction happened to work against it, its less-strong factor 2 exposure could not save it from losing.[24]

---

[24] Also in October 2010, there was a high correlation to factor 1, but this time the direction worked in favor of the steepening trade. Thus, in 2010, the trade made money, but for the wrong reason: not because it was a factor 2 position hedged against factor 1 as intended but because we were lucky that the direction worked in our favor.

Compare this situation with the regressions depicted in Figure 3.14, where we have argued against BPV-neutral weighting due to its factor 1 exposure: in times of ephemeral correlation between the factors, a PCA-neutral trade shares the fate and criticism of BPV-neutral trades.

The good news is that in many cases correlation between factors during subperiods can be spotted before entering into a trade. To do so, it is crucial to run the regressions (step 5 of the flow above). Often, a potential problem with factor correlation announces itself, as in the current example. Thus, if there has been a high correlation between the factors in the time period before (as in Figure 3.23), caution is advisable. By contrast, the 2Y-5Y-7Y butterfly entered on 3 Oct 2011 did not exhibit a significant correlation of factors before entry: the entry level is the isolated point in the lower left corner of Figure 3.14. Unlike the cloud of points along a regression line in Figure 3.23, in the case of the butterfly from Figure 3.14, there is no correlation problem visible – and this was one reason why one trade worked (Figure 3.21) and the other did not (Figure 3.22).

In recent times, the reason for correlation of factors between subperiods is often the shift in the credit assessment of sovereign issuers. Imagine that a PCA is calculated on data before credit risk became an issue in Western government bond markets. From the point in time onwards when it did become an issue, it will impact factor 1 (the yield level tends to increase when credit risk increases) *and* factor 2 (since the longer the maturity, the more it will be affected by increasing credit risk,[25] thus an increase in credit risk tends to lead to a higher non-directional steepness of the yield curve). Consequently, the emergence of credit concerns has often resulted in significant correlation between factors 1 and 2. We shall address this issue in detail in Chapter 15 and show how running a PCA on CDS-adjusted yield curves (bond yield minus CDS) can solve the problem.

In our experience, ephemeral correlation between factors is the main pitfall of PCA. Conversely, consistently checking for factor correlation, for example through the method described above, reduces the risk of PCA leading to unsatisfactory trades significantly. When we started using PCA systematically as a tool to find and construct trades in global bond markets about 15 years ago, we did not pay enough attention to the correlation problem and produced a ratio of profitable to overall PCA-based trade

---

[25] As can be seen from Moody's transition matrix, for example, this statement is true for good credits, such as Western government bonds at the start of the recent crisis. When the credit becomes bad, however, the dynamics can change and increasing credit risk can then affect shorter maturities more. See Chapter 15 for more details.

ideas of 82%.[26] After figuring out that many of the 18% of losing trades were due to the correlation issue, we avoided this trap better and could increase the success ratio to just over 90%, with the number of trades obviously going down. In general, experience is required to strike the right balance between having too many trades and being overly cautious. In the current case, striking this balance requires experience to judge the level of correlation between factors in the subperiod that is acceptable before entering a trade. As a rough guide, Figure 3.14 (isolated current point out of cloud of points with no correlation) and Figure 3.23 (correlated cloud of points leading to current point) provide an illustration of unsuspicious and suspicious situations.

Problems and Pitfalls of PCA 2: Instability of Eigenvectors over Time

If eigenvectors change after entering into a trade with PCA hedge ratios, the trade will become exposed to unintended factor risk. Imagine again that we have entered into a trade on factor 2 and hedged against factor 1. If the first eigenvector for the time period during which we hold the trade turns out to be different from the first eigenvector calculated on the sample period before the trade (and thus used for determining the hedge ratios for factor 1 neutrality), then we will be hedged against the "wrong" first eigenvector and exposed to the first factor. Thus, a change of the first eigenvector results in the hedge breaking down and in directional exposure. While the cause can be different, the problem is the same as in the case of correlation between factors occurring after entering into a PCA-neutral position: it loses its neutrality and becomes exposed to factors it was not intended to.

First of all, it is important to distinguish changes in factors from changes in factor loadings: changes in factors occur all the time and are no problem for the PCA model and hedges based on it. For example, yields could fluctuate between 1% and 10% (i.e. α_1 exhibits a high volatility), while the eigenvectors remain stable. If the central bank is driving yields both up and down, then the first eigenvector should maintain its downward sloping shape (depicted in Figure 3.6). However, if the central bank were to cut rates to zero and then announce that it would maintain a zero policy rate for a number of years, the sensitivity of

---

[26] We generated these trade ideas by screening mainly Western government bond markets through an approach similar to the step-by-step guide from above, including macroeconomic analysis (as in Table 3.1) when necessary. A trade was counted as profitable when it reverted back to its mean before hitting the stop loss. Since we pursued an analytical goal, we disregarded issues arising in a trading context, such as bid–ask spreads and capital charges.

short rates to directional moves would be expected to decrease versus the sensitivity of long rates. This corresponds to a change in the first factor loading.

Moreover, sometimes a perceived instability of eigenvectors is the result of a too-short sample period for the PCA calculation. This can be easily avoided by choosing a longer time period (step 1) (in case of yield curve analysis usually at least one year).

In order to get a sense of the empirical stability of eigenvectors, we have run a PCA on yield data for consecutive five-year periods and calculated the eigenvalues and eigenvectors. The charts in Figure 3.24 depict the evolution of eigenvalues and eigenvectors over time for the Bund, USD swap, and JPY swap markets.

In general, the result of this empirical study comes as a relief: despite the sea-changing events that occurred during the last 20 years, eigenvalues and eigenvectors have been remarkably stable (i.e. the factors changed and not the factor loadings), just as a factor model like PCA assumes and requires.

FIGURE 3.24   Evolution of eigenvalues and eigenvectors from 1993 to 2012 in several rate markets.

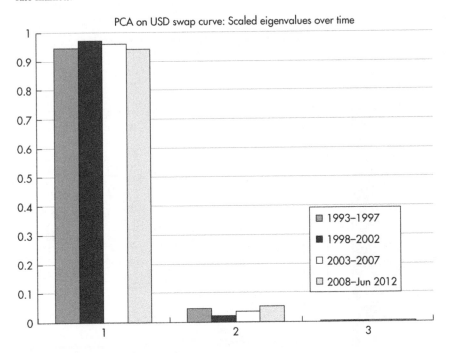

Sources: data – Bloomberg; chart – Authors.
Data period: 1 Jan 1993 to 14 Jun 2012, weekly data, broken down in four five-year sections.

FIGURE 3.24   Continued.

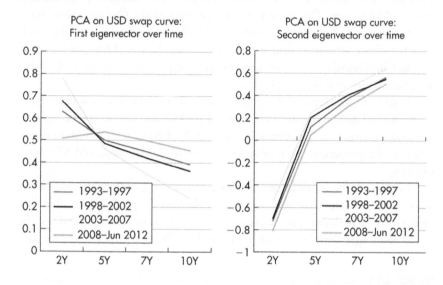

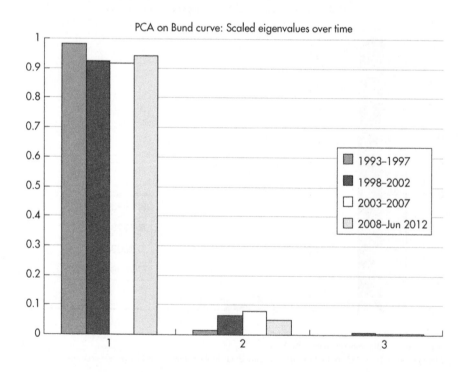

FIGURE 3.24 Continued.

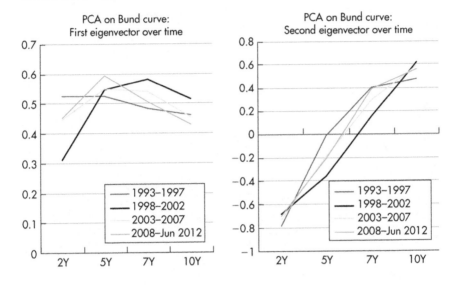

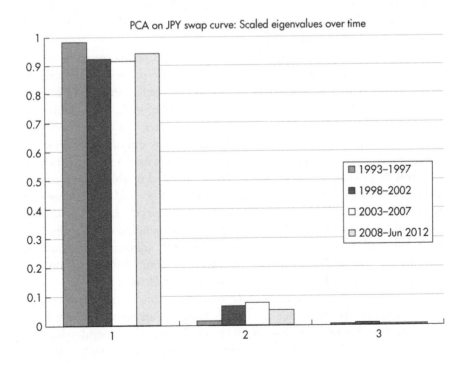

FIGURE 3.24 Continued.

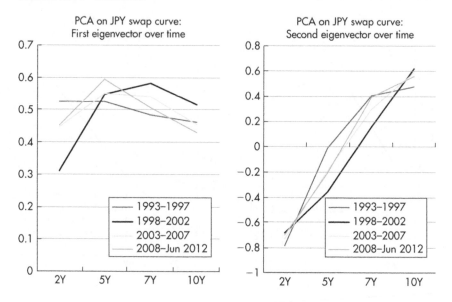

With the exception of the short end, this is even the case for Japan, which saw the transition from a very active central bank to a BoJ which has removed virtually all volatility from its policy rates.

In particular, the recent debt crisis did not leave significant traces in the eigenvectors – while it is an important cause for the problem of correlation between factors during subperiods (see above). Overall, correlation between factors, not eigenvector instability, is the main pitfall of PCA. Accordingly, the crisis starting in 2008 produced a break in the market that often manifested itself in a changing correlation pattern between factors and not so much in an instability of factor loadings. PCA-based trades which used a sample period of pre-crisis data to calculate hedge ratios sometimes faced trouble when the crisis erupted, but almost always due to the factors becoming correlated, seldom due to eigenvectors changing shape. As the problem of factor correlation has receded afterward, we recommend avoiding basing a PCA on sample data which include both pre- and post-crisis data (or using the CDS adjustment outlined in Chapter 15). For analyzing the current market situation, a starting point like January 2010 (as in the butterfly trade example) could work well.

The one exception from stability of eigenvectors is the short end of the curve. This is probably due to the high impact of an external driving force (i.e. central bank action) on that part of the yield curve. Correspondingly, with central banks keeping to a low rate policy and thereby intentionally removing uncertainty, equal volatility, and equal sensitivity from the short end of the yield curve, we currently observe in all major rates markets a relatively low sensitivity of 2Y rates to the first factor. One can react in a couple of ways to this finding:

- Refrain from PCA-based trades on the short end. For example, restrict the input variables to a PCA (step 1) and thus the universe of trades analyzed to maturities above 3Y or 5Y.
- If, nevertheless, a PCA-based trade involves the short end, ensure that its speed of mean reversion is high enough for it to be likely to perform before a (rather long-term) change in central bank policy could affect the eigenvector. Our butterfly trade example from above could fall into that category.
- Intentionally position for the short end of the eigenvector to change. We know that a change in the eigenvector will result in the PCA hedge breaking down. But if we can forecast how the eigenvector is going to change, we can position ourselves in such a way that we will end up being overhedged in a falling and underhedged in a rising market (i.e. turn the problem of changing eigenvectors into a profitable trading strategy that has similarities with delta hedging a long option position). For example, if BoJ ends the zero interest rate policy, an increase in rates (factor 1) should be linked to the short end becoming more volatile (sensitivities in first eigenvector increasing at the short relative to the long end). A curve-flattening position dynamically hedged against (the changing) factor 1 should therefore in fact be overhedged in declining and underhedged in increasing markets.[27]

While these results can serve to increase the confidence of analysts in the stability of eigenvectors of yield curves, it is important to note that in other markets the stability could be less pronounced. In this case, one could compare the stability of eigenvectors with the expected holding horizon of a trade and focus on those positions, which are expected to perform before eigenvectors become unstable. For example, if a PCA-based trade shows an expected holding horizon of a few weeks (step 9 above), it requires the eigenvectors to be stable over at least that period of time (and ideally longer). In markets where stability of eigenvectors could be an issue, an investor may want to refrain from that trade if he sees a risk of eigenvectors changing during the next few weeks, but may still feel comfortable enough, if he perceives potential instability to be a longer-term issue only.

---

[27] This strategy has first been published in the ABN AMRO Research note from 17 Nov 2006 "Exploiting the regime shift with PCA weighted flatteners" and is mentioned here with kind permission from RBS.

PCA as a Tool to Construct New Types of Trades

Finally, we provide an example of how PCA could be used in the currency market, thereby underlining its universal applicability. At the same time, we shall illustrate how creatively a PCA can be applied, using the step-by-step guide from above as stepping stones to a trade idea, which only PCA enables but in which PCA is just one of several parts.

When running a PCA on JPY, GBP, SEK, CHF, AUD, and SGD (versus USD), it is useful to adjust the series for the difference in absolute values in order for the charts to be legible (otherwise, 100 JPY per USD versus 0.6 GBP per USD would show up as huge difference in sensitivities to the eigenvectors, for example). Thus, we have run the PCA on synthetic currencies, starting all at a value of 1 on 4 Jan 1999. The PCA then uses weekly data of these synthetic series from 4 Jan 1999 until 25 July 2011 and can be seen on the Excel sheet on the website accompanying this book.

Figure 3.25 depicts the scaled eigenvalues. It turns out that the relative explanatory strength of the first and second factor in the FX market is similar to the bond market, while the eigenvalues above 3 decrease slower than in the case of bonds.

In Figure 3.26, the eigenvectors are displayed. As in the case of a PCA on bonds, the first eigenvector has only positive entries (i.e. a change in factor 1 affects all currencies similarly). However, the sensitivities may seem puzzling:

FIGURE 3.25   Scaled eigenvalues of a PCA on currencies.

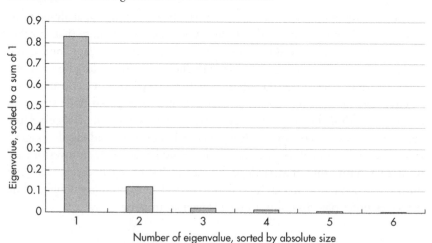

Sources: data – ECB; chart – Authors.
Data period: 4 Jan 1999 to 25 Jul 2011, weekly data.

FIGURE 3.26 Eigenvectors of a PCA on currencies.

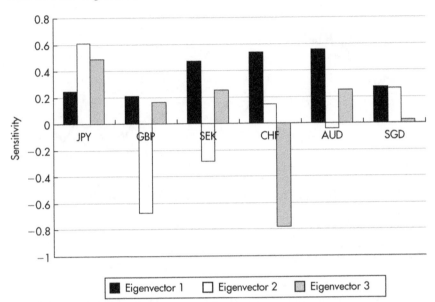

Sources: data – ECB; chart – Authors.
Data period: 4 Jan 1999 to 25 Jul 2011, weekly data.

if factor 1 increases, SEK, CHF, and AUD increase a lot, while JPY, GBP, and SGD less so. Since few FX traders think of grouping currencies in such a manner, this puzzle may represent an interesting, PCA-induced insight, but requires further examination, which will be provided below by looking simultaneously at the time series of factor 1.

Likewise, factors 2 and 3 cause differentiation among currencies (e.g. if factor 2 rises, JPY, CHF, and SGD increase, while GBP, SEK and AUD decrease). This grouping may sound more familiar, as it puts "low risk" and "high risk" currencies together.

Since the interpretation of eigenvectors (i.e. market mechanisms) is less straightforward than in the case of Bunds, we need to consider additionally the time series of the factors and their link to external variables in order to be able to complete the interpretation of the PCA results. The evolution of the factors is shown in Figure 3.27.

This graphical representation may well evoke the visual memory of the analyst. For example, he may find that the evolution of factor 1 is almost a mirror image of the USD–EUR FX rate. This visual discovery can be confirmed (e.g. via a regression, which returns a correlation of −0.94

FIGURE 3.27  Factors of a PCA on currencies.

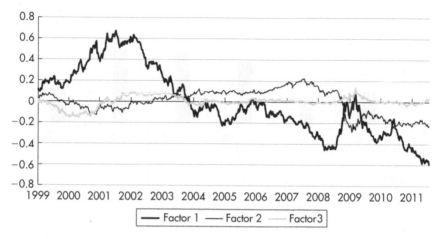

Sources: data – ECB; chart – Authors.
Data period: 4 Jan 1999 to 25 Jul 2011, weekly data.

between factor 1 and the EUR exchange rate). Thus, an increase of factor 1 is strongly linked to the EUR weakening versus the USD. An interesting consequence of that result is that the exchange rate of the USD versus the EUR (which we excluded from the PCA input series) explains 83% (scaled first eigenvalue) of the moves of the USD versus the other currencies. Hence, one may conclude that the USD–EUR rate is by far the most important driving force of all USD FX rates. Moreover, the sensitivities versus the first factor (first eigenvector) group the currencies with a strong (SEK, CHF, AUD) and not so strong (JPY, GBP, SGD) tendency to weaken versus the USD in case of factor 1 going up (i.e. the EUR weakening against the USD).

The time series of factor 2 corresponds well to a more psychological variable like "risk on/risk off". And as expected, factor 2 falling significantly in 2009 (and staying low) has resulted in those currencies with a positive sensitivity to factor 2 ("safe havens") (JPY, CHF, SGD) to outperform those with a negative sensitivity to factor 2 ("risky") (GBP, SEK, AUD). This is probably the picture most traders have in mind when they think about the FX market. Note, however, that a PCA relegates this market mechanism to number two, revealing that it only explains 12% of the FX market action – and reveals the more important structure given by eigenvector 1.

In cases of puzzling eigenvectors, it is often useful to calculate a table of heuristic regressions, with the factors as dependent variables and with various

TABLE 3.2 Correlations of the First Three Factors of a PCA on Currencies versus Candidates for External Explaining Variables

	Factor 1	Factor 2	Factor 3
EUR	−0.94	−0.01	0.13
S&P500	−0.20	0.27	−0.66
VIX	0.15	−0.46	0.28
US swap PCA factor 1	0.64	0.55	−0.49
US swap PCA factor 2	0.42	−0.10	0.16
US swap PCA factor 3	−0.13	−0.04	−0.41
Oil	−0.86	−0.12	−0.07

candidates serving as independent or explanatory variables. We have tried a couple of those regressions and present the results in Table 3.2.[28]

This table confirms our optical interpretation of factor 1 being closely linked to the EUR and factor 2 being a "risk on/risk off" factor, which has therefore some correlation to the direction of USD interest rates (as represented in the first factor of a PCA on USD swaps) and the VIX. Furthermore, this table reveals that the third factor is linked to the S&P500 index – and, indeed, taking another look at the time series of factor 3 in the chart above confirms that it is a close mirror image to the stock market. This relationship is depicted in Figure 3.28 in more detail.

These new insights, which a PCA provides into the FX market, could be used to model currencies by a three-factor model, with the factors linked to external variables like EUR, risk adversity (e.g. VIX), and stock prices.

In the following, however, we would like to show how the insights of a PCA into market mechanisms can be used to construct new trading positions, which would not be possible or understandable outside of the PCA framework.

While there is a reasonable correlation between factor 3 and the S&P500, currently (25 July 2011), the residual of a regression is rather high. Figure 3.29 illustrates that the current point is quite far away from the regression line. Note that in case we use shorter time horizons for the regression we still witness a significant residual. This means that the relationship between factor 3 and stock prices, which has been relatively stable over the past 12 years, is currently disturbed. Thus, in case we believe that the

---

[28] For some series, the time period for the regression is slightly different.

FIGURE 3.28 Factor 3 of a PCA on currencies versus the S&P500 index.

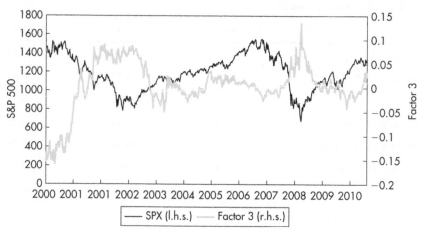

Sources: data – ECB, Bloomberg; chart – Authors.
Data period: 3 Jan 2000 to 25 Jul 2011, weekly data.

FIGURE 3.29 Regression of factor 3 of the PCA on currencies versus the S&P500 index.

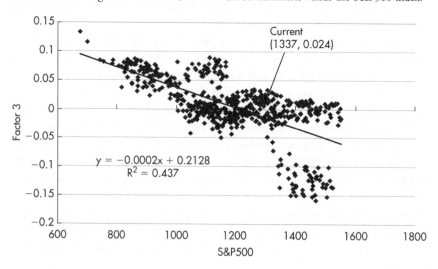

Sources: data – ECB, Bloomberg; chart – Authors.
Data period: 3 Jan 2000 to 25 Jul 2011, weekly data.

FIGURE 3.30 Two-factor residuals of a PCA on currencies.

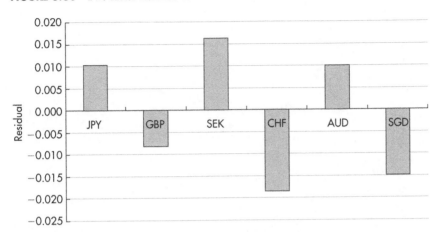

Sources: data – ECB; chart – Authors.
Data period: 4 Jan 1999 to 25 Jul 2011, weekly data; current residuals as of 25 Jul 2011.

long-term relationship will hold in future (and we see no reason not to do so), we may want to bet on the residual disappearing.[29] Hence, we investigate for a trade of factor 3 of a PCA on currencies versus the S&P500 index.

Since we cannot trade factor 3 directly, we need to find a portfolio of three currencies, hedged against factors 1 and 2 and highly correlated to factor 3. Given the relatively high strength of factor 4 in particular, not every two-factor neutral combination of currencies can be expected to work, as it could be mainly a function of factor 4 rather than factor 3. In addition, we would like to improve our return by choosing a combination of currencies with a high two-factor residual. These residuals are shown in Figure 3.30, and thus both a JPY–CHF–SEK and a JPY–SGD–SEK PCA-neutral combination of currencies (similar to a butterfly on the yield curve) seem attractive. However, only the first one has a strong correlation to the third factor, so we choose this one.

Now, we can formulate our trading strategy, which is to trade a two-factor PCA-neutral portfolio of JPY, CHF, and SEK versus the S&P500 index. The hedge ratio between the portfolio of currencies and the S&P500 index is given by the slope of the regression line, while the weightings of the currencies in the portfolio are determined by the conditions of neutrality versus factors 1 and 2 of the PCA on currencies. The result is the exposure to the residual of a regression between the portfolio of currencies and the S&P500 index, whose time series is shown in Figure 3.31.

---

[29] Ideally, we would like to see an even higher correlation, though.

FIGURE 3.31   Residual of a regression between a PCA-neutral portfolio of currencies and the S&P500 index.

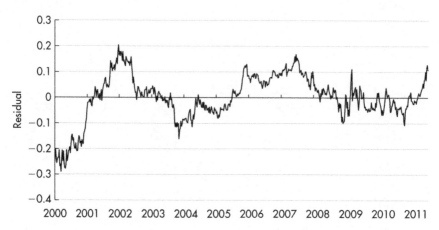

Sources: data – ECB, Bloomberg; chart – Authors.
Data period: 3 Jan 2000 to 25 Jul 2011, weekly data.

FIGURE 3.32   Actual performance of the trade versus the OU model forecast.

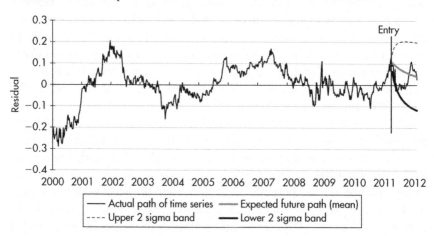

Sources: data – ECB, Bloomberg; chart – Authors.
Data period: 3 Jan 2000 to 25 Jul 2011, weekly data as input in OU model; forecast period as output of OU model versus weekly market data from 1 Aug 2011 to 4 Jun 2012.

Of course, we can now run a mean reversion model on that series and judge whether the statistical properties, like speed of mean reversion, seem sufficiently good to enter the trade. Figure 3.32 depicts the actual performance of the trade versus the forecast of the OU model. Since the actual performance followed the lower 2-sigma band of the OU simulation closely, one can say that an investor entering the trade was quite lucky to be able to realize the profit potential from the time series returning to its mean (i.e. the residual of the regression disappearing) soon.

This example demonstrates how PCA both yields new insights into a variety of markets and is the basis for new trading opportunities. By producing time series (like factor 3) that are not directly observable in the market but can be traded nevertheless (in this example through a two-factor neutral portfolio), PCA opens the door to a multitude of new and creative analyses and trading opportunities. The advantages of these new positions, besides their analytical challenges and illuminating results, are that they offer:

- a good chance to find a source of profit which is uncorrelated to more common positions;
- trading ideas that are unlikely to be analyzed by many people and therefore likely to be profitable. While lots of analytical effort is invested in 2Y-5Y-10Y butterflies on the yield curve, probably no one ever thought of the trade developed above. Hence, PCA is also a tool to find value off the beaten track, as it allows constructing new trade ideas individually.

Our goal is not to promote trading stock indices versus portfolios of currencies but to encourage using PCA as a compass to venture into unknown territory, where golden fruits may be growing on the trees.

PART II

Financial Models

CHAPTER 4

Some Comments on Yield, Duration, and Convexity

Introduction

This book is intended for somewhat experienced fixed income analysts, traders, and portfolio managers, so we assume the reader has more than a passing familiarity with the concepts of yield, duration, and convexity. However, we do come across some confusion concerning these concepts from time to time, so we'll offer a few thoughts in this chapter, designed to help clarify potential misunderstandings.

Some Brief Comments on the Yield of a Coupon-Paying Bond

A bond that pays a coupon is simply a portfolio of zero-coupon bonds, and the price of the coupon bond is the sum of the prices of the zero-coupon bonds.

However, the yield of a coupon bond generally can't be expressed as a linear combination of the yields of the constituent zero-coupon bonds. Nevertheless, many investors would like to be able to talk about the yield or the rate of return of a coupon bond. To that end, the yield of a coupon bond is typically defined as the discount rate that when applied to all cash flows produces a net present value equal to the invoice price of the bond. In other words, it's the value of y that satisfies

$$P = \sum_{i=1}^{K} \frac{X_i}{\left(1 + \frac{y}{c}\right)^{cT_i}}$$

Where P is the price of the bond; K is the number of cash flows, X_i is the size of cash flow i, $c =$ the compounding frequency, and T_i is the time until the i-th cash flow is due to be received.

In the limit, as the compounding frequency increases, we have

$$P = \sum_{i=1}^{K} X_i e^{-yT_i}$$

At this point, it's worth mentioning a few issues with the concept of yield for a zero-coupon bond.

- For a zero-coupon bond, the yield has the straightforward interpretation as the rate of return. For a coupon bond, this interpretation is not straightforward. For example, the yield is the rate of return of the coupon bond under the assumption that all cash flows are reinvested until maturity at a rate of return equal to the yield of the coupon bond. But why would we assume that the bond coupons could be reinvested at the bond yield? It would seem more realistic to assume that the bond coupons are reinvested at the forward rates corresponding to each coupon. For example, for a coupon bond maturing in 10 years, we might assume that the coupon paid at the end of the fifth year could be reinvested for another five years at the current five-year (5Y) rate five years forward. The useful point to note here is that the yield is unlikely to be the rate of return of the bond, even if the bond is held to maturity.
- In general, the yield of a coupon bond is not equal to the yields of any of the constituent zero-coupon bonds. In fact, the yield of a coupon bond isn't even a weighted average of the yields of the constituent zero-coupon bonds.

Strictly speaking, the yield of a coupon bond is simply a nonlinear transformation of price and time that makes it easier for investors to compare the relative values of bonds. But while there's nothing wrong with applying a nonlinear transformation to prices to make investing easier, investors too often apply the concept of the bond yield in ways that are misleading and can lead to incorrect or otherwise unjustified inferences.

For example, consider two coupon-paying bonds, with the same maturity date and the same issuer, and assume that one has a greater coupon than the other. Assume also that each of the two bonds is priced exactly in line with the yield curve, in the sense that there are no reconstitution arbitrage opportunities available.

If the yield curve is upward-sloping, it's very likely that the bond with the greater coupon will have a lesser yield than the other bond. And if the yield curve is downward-sloping, it's very likely that the bond with the greater coupon will have a greater yield than the other bond. In this case, it would be inappropriate to use the unadjusted yield spread between the two bonds as an indication of the relative value between the two bonds. Likewise, as we'll see in Chapter 10, it also would be inappropriate to use interpolated swap spreads to assess the relative values of the two bonds. Yet we see these sorts of comparisons being made by analysts and traders more often than we'd like.

A Brief Comment on Duration

Macaulay Duration

In 1938, Frederick Macaulay published an article in which he discusses the weighted average time to maturity of a stream of payments. Since then, Macaulay's duration has been taught to almost every bond analyst and trader.

In particular, the standard formula for the Macaulay duration of a coupon-paying bond is:

$$D_M = \sum_{i=1}^{K} T_i \frac{\frac{X_i}{\left(1+\frac{z}{c}\right)^{cT_i}}}{P}$$

which gives the weighted average time to maturity of a coupon-paying bond, assuming the present values of the cash flows are obtained by discounting each cash flow using the yield to maturity of the coupon-paying bond. For a zero-coupon bond, the Macaulay duration is simply the maturity of the bond.

However, there is no reason to discount each cash flow at the same yield, unless somehow the individual prices of the constituent zero-coupon bonds are unknown. As long as we know the prices of the individual zero-coupon bonds, we could calculate the weighted time to maturity of the bond directly.

Fisher–Weil Duration

In 1971, Lawrence Fisher and Roman Weil, of the University of Chicago, published an article in which they discuss another measure of duration, similar to Macaulay duration but with the price of each cash flow corresponding to the actual term structure of interest rates. In other words, the present value of each cash flow corresponded to the actual prices of the zero-coupon bonds that constitute the coupon-paying bond. In this respect, the Fisher–Weil duration is a more accurate reflection of the weighted average maturity of the bond.

The standard formula for the Fisher–Weil duration is similar to the formula for the Macaulay duration but with the yield of each cash flow used in place of the yield for the entire bond.

$$D_{FW} = \sum_{i=1}^{K} T_i \frac{\dfrac{X_i}{\left(1 + \frac{y_i}{c}\right)^{cT_i}}}{P}$$

The Fisher–Weil concept of duration provides a more accurate measure of the weighted time to maturity of a coupon-paying bond, yet the formula for the Macaulay duration is still used far more frequently in our experience, perhaps given the view that it's easier to implement, given it requires only a single yield.

In our view, the additional steps required to calculate the Fisher–Weil measure of duration are worth the effort, and we suggest using this measure in place of the Macaulay measure.

A Common Misapplication of Convexity

As the price of a bond is a convex function of its yield, its price will change more in the event its yield decreases by 25 bp than if its yield increases by 25 basis points (bp). For example, the German Bund with a coupon of 3.25%, maturing on 4 Jul 2032, currently has a price of EUR 122.713 and a yield of 2.197%. At a yield of 1.947, its price would be higher by EUR 6.36, and at a yield of 2.447%, its price would be lower by EUR 5.96. If there were an equal chance of either scenario today, the expected return of the bond would be +0.2% (non-annualized), despite the fact that the yield distribution in this case was presumed to be symmetric.

This is the case not only in this example but in general, due to *Jensen's inequality*, which states that the expected value of a convex function of a random variable is greater than or equal to the function evaluated at the expected value of the random variable.

The impact of Jensen's inequality is an increasing function of the volatility of the random variable. For example, if there were an equal chance that the yield of our bond would increase or decrease by 50 bp rather than by 25 bp, the expected return would be +0.7%. If the potential yield change were 75 bp, the expected return would be +1.5%, and if the potential yield change were 100 bp, the expected return would be +2.6%.

Since the favorable impact of convexity appears to be an increasing function of volatility, many analysts compare this convexity effect to an option, which also has a convex return structure. Just as the fair price of an option increases with the volatility of the underlying asset, so too should the fair value of this convexity effect increase with the volatility of the bond's yield.

But, as we'll soon see, there's a problem with this argument.

All else being equal, the convexity of a bond price as a function of its yield is an increasing function of the time to maturity of the bond. That is, longer-dated bonds have greater convexities than shorter-dated bonds, all else being equal.

For instance, a 30-year (30Y) zero-coupon bond with a yield of 2.25% and with an equal chance of experiencing a 100 bp yield increase or decrease would have an expected return of +4.5%. If the same bond matured in 50 years, the expected return would be 12.8%. If the bond matured in 100 years, the expected return would be a remarkable 54.3%.

To illustrate our point, let's consider hypothetical bonds with even greater times to maturity. For example, if the bond had a 200Y maturity, the expected return in our example would be 276.2%. If the bond had a maturity of 500 years, the expected return would be 7,320%. And if there were such a thing as a millennial bond (i.e. a zero-coupon bond that matured in 1,000 years) its expected return would be more than one million percent. One million dollars invested in this bond would be associated with an *expected* value of more than 22 billion dollars. It's clear that there is something seriously problematic in this example.

In our example, we held constant the probabilities of our two yield scenarios, and we observed the effect on the expected return when the maturity of the bond was increased. As an alternative, let's hold constant the expected return on the bond and observe the effect on the probability of a yield decrease as the maturity of the bond is increased.

A 30Y zero-coupon bond with a yield of 2.25% would have an expected return of 4.53% (non-annualized) if there were a 50% chance of a 100 bp yield increase and a 50% chance of a 100 bp yield decrease. If the bond had a maturity of 50 years, then to keep the expected return equal to 4.53% the probability of a yield decrease would have to decline to 42% (with the probability of a 100 bp increase at 58%). If the maturity of our zero-coupon bond were 75Y, the probability of the lower yield would decline to 35%.

With a 100Y bond, the probability of a 100 bp yield decrease would be only 29%.

Continuing toward the limit, the probability in the case of a 200Y bond is 12.5%; the probability in the case of a 500Y bond is seven-tenths of 1%, and the probability in the case of our hypothetical millennial bond is only 0.0000485.

These examples highlight an important point made in the 1990s by Philip Dybvig, Jonathan Ingersoll, and Stephen Ross, who showed that *in the limit* the long zero-coupon rate could never fall.[1]

Of course, bonds with the sorts of maturities used in these examples simply don't trade in the real world. But by considering the traditional convexity argument in the limit, we've come upon an interpretation of convexity that makes far more economic sense than the traditional interpretation does.

The traditional interpretation is that convexity transforms symmetric yield distributions into asymmetric return distributions, which increase the value of highly convex bonds. *Our interpretation is that convexity transforms symmetric return distributions into asymmetric yield distributions.* And this interpretation makes far more economic sense, in our view.

Note that this result helps explain the typical shape of the first eigenvector obtained when conducting principal component analysis (PCA) of yield curves. Long rates tend not to be as volatile as short rates are, which means that short rates are more sensitive to changes in the first principal component in the context of a PCA. This result is intuitive once we realize that the asymptotic rate can never decrease, since a rate that can never decrease must not spend much time increasing either.

Note too that this convexity result is consistent with the mean reversion of short rates. If there's a sense in which long rates are (potentially complicated) averages of the overnight rate, then mean reversion in the short rate will lead to long rates being less volatile than short rates as a simple statistical result. In the limit, the average of a mean-reverting short rate is the unconditional mean of the short rate process.

---

[1] Philip H. Dybvig, Jonathan E. Ingersoll, Jr., and Stephen A. Ross (1996) Long Forward and Zero-Coupon Rates Can Never Fall. *Journal of Business*, Vol. 69, No. 1, pp. 1–25.

CHAPTER 5

Bond Futures Contracts

Futures Price and Delivery Option

The key difference between a bond forward and a bond futures contract is the existence of a *set* of deliverable bonds, called the *deliverable basket*. In particular, the person with a short position in a bond futures contract (i.e. the short) has a choice of bonds he can deliver. Since the bonds in the deliverable basket have different coupons and maturity dates, the exchanges introduce the concept of a *conversion factor* (CF), which is applied to the price of each bond when determining the invoice price that the short receives when delivering a particular bond into a particular futures contract. In order to make all deliverable bonds comparable, a CF is defined for each, which roughly corresponds to one-hundredth of the price of the deliverable bond at a certain yield level (often 6%). This yield level is called the *notional coupon* of the bond futures contract.

Technical points regarding the conversion factor

- The CF is a constant for each individual deliverable bond.
- The CF of a bond will depend on the expiration date of the futures contract. For example, if a bond is deliverable into both the March and the June contracts, it will have a different CF for each expiration month.
- In general terms, the CF of a bond is one-hundredth of the price the bond would have at expiration of the futures contract if the bond yield was equal to the notional coupon for that contract.
- The notional coupon of the futures contract is defined at the time the contract is first listed by the exchange. Like the CF, once the notional contract for a particular expiration month is defined, it does not change.

- However, exchanges can and do sometimes switch to a new notional coupon when listing a new futures contract, particularly when the yields of the bonds in the deliverable basket are far from the notional coupon used most recently.
- Changes to the notional coupon can have a material effect on the value of the delivery option and the value of the futures contract, as discussed below.
- Note that the calculation of the CF as specified in the contract documentation may not correspond exactly to one-hundredth of the bond price at the yield of the notional coupon. The exchanges publish formulae that analysts can use to predict the CF before a contract is listed, but the analyst should be careful to confirm the CF for each contract when it is listed, as the CF published at the time of listing is determinative, irrespective of any formulae the exchange may have published to assist analysts.

The Delivery Process

At delivery, the person with the short position in the bond futures contract can choose to deliver any bond in the deliverable basket and will receive a payment of the futures price, F, multiplied by the CF for the bond he has chosen, in exchange for delivery of the bond. Thus, if the yield at delivery equals the notional coupon of the bond futures contract, and if the CFs represent exactly one-hundredth of the prices of the bonds at that yield level, then the futures contract should trade at 100, and the prices of all deliverable bonds should be equal to the compensation received for their delivery into the futures contract. In that case, the short would be indifferent about the bond he chooses to deliver. In general, however, there are differences with regards to the payoffs at delivery between the deliverable bonds. Assuming the short buys a deliverable bond right at delivery at price P, and delivers it immediately into the futures contract, his P&L will be $F \times CF - P$. If there are n deliverable bonds in the basket with prices $P_1, \ldots, P_n$ and conversion factors $CF_1, \ldots, CF_n$, he can compare the payoffs for buying and delivering each of them with a table like this:

$$\text{Bond 1: } F \times CF_1 - P_1$$

$$\ldots$$

$$\text{Bond n: } F \times CF_n - P_n$$

The deliverable bond with the best payoff (i.e. the largest number in the table above) is called the *cheapest-to-deliver* (CTD), and the short will usually deliver that bond. If the yields of all deliverable bonds at delivery were equal to the notional coupon of the bond futures contract, and if the CF of each bond was exactly equal to one-hundredth of the price of the bond at that

FIGURE 5.1   CTD situation as a function of the yield level.

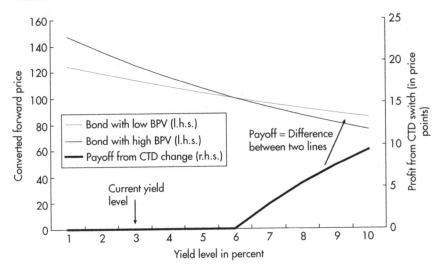

Source: Authors.

yield level, then all deliverable bonds would be equally CTD.[1] At higher yield levels, only the bonds with largest basis point values (BPVs) in the basket tend to be CTD, while at lower yield levels only the bonds with the smallest BPV in the basket tend to be CTD. The reason for this behavior is illustrated in Figure 5.1. When the general level of yields is high, the converted prices (*P/CF*) of large BPV bonds tend to be low relative to the converted prices of bonds with a smaller BPV. If the two bonds of Figure 5.1 were the only ones that were deliverable, the one with the lower converted price would be CTD at a given yield level. Thus, the CTD would switch between the bond with a small BPV to the bond with a large BPV at the notional coupon (6% in this example). This switching point is also called the *inflection point*.

CTD Switches and the Delivery Option

Since the short has the right to choose the bond he delivers, he can profit from changes in the CTD. The monetary value of that right is called the *delivery option* (DO) value of the bond futures contract. Using the illustration from above as an example, imagine we are three months before delivery and

---

[1] In this scenario, a difference in coupons would result in some bonds being rich relative to others given the coupon effect, perhaps even allowing reconstitution arbitrage (via the strip market).

at a yield level of 3%. At that yield level, the bond with a small BPV is CTD, so we could buy that bond on a forward basis and sell the futures contract. If at delivery the same bond is still CTD, we can deliver it and close our positions at zero cost. If, however, a rise in yields has caused the CTD to switch to the bond with a large BPV, we could sell our bond, buy the new CTD, and deliver this cheaper bond into our short position in the futures contract. A switch in CTD is equivalent to a profit from our bond switch operation, with the amount of profit given by the difference of the converted forward prices of the two bonds (the difference of the two lines in Figure 5.1).

To prevent arbitrage at delivery, the futures contract must settle at a price such that there is no profit or loss from buying the CTD in the bond market and delivering it into the contract. Thus, at delivery, the equation $F \times CF_{\text{CTD}} - P_{\text{CTD}} = 0$ holds and implies a fair futures price of $\frac{P_{\text{CTD}}}{CF_{\text{CTD}}}$. Likewise, before delivery, the fair futures price is a function of the converted forward price of the CTD. But as the CTD can still change, it needs to be adjusted for the DO value, and the fair futures price is given as $\frac{FwdP_{\text{CTD}}}{CF_{\text{CTD}}} - DO$.

Net and Gross Bond Basis

That arbitrage relationship at delivery is the key for basis trades between deliverable bonds and the future, with the following conventions:

$$\text{Gross basis} = P - F \times CF$$
$$\text{Net basis} = FwdP - F \times CF$$

Note that the fair value of the CTD net basis is equal to $DO \times CF_{\text{CTD}}$. Thus, if there is no DO, in particular at the delivery date, then the fair value of the CTD net basis is 0. And as the DO is never negative, the fair value of any net basis is always greater than or equal to zero.[2]

From these equations, it is clear that the DO is key to pricing and trading bond futures contracts. All other aspects of the contract can be hedged in the markets. For example, the forward price of a deliverable bond is a direct function of the bond and of the repo market. (The CF is a pre-defined constant.) Thus, the model used to calculate the fair value of the DO will determine the fair value of the futures contract and therefore whether basis trades are attractive. In addition, the better the DO is understood, the better the futures contract can be applied for hedging purposes, and the more

---

[2] At times, specific situations like penalties for failing to deliver might result in a negative net basis being observed in the market.

informed the appropriate time for rolling over front into back month contracts can be decided.

Imagine that the net basis of the CTD quotes in the market at 5 cents and that the CF of the CTD is 1. If the model used to evaluate the DO returns a fair DO price of 2 cents, selling the CTD net basis (i.e. selling the CTD in the forward market and buying the futures contract) appears attractive. If another model returns a fair DO price of 10 cents, however, buying the CTD net basis looks profitable. This illustrates the crucial importance of the model used to price the DO for correctly evaluating the fair value of the futures contract and for ensuring that one is on the right side of basis trades.

As the futures price observed in the market in some sense should reflect the average pricing model used by market participants, having a better model enables us to exploit the shortcoming of the average model. The CTD net basis in the market is a function of the DO models of the other market participants, which we can compare with the results of our DO model. If we have a superior DO model and the market price is not in line with its results, we can translate the superiority of our model directly into profitable trading strategies by entering into CTD net basis positions. For example, if the DO model used by market participants gives a fair value of the DO of 5 cents, and if the CF of the CTD is 1, then the CTD net basis should trade at 5 cents. If our better model gives us a fair value for the DO of 10 cents, then we can translate the theoretical advantage of our model into trading profit by buying the CTD net basis in a market that underestimates its value.

We shall therefore describe two different DO models. The first one is the one-factor DO model commonly used in the market, while the second one is a superior multi-factor DO model we developed while working at ABN Amro. The model arbitrage mentioned in the previous paragraph will therefore consist in assessing the market price for the DO (CTD net basis/CF), calculated by one-factor models, through the lens of a multi-factor model.

One-Factor Delivery Option Models[3]

Figure 5.1 can serve as the basis for a straightforward DO model. Since the payoff profile from a CTD switch is a function of the yield level, the value of the DO can be estimated by using an option pricing model.

---

[3] To our knowledge, that model was first described in *The Treasury Bond Basis* by Galen Burghardt, Terry Belton, Morton Lane, and John Pappa, published by McGraw-Hill in 1989.

- The payoff profile of the DO is almost that of a put or call.[4] In the example of Figure 5.1, buying the CTD net basis is like buying a fraction of puts on the future. Note that this relationship in principle allows trading the CTD net basis versus options on the bond futures contract. Usually, however, the CTD switch situation is more complex than in Figure 5.1, which makes that arbitrage rarely practicable, as discussed below.
- The strike price of the DO is determined by the CTD inflection point. Note that the DO is always an OTM (Out-of-the-money) option, as the CTD needs to change (i.e. something needs to happen) for the DO to produce profit. This means that the DO has only time value and is the reason that the DO value is equal to zero at the delivery date.
- The market consensus about yield level volatility until delivery is reflected in the option prices quoted in the market (e.g. from the options on bond futures).

With this information, the DO can be calculated through an option model like Black–Scholes, using the payoff profile from Figure 5.1 and the expected volatility of the market until delivery (e.g. as reflected in the bond futures option quotes) as inputs. Qualitatively, the DO value will be large, if:

- The CTD switching point is close to the current yield level. This corresponds to the strike price of an OTM option being close to the current market price. In this case, not a lot needs to happen for the CTD to change and there is a high likelihood for a CTD switch to occur before delivery.
- The delivery date is far away. In this case, there is considerable time for a CTD switch to occur and thus there is a high likelihood for a CTD switch to occur before delivery.
- The volatility is high. In this case, there is a high likelihood for a CTD switch to occur before delivery.
- The difference between the converted BPV of the old CTD and that of the new CTD (after a switch takes place) is large. In this case, a given amount of change in yield level causes a high profit from switching out of the old into the new CTD. In Figure 5.1, a large difference between the converted BPVs corresponds to a large difference in the slope of the converted forward price lines and hence to a larger payoff in the case of a CTD switch. Therefore, the profit from a CTD switch tends to be an increasing function of the difference between the converted forward BPVs.

The first feature of our list means that for a given bond futures contract at a given date, the DO value is largest when the price of the futures contract is

---

[4] Due to convexity effects, the relationship of the payoff to the yield level is not exactly linear.

FIGURE 5.2 Fair futures price as a function of the yield level.

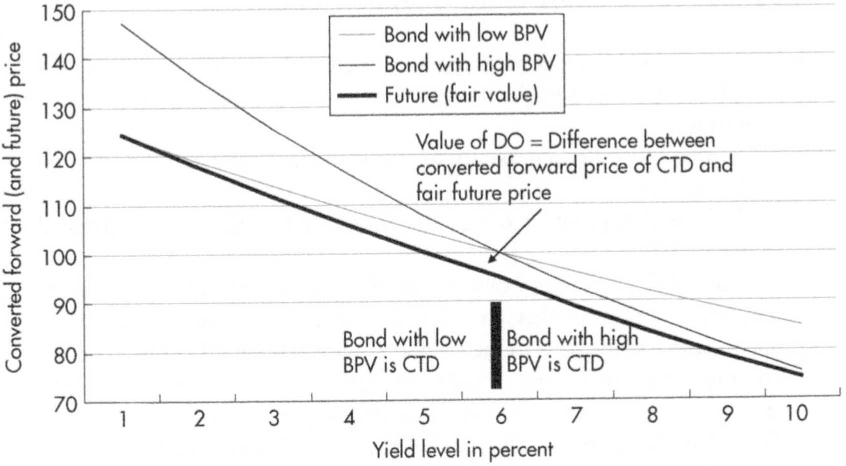

Source: Authors.

at the CTD inflection point. In other words, the impact on the fair futures price is a decreasing function of the distance between the yield of the current CTD and the inflection point. This result is illustrated in Figure 5.2.

Given the use of futures contracts for hedging bonds, an important application of this model is the calculation of the correct BPV for the futures contract. Simply assuming that the BPV of the futures contract is equal to the converted forward BPV of the CTD, $\frac{FwdBPV_{CTD}}{CF_{CTD}}$, ignores the impact of the DO on the futures price and might only be an acceptable approximation, particularly when the yield of the CTD is far from the inflection point. In addition, that number changes in a discontinuous fashion at the inflection point, which is a major problem for bond hedges using futures contracts. It is therefore necessary to use the slope of the "Future (fair value)" line in Figure 5.2 as the BPV for the futures contract in hedging operations. That number is called the option-adjusted BPV (OABPV) and can be obtained by calculating the fair value of the future (i.e. $\frac{FwdP_{CTD}}{CF_{CTD}} - DO$) at two slightly different yield levels, thereby taking the impact of the change of the yield level on the DO into account.

Since changes in the absolute yield level may impact different deliverable bonds to a different extent, one should adjust the calculation for this effect, for example by using the betas of a regression of the yield level of a deliverable bond versus the yield level of the CTD. The DO calculation then looks like the one shown in Box 5.1.

Box 5.1   One-factor delivery option model

- For a reasonable range of yield levels for the CTD at delivery, calculate the yield levels of all deliverable issues at delivery (e.g. by using the betas from a regression).
- Determine the inflection points for CTD switches and the payoff from CTD switches.
- Decompose that payoff into a combination of puts and calls, as illustrated in Figure 5.1.
- For each of these puts and calls, obtain the relevant implied volatility from the futures options market. In order to account for the skew, use a futures option with a strike close to the yield level, at which the CTD switch occurs (i.e. the "strike" of the put or call from Figure 5.1). Thus, each of the puts and calls are priced with an individual implied volatility.
- For each of these puts and calls, calculate the value. This could be done by using the implied volatility and "strike" levels as input into the Black–Scholes formula.
- The DO is the sum of the option prices obtained in the previous step.
- Alternatively, the payoff function (Figure 5.1) could be numerically integrated over the probability density for the CTD yield, which again can be obtained from the futures options market. This alternative is preferable in case of the payoff function exhibiting a significant convexity. On the other hand, as it is easier to account for the skew through individual puts and calls rather than through an adjustment of the probability density for the CTD yield, this alternative is not advisable in the presence of a large skew.

The Need for Multi-Factor Delivery Option Models

By construction, the DO model described above is a one-factor model. It can only assess the impact of changes in the absolute yield level on the DO; it cannot consider CTD switches that occur due to reasons other than a change in the overall yield level. Thus, those CTD switches that happen without a change in absolute yield level are outside of the scope of that model, which may therefore underestimate the value of the DO. In other words, as the model only assesses the DO coming from changes in the absolute yield level, it is conceptually ignorant of DO value coming from other sources, for example from a bond becoming CTD due to only its individual repo rate decreasing.

In general, the DO value arises from the volatilities of the differences between the prices of deliverable bonds, which thereby determine the like-lihood of and profit from CTD switches. The prices of the deliverable bonds, and hence the differences in prices, can be modeled indirectly by modeling the yields of the deliverable bonds.

In the one-factor model discussed above, all changes in the yield spreads between deliverable bonds were the result of the different yield betas associated with each bond. When our main yield factor increased, the yields of bonds with large betas would increase by more than would the yields of bonds with smaller betas. So while the one-factor model is capable of producing varying yield spreads, the entirety of the variation in yield spreads is the result of an increase or decrease in the general level of yields.

But while the results of our PCA chapter indicate that roughly 95% of the variation in yields generally can be attributed to a single factor (see Figures 3.4 and 3.24), it is *not* the case that the vast majority of the variation in yield *spreads* can be attributed to a single factor. In fact, the proportion of yield *spread* variation that can be attributed to changes in the overall level of yields depends on the situation.

- If the market yield level is close to the notional coupon of the bond futures contract, CTD switches between the short end and the long end of the basket can occur. These switches are usually caused by a change in the overall yield level and therefore captured by a one-factor model. Correspondingly, they show up in Figure 5.1 and Figure 5.2, which depict the perspective of one-factor models.

  As explained above, these CTD switches between the short and long end of the basket result in a large DO value due to the big difference in converted BPVs. Thus, when the market yield level is close to the notional coupon of the bond futures contract, one-factor models can be expected to capture the most important source of the DO value.

- The further the market yield level is away from the notional coupon of the bond futures contract, the less likely those CTD switches between the long and short end of the basket become. As a consequence, the DO value calculated by a one-factor model decreases and converges to zero. In the example of Figure 5.1, at a yield level of 3%, it is extremely unlikely to reach the 6% needed for a CTD switch caused by changes in the overall yield level in the few months until delivery, and thus the model based on Figure 5.1 will return a negligible DO value.

- Thus, the relative importance for yield spread volatility of factors other than the overall yield level is an increasing function of the distance between the CTD yield and the notional coupon of the bond futures contract. Consequently, there is a tendency for one-factor DO models to understate the value of the DO when the yield of the CTD is far from the notional coupon.

As a result, when yields dropped globally toward levels far below the notional coupons, the one-factor DO models working well at a 6% yield level became less useful. Since most market participants did not adjust their models to reflect the new source of DO value, the net bases quoted in the market nowadays systematically underestimate the real value of the DO (i.e. tend to be too low).

As an illustration, we consider the source of yield spread volatility between deliverables in a low-yield environment for the case of JGB futures, for which this situation first was relevant. While the deliverable basket extends from seven to 10.5 years, the low yield level in Japan means that the bond with the shortest maturity is always clearly CTD and that there is practically no chance for a bond with a longer maturity to become CTD, as seen in Figure 5.1. However, there are often two or even three bonds with the same shortest maturity and only a minimal difference in coupon, thus with almost the same BPV. These two or three bonds can all easily become CTD, thus there can be CTD switches between the two or three candidates with the same maturity. In fact, because the CTD candidates are so similar, CTD switches between them are quite common. Seen through the perspective of a one-factor model, a change in the overall yield level impacts all CTD candidates in almost the same manner, given the almost identical BPV and sensitivity. Thus, even if a CTD switch occurs, the profit is negligible, as argued above. In other words, while the similarity of CTD candidates may make CTD switches between them likely, the similarity of converted BPVs also means that the impact of a change in the overall yield level on the yield spread volatility between them is only marginal. Hence, applying a one-factor model to the basket of JGB futures returns a DO value close to zero.

In reality, however, the yield spread volatility between CTD candidates can be quite large, in part because the delivery situation can magnify the natural yield spread volatility. Imagine that many investors have a short CTD net basis position on their books. If the CTD switches to another candidate, which initially may be just a little bit cheaper, they need to be concerned about being delivered the new CTD into their long futures position. Thus, in order to hedge their risk, they need to sell the new and buy back the old CTD, an operation that may magnify an initially small yield spread between the two CTD candidates and may cause more investors to close their positions, leading to a reinforcing cycle. Note that this potentially significant yield spread volatility between deliverables is not caused and not even accompanied by any change in the overall yield level. Hence, by construction it cannot contribute toward the DO value in the context of a one-factor model, even though a long net basis position could yield significant profit in this scenario.[5]

When yields are far below the notional coupon, the yield spread volatility between deliverables is therefore not a function of the 95% of overall yield volatility explained by the overall yield level (and captured by one-factor models) but rather of the 5% of overall yield volatility not explained by the overall yield level (and not captured by one-factor models). Hence, at current yield levels, it is the 5% of overall yield volatility explained by greater factors (2, 3, . . .), which matters for the yield spread volatility between deliverables. Consequently, a DO model claiming applicability in any yield environment needs to take more factors into account. DO modeling therefore needs to respond to the drop in yield levels far below the notional coupon by moving from one-factor to multi-factor models.

A Flexible Multi-Factor Delivery Option Model[6]

Since it is impossible to determine ex ante *which* factor will be responsible for yield spread volatility between deliverables, we advise using *all* factors. That is, we replace the one-factor model by a model that has as many factors as there are bonds in the deliverable basket. The full information needed to assess the yield spread volatility between deliverables and thus the value of the DO can be represented for a deliverable basket with n bonds with the yields $y_1, \ldots, y_n$ by the variables

- y_1: the absolute yield level of the first deliverable bond. The designation "first" is arbitrary. For example, the bond with the shortest maturity in the basket could be considered the first bond, as could the CTD.
- $y_2 - y_1, \ldots, y_n - y_1$ (i.e. the yield spread between every other bond and the first one).

Note that this set of variables is just a different way of modeling all yields $y_1, \ldots, y_n$. The reason for this particular representation will become clear later on. While we can make reasonable assumptions about how yield spread

---

[5] This is also the reason why an arbitrage between the net basis and futures options is only practicable when CTD switches between the short and long end of the basket are the main driving force of the net basis.

[6] That model was developed by us as employees of ABN Amro and first published in the ABN Amro research note "Exploiting the ignored delivery option in JGB contracts" from 21 February 2002. It is reproduced here with kind permission from RBS.

variables behave in a delivery situation, expressing that impact of a futures contract on the relationships between deliverable bonds in the form of correlations between $y_1, \ldots, y_n$ would be a major and unnecessary challenge.

We allow for correlation between all of the variables (i.e. both between the absolute yield level and yield spread variables[7] and between different yield spread variables). Furthermore, we assume all variables are normally distributed. Note that this is the only assumption of the model and in our view not a very strong or particularly restrictive assumption. If a particular market was found to behave differently, the following simulation could be adjusted accordingly. (For example, one could replace the normal distribution with a lognormal distribution.) We can now obtain an estimate for the DO through the steps shown in Box 5.2.

Box 5.2   Multi-factor delivery option model

- Define the yield volatility of the first deliverable bond.
- Define the yield spread volatility for the variables $y_2 - y_1, \ldots, y_n - y_1$.
- Define the correlations between all of the variables $y_1, y_2 - y_1, \ldots, y_n - y_1$. We shall discuss ways to set these input parameters below.
- Run a Monte Carlo simulation with normally distributed random variables each with zero mean and with standard deviations and correlations defined as above, simulating the evolution of the yield (spreads) of all deliverable bonds until the delivery date.
- Translate the results of each simulation into a table of yields $y_1, \ldots, y_n$ at delivery and calculate the corresponding converted prices. In order to adjust for the difference between forward and spot prices, add the difference between the current converted forward price and the average of the future converted prices at delivery generated by the simulation to each of the simulation results. In this way, the mean of the simulated prices on the delivery date for each bond will equal the forward price for each bond.
- For each of the mean-adjusted simulation results, identify the bond that is CTD and the extent of any profit from a CTD switch.
- Calculate an estimate for the DO value as the average of the profit from CTD switches over all simulations, taking the CFs into account.
- Calculate for each deliverable bond an estimate for the probability of being CTD at delivery date by dividing the number of simulations in which it finishes as CTD by the number of all simulations.

---

[7] The yield beta of a one-factor model would show up via the covariance matrix in the multi-factor model.

Based on these results, one can repeat the calculation of the fair value of the future and related numbers from above with a better estimation for the value of the DO. In particular:

- Calculate the fair futures price as $\frac{FwdP_{CTD}}{CF_{CTD}} - DO$.
- Repeating the exercise for the back month contract, calculate the fair futures roll (calendar spread).
- Calculate the OABPV (with reference to the first bond) by repeating the Monte Carlo simulation on a set of yields y_i as starting points, which reflects the typical impact of a 1 bp increase in y_1 on the yields of all deliverables. Then, the OABPV is the difference between the fair futures price and the fair futures price of the simulation starting with the shifted yields. As required, this calculation takes the impact of a different yield level on the DO into account.

One way to obtain the set of yields y_i, which reflects the typical impact of a 1 bp increase in y_1 on the yields of all deliverables, is to perform a PCA on the covariance matrix given by the input parameters. Then, the sensitivities to the first factor show how a 1 bp increase of y_1 is expected to influence the yields of the other deliverables. This is an application of the curve reconstruction technique through PCA outlined in Chapter 3.

A good graphical representation of both the input parameters into that Monte Carlo simulation and its output can be obtained by using the change in the yield spread variables until delivery as coordinates and plotting the resulting CTD of each simulation as a specific mark (such as points for the first bond, crosses for the second, etc.) into that coordinate system. An example for such a chart is given in Figure 5.3, which provides immediate intuition of the scenarios under which each bond is likely to be CTD.

The shape of the scatterplot in Figure 5.3 is determined by the two yield spread volatilities and by the correlation between the two yield spreads.

The CTD probability for each bond corresponds to the relative frequency of the symbols in the scatterplot depicted in Figure 5.3. Also, by assessing the positions of the symbols, one can get an understanding of the way a shift in yield spreads influences the CTD situation or, conversely, which yield spread move would need to happen in order for a particular bond to become CTD.

Choosing Input Parameters for the Multi-Factor DO Model

After outlining the model, we now discuss ways to choose its input parameters. The yield volatility, which is the only parameter involved in

FIGURE 5.3 Results of a Monte Carlo simulation of the CTD situation at delivery date as a function of the yield spread changes between CTD candidates until delivery.

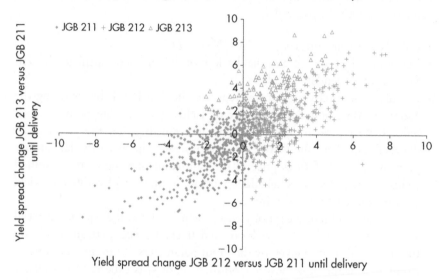

Yield spread change JGB 212 versus JGB 211 until delivery

Source: ABN Amro (reproduced here with permission from RBS).

one-factor models, can be set equal to the implied volatility of options on bond futures. With regards to defining the parameters for yield spread volatilities, we face a basic problem in that historical yield spread volatility is of limited value.

Outside of the context of a deliverable basket, there is usually little reason for very similar bonds to exhibit significant yield spread volatilities. For example, why should an investor's preference for JGB 212 1.5% maturing on 22 June 2009 and JGB 213 1.4%, also maturing on 22 June 2009, suddenly change? In fact, these very similar issues are not considered as *individual* bonds but rather as almost identical representations of the same issue. Therefore, before becoming relevant for delivery into a futures contract, the yield spread volatility between deliverables is typically small.

But this situation changes when the bonds enter into competition for CTD status. JGB 212 might be CTD, but JGB 213 is not, which has a major impact on the treatment of both issues in the repo market and in basis trades. We have given an example earlier of the way a CTD switch can impact the yield spread between the two deliverable bonds involved. Hence, bonds gain an individuality, an individual treatment in the bond and repo markets, through the context of a deliverable basket. And consequently, the

FIGURE 5.4 Evolution of the yield spread volatility between CTD candidates as they approach delivery in the example of JGB futures contracts.

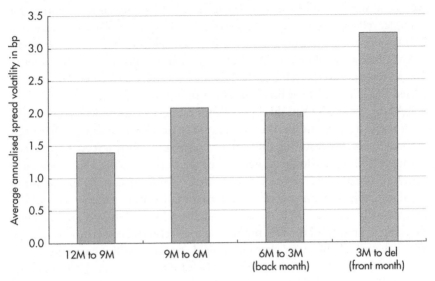

Source: ABN Amro (reproduced here with permission from RBS).

CTD situation is a major (most of the times the only) reason for a significant yield spread volatility between otherwise very similar bonds. Figure 5.4 shows the way the yield spread volatilities between CTD candidates increase as the delivery date approaches. On average, the yield spread volatility more than doubles in the year prior to delivery, reflecting the strong impact of a delivery situation on *individual* bonds versus their peers. In the case of a squeeze situation, the increase of yield spread volatility can be far above that in typical circumstances.

The calculation of the DO value through a multi-factor model requires an input parameter for the yield spread volatilities before delivery (i.e. before the actual impact of the specific delivery situation on the yield spread volatilities can be known). In addition, that input parameter has a significant importance for the resulting DO value, which (in case of a large distance between the actual yield level and the notional coupon) often depends almost exclusively on that input variable. Actually, drawing the estimated DO value as a function of the yield spread volatility used in the Monte Carlo simulation often reveals an almost linear relationship, with the line crossing through the origin of the coordinate system.

A possible solution to this problem could be first to calculate the historical yield spread volatility between the deliverable issues before they became part of the deliverable basket and then to adjust that yield spread volatility by the factor of its average increase into delivery, as shown in Figure 5.4. This main or average scenario could further be complemented by alternative scenarios, for example, reflecting the expected increase of yield spread volatility in case of a CTD squeeze. As a general remark, it is advisable to run the DO model described above several times for a set of different input parameters in order to gain an insight into the value of the DO and thus the expected performance of related trades (such as net basis positions) under various scenarios.

All the correlations in this multi-factor model usually remain stable in the context of a delivery, unlike the yield spread volatilities themselves. Moreover, in many cases, the resulting DO value is not significantly affected by a small change in the correlation parameters. For the purpose of the DO model, it is therefore usually fine to use the historically observed correlations as input variables. Still, as the impact of changes to the correlation parameters could be exceptionally strong in a particular delivery situation, we recommend checking the results of the DO model also for alternative correlation scenarios, just as described above for alternative yield spread volatility parameters.

The reward for these efforts is the ability to detect DOs that are undervalued in a market whose participants stick mostly to one-factor models. In the example of the JGB futures contract of Figure 5.3, the one-factor model outlined at the beginning of this chapter returned a DO of less than 1 sen, while the multi-factor DO model[8] suggests it is in fact worth 7 sen. Thus, the methodological progress can be exploited by finding and buying valuable DOs at a bargain price. As long as the majority of market participants continue using one-factor models, the profit from buying undervalued DOs (e.g. through long CTD net basis positions) must come from actual CTD switches. The downside in case there is no CTD switch is very limited if the DO can be bought almost for free, as in the JGB futures example above. In addition, however, the increasing application of multi-factor models should result in a general trend, correcting the current undervaluation of DOs toward an overall increase in net bases.

In summary, a better estimation for the DO value allows a better estimation for the fair value of the futures contract, which enhances:

- basis trading
- hedging of bonds with the future (using the OABPV)
- rolling over from the front in the back month contract.

---

[8] Using the same yield volatility as the one-factor model and historical yield spread volatilities and correlations, with the yield spread volatilities adjusted by the factor from Figure 5.4.

CHAPTER 6

LIBOR, OIS Rates, and Repo Rates

Introduction

Given the severe disruptions that occurred in many of the world's money markets with the onset of the financial crisis in 2007, LIBOR, OIS rates, and repo rates are of considerable interest in their own right. But for the relative value analyst, they're also of interest because they serve as the building blocks for term structures of government bond yields, LIBOR swap rates, and OIS swap rates. If we're to understand the relative valuations between government bond yields and swap rates, we need to understand the relative valuations between their respective components in the money markets.

As this book assumes a familiarity with these rates, we'll provide only brief definitions of these rates here, focusing instead on the differences between these rates and the implications that these differences have for relative value models linking these rates.

Brief Definitions

Repo

A repurchase agreement, or repo, in its most basic form is a type of secured loan. One party lends money for a specified term to a second party, who posts collateral to the first party for the duration of the loan and who pays an agreed interest rate – the repo rate – to the first party on the funds lent.

LIBOR

In contrast, an unsecured interbank loan is not collateralized, so the London Interbank Offered Rate (LIBOR) reflects the credit risk of the banks active in this market. For most currencies, LIBOR is calculated by the British Bankers' Association (BBA) using a trimmed mean of the rates at which banks believe they can borrow in the interbank market. For EURIBOR, this process is managed by the European Banking Federation (EBF).

OIS

An overnight index swap (OIS) is a derivative security in which one party agrees to pay a fixed rate to a second party in exchange for the daily accrual on a notional sum between the start date and end date of the swap. The rate used to calculate this daily accrual is the overnight index rate.

For example, the euro overnight index average (EONIA) is the rate applicable to the euro area, calculated as the volume-weighted average of actual overnight, unsecured loans among a group of banks, who are required to report such transactions to the European Central Bank (ECB). The sterling overnight index average (SONIA) and the Fed Funds rate are determined in similar manners.

OIS swaps can assume a variety of tenors, as short as a few days and as long as 30 years.

Differences between LIBOR and OIS Rates

While LIBOR and OIS rates are similar in that they both apply to unsecured transactions, there are a number of differences between LIBOR and OIS rates. We focus here on the differences that are most important from a relative value perspective.

The Effect of Short Rate Expectations

The most obvious effect of a longer tenor is that expectations of future short rates are reflected in LIBOR, whereas expected future short rates are not incorporated into OIS rates.[1] Over long periods of time, short rates appear to

---

[1] Strictly speaking, the expectation of high short rates in the remainder of a current reserve maintenance period could induce banks to pay a higher rate on overnight funds, but since this effect is symmetric and not systematic it will not be addressed in this analysis.

increase as often as they decrease, so this effect should not explain persistent differences between OIS rates and LIBORs over long periods of time or persistent differences between longer-dated LIBOR and OIS swap rates.

The Effect of Interest Rate Compounding

Another difference is that OIS rates must be compounded in order to be compared to LIBORs of longer tenors. For example, even if OIS rates were certain to be 5% every day for an entire year, the six-month (6M) LIBOR rate would be 4–5 basis points (bp) above this rate to reflect the difference in the compounding frequencies.

The Effect of Interest Rate Compounding Convexity

One additional conceptual difference relates to the fact that compounding of any frequency introduces a convexity that links interest rate volatility to the expected growth rate in overnight deposits. For example, consider two scenarios in which the expected OIS rate was 5% indefinitely: one in which the volatility around this rate was high, and another in which the volatility of the OIS rate was low. In each scenario, an investor makes the same initial deposit, which is re-invested every night at the prevailing OIS rate in each scenario for an investment horizon of six months.

The expected terminal value of this deposit is greater in the high-volatility scenario than in the low-volatility scenario, simply due to the convexity inherent in the compounding process. All things being equal, longer-term rates should be lower in high-volatility environments than in low-volatility environments. And with any volatility at all, there is a conceptual downward bias in longer-term rates for this reason. In theory, this convexity effect might lower LIBORs relative to OIS rates. However, the magnitude of this effect for the tenors considered here is very small (much less than a basis point), and this effect will not be addressed further in this book.

The Effects of Risk and Term Premia

Of course, risk premia and term premia are often invoked to explain the difference between overnight rates and rates with longer tenors. These terms are often used by market analysts as catchall terms to refer to the additional return or yield that investors might demand to be compensated for various risks.

In this book, these terms are reserved for the more academic usage. In particular, these premia refer here to the compensation that investors demand in the expected return for accepting systematic risks (e.g. consumption risk) resulting from the covariance between the marginal utility of the investor and the return of the asset.

Though a truly comprehensive analysis would include these sorts of risk and term premia, they will not be considered explicitly in this book, for two reasons. First, these premia are not observable ex ante, and a comprehensive treatment of these premia is simply beyond the scope of this book.

Second, this book deals primarily with the systematic difference between interest rates along three yield curves with maturities of up to fifty years in some cases. It's unlikely (though not inconceivable) that these risk and term premia could explain temporary anomalies between spreads in isolated and long-term segments of these yield curves.

The Effect of Default Risk

Perhaps the most important reason for the systematic difference between LIBOR and OIS involves default risk. The OIS rate is the interbank rate for overnight lending between banks, all of which are healthy on the day the transaction is initiated. The scope for a bank to transition overnight from being healthy to being bankrupt is fairly limited. In contrast, there is greater scope for a healthy bank to transition to bankruptcy over, say, six months, a common tenor for LIBOR.

For example, if the 60 bp spread between 6M LIBOR and the 6M riskless rate was attributed to the default risk of banks over the 6M horizon, then the implied 6M default probability would be 74/100ths of one percent, under the conservative assumption that the recovery rate in the event of default would be 80%. (If the recovery rate was assumed to be zero, the implied default probability would be only 15/100ths of one percent.) Assuming that the one-day probability of default is the same every day, this 6M default probability corresponds to a one-day default probability of only 0.000041. For any practical purpose, therefore, the EONIA rate can be effectively considered to be a riskless rate.[2]

As this concept is particularly important, we'll reiterate the importance of these credit "refreshes". If an investor lends at the 6M interbank deposit rate, he subjects his deposit to the possibility that the borrowing bank will default at some point during those six months, and his deposit rate reflects that risk. If, as an alternative, he sticks with one-month deposits, which he rolls five

---

[2] Of course, this argument doesn't suggest that the probability of bank defaults is effectively zero, merely that the probability of a large, healthy bank defaulting on its overnight deposits is very small, at least as implied from interest rate spreads.

times after the initial deposit, then he subjects his deposit to less default risk, since an institution whose credit deteriorates after, say, three months can be avoided when rolling the deposit in the latter scenario, while our investor would be subject to this credit deterioration in the former scenario.

In other words, 6M LIBOR reflects the risk that institutions in the LIBOR fixing panel might default during those six months. But by dealing with LIBORs of lesser tenors, we limit the extent of default risk, as subsequent LIBOR fixings are in some sense "refreshed" by the fact that poor credits are removed from the fixing panel. So exposure to two 3M LIBORs in sequence will expose a trader to less credit risk than will a single 6M LIBOR. And a series of overnight index swaps will subject the trader to far less credit risk, as each overnight rate in the sequences exposes the trader only to one day's worth of credit risk.

The implication here is quite important. As credit conditions in the banking sector deteriorate, LIBORs should increase relative to OIS rates, all things being equal. And, of course, this is precisely the behavior observed in practice.

Repo Rates in Greater Detail

Unlike LIBOR and OIS rates, repo rates apply to loans that are secured by collateral. While the collateral enhances the security of the loan, it also introduces some additional issues of which the relative value analyst should be aware.

Repricing

Once the initial exchange of repo funds and repo collateral has been made, it's possible, even likely, that the value of the collateral will change before the end of the repo agreement. If the value of the collateral increases, the lender will be holding more collateral than is required to secure the loan and will be asked to return the surplus collateral. If the value of the collateral decreases, the lender will be holding less collateral than is required to secure the loan, and the borrower will be required to post additional collateral. This process is referred to as repricing and occurs throughout the term of the repo transaction along terms set out in the initial repo documentation.[3]

Repricing is an issue too often neglected by analysts when calculating carry and cash flows. For example, imagine a trader has purchased bonds financed via a term repo transaction and has sold bond futures against the

---

[3] The rules governing acceptable collateral usually are negotiated between counterparties and will specify which instruments are acceptable as collateral and under what conditions repricing is to occur.

long bond position. If the price of the bonds declines, the repo counterparty is likely to ask for more collateral. At the same time, the price of the futures contracts is likely to have decreased, resulting in a positive inflow of cash in the futures margin account. The cash in the futures margin account can be provided directly to the lender to satisfy the call for additional collateral, or the cash could be used to purchase additional bonds, which could be used as collateral. Either way, the additional transaction is likely to have at least some impact on the interest receipts and/or payments made by the trader.

Many larger financial institutions have collateral management desks that consolidate the process of posting collateral, including repricings, insulating the bond trader from the need to worry about these considerations. But that won't be the case for every trader. And even traders who benefit from a central collateral management operation should be aware of the mechanics affecting the financing of their positions.

Specialness

Repo desks typically accept a large number of bonds as collateral for a repo loan, with no real preference for any specific issue. We refer to such bonds as "general collateral" (GC). However, there are some scenarios where a repo desk or the market in general will have a preference for a particular bond.

For example, consider a scenario in which a trader has borrowed a particular bond from a repo desk so that he could sell the issue short. The repo desk will need to acquire this bond in the market on or before the day it is scheduled to be returned to the original counterparty who previously submitted the bond as collateral.

It may be a simple matter for the repo desk to find that bond and persuade another of its clients to provide that bond as collateral. But that won't always be the case. If the repo desk is finding it difficult to obtain the bond, it can offer to lend funds at a reduced interest rate for any borrower who is able to provide that bond as collateral. In this case, we say the bond has become "special collateral". Equivalently, we may say that the bond has "gone special".

A bond that confers a borrowing advantage to its owner is worth more than a bond that is trading as GC in the repo market. As a result, for traders to be indifferent between the two bonds, the bond that is special in the repo market needs to trade with a spot price that is greater than that of the GC bond by an amount that exactly offsets the advantage the special bond provides in the repo market.

Some bonds are more likely than others to experience periods of specialness. For example, bonds that are deliverable into futures contracts are more likely to be special than are other bonds. Even if a bond isn't part of a futures delivery basket at the moment, the prospect that it will become eligible for delivery and possibly experience a period of specialness may give it additional value in the spot market today. In this sense, repo specialness is asymmetric and therefore exhibits some similarities with call options.

Owning a bond that becomes special is a bit like winning the lottery in this sense. And the price premium that a bond enjoys in the spot market is related to the likelihood and extent of any specialness it might enjoy over its life.[4]

Repo "Fails"

In the above example, a repo dealer lent a particular bond to a trader who wished to sell the issue short. In this transaction, the trader was lending money, and the repo dealer was lending the bond as collateral to this trader, who was able to sell the bond in the spot market.

The repo dealer in this example was able to provide the bond to the trader because it previously had been posted to the dealer as collateral for another transaction. And at some point, the dealer will need to return this bond to the original counterparty.

Of course one possibility is that the dealer will receive the bond from the short-seller before he's scheduled to return it to the original counterparty. But that need not be the case. For example, the repo dealer may have entered into a term repo with the short seller for a date that falls after the date on which the collateral is scheduled to be returned to the original counterparty. In that case, the repo dealer will have to find the bond elsewhere – perhaps in the portfolio of another customer or perhaps from the street (e.g. through an interdealer broker).

If the repo dealer has trouble finding the bond, he can provide an incentive to the market by lowering the repo rate on the bond. If he's having considerable difficulty, he may have to lower the repo rate quite a bit.

But in some circumstances, despite his best efforts, the dealer simply may not be able to find the bond in time to return the bond to the original counterparty. In that case, the dealer is said to have "failed" to the original counterparty.

Repo failures typically carry a penalty to provide an incentive against failure, and these penalties have varied over time and in different markets. In some markets (e.g. Japan), failure could result in a suspension of the repo desk from the market. In some markets, the failure penalty was that the person borrowing money could hold onto the funds at an interest rate of zero

---

[4] For more on repo specialness, see Darrell Duffie (1996) Special Repo Rates. *Journal of Finance*, Vol. 51, No. 2, pp. 493–526.

until the collateral was returned. Of course, this penalty is more effective when interest rates are high than when they're low.

Haircuts

Since government bond prices can be volatile, repo transactions often require the party borrowing cash to post as collateral bonds having a somewhat greater market value than the cash being lent. The difference between the value of the cash and the value of the bonds is referred to as the haircut of the collateral.

If repo counterparties can fund the haircuts at the repo rate, then the haircuts should be of no consequence when considering valuations along the curve. However, if repo counterparties have to fund the haircuts at a cost of capital in excess of the repo rate, then these haircuts may have some effect on the relative pricing of bonds across the curve.

As an example, consider the repo haircut schedule that applies for collateral submitted with the ECB, shown in Table 6.1.

To see the implications of this haircut schedule on the valuation of government bonds, consider the term structures of yield premiums shown in Figure 6.1. Each curve shows the additional premium, in basis points, that would be required in the yield of a zero coupon bond, to offset the effect of the required haircuts shown in Table 6.1, assuming various incremental costs of capital.[5]

TABLE 6.1 ECB Haircut Schedule for "Category 1" Collateral (% of Par)

Residual maturity (years)	Fixed coupon	Zero coupon
0-1	0.5	0.5
1-3	1.5	1.5
3-5	2.5	3
5-7	3	3.5
7-10	4	4.5
> 10	5.5	8.5

Source: ECB.

---

[5] These calculations assume the haircut applicable to each bond changes as a function of the maturity of the bond as time passes, as per the haircut schedule in Table 6.1.

FIGURE 6.1 Yield premiums due to financing of ECB haircuts.

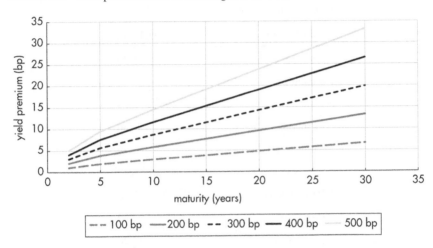

Source: Authors.

For example, a 30Y bond would require an additional 33 bp in yield if the cost of funds required to finance the haircut was 500 bp greater than the repo rate at the ECB over the life of the bond.

The impact tends to decrease as a function of the maturity of the bond and of the incremental funding premium. For example, in the case of a 10Y zero-coupon bond, with a haircut financed at a rate 200 bp greater than the ECB repo rate, the yield premium would be 5.8 bp. This may seem like a modest amount, but 5.8 bp often matters when conducting relative value analysis for government bonds, and the impact of haircuts shouldn't be ignored.

And in some cases, the impact is even greater. For example, the haircut schedule for Spanish government bonds used as collateral with LCH Clearnet is shown in Table 6.2.[6]

In this case, a 10Y Spanish bond whose haircut was financed at a premium of 200 bp above the ECB repo rate would have a yield premium of 16.6 bp. A 30Y bond whose haircut was financed at a premium of 500 bp above the ECB repo rate would have a yield premium of 79 bp. Clearly, there are times when these repo haircuts have a significant impact on the relative

---

[6] LCH Clearnet revises collateral schedules based on market conditions. This table was published on 26 November 2012. Haircuts for Spanish bonds have been even higher in the recent past.

TABLE 6.2   LCH Clearnet Haircut Schedule for
Spanish Bonds (% of Par)

Residual maturity	Haircut (%)
0-1 month	0.70
1-3 months	1.25
3-9 months	2.25
9-15 months	3.30
15 months-2 years	4.40
2-3.25 years	6.40
3.25-4.75 years	7.00
4.75-7 years	9.50
7-10 years	12.20
10-15 years	18.35
15-30 years	20.00

Source: LCH Clearnet.

valuations of government bonds, and the relative value analyst should be aware of this issue.

Right of Substitution

In some cases, the party who borrows cash and provides collateral will retain the right to substitute new collateral for existing collateral during the course of the repo loan. In this case, we say that the borrower has the *right of substitution*.

The right of substitution is an option that benefits the cash borrower in the event that the bonds submitted as collateral become special during the term of the repo transaction. Like most options, its value ex ante depends on the extent to which the bonds in question are likely to "go special".

As this right is valuable to the party borrowing cash, the owner of this right pays for it by agreeing to pay a higher repo rate to the party lending the cash.

Many analysts ignore the right of substitution in their calculations, and we admit that the issue may seem a bit esoteric in many cases. But there are times when additional relative value can be derived by being smart about this issue, and we suggest being aware of the issue when looking carefully at repo calculations.

Credit: Counterparty and Collateral Combined

One of the key features of repo transactions is that they rely on more than a single source of credit. For example, for a lender of cash in a repo transaction not to get paid requires that the borrower default at the same time that the collateral drops precipitously in value.

Consider the case of a US bank submitting German Bunds as collateral against a loan of EUR cash from a Japanese bank. If the US bank is unable to repay the EUR cash to the Japanese bank at the end of the repo transaction, the Japanese bank should be made whole as a result of the German Bunds it holds as collateral against the loan. The risk to the Japanese bank is that the German Bunds plummet in value at precisely the time the US bank goes bankrupt.

While this scenario is not impossible, it's typically viewed as being very unlikely, and most repo desks can manage this risk to some extent by judiciously diversifying collateral types with respect to counterparty.

For example, in recent years, many international banks have been wary about lending cash to Spanish banks in exchange for Spanish government bonds, given the apparent linkages between the sovereign and financial sectors in Spain. Instead, Spanish banks have submitted their Spanish government bonds as collateral against loans of EUR cash from the ECB. If the Spanish banks need cash in other currencies, they've been able to use EUR cash as collateral against loans of cash in these other currencies, such as USD, in the form of shorter-term FX swaps or longer-dated cross-currency basis swaps.

Tri-Party or Custodial Repo

In a bilateral repo transaction, the party receiving collateral typically is able to make use of that collateral in a variety of ways. For instance, in the example above, the repo dealer lent bonds that it was holding as collateral to a trader, so that the trader could sell the bond short.

And as we continued with this example above, we saw that the repo dealer might be caught short himself, unable to return the bonds to the original counterparty, resulting in a repo fail.

To continue with this example, let's imagine that this repo dealer went bankrupt before being able to return the collateral to the original counterparty. In this case, the original counterparty may have to spend considerable time, effort, and money in order to replace the missing bonds. Many repo counterparties consider this risk to be small and manageable, but some participants in the repo market are concerned about it.

One way to mitigate this risk is to use a custodial bank to hold the collateral, in which case the custodial bank is a third party to the transaction, which is then referred to as a tri-party repo.

Most relative value analysts tend not to concern themselves with tri-party repos, but there are times when it's useful to consider the implications of tri-party vs. bilateral repo. For example, there have been times when haircuts on bilateral repo transactions have tended to be considerably wider than in the tri-party market. And as we've seen above, the size of any haircut applied in a repo financing typically impacts the all-in cost of carrying a position, as the haircut typically must be financed at a higher cost of funds.

Capital Treatment for Secured and Unsecured Loans

In most regulatory jurisdictions, the capital requirements that banks face for unsecured loans are different from the requirements they face for secured loans. These requirements typically conform to the Basel directives, which have evolved over time since the Basel capital accords of 1998, and the Basel Committee is currently working on a set of revised accords, collectively known as Basel III.

Some of the specific requirements in Basel III have not yet been agreed. And in fact, Andrew Haldane, the Bank of England's Director of Financial Stability, recently suggested scrapping Basel III in favor of a simpler regime.

Given the ongoing changes to Basel III, we'll discuss the capital treatment of secured and unsecured loans as it has been. Even if the specific calculations change over time, the principles outlined here are very likely to apply under any regime.

In general, unsecured lending between banks carries a risk weighting under Basel rules. The precise risk weights depend on a variety of factors but usually involve a minimum risk weighting of 20% in most cases. So, for example, an asset with a 20% risk weight would require capital of 1.6% for a bank with a core capital requirement of 8%. In this case, 1.6% of the interbank loan needs to be funded at the lending bank's cost of equity (or other core) capital.

The Bank for International Settlements' (BIS) risk weighting for a secured repo transaction, however, is less in most cases. In fact, for repos involving high-quality government bonds as collateral, the BIS risk weighting is zero in many jurisdictions. For a fixed default probability, therefore, a higher cost of equity capital should lead to a higher spread between LIBOR and the repo rate.

A Model Relating LIBOR and Repo Rates

These general ideas can be expressed algebraically to produce a simple equation that can be used to model LIBOR–repo spreads.[7]

Assume a bank wants to make a loan for a single period. If the loan is to be secured via repo collateral, the pre-tax return at the end of the period will be $[1 + R]$, where R is the repo rate for this single period. Assuming the loan is collateralized with a high-quality government bond, the bank can use a low-cost source of funds (e.g. bank retail deposits) to provide for the loan. If the cost of this capital is given by b, the cost of the loan is $[1 + b]$. The profit on this transaction is then $[1 + R] - [1 + b]$.

If the bank makes an unsecured interbank loan instead, it will have to finance dq of this loan at its higher cost of equity capital, g, where q is the BIS risk-weighting for interbank loans and d is the BIS guideline for the capital adequacy ratio for a 100% risk-weighted asset (typically 8%). The cost of capital will then be given by the expression $(1 - qd)[1 + b] + qd[1 + g]$.

If the probability of default is given by p, and the recovery percentage is given by c (percentage of terminal liability recovered rather than percentage of the current market value), then the expected return of the interbank loan L is given by $pc[1 + L] + (1 - p)[1 + L]$. Then the expected profit is given by $pc[1 + L] + (1 - p)[1 + L] - (1 - qd)[1 + b] - qd[1 + g]$.

Assuming that the default probability is a risk-neutral default probability (i.e. it already incorporates the effect of any covariance-related risk premia), the expected profits of the secured and unsecured transactions can be equated to obtain an expression relating LIBOR and the repo rate. In particular:

$$[1 + R] - [1 + b] = pc[1 + L] + (1 - p)[1 + L] - (1 - qd)[1 + b] - qd[1 + g]$$

This equation can be solved in terms of LIBOR.

$$L = \frac{R}{1 - p(1 - c)} + \frac{p(1 - c)}{1 - p(1 - c)} + \frac{qd(g - b)}{1 - p(1 - c)}$$

---

[7] This model is constructed from the perspective of a bank lending cash. We ignore any possible impact of haircuts for simplicity at this point. From the perspective of the bank, this would be valid, for example, in a case in which the loan was over-collateralized with government bonds, with the borrower of cash receiving any interest payments on the bonds.

The first term on the right-hand side of this equation is an amount to act as insurance against the default on the interest payment. In the degenerate case that $R = 0$, there is no interest payment against which to insure, and this term equals zero. And in the case that the recovery rate in the event of default is 100% (again, as a percentage of terminal value rather than nominal value), then the denominator in the first term equals 1, in which case this term contributes nothing to the LIBOR–repo spread. And if $p = 0$, so there is no probability of default, then the denominator of this expression is also 1, and this first term contributes nothing to the spread.

Note also that as long as there is some probability of default ($p > 0$) and the recovery value, c, is less than 100%, the denominator of this first term is less than one, so that LIBOR increases at a rate faster than the repo rate. As a result, the LIBOR–repo spread in general should be an increasing function of interest rates, all things being equal.

The second term on the right-hand side of the equation is an amount to insure against the principal of the loan. Note that this term equals zero if the recovery value is 100% ($c = 1$) or if the default probability is zero ($p = 0$).

The third and final term on the right-hand side of the expression reflects the additional amount that needs to be charged to compensate for the higher cost of equity capital on the portion of the unsecured loan that needs to be funded with core capital to satisfy the bank's regulatory capital requirement. If the cost of equity capital, g, happens to be the same as the marginal cost of borrowed funds, b, then this term is zero. Likewise, if the regulatory risk weighting for the unsecured loan is zero ($g = 0$) or if the capital adequacy ratio is zero ($d = 0$), then this term is also zero.

This equation is helpful in thinking about the spread between LIBOR and repo rates. In fact, we've used it in the past to implement fair-value models for LIBOR–repo spreads. And we'll see in Chapter 8 on the theoretical determinants of swap spreads that the model can serve as the foundation of a fair-value model for swap spreads as well.

Conclusions

All in all, our consideration of repo rates, LIBORs, and OIS rates allows us to offer a few general conclusions:

- GC repo rates should be lower than LIBORs of the same tenor.
- Overnight GC repo rates should be slightly lower than OIS rates.
- OIS rates generally should be lower than LIBOR rates, on average, over long periods of time, though this need not always be the case.

- The spread between LIBORs and repo rates should be:
  - an increasing function of the level of interest rates;
  - an increasing function of the cost of core capital;
  - an increasing function of required capital ratios.

As an empirical matter, these conclusions tended to be consistent with the observed money market data prior to the onset of the financial crisis in Q3 2007. But as the crisis worsened, the capital positions of the banking sector deteriorated significantly, to the point that there was relatively little capital that could be committed to pursuing arbitrage opportunities in the money markets.

As a result, we have seen some violations of these pricing relations in recent years. For example, there have been times in the Eurozone money markets that repo rates for GC in the German market have been quite a bit lower than EONIA rates of corresponding terms.

As the capital positions of the banks have been improving over time, we're observing fewer apparent anomalies in the money markets. But we're also observing that LIBOR–repo spreads in the main markets appear to be stabilizing at levels somewhat wider than their pre-crisis levels. Our model of LIBOR–repo rates provides a useful framework for considering reasons for today's wider levels.

The level of short interest rates in these markets is at a record low, which would argue for *narrower* LIBOR–repo spreads, all things being equal. But of course everything else isn't the same in this case. For example, given the ubiquity of bank bailouts, the probability of outright bank defaults appears to be lower now than it was before the crisis.

But if rate levels and default probabilities don't explain today's wider spreads, what factors are likely to be responsible? According to our model, the two most likely candidates are capital requirements and the cost of core capital.

Regulators in most jurisdictions have responded to the financial crisis by requiring banks to increase their capital ratios. For example, the current Basel III requirements are for banks to have total capital of 10.5%, with 7% in the form of common equity. The Swiss National Bank has gone much further, announcing that its two largest banks, UBS and CSFB, will be required to maintain core capital ratios of 19%, with 10% consisting of common equity.

The ex ante return on core capital is unobservable, but our sense is that this has been increasing as well, despite the fact that ex post returns on equity have been declining for many banks in the sector. The continuing underperformance of bank shares in many markets (relative to broad market indices) is consistent with an increase in the ex ante cost of core capital.

All in all then, our sense is that banks are having to set aside more capital for interbank loans than they used to and that the ex ante marginal cost of this capital relative to their marginal cost of funds (e.g. retail deposits) is higher than it used to be. Both factors would argue in favor of wider LIBOR–repo spreads.

Looking further ahead, a number of Western governments appear to be transforming their banks into quasi-utilities, with considerably less risk and earning considerably lower returns on equity than they've earned in the past. In this case, ex ante costs of equity are likely to decline relative to general funding costs, exerting downward pressure on LIBOR–repo spreads. Time will tell whether the impact of this trend will counter the impact of the increase in required capital ratios also taking place.

CHAPTER 7

Intra-Currency Basis Swaps

Definition

An intra-currency basis swap (ICBS) is a derivative security in which each of two parties agrees to pay the other a different floating rate, with both rates denominated in the same currency. For example, one party might agree to pay six-month (6M) LIBOR to the other party in exchange for being paid 3M LIBOR less a spread.

Were we to apply this definition strictly, we'd also characterize as ICBS an agreement to exchange 3M LIBOR for the 3M OIS rate in the same currency. However, we won't treat such swaps in this chapter, as they can be constructed synthetically by combining swaps discussed here and in other chapters in this book.

Factors that Determine Pricing

In Chapter 6, we discussed a few of the factors that influence the spreads between LIBOR and OIS rates, as both are unsecured lending rates between banks. As ICBS are a function of lending rates with different terms, the same considerations affect the pricing of ICBS. Rather than discuss these factors again in detail in this chapter, we'll simply remind the reader that these include a minor effect for short rate expectations, a minor effect due to interest rate compounding frequencies, and a catchall term that often is referred to as "risk premia".

As with the difference between LIBOR and OIS rates, the key difference is the differing probabilities of default between rates with different terms. For example, there is a greater probability for an individual bank to default over six months than there is for the same bank to default over three months, simply due to the additional three months over which a default could occur.

To provide intuition about the nature of the credit risk in basis swaps, Figure 7.1 shows the five-year (5Y) basis swap spread between 3M EURIBOR and 6M EURIBOR since 2003. The positive spread shown in this graph depicts the spread attached to the 3M rate in this case. For example, in June of 2010, one could agree to pay 6M EURIBOR for five years in exchange for receiving 3M EURIBOR + 18 basis points (bp) for five years.

A few points to note:

- The basis swap was almost always within 1 bp of zero prior to the onset of the subprime crisis in July of 2007.
- Subsequent to the onset of the crisis, the spread widened considerably, reflecting the perception that the risk of bank default had increased.

To further illustrate the relation between the level of the EUR 3M/6M basis swap and overall perceptions of crisis-related credit risks, we show the 5Y EURIBOR 3M/6M basis swap along with the euro exchange rate in Figure 7.2. In Figure 7.3, we show this ICBS along with the 5Y basis swap between 3M EURIBOR and 3M USD LIBOR.

FIGURE 7.1 5Y basis swap spread between 3M EURIBOR and 6M EURIBOR.

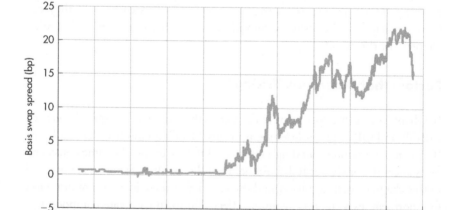

Source: Bloomberg.

FIGURE 7.2   EUR exchange rate and 5Y basis swap spread between 3M EURIBOR and 6M EURIBOR.

Source: Bloomberg.

FIGURE 7.3   5Y basis swap spread between 3M EURIBOR and 6M EURIBOR and 5Y basis swap between 3M EURIBOR and 3M USD LIBOR.

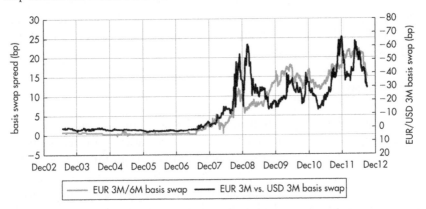

Source: Bloomberg.

Prior to the onset of the subprime crisis, there was no correlation between the euro and the ICBS, but after the onset of the crisis, the correlation between these two variables has been 0.68.

Prior to the onset of the subprime crisis in July of 2007, the two basis swaps were both very close to zero. Subsequent to the start of the crisis, the spreads have tended to widen and narrow together. Over the entire period, the correlation between these two variables has been −0.62. (The convention is to quote the EUR 3M vs. USD 3M basis swap as a spread to the EUR leg, and the cross-currency basis swap is shown on an inverted axis in Figure 7.3.)

The overall impression is that this EUR ICBS has widened and narrowed in recent years along with general perceptions of credit risk within the European banking system.

Role as Building Blocks

ICBS are of interest in their own right, as instruments for hedging various transactions and as a means for trading perceptions of credit risk in the banking sector. But for the relative value analyst, their most interesting role is as a building block for other structures, primarily bonds that are cross-currency basis swapped into other currencies.

For example, US Treasuries typically pay a semi-annual coupon, and USD interest rate swaps typically involve semi-annual fixed payments against quarterly floating payments. In contrast, German Bunds typically pay an annual coupon, and EUR swaps typically involve annual fixed payments against semi-annual floating payments. As a result, if an analyst wishes to compare German Bunds and US Treasuries on a like-for-like basis, at some point he'll need either to include a USD 3M/6M basis swap or a EUR 3M/6M basis swap in the analysis.

Conclusion

We'll illustrate the application of the ICBS as a building block in relative value comparisons later in the book, once we've discussed some additional concepts. But for now the two key points to note from this chapter are:

- The ICBS is a function of perceived credit risks in the banking sector.
- ICBS constitute one of the building blocks required to compare bonds that pay with differing frequencies.

CHAPTER 8

Theoretical Determinants of Swap Spreads

One of the fundamental relative value relations in the fixed income markets is that between government bond yields and the fixed interest rates of plain vanilla interest rate swaps. These swap spreads have been traded and studied extensively since the advent of the first interest rate swap in 1981, and in this chapter we discuss the theoretical determinants of swap spreads.

Old Approach: Looking at Default Risk of Swap Counterparties

Until the mid-1990s, most analysts and academics attributed the spread between swap rates and government bond yields to the credit risks of the two counterparties in the swap. In this framework, swap rates were like corporate bond yields, which are higher than government bond yields in large part due to the credit risk of the corporate issuers.

There are a few problems with this approach.

First, while a corporate bond has a single issuer, an interest rate swap has two counterparties, with interest payments netted and with no principal changing hands. In order to explain observed swap spreads, researchers had to appeal to a significant credit asymmetry between the two counterparties.

Second, unlike a corporate bond, the rate of a swap at inception is typically set so that the net present value (NPV) of the swap is zero. Since there is no value to be lost in the event of default immediately after the start of the swap, it seems unlikely default risk could be responsible for the swap spread at inception.

Of course, over time, the NPV of a swap tends to move away from zero, but it's not known in advance whether the swap will become more valuable to

157

the fixed rate payer or to the floating rate payer. In this case, it seems unlikely that expectations of future credit risk could explain the size of swap spreads.

On the other hand, when the yield curve is very steep, the party receiving fixed rates is likely to experience positive net inflows in the early years of the swap and net cash outflows in the latter years of the swap. In this case, there may be a risk that the party receiving a fixed rate would collect net payments in the early years of the swap but then fail to perform once the LIBOR rate increased to the point that the net cash flows became negative for this party. And this brings us to our third problem with the traditional valuation approach: the fact that collateral is exchanged in most swaps in order to protect against default when the NPV of the swap favors one party over another.

These concerns motivated us and others in the mid- to late 1990s to find alternative perspectives on swap spread valuations. In the approach we developed, fixed swap spreads were explained by focusing on LIBOR and repo rates. In particular, the swap spread was seen as the amount that caused traders to be indifferent between buying a government bond financed in the repo market and receiving a fixed rate in a swap against floating payments of LIBOR.

The Modern Approach

The Fixed Rate Perspective

Consider a trader who wants to be long a fixed rate instrument and is considering buying a bond or receiving fixed in the swap market. In one case, he could buy a 10Y par-coupon bond and finance it over its life by rolling it over in the repo market until maturity. In the second case, he could receive a fixed rate in the swap market for 10 years and pay 3M LIBOR against it for 10 years.

For reasons we discussed earlier, LIBOR is almost certainly going to be greater than the repo rate of the same term over time. If the swap rate and the par-coupon government bond yield are identical, this trader always would prefer to buy the bond, as he's very likely to experience lower floating rate payments in this scenario. Only if he can receive a fixed swap rate greater than the par-coupon government bond yield would he be indifferent between buying the bond and receiving fixed in the swap. In particular, the fair swap spread in this case will be the size of annuity that has the same present value as the difference over time between LIBOR and the repo rate.

The Floating Rate Perspective

We can also view the situation from the perspective of an investor wanting floating rate exposure over time. For example, consider an investor who owns a 10Y government bond trading at par and decides he would rather have floating rate exposure. He could sell the bond and invest the proceeds in the repo market, holding a bond (perhaps even his original bond) as collateral. Alternatively, he could swap the bond and receive LIBOR for the next 10 years. As LIBOR is expected to be greater than the repo rate, he would be indifferent between these two alternatives only in the event that the swap rate was greater than the par-coupon government bond yield.

In fact, he would be indifferent only if the difference between the fixed swap rate and the par-coupon bond yield had a net present value that compensated for the anticipated difference between LIBOR and the repo rate over the life of the swap. Again, the fair value for this swap spread would be the size of an annuity that had the same present value as the difference over time between LIBOR and the repo rate.

Viewing the Swap as a Derivative

The fixed and floating rate perspectives provide intuition about the fair value of a swap spread, but it's particularly useful to consider swap spreads from the perspective that the swap is a derivative security. In this case, we could value the swap using no-arbitrage considerations.

A Preliminary Analogy

As a useful analogy, consider the no-arbitrage valuation relation between government bond futures and the underlying government bonds. In particular, to simplify the analysis, let's consider a hypothetical example in which only one bond is deliverable into a particular contract.

We know from previous discussions that the prices of the futures contract and the bond should preclude arbitrage. There will be no free lunch from selling the futures, buying the bond, and financing the bond in the term repo market until the delivery date of the futures contract. Likewise, there will no free lunch from buying the futures, selling the bond via the repo market, earning the repo rate on the proceeds, and then accepting delivery of the bonds at the end of the futures contract. In other words, the spread or basis between the futures contract and the bond will depend on the term repo rate so as to preclude arbitrage.

Before considering the case of the swap, it's useful to consider the relation between the bond futures price and the bond price in the event that there is no term repo market.

For example, imagine that an active overnight repo market existed but that there simply was no repo market available for terms greater than overnight. What would happen to the bond/futures basis in this case?

The first thing to note in this case is that the futures can no longer be priced relative to the bond via no-arbitrage considerations. As the overnight repo rate can change over time, it's not possible to construct a true arbitrage in this case. On the other hand, we still can say something about the relative values of the futures contract and the bond.

For example, imagine that the bond futures price was very much lower than the bond price. This would imply that a trader could create a relatively low-term repo rate synthetically by selling the bond and buying the futures. If this synthetic term repo was quite a bit lower than the expected overnight repo rate until expiration, many traders would be motivated to borrow synthetically in this way and to invest the proceeds in the overnight repo market, with the expectation of earning a positive spread until delivery.

Similarly, consider a case in which the bond futures price was quite a bit higher than the bond price. In this case, a trader could create a relatively high-term repo rate synthetically by buying the bond and selling the futures. If this synthetic term repo rate was quite a bit higher than the expected overnight repo rate until expiration, many traders would be motivated to lend synthetically in this way and to borrow the needed funds in the overnight repo market, with the expectation of earning a positive spread until delivery.

The point of this example is that we should expect the futures price and the bond price to reflect expectations regarding the future path of the overnight repo rate, even in cases in which a term repo market doesn't exist. In this case, the futures and cash prices may not conform to true no-arbitrage principles, but they are likely to conform to reasonable expectations about the overnight financing rate.

The Cash and Carry Arbitrage for a Swap

As with government bond futures contracts, we can apply no-arbitrage pricing considerations to swaps as derivatives.

For the sake of argument, assume that an active and liquid market existed for basis swaps between 3M LIBOR and 3M repo rates, in which one party pays 3M LIBOR less a fixed spread, X, over time and the other party pays the 3M, general collateral repo rate over the same period. (Assume for now that no bonds ever trade special in the repo market.)

In this case, it would be possible to create a synthetic swap by combining a bond, financed in the repo market, with a position in this LIBOR–repo basis swap. For example, if we wanted to receive fixed and pay LIBOR in our synthetic swap, we could buy a par-coupon bond, financed in the repo market, and then agree to pay LIBOR less X in exchange for receiving the repo rate in a LIBOR–repo basis swap. Our net position is that we would receive a fixed rate equal to the bond coupon plus X in exchange for paying LIBOR, as the repo interest we pay to finance our bonds is equal to the repo interest we receive in the LIBOR–repo basis swap. In this case, our swap spread is X.

Similarly, we could construct a synthetic swap in which we receive LIBOR. For example, imagine we sell a par-coupon bond and invest the proceeds in the repo market, earning the repo rate over the life of the bond. We then could enter a LIBOR–repo basis swap in which we pay the repo rate and receive LIBOR less the fixed rate, X. In this case, our net position is that we receive LIBOR and pay a fixed swap rate equal to the par coupon of the bond plus X. In this case as well, our swap spread is X.

Just as we saw when considering swap spreads from the fixed and floating rate perspectives earlier, the swap spread from this derivative perspective turns out to be the value of an annuity, X, whose present value is equal to the present value of the difference between LIBOR and the repo rate over the life of the swap. In other words, the swap spread is equivalent to the LIBOR–repo basis swap spread, assuming such a basis swap market existed.

Applying the Concept without a Market for LIBOR–Repo Basis Swaps

In fact, there isn't an active, liquid market for LIBOR–repo basis swaps. But in this case, we can think about swap valuation the same way we thought about valuation of bond futures and cash bonds in the absence of a market for term repo. In other words, we could create a synthetic LIBOR–repo basis swap simply by trading a swap against a par-coupon bond. In the case of a long bond position and a pay fixed position in the swap market, we receive the LIBOR less the repo rate over the life of the swap in exchange for the swap spread. In the case of a short bond position and a received fixed position in the swap market, we pay LIBOR less the repo rate over the life of the swap in exchange for the swap spread.

If the swap spread is wide relative to our expectations for LIBOR and the repo rate over time, many traders would attempt to profit by earning the swap spread and paying the LIBOR–repo spread over time. If the swap spread is narrow relative to expectations for LIBOR and the repo rate over time, many traders would attempt to profit by paying the swap spread and receiving the LIBOR–repo spread over time.

In the absence of an active and liquid market for LIBOR–repo basis swaps, we're unable to use no-arbitrage principles for valuing swaps. But we are able to compare swap spreads to our expectations for LIBOR–repo spreads over time to assess the relative values between swap rates and bond yields.

In this example, we were careful to refer to par-coupon bonds. The situation becomes a bit more complex in the case of bonds trading at a discount to par, as we'll see in a subsequent chapter. But fair swap spreads for off-coupon bonds can be calculated by first calculating a fair swap spread for a par-coupon bond and then determining the fair yield spread between the par-coupon bond and the off-coupon bond.

Also, in this example, we ignored some of the real-world issues in the repo market that we discussed in Chapter 6. For example, current par-coupon bonds are likely to trade away from par at some point, in which case they will be re-priced in the repo market, as we discussed in our earlier chapter. If the swap spread for the bond remains constant, then the NPV of the swap is very likely to move in the opposite direction and by a similar magnitude. Provided the swap is being margined (as almost surely will be the case), then the change in margin for the swap is very likely to offset the change in margin for the bond. For example, if cash were acceptable as margin for the bond position and the swap position, then we could shift the cash from our swap margin account to our repo margin account, and vice versa.

However, the swap spread is likely to move over time as well, in which case there will be times when our repo margin and swap margin don't offset.

Insurance Properties of LIBOR–Repo Spreads

So far in our discussion, we've addressed the notion of random and time-varying LIBOR–repo spreads by focusing on the expectation of those spreads over the lives of the bond and the swap. In theory, we might also care about the covariance between these LIBOR–repo spreads and the marginal utility of a typical investor. This issue is particularly important given the behavior of LIBOR–repo spreads in the financial crisis that started in 2007.

When considering this issue, it's useful to draw an analogy to popular types of insurance contracts, such as fire insurance. For most homeowners, the expected return on a fire insurance policy is negative, in that they are required to pay more in insurance premiums than the payouts they expect to receive from the policy, given the likelihood of a fire. Nevertheless, most homeowners are happy to buy fire insurance, because the payouts from a policy come at precisely the time that the homeowner most needs money to rebuild a home destroyed by fire. In other words, the covariance between the payout and the homeowner's marginal utility is relatively high.

Now let's apply this consideration to LIBOR–repo spreads and therefore to swap spreads.

As discussed in an earlier chapter, LIBOR–repo spreads should be an increasing function of the level of interest rates. As interest rates tend to be pro-cyclical, they would be expected to contribute to the pro-cyclicality of LIBOR–repo spreads. In this case, LIBOR–repo spreads would be expected to be negatively correlated with the marginal utility of the typical investor. In other words, receiving LIBOR and paying repo increases rather than decreases the portfolio risk of most investors, so investors require a return greater than they would earn if the LIBOR–repo basis swap were priced at actuarial fair value. As a result, the LIBOR–repo basis swap spread should be lower than its actuarial fair value. (Recall the investor receives LIBOR – X in the swap, where X is the quoted basis swap spread.)

On the other hand, LIBOR–repo basis swaps should also be an increasing function of default probabilities for banks in the LIBOR fixing panel, and we would expect these probabilities to be countercyclical (i.e. we'd expect them to be relatively high during recessions). In this case, the argument above works in reverse, and we'd expect the LIBOR–repo basis swap spread, X, to be wider than if it were priced at actuarial fair value.

While the level of interest rates and the default probabilities of banks are related to the correlation between swap spreads and marginal utility, our theory suggests we should focus on the covariance between these spreads and marginal utility, in which case we also need to focus on the volatilities of LIBOR–repo spreads and of marginal utility generally.

In general, volatilities tend to be higher during recessions than during expansions, so we'd expect the insurance component of LIBOR–repo basis swap spreads to be greater during times of recession than they would be when the economy was expanding. Whether this premium increases or decreases basis swap spreads and hence swap spreads relative to actuarial fair value will depend on whether the pro-cyclical factors (e.g. interest rates) are dominating or whether the countercyclical factors (e.g. default probabilities and volatilities) are dominating at the time.

Implications of the Insurance Perspective

With this conversation in mind, we can summarize the implications of taking into consideration the covariance between LIBOR–repo spreads and marginal utility.

- LIBOR–repo basis swap spreads and hence swap spreads are probably wider than actuarial fair value, as investors are willing to accept a lower expected return from receiving LIBOR, given that this position helps hedge against recessions and is therefore positively correlated with marginal utility. This result assumes the cyclical impact of default probabilities is greater than the countercyclical impact of interest rates, though this needn't be the case at all times. This result is also irrespective of any time variation in volatility.

- Since volatilities do change over time, LIBOR–repo spreads are likely to be high when volatility is high, all things being equal.
- Risk aversion and hence the market prices of many risks are likely to be high when wealth is low, so we expect LIBOR–repo basis swap spreads and hence swap spreads to be high when there has been a negative shock to wealth, as in the recent financial crises.

Other Practical Modeling Issues

There are a few other practical issues that we should consider as well.

Capital Requirements

Amount of Capital Required

Even if there were no regulatory capital requirements from these swap spread trades, we would still be prudent in backing these trades with capital, and the cost of capital will affect our ability to allocate arbitrage capital in pursuing opportunities. All things being equal, allocating larger amounts of capital to this trade will increase our capital costs and increase the size of the no-arbitrage band applicable to the pricing of swaps and bonds.

Similarly, an increase in the cost of capital will increase our capital costs and have the same effect on the relevant no-arbitrage bands.

Repo Haircuts

We assumed there were no repo haircuts in these examples. In practice, many traders will face repo haircuts when financing bond positions, and the no-arbitrage arguments should be modified to reflect these.

For example, consider a situation in which a swap spread was narrow relative to a trader's expectation of LIBOR–repo spreads in the future. Absent a haircut,[1]

---

[1] A haircut is the difference between the face value of a loan and the agreed value of the collateral backing the loan. For example, if a bank lends USD 900,000 against a house with a value of USD 1MM, then the haircut is USD 100,000 (1MM less 900,000), equal to 10% of the value of the house.

we saw that the trader could buy the bond, financed in the repo market, pay the fixed swap rate, and receive LIBOR. The net position would be for the trader to pay the swap spread and receive the LIBOR–repo spread over the life of the swap.

But if the repo position required a significant haircut, the trader would have to fund the haircut with more expensive capital, in which case the net floating rate interest payments received by the trader would be lower than they would be without the haircut. In this case, the fair value for the swap spread also would be lower.

In fact, if the LIBOR–repo spread is already fairly narrow, and if typical haircuts in a particular bond market are relatively large, and if the cost of the capital required to fund the haircuts is relatively high, then it's possible that the net floating rate interest received would be negative, in which case the swap spread that would make a trader indifferent between the swap and the bond might even be negative, with the "fair" swap rate less than the yield of the par-coupon bond.

The Subprime Crisis as a Brief Case Study

As it was a relatively extreme event, the subprime crisis is an opportunity to consider these factors in practice.

As the crisis materialized in July 2007, concerns about bank solvency emerged, effectively raising default probabilities for banks in the fixing panel. At the same time, volatility increased, with, for example, 1Y options on the 1Y USD swap rate increasing from 72 bp/year to 110 bp/year by September. The 3M LIBOR–repo spread increased from single digits in early July to 95 bp by September. Not surprisingly, the 2Y US swap spread increased from 48 bp in July to nearly 80 bp in September.[2]

In September, the Fed began cutting rates, lowering the target rate from 5.25% at the beginning of the month to 4.25% at the end of the year. 1Y1Y[3] swaption volatility increased to 125 bp/year by the end of the year. Three-month LIBOR–repo spreads increased to 106 bp in December. Repo haircuts were increased in a number of instances, particularly for bilateral repos

---

[2] When we say "the swap spread widened", we mean the bond yield declined relative to the swap rate. For example, if a bond could be asset swapped for LIBOR −20 bp at the start of the month and then could be asset swapped at LIBOR −30 bp at the end of the month, we would say that the swap spread widened by 10 bp, having increased from 20 bp to 30 bp. Note that in Chapters 14 and 16 a different convention will be used.

[3] When discussing swaptions, the notation is such that by, for example, "3Y4Y" we mean *an option that expires in three years on an underlying instrument that will have four years to maturity at the time the option expires.*

and for bonds with longer maturities. Again, not surprisingly, the 2Y US swap spread widened to just over 100 bp.

As the crisis continued in 2008, the Fed cut rates to a historic low of 0.25%, and 1Y1Y implied volatility reached a high of 200 bp. At one point in 2008, the 3M LIBOR–repo spread reached a high of 365 bp. And again, not surprisingly, the 2Y US swap spread widened to about 165 bp.

Since then, as the crisis abated, the 1Y1Y implied volatility decreased and is now 29 bp/year. The Fed Funds rate is still targeted to be between 0 and 0.25%. The LIBOR–repo spread has returned to a more typical level of 25 bp. Repo haircuts have gradually moderated, though in many cases they're still higher than pre-crisis levels. And, not surprisingly, the 2Y US swap spread is currently 12 bp.

In general, this brief case study suggests our conceptual framework is consistent with the changes in swap spreads and other relevant variables actually observed in practice. We'll take a closer look at some of these empirical aspects in the next chapter.

Conclusions

Our conceptual approach toward the relative valuations of swap spreads has identified a number of factors that would be expected to determine swap spreads. In particular, we find swap spreads should be:

(1) an increasing function of the level of repo rates expected over the life of the swap;
(2) an increasing function of the default probabilities of banks in the LIBOR fixing panel;
(3) an increasing function of the amount of core capital that needs to back an unsecured interbank loan;
(4) an increasing function of the cost (relative to LIBOR) of the capital required to back an unsecured interbank loan;
(5) an increasing function of the correlation between LIBOR–repo spreads and marginal utility;
(6) an increasing function of the volatility of LIBOR–repo spreads and of marginal utility;
(7) a decreasing function of haircuts, which typically increase during periods of high volatility and financial stress;
(8) a decreasing function of the cost (relative to the repo rate) of the funds used to finance the haircut.

Factors (1)–(4) pertain to the actuarial fair value of swap spreads. Factors (5) and (6) pertain to the insurance role of swap spreads given their covariance with marginal utility. And factors (7) and (8) pertain to the microstructure of the market for government bond financing.

In the next chapter, we'll consider further the empirical support for the conceptual framework outlined in this chapter.

CHAPTER 9

Swap Spreads from an Empirical Perspective

To this point in the book, our discussion of swap spreads and LIBOR–repo spreads has been largely conceptual. In this chapter, we consider swap spreads from an empirical perspective. In particular, we're looking for relations among variables that would help support or perhaps refute the conceptual framework for modeling swap spreads presented in the previous chapter.

Empirical Analysis of Swap Spreads

In the previous chapter, we used no-arbitrage principles to conclude that the swap spreads should be equal to LIBOR–repo basis swap spreads. Since there is no liquid market for LIBOR–repo basis swaps, we used basic results of financial economics to characterize the observable factors on which swap spreads should depend.

In particular, swap spreads should be an increasing function of spot LIBOR–repo spreads, given the reasonable expectation that LIBOR–repo basis swaps of different tenors would be positively correlated with spot LIBOR–repo spreads.

In addition, as spot swap spreads should be increasing functions of the level of interest rates, all things being equal, we would expect LIBOR–repo basis swaps and hence swap spreads to be an increasing function of forward rates.

Also, to the extent LIBOR–repo spreads are correlated with the marginal utility of the typical investor, we would expect LIBOR–repo basis swaps and hence swap spreads to be somewhat wider than actuarial fair value, to reflect the ability of LIBOR–repo basis swaps and therefore swap spreads to help insure against adverse shocks to investor utility.

Finally, we would expect swap spreads to be a decreasing function of the size of the haircut involved in the repo financing and of the cost of financing this haircut, above and beyond the cost of financing the rest of the bond.

Some of these variables, such as spot LIBOR–repo spreads, are quantifiable and observable. As a result, it would be possible to incorporate them into an empirical model for swap spreads.

In contrast, some of these variables are either not quantifiable or not observable. For example, we aren't able to observe the marginal utility of the typical investor or the correlation between this marginal utility and LIBOR–repo spreads. As a result, some of these variables are not practicable for inclusion in an econometric model.

As a result, in this chapter we'll appeal to the data to help confirm or refute the concepts presented in the previous chapter, on the theoretical determinants of swap spreads, rather than attempt to build a formal econometric model of swap spreads.

Swap Spreads over Time

Figure 9.1 shows swap spreads for US Treasuries with maturities of two, five, ten, and thirty years since November of 1988.

FIGURE 9.1   US swap spreads.

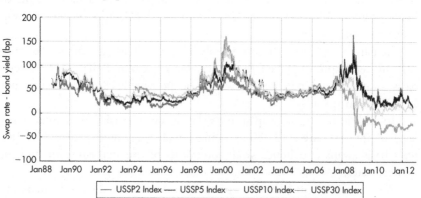

Source: Bloomberg.

There are a few key points to note from this figure:

- In general, swap spreads appear cyclical, widening during periods of growth and narrowing during periods of relatively weak growth.
- Swap spreads generally appear to revert around a long-run mean.
- The start of the subprime crisis in 2007 appears to be a structural break, in particular with longer-maturity bonds significantly cheaper relative to swaps than at any time previously.

A Brief Comment on the Cyclicality of Swap Spreads

Before we examine the empirical relation between swap spreads and the variables previously identified as theoretical determinants of swap spreads, it's useful to comment on the cyclical nature of swap spreads apparent already from Figure 9.1.

To highlight the cyclical nature of swap spreads, Figure 9.2 shows the thirty-year (30Y) US swap spread along with the US unemployment rate (on an inverted axis) since 1998.

The cyclical nature of swap spreads raises an important point. Almost any cyclical or countercyclical variable will correlate with swap spreads over longer periods of time. But of course correlation doesn't imply causality, and we should be careful not to build empirical models of swap spreads using variables chosen simply because of their correlations with swap spreads.

A case in point involves government bond supply, which figures in many of the empirically based models of swap spreads we've seen over the years.

FIGURE 9.2 30Y swap spread and US unemployment rate.

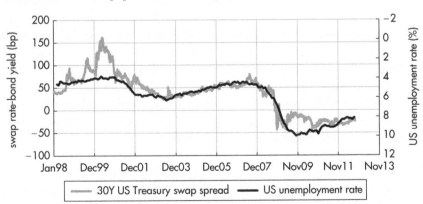

Source: Bloomberg.

FIGURE 9.3   30Y swap spread and US Treasury debt sold to the public.

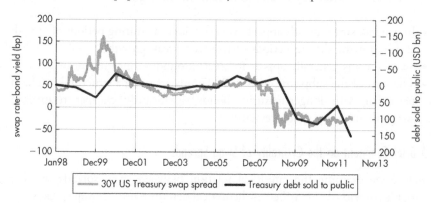

Source: Bloomberg.

Figure 9.3 shows the 30Y US swap spread along with the amount of US Treasury debt sold to the public over time.

Government bond supply correlates less well with the swap spread than does the unemployment rate, yet many analysts are happy to include Treasury supply in their swap spread models, despite the difficulty in motivating Treasury supply for economic reasons.[1]

The intuition for including government supply involves a general appeal to supply and demand. If the government issues a large number of bonds, the supply of bonds increases, the prices of the bonds decline, and the yields of the bonds increase, narrowing swap spreads.

But while this explanation is intuitive, it completely ignores the fact that the swap is a derivative. We don't expect the bond futures basis to narrow when the government issues more bonds, unless increased government bond issuance somehow increases repo rates. Similarly, we shouldn't expect swap spreads to narrow when the government issues more bonds, unless increased government bond issuance somehow narrows LIBOR–repo basis swaps.

In our view, it makes no more sense to include government bond supply in a model of swap spreads than it does to include the unemployment rate. Nevertheless, analysts continue to point to the observed correlation between government bond supply and swap spreads, inferring causality from correlation, without considering alternative hypotheses.

---

[1] It is possible that the unemployment rate and government bond supply are both serving as proxies for any credit risk that may be reflected in the prices of US Treasury bonds. We'd like to thank Antti Ilmanen for making this point. We address sovereign credit risk briefly later in this chapter and in greater detail in Chapter 15 and Chapter 16.

It will be useful to keep these points in mind as we focus on more detailed relations through the remainder of this chapter, starting with the relation between swap spreads and LIBOR–repo spreads.

Swap Spreads and LIBOR–Repo Spreads

As discussed in our earlier chapter on the theoretical determinants of swap spreads, the main driver of swap spreads should be LIBOR–repo basis swaps. But as there is no liquid market for these, we'll compare swap spreads to spot LIBOR–repo spreads as a proxy for LIBOR–repo basis swap spreads.

Figure 9.4 shows the 2Y US swap spread since 15 Feb 1989 along with the spread between three-month (3M) LIBOR and the 3M Treasury bill rate, which we use here as a proxy for the 3M repo rate, as our repo data extend only to 26 Mar 1998. As the LIBOR–bill spread has been fairly noisy, we plot the 30-day average of this spread, so as not to obscure the underlying relations between the LIBOR–bill spread and the swap spread.

There are a few points worth noting in this graph:

- Overall, the correspondence between the LIBOR–bill spread and the 2Y swap spread is quite close.
- The swap spread was somewhat less than the LIBOR–bill spread in 1995–1997.
- The swap spread was somewhat greater than the LIBOR–bill spread in 2001 and 2002.

FIGURE 9.4 2Y US swap spreads and 3M spot LIBOR–bill spreads.

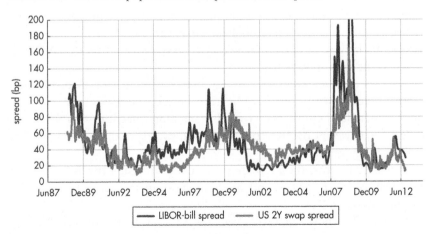

Source: Bloomberg.

FIGURE 9.5 2Y US swap spreads and 3M spot LIBOR–repo spreads.

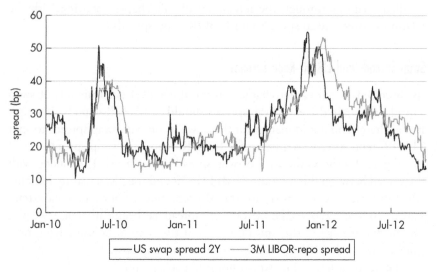

Source: Bloomberg.

Figure 9.5 shows the 2Y swap rate since January of 2010 along with the 3M LIBOR–repo spread rather than the average of the 3M LIBOR–bill spread.

It's clear from Figure 9.5 that 2Y swap spreads have been tracking spot LIBOR–repo spreads quite closely. In fact, regression analysis of the data in this figure produces a coefficient estimate of 0.98, meaning the swap spread has moved nearly one-for-one with the LIBOR–repo spread over this period, consistent with our discussion of the theoretical determinants of swap spreads. With this in mind, it's likely that the latest LIBOR–bill spread appeared relatively elevated because the 3M average hadn't yet declined by as much as the spot spreads had.

As we consider swap spreads for bonds with greater maturities, the correspondence with spot LIBOR–repo spreads decreases somewhat, an understandable circumstance given that it's more practical to arbitrage the difference between LIBOR–repo spreads and swap spreads for two years than it is for thirty years.

Figure 9.6 shows the 5Y swap spread along with the LIBOR–bill spread. Here too we see the correspondence between swap spreads and LIBOR–bill spreads is very close.

Figure 9.7 shows the 10Y swap spread along with the LIBOR–repo spread. From this figure, we see the 10Y spread is particularly elevated relative to the LIBOR–repo spread in 2000. In our view, this is likely due to two

FIGURE 9.6 5Y US swap spreads and 3M spot LIBOR–bill spreads.

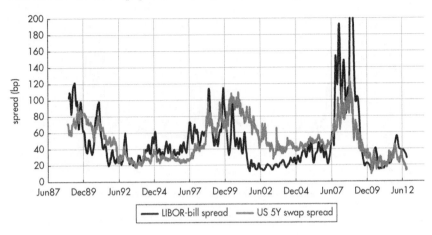

Source: Bloomberg.

FIGURE 9.7 10Y US swap spreads and 3M spot LIBOR–bill spreads.

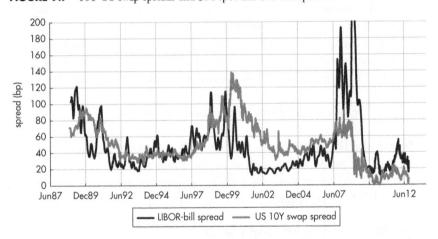

Source: Bloomberg.

factors. First, the LTCM crisis in 1998 had pushed longer-dated spreads to fairly elevated levels already in late 1998 and 1999.[2] And then second, auctions of the European UMTS spectrum in the spring of 2000 raised more

---

[2] Long Term Capital Management was a hedge fund that lost a substantial amount of money on very large, leveraged positions in global fixed income markets. The ensuing impact on financial markets resulted in a financial crisis in 1998 that ended with a government-orchestrated bailout consisting of funds contributed by fourteen large banks.

FIGURE 9.8   30Y US swap spreads and 3M spot LIBOR–bill spreads.

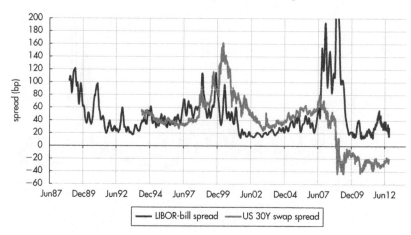

Source: Bloomberg.

funds than had been anticipated, catching some market participants off-guard and causing them to close short bond positions as a result.[3] As European debt richened, so too did US debt.

It's also useful to note that the latest 10Y swap spread is somewhat lower than one would expect given the latest value for the LIBOR–repo spread.

The 30Y swap spread is shown along with the LIBOR–repo spread in Figure 9.8.

There are two observations worth noting in this case.

- As with the 10Y swap spread, the 30Y swap spread was elevated relative to the level we would have expected in the spring of 2000.
- The latest 30Y swap spread is well below the level we'd expect given the latest LIBOR–repo spread.

Taking Stock of Our Empirical Analysis So Far

At this point, it's useful to summarize our empirical findings so far.

(1) Overall, we find a very close correspondence between swap spreads and LIBOR–repo spreads, as we would expect given our theoretical discussion.

---

[3] UMTS stands for Universal Mobile Telecommunications System, the third generation of communication protocols used for mobile phones. In 2000, a number of European governments auctioned this "3G" spectrum, with proceeds well in excess of expectations. This led to a one-off windfall for national governments, which responded by reducing the number of government bonds they planned to issue.

(2) In general, the correspondence between swap spreads and LIBOR–repo spreads is greater for shorter maturities than for longer-maturities. This is not surprising, given that our theoretical discussion was motivated by no-arbitrage considerations, and it's far more practical to construct an arbitrage for two years than it is for thirty years.

(3) Long-dated swap spreads were greater than we would have expected in 1995 through 1997, and they were narrower than we would have expected given the level of LIBOR–repo spreads in 2001 and 2002.

(4) The latest long-dated swap spreads are narrower than we would have expected (with bonds cheap relative to swaps), given the latest level of LIBOR–repos spreads. This is particularly true for 30Y swap spreads.

Point (4) is especially useful to address at this point. In particular, we can put forward three hypotheses to help explain the fact that since the advent of the subprime crisis 30Y swap spreads have been surprisingly narrow, with 30Y bonds surprisingly cheap relative to swaps.

Hypothesis 1: Repo haircuts have increased for long-dated bonds, and the cost of financing the haircuts has increased relative to the repo rate.

Hypothesis 2: The costs to banks of financing bond purchases, particularly long-dated bonds, are now higher than the repo rate would suggest, given new regulatory constraints on capital, leverage, and liquidity.

Hypothesis 3: While our swap spread model thus far has been developed with the assumption that the bonds in question are free from default risk, this assumption may have become inappropriate for some sovereigns, including the US, after the subprime crisis.

We'll discuss each of these hypotheses in turn.

Repo Haircuts

We discussed this issue in our chapter on the theoretical determinants of swap spreads. We do believe that increased haircuts and the increased cost of financing haircuts relative to repo rates have cheapened bonds relative to swaps. In particular, because for many market participants the haircut schedule for long-dated bonds has increased relative to that of short-dated bonds, we would expect this effect to be greater for long-dated bonds than it would be for shorter-dated bonds.

Given the scarcity of data, it's difficult for us to test this hypothesis empirically, but we do believe it's a contributing factor in the relative cheapening of long-dated debt with the advent of the subprime crisis.

Capital Costs under Constraints on Capital, Leverage, and Liquidity

The regulatory responses to the series of financial crises that began in July 2007 have included requirements that banks increase the amount of capital available on their balance sheets for absorbing losses, variously referred to as equity capital, core capital, or tier one capital. More precisely, regulators have been requiring that banks increase the amount of loss-absorbing capital on their books relative to the amount of assets and liabilities on their balance sheets. At the same time, regulators have tightened restrictions on leverage and liquidity ratios.

In the early days of the crisis, banks were able to raise new capital from various sources in the private sector. For example, Citigroup raised USD 7.5 bn from the Abu Dhabi Investment Authority in November of 2007. Goldman Sachs raised USD 5 bn from Warren Buffet in September of 2008. And Morgan Stanley raised USD 9 bn from Mitsubishi UFJ in October of 2008.

But as the markets continued to tumble in the wake of the Lehman bankruptcy in September of 2008, it became increasingly difficult for banks to raise capital from the private sector, and most large Western banks received capital injections from their governments rather than from the private sector.[4]

As time passed, the regulatory requirements imposed on banks became more onerous and in many cases more uncertain, so that private capital has been more difficult for banks to obtain. As a result, most large banks have adopted a capital strategy that combines two important tactics. The first is to add to capital over time via retained earnings. And the second is to shed assets and reduce the size of the balance sheet. At the same time, banks have been responding to tighter regulatory restrictions on leverage and liquidity of bank balance sheets.

With these developments in mind, let's consider the way these constraints might affect the pricing of bonds relative to swaps.

In our conceptual framework, the cost of buying a bond is a function of the financing cost, determined by the repo rate and by the cost of financing the haircut. An implicit assumption in this case is that the bank's balance sheet is unconstrained. For example, if the bank wishes to hold another bond it can allow its leverage and capital ratios to increase, or it can raise additional

---

[4] These government injections generally have been referred to as capital, but in many cases they took the form of loans that needed to be repaid rather than the form of equity that would have the potential to genuinely absorb losses.

capital so that leverage and capital ratios remain unchanged due to the purchase of the bond.

However, the situation is different when a bank's balance sheet is constrained. In that case, the cost that a bank incurs in holding an asset on its balance sheet is not simply a function of the cost of financing that asset. Rather, it's also a function of the opportunity cost of the profit foregone by not holding a different asset on the balance sheet, given the constraints facing the bank.

For example, consider a somewhat contrived example in which a bank faces a hard capital constraint. Unable to raise new capital, if it wishes to buy USD 100 MM of a 30Y government bond, the bank must first dispose of an asset worth USD 100 MM. In order for the bank to proceed with the transaction, the expected rate of return of the government bond must be greater than the expected rate of return of the asset the bank must sell to make room for the government bond on its balance sheet. If the expected rate of return on this other asset is, say, 12%, then the cost of capital applicable to the bond purchase is 12%, irrespective of the repo rate or the cost of the funds used to finance the bond's haircut.

Before the crisis, bank balance sheets were relatively unconstrained, so the marginal cost of owning a bond was a function of the repo rate and the cost of the funds used to finance the bond's haircut. But currently, when bank balance sheets are constrained by required capital, leverage, and liquidity ratios and the difficulty of raising capital, the relevant cost of capital is the opportunity cost under these constraints. Economists would refer to this as the "shadow cost" for the capital (i.e. the marginal increase in profits that would be expected by relaxing the capital constraint by one unit).

For the past few years, many banks, particularly larger banks, have been shedding assets in an attempt to reduce both leverage ratios and capital ratios to levels required by their regulators. In such a constrained environment, the relevant cost of holding a 30Y bond is considerably greater than it used to be, particularly because 30Y bonds tend to have greater price volatility than shorter-dated bonds.

In contrast, swaps are "off balance sheet" instruments in that only the gain or loss on the swap is recorded on the balance sheet. So whereas buying USD 100 MM of a 30Y bond and financing it in the repo market will increase the asset and liability sides of a bank's balance sheet by USD 100 MM, agreeing to pay LIBOR in exchange for a fixed swap rate for thirty years will have no initial impact on the size of the balance sheet.

Of course, the swap and the bond have similar risk characteristics. For example, the swap and the bond may each have the same value at risk, in which case a bank would be well advised to allocate a similar amount of capital to support the market risk of each transaction. But the two transactions won't expose the bank to a similar amount of credit risk, as the swap involves no exchange of principal and all interest payments are netted. Neither will they have the same impact on simple leverage ratios for most banks.

As a result, the relative pricing of bonds and swaps that made investors indifferent between the two before the crisis, when bank balance sheets were relatively unconstrained, was different than it is now, given existing constraints involving capital, leverage, and liquidity ratios. Before the crisis, the pricing that would make an investor indifferent between a bond and a swap was given by the fair value considerations outlined in the previous chapter. In recent years, the situation has changed. The same conceptual framework applies now as it did before the crisis, but the cost of the capital in holding a bond is now higher and includes the "shadow cost" in addition to the cost of financing.

Observant readers will note that this argument applies not only to long positions in bonds but also short positions in bonds, as a short position will also increase the balance sheet of the bank. As a result, the shadow cost of capital for a bank with a constrained balance sheet should increase the no-arbitrage bands around fair value rather than skew the fair value in any particular direction.

However, most banks are naturally long a large number of bonds. As a result, the relevant side of the arbitrage bounds is probably the side that involves the cheapness of bonds relative to swaps. In other words, in an era of constrained and sometimes shrinking balance sheets, bonds can cheapen relative to swaps in the current environment by more than they could have otherwise before they violate effective arbitrage bounds.

Increased Sovereign Default Risk

The perception is widespread that the credit quality of the US government has deteriorated since the onset of the subprime crisis, consistent with Standard & Poor's downgrading the credit rating of the US government to AA+ in August 2011 and with the gradual widening of CDS rates for US debt.

The issue for us is the extent to which this credit deterioration explains the relative cheapening of long-dated government bonds to the swap curve, beyond the level one would expect given the level of LIBOR–repo spreads.

As it happens, sovereign CDS for the US haven't traded actively for very long. In particular, our data set starts only in November of 2007. While this might not be long enough to conduct formal hypothesis tests, we can provide some evidence about the ability of credit deterioration to explain the relative cheapness of the long end of the Treasury curve.

FIGURE 9.9 30Y US swap spread and 10Y US CDS rate.

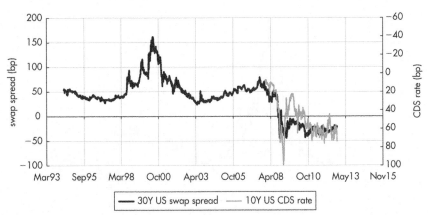

Source: Bloomberg.

Figure 9.9 shows the 30Y swap spread along with the 10Y CDS rate for US government debt. (The 10Y CDS rate will have to serve as a proxy, as 30Y CDS isn't liquid.)

The figure highlights the significant correlation (–0.80) between the two series over the period for which we have CDS data.

To see the extent to which the CDS rates help explain the cheapness of the 30Y bonds relative to swaps, we plot the LIBOR–repo spread along with an adjusted series for the 30Y swap spread in Figure 9.10. In particular, this adjusted 30Y spread increases the swap spread (richening the bonds relative to swaps) by adding the CDS rate to the swap spread.

Comparing Figure 9.8 to Figure 9.10, we see that the 30Y swap spread doesn't appear anomalous relative to the LIBOR–repo spread once we've made an adjustment for default risk via the CDS rate. In fact, if anything, the latest value for the 30Y swap spread appears somewhat greater than the level we'd expect given the latest value of the LIBOR–repo spread.

There are a few caveats we would offer at this point.

(1) While it would be preferable to adjust with 30Y CDS rates, we're having to use 10Y CDS rates as a proxy, making our results less precise than would be ideal. In particular, we may be under-adjusting by using 10Y CDS rates, as 30Y rates are likely to be at least as large if not larger than 10Y CDS rates.

(2) As we'll discuss in a later chapter, CDS rates for most sovereigns are quoted in currencies other than the currency in which the bonds are denominated. In our case, the US CDS rates we're using are for CDS

FIGURE 9.10 LIBOR–repo spread and CDS-adjusted 30Y swap spread.

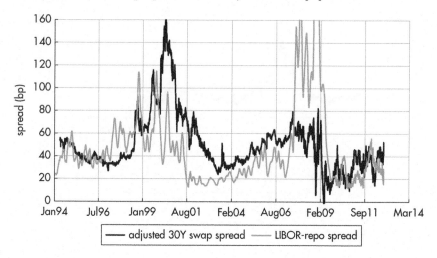

Source: Bloomberg.

quoted in euros. This introduces some FX optionality into the CDS rate, which reduces the precision of our analysis. We'll discuss this issue in greater detail in our chapter on CDS (Chapter 15). But for now it's sufficient to note that we may have over-adjusted the swap spread by using a CDS rate that includes exchange rate risk along with default risk.

Of course, point (1) suggests we may have under-adjusted and point (2) suggests we may have over-adjusted. But the net impact is somewhat ambiguous unless we're able to compare 30Y CDS rates to 10Y CDS rates and unless we're able to quantify the impact of the FX risk in the CDS rate. For now, we'll simply note that the adjustment we've made produces a swap spread series that appears largely in line with the figures we'd expect, given LIBOR–repo spreads.

It's also possible that credit considerations help explain our earlier observations that swap spreads appear a bit greater than one would expect in 1997–1999 and that they appeared somewhat narrower than one would expect given the level of LIBOR–repo spreads in 2001 and 2002. In particular, the US was experiencing a record fiscal surplus in the earlier period, which reversed quickly with the advent of the recession in 2001.

Conclusions

Overall, the empirical data are consistent with the conceptual framework we discussed in the previous chapter, on the theoretical determinants of swap spreads. In particular, we see that swap spreads over long periods of time tend to correspond fairly closely with LIBOR–repo spreads.

It's possible that the tightening regulatory requirements regarding bank capital, leverage, and liquidity explain the fact that swap spreads have appeared relatively cheap in recent years. The fact that repo haircuts have increased also may help explain this relative cheapening.

In addition, the simple CDS adjustment we've made to the 30Y US swap spread suggests that the deteriorating credit quality of the US government may be partially responsible for the relative cheapening of longer-dated bonds relative to swaps in the United States.

We'll discuss this particular issue in greater detail in subsequent chapters.

CHAPTER 10

Swap Spreads as Relative Value Indicators for Government Bonds

Introduction

Swaps spreads are commonly used to assess relative values between bonds. For example, many investors comparing par asset swap spreads between two bonds will conclude the bond with the wider spread is the richer of the two issues. Initially, such a conclusion seems intuitively reasonable. Since the bond with the wider par asset swap spread will pay the investor less for the same initial investment, it should be viewed as the richer bond. However, we'll see in this chapter that such comparisons are fraught with complications, and investors are urged to use caution when attempting to use the swap curve to assess relative values between bonds. In fact, we argue that the swap curve should never be used for assessing relative values between bonds. Before we discuss our reasons for such a strong conclusion, we review the way investors typically use the swap curve to judge relative values between sovereign issues.

Typical Use of Swap Spreads as a Relative Value Indicator for Government Bonds

Par Asset Swap Spreads

Initially, the par asset swap spread would seem to be an ideal measure of relative value between bonds. For example, consider two bonds with identical maturity dates but with different coupons, say 5% and 10%. If the 10% issue is trading as a par asset swap at LIBOR − 40 basis points (bp) and the 5% bond is trading at a par asset swap spread of LIBOR − 35 bp, the 10% bond would appear to be the richer bond. For the same initial investment of USD 100, the payoff of the 10% bond is lower than that of the 5% bond. The clean structure of the par asset swap spread makes such comparison relatively straightforward.

Interpolated Asset Swap Spreads

Some investors are concerned that the comparison of the bonds in the above example is complicated by the fact that the two par asset swaps involve up-front payments of different sizes by the swap dealer. For example, if the 5% issue is trading at par, no up-front payment will be required, while the 10% issue is likely to involve a substantial up-front payment from the dealer.

In order to mitigate any problems that might result from these differing up-front payments, some investors prefer to compare the yields of a bond to the par swap rate with the same maturity as the bond. This difference generally is referred to as the interpolated swap spread, since the maturity of the bond is unlikely to fall on a yearly swap point quoted in the market, and therefore the corresponding swap rate will need to be interpolated. In the example above, let's assume the yield of the 10% is 4.98%, the yield of the 5% bond is 5%, and the swap rate with the same maturity as these bonds is 5.35%. In this case, the interpolated swap spreads of the 10% and 5% bonds are 37 bp and 35 bp, and the 10% issue again appears to be the richer of the two issues.

Notice in this example that we could have reached the conclusion that the 10% issue is richer than the 5% issue simply by comparing their yields, since the two bonds in this example are assumed to have the same maturity dates. Of course, this would not be the case more generally.

Full Asset Swap Spreads

While some investors use the interpolated swap spread to mitigate possible difficulties with the par asset swap spread, other investors will use the full asset swap spread. Like the interpolated swap spread, the full asset swap spread involves no up-front payments. Like the par asset swap, the full asset swap is a cash flow matched structure (i.e. the fixed cash flow dates and amounts in the swap are identical to the coupon dates and the coupon size of the bond).

Problems with the Use of Swap Spreads as Relative Value Indicators for Government Bonds

Interpolated Swap Spreads

The problem with the interpolated swap spread as a relative value indicator for bonds is the easiest to identify, so we start with this case. In the example of the 5% and 10% bonds above, let's assume the yield curve is upward sloping. Let's also assume that both bonds are fairly valued to the government bond curve. For example, this would be the case if these two bonds, which we assume to have identical maturity dates, were strippable and there was no reconstitution arbitrage, even under the assumption of zero bid/ask spreads for the bonds and their strips.

Under these assumptions, it can be shown mathematically that the 10% bond has to have a lower yield than the 5% bond. Intuitively, this result is due to the fact that the 10% issue has more of its cash flows discounted at relatively lower rates, since it has the greater coupon. As a result, the 10% bond has to have the wider interpolated swap spread. In this case, it will always appear to be the richer bond, according to the interpolated swap spread, even though both bonds are fairly valued in this example by construction. As this simple example demonstrates, the interpolated swap spread is a fundamentally flawed measure of relative value between two bonds.

Par Asset Swap Spreads

The par asset swap is a cash flow matched structure. As a result, the par asset swap spread doesn't suffer from the same defect as does the interpolated swap spread. However, it does suffer from a more subtle problem relating to the coupon.

The problem with the par asset swap spread as a measure of relative value between bonds can be seen by conducting a thought experiment. Let's start the experiment by assuming the 5% bond has a perfectly fair value, in the sense that there is no reconstitution arbitrage between it and the strips in the market, even assuming zero bid/ask spreads. Now let's increase the coupon of the 5% bond incrementally, until it becomes a 10% bond, and let's assume that the bond continues to have a perfectly fair value to the strips throughout the experiment. We'll watch the behavior of the par asset swap spread as the coupon of the bond is increased.

When the coupon of the bond is increased by 10 bp, from 5% to 5.10%, the price of the bond also increases. Let's assume the bond price increases by

70 cents, from 100.00 to 100.70. In order to see the impact, if any, on the par asset swap spread, let's review the way this spread is calculated.

The par asset swap spread is calculated by discounting the cash flows of the bond to determine a present value for the bond using the swap curve as the source of the discount rates.[1] Let's call this present value the bond's "swap curve present value". The par asset swap spread is the size of an annuity that has the same present value as the difference between the bond's market price and its swap curve present value.

If the term structure of swap rates is uniformly greater than the term structure of government bond yields, a bond's market price will increase by more than a bond's swap curve present value as we increase the coupon of the bond, since the swap curve will involve higher discount rates and lower discount factors than will the government bond curve. In our example, the bond price increased by 70 cents when we added 10 bp to the coupon, but the swap curve present value would increase by a lesser amount, say 65 cents. As a result, the difference between the market price of the bond and its swap curve present value increased by 5 cents. Therefore, the present value of the par asset swap spread as an annuity must increase by 5 cents. Since the swap curve doesn't change in this example, the only way for this present value to change is for the size of the par asset swap spread to increase. In other words, increasing a bond's coupon will increase its par asset swap spread, even if the bond is assumed to have a perfectly fair value as measured by the government bond curve. The necessary conclusion from this example is that two fairly valued bonds almost always will have different par asset swap spreads if they have different coupons, even if they have the same maturity date. For this reason, the par asset swap spread as a measure of relative value between two bonds also suffers from a coupon effect and is therefore an inappropriate measure.

Note that this coupon effect is not the same as the coupon effect we discussed above. The "yield" coupon effect is not an issue when the yield curve is flat, but this "par asset swap spread" coupon effect is an issue even if the yield curve is flat. The only time this par asset swap spread coupon effect isn't an issue is when the swap curve is identical to the government bond curve, in which case all par asset swap spreads trivially are equal to zero.

---

[1] This argument can be generalized to the case in which an OIS curve is used for the discounting of all cash flows. The conclusion is the same as long as the term structure of OIS rates and the term structure of government bond yields are not identical.

Full Asset Swap Spreads

To see that the full asset swap spread suffers from a similar defect, recall that the full asset swap spread is equal to the par asset swap spread multiplied by par and divided by the dirty price of the bond.[2] As basis points are added to the bond's coupon, the par asset swap spread increases by a constant amount per basis point. The full asset swap only can remain unchanged in this thought experiment if the change from par asset swap spread to full asset swap spread involved the par asset swap spread decreasing by the same constant amount per basis point. Since this is not the case, the full asset swap spread also is seen to change as basis points are added to the bond's coupon. As a result, the full asset swap spread suffers from a similar defect, and we can conclude it too is an inappropriate measure of relative value between bonds.

Attempts to Solve these Problems

Zero Coupon Asset Swap Spreads

Approach

So far, we've focused on coupon effects as the sources of concern in using swap spreads for relative value comparisons between bonds. Since zero-coupon bonds are free from such problems, it's worth considering whether the relative values between zero-coupon bonds can be determined by comparisons to the swap curve. For example, let's assume we have two zero-coupon government bonds, a 10-year (10Y) bond with a 50 bp swap spread and a 9Y bond with a 45 bp swap spread, assuming each swap spread is computed as the difference between the bond's yield and the zero-coupon rate with the same maturity as the bond calculated using the swap curve. Would we be justified in claiming the 10Y zero-coupon bond was rich to the 9Y bond?

Problem with this Approach

In this case, the answer is an unequivocal no. As we saw in the previous chapter, the fair swap spread is a function of expected LIBOR–repo spreads, and there will be a presumed forward LIBOR–repo spread that will cause both the 9Y and the 10Y swap spreads to appear to be fair value.

---

[2] The dirty price is the clean price plus accrued interest.

The only time at which we might be tempted to use the relative swap spreads as a guide to valuation is if the forward LIBOR–repo spread were negative (i.e. the forward repo rate were greater than the forward LIBOR). Unless there are special circumstances involved, such as different tax treatments, the unsecured LIBOR should never be less than the secured repo rate and the LIBOR–repo spread should never be negative, even on a forward basis.[3]

Another problem with this approach is that the spread between LIBOR and the repo rate should be a function of the level of interest rates. Even if the default probability implied by LIBOR remained the same, the LIBOR–repo spread would be expected to increase as the level of the repo rate increases, as discussed in Chapter 8.

If the 1Y rate nine years forward is higher than the present-value weighted averages of the first nine 1Y forward rates along the curve, then the fair 1Y LIBOR–repo spread nine years forward will also be larger than the first nine 1Y LIBOR–repo spreads along the curve. In this case, the fair zero-coupon swap spread for a 10Y bond will be greater than the fair zero-coupon swap spread for a 9Y bond. From this example, we see that a simple, unadjusted comparison of zero-coupon swap spreads is inappropriate for assessing the relative values between zero-coupon bonds.

Calculate Implied Default Probability to Control for Level-Dependence

Approach

In an attempt to control for the fact that LIBOR–repo spreads are increasing functions of short rate levels, we can calculate the term structure of default probabilities implied by the term structure of swap spreads, assuming default probabilities are not random. For example, 1Y zero-coupon rates on the swap and government curves may indicate an implied default probability in LIBOR for the first year of 1%. If we knew the implied probability of default by the end of the second year was 3%, we could calculate that the probability of default during the second year, conditional on no default having occurred during the first year, was 2.02%. In this way, a term

---

[3] As we discuss in Chapter 9, since the onset of the subprime crisis in 2007 some bond yields have been observed to be greater than swap rates of corresponding maturity, consistent with a variety of factors, including non-negligible sovereign default risk; significant haircuts having to be financed at elevated rates; and regulatory constraints on bank capital, leverage, and liquidity.

structure of conditional default probabilities for LIBOR can be constructed from the swap spread term structure. The resulting term structure will control for the fact that the fair LIBOR–repo spread (and therefore the fair swap spread) is an increasing function of interest rate levels.

Problem with this Approach

Unlike the zero-coupon swap spread approach, this method does control for the effect of changing interest rate levels along the yield curve. However, this method suffers from a similar defect in that it doesn't tell us what the fair conditional default probability should be. A figure of 5% may seem large relative to historical default rates for the banking sector, but we need to remember that these implied default probabilities are not subjective probabilities (i.e. probabilities that represent the observable frequency of occurrences in the real world). As we discussed in the chapter on the theoretical determinants of swap spreads, these probabilities are merely risk-neutral probabilities. In other words, they're probabilities after being adjusted by risk premiums. Unless we know the size of the risk premium adjustments, we can't determine the subjective probabilities presumed to represent the collective uncertainty of the market about future defaults.

As a lower bound on these probabilities, we can say they should be positive. A negative conditional default probability implied by a swap spread term structure would indicate certain swap spreads along the curve were too narrow relative to swap spreads with lower maturities.

A Note on Cross-Currency Swap Spread Comparisons

Before we discuss our general conclusions about assessing relative value between bonds across the same curve, we'll offer a brief thought about using swap spreads to assess relative value between bonds in different currencies.

The first point to note is that cross-currency swap spreads suffer from all the deficiencies we discussed above. Therefore, we can't recommend their use as indicators of relative value between bonds denominated in different currencies. However, cross-currency swap spread comparisons suffer from an additional defect.

To see the nature of this additional defect, let's conduct another thought experiment. Assume that we knew that all German Bunds always would have repo rates 15 bp below EURIBOR and that all US Treasury bonds always would have repo rates 25 bp below USD LIBOR. Assume also that the basis swap margin between EURIBOR and USD LIBOR always was equal to zero.

Then the German bund might have a cross-currency asset swap margin of LIBOR less 15 bp. Initially, it would seem that the German Bund is somehow cheap to the US Treasury bond with an asset swap margin of LIBOR less 25 bp. But if the German Bund could be financed in euros at EURIBOR less 15 bp, and if the EURIBOR–LIBOR basis swap were always equal to zero, then the euro financing of the Bund could be swapped into dollars at LIBOR less 15 bp. Therefore, the carry between the repo rate and the asset swap would be zero in both currencies, and the Bund would appear fairly valued.

The lesson of this thought experiment is that one should not compare the asset swap spreads of two bonds in the same currency directly. Rather, the net carry of the financed asset swaps should be compared in the same currency.

Conclusions

As we mentioned in the introduction, the use of the asset swap spread as a relative value indicator between bonds is now ubiquitous. We argue in this article that it is also very problematic. In fact, we believe the problems are too great to allow for the rehabilitation of swap spreads as a relative value indicator for bonds.

In our view, there is no acceptable way of determining relative value between two bonds by using the swap curve. Given the popularity of swap spreads as relative value indicators, this conclusion may seem a bit radical. Nevertheless, the problems we've discussed in this article suggest the swap curve is an inappropriate tool for assessing relative values between bonds.

In our view, the better method for assessing relative values between bonds along a curve is to use the tried-and-true method of fitting a zero-coupon curve to observable government bond prices. While this method is fraught with its own set of difficulties, these problems are of a practical rather than a theoretical nature, and they can be overcome by careful work on the part of the bond analyst, as discussed in the next chapter. As we've seen in this chapter, such is not the case for asset swap spreads.

CHAPTER 11

Fitted Bond Curves

Introduction

Which of an issuer's bonds are rich, and which are cheap? And how do we know? To answer these questions, we first need to better define the terms rich and cheap in this context.

Not surprisingly given that our subject matter is relative value, we'll define these words in relative terms rather than in absolute terms. In particular, we say that a bond is rich if its price is greater than we'd expect conditional on the available information, including but not limited to the prices of the issuer's other bonds. Other information might include whether the bond is special in the repo market, whether the bond is deliverable into a futures contract, and the liquidity of the bond as proxied by the bid–ask spread.

Framework of Analysis

Whenever we're dealing with expectations conditional on a set of information, we're in the realm of regression analysis. In particular, at any point in time, we'll specify the price of each bond in our data set as the dependent variable and the relevant conditioning information as the independent variables, as in the cross-sectional regression given by:

$$P_i = A(\Theta_i; \alpha) + B(\Psi_i; \gamma) + \varepsilon_i \qquad (11.1)$$

Where P_i is the price of the i-th bond in our data set, $i = 1, \ldots, N$; $A(\Theta_i; \alpha)$ is a function of the parameter vector α, and of Θ_i, an array of dimension $2 \times M_i$ that represents the dates and sizes of the M_i cash flows that constitute bond i; $B(\Psi_i; \gamma)$ is a function of the $k \times 1$ parameter vector, γ, and of the $k \times 1$ vector Ψ_i, which contains the independent variables other than the cash flow dates

193

and amounts on which we condition our expectations of the bond prices; and ε_i is a random error term, unique to each bond in our data set.

In this equation, we suppress any notation to indicate that this regression applies at any and all times. For example, without loss of generality, we could subscript all the variables and parameters in Equation 11.1 with a time index.

The ε_i terms, for all $i = 1, \ldots, N$ are the terms that represent the richness and cheapness of the bonds in our data set, with positive values indicating the bond in question as rich.

Because $A(\Theta_i; \alpha)$ is a function involving the cash flows of the coupon bond, and because the value of a coupon bond is a linear function of the values of the individual cash flows, $A(\Theta_i; \alpha)$ generally will have a form given by:

$$A(\Theta_i; \alpha) = \sum_{l=1}^{M_i} C_{il} \phi(\tau_{il})$$

where C_{il} is the size of the i-th cash flow for bond i, and $\phi(\tau_{il})$ is the discount factor associated with the i-th cash flow for the i-th bond, to be received at time τ_{il}.

With this in mind, we see that the key to taking a view as to the richness or cheapness of specific bonds among a collection of bonds is to ascertain an appropriate discount function $\phi(\tau)$ that is presumed to apply generally to the collection of bonds at any particular point in time.

As with standard regressions, we can proceed once we've made some distributional assumptions on the error terms. In particular, we'll assume that the error terms in Equation 11.1 are independent of one another and that they're normally distributed, each with a mean equal to zero. For now, we'll also assume that all the error terms have variances that are identical to each other. In this case, the maximum likelihood estimators for α and γ are identical to the estimators obtained via ordinary least squares (OLS). If we have reason to believe that the error terms are in some sense heteroscedastic, we can use weighted least squares (WLS) in place of OLS.

To make the regression in Equation 11.1 operational, we need to specify two more aspects of our regression. First, we need to decide on a functional form for the discount factor function $\phi(\tau)$. Second, we need to specify the independent variables on which we believe the bond prices are conditioned.

Specifying a Function for Discount Factors

We use the term *discount factor* to refer to the price of a zero-coupon bond as a percentage of its face value. In the context of our exercise, we assume that at any point in time there exists one and only one discount factor corresponding to every future date on which a zero-coupon bond could mature. An absence of arbitrage ensures the uniqueness of each discount factor and that all discount factors are non-negative.

In the past, it was common to make the additional assumption that all discount factors were no greater than one, in order to preclude negative interest rates. The argument was that investors could choose to keep their money under a proverbial mattress rather than on deposit earning a negative interest rate. But the spate of negative interest rates in recent quarters suggests there aren't enough mattresses under which to keep funds safe from negative interest rates. In more economic terms, banks clearly provide services for which depositors are willing to pay in the form of below-market interest rates, even if that means accepting negative nominal interest rates.

When choosing a functional form for $\phi(\tau)$, there are two conditions we'd like to satisfy.

Criterion 1: We'd like a discount function that approaches zero in the limit as time increases. That is, $\lim_{\tau \to \infty} \phi(\tau) = 0$, where ϕ is the discount function and τ is the time until the relevant cash flow is received.

Criterion 2: To prevent arbitrage, we also require $\lim_{\tau \to 0} \phi(\tau) = 1$. Otherwise, an investor would be able to purchase (or sell) a zero-coupon bond an instant before maturity and earn a riskless profit well in excess of the riskless rate.

In our experience, exponential functions are useful for this purpose, and they clearly satisfy criteria 1 (C1) and 2 (C2).

For example, if we specify yields in terms of continuously compounded rates, we could use the general specification

$$\phi(\tau) = e^{-h(\tau)} \tag{11.2}$$

where $h(\tau)$ is a continuous function of τ.

As long as $h(\tau)$ is bounded, Equation 11.2 will satisfy C1 and C2 above. Actually, boundedness is too strong a condition in this case. For example, if $h(\tau)$ is a polynomial in τ, it will also satisfy C1 as all polynomials increase at a slower rate than the exponential function. Nevertheless, the concept of an unbounded yield curve presents difficulties with economic interpretation if not necessarily with the mathematics, and we strongly advise using bounded functions in this setting.

It's also nice, if not necessary, for $h(\tau)$ to have a limit as $\tau \to \infty$. (Note that polynomials do not satisfy this criterion.)

Depending on the functional form used for $h(\tau)$, there can be a number of advantages in specifying a functional form for the yield curve rather than for the discount factor function directly. In addition to the ease with which conditions C1 and C2 can be satisfied, specifying a functional form for the zero-coupon yield curve tends to offer greater intuition to the analyst during the curve-fitting exercise. For example, if a particular attempt to fit the curve is producing modeled yields that are systemically too high for bonds maturing between seven and 10 years, it's typically easier to ascertain the desired changes to make when specifying a yield curve than it is when specifying a discount factor function that may contain upward of 10 constituent functions, all specified in terms of zero-coupon bond prices.

Ultimately, however, the choice is a function of the quality of the fit and of the ease with which the analyst is able to implement the model.

Weights

Thus far, we've maintained the assumption that the error terms have identical distributions, with zero means and with variances equal to one another. If there are reasons to believe that the variances of the error terms are not equal, we can modify our approach to accommodate WLS. In other words, we can choose parameters to minimize:

$$\sum_{i=1}^{N} \frac{\varepsilon_i^2}{U_i}$$

where U_i is the weight assumed to be proportional to the variance of ε_i.

In our experience, there are a few criteria that could help guide the choice of weights in this context:

- **Basis point values:** Some analysts take the view that bonds with large basis point values have prices that are measured with less precision and therefore with greater error than bonds with smaller basis point values. In particular, if the variances of the error terms for the fitted yields were assumed to be equal, then the variances of the fitted prices would be roughly proportional to the basis point values of the bonds.

- **Deliverability:** As discussed in the chapter on future delivery options, bonds that are deliverable into a futures contract may experience greater price volatility than similar bonds that are not deliverable.
- **Repo specialness:** Bonds that are experiencing episodic specialness in the repo market have a tendency to have greater spot price volatility than other bonds.

Ultimately, the heteroscedasticity of the error terms is an empirical matter. We suggest analysts use judgment in deciding what forms of heteroscedasticity are likely to be present in the markets they're analyzing.

Example: Fitting the German Bund Curve

The Setting: German Bunds, Using Size, Age, and CTD Status as Additional Conditioning Variables

The best way to illustrate these concepts is to work through a specific example. In this case, we use the closing prices of coupon-paying German Bunds, OBLs, and Schatze on 7 Dec 2012. As additional independent variables, we'll include:

- **Time since issuance:** New issues may be in greater demand than older issues.
- **Issue size:** To achieve benchmark status, a bond needs to be issued in sufficient size.
- **CTD status:** Bonds that are cheapest-to-deliver (CTD) into futures contracts may be priced differently from other bonds.

Note that theoretical arguments can be made for the coefficients on these three variables to be positive or negative. For example, benchmark issues may be easier to sell short, making them less expensive than otherwise comparable issues. Likewise, if a CTD issue is easier to sell short, its price might be less than it would be otherwise. So ultimately, the signs of the coefficients will be determined by the data.

Our list of explanatory variables isn't meant to be exhaustive. There are reasons to include repo specialness as a variable. It's also useful to consider whether recent CTDs might maintain residual richness of cheapness for a period and whether likely future CTDs might contain some anticipatory richness or cheapness. For illustrative purposes, however, we'll focus on the explanatory variables listed above.

FIGURE 11.1   Bund yields as of 7 Dec 2012.

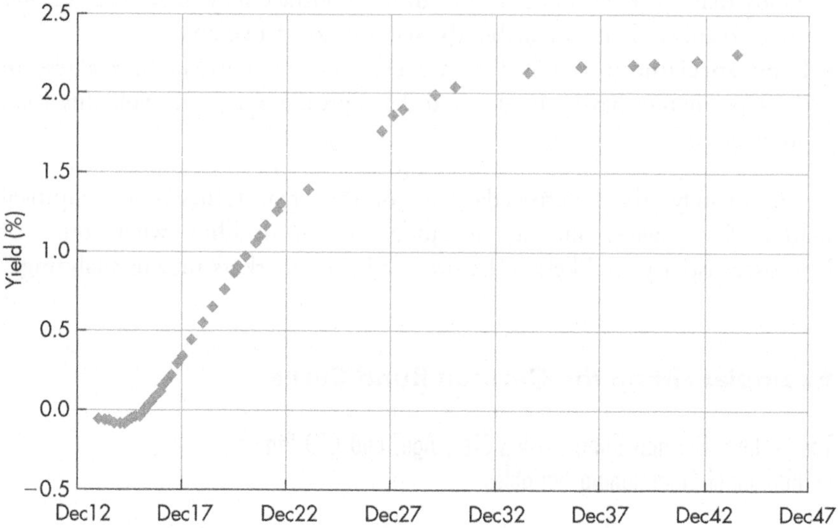

TABLE 11.1   Deliverable Issues into March 2013 Futures Contracts

Schatz	Bobl	Bond	Buxl
BKO 0% 12-Dec-14	DBR 4% 4-Jan-18	DBR 2% 4-Jan-22	DBR 4.75% 4-Jul-40
DBR 3.75% 4-Jan-15	OBL 0.5% 13-Oct-17	DBR 1.75% 4-Jul-22	DBR 4.25% 4-Jul-39
OBL 2.5% 27-Feb-15	DBR 4.25% 4-Jul-18	DBR 1.5% 4-Sep-22	DBR 3.25% 4-Jul-42
OBL 2.25% 10-Feb-15			DBR 2.5% 4-Jul-44

Source: Bloomberg.

Figure 11.1 shows the term structure of yields for coupon-paying German Bunds as of the close of trading on Friday, 7 December. We exclude bonds with times to maturity of less than one year, as we find money markets are best modeled separately.[1]

Table 11.1 shows the issues that are deliverable into the Schatz, Bobl, Bund, and Buxl futures contracts expiring in March 2013.

---

[1] Money market instruments, including bonds with less than a year to maturity, require a greater degree of analytical precision than longer-dated bonds, for a number of reasons. For example, money market instruments are particularly sensitive to central bank policy, and at times we observe sharp discontinuities between instruments maturing before particular central bank meeting dates and those maturing after.

We define our deliverability variable in such a way that the deliverability variable is not simply one if a bond is deliverable and zero otherwise. Rather, this variable is set equal to the price value of a basis point for the bond if the bond is deliverable, and it's set to zero otherwise. As a result, the coefficients for these variables have the interpretation of being the number of basis points by which an issue tends to be rich when it is the deliverable issue into one of the futures contracts.

Choosing a Functional Form for the Yield Curve

The next step in implementing this approach is specifying a suitable functional form for $h(\tau)$, in particular in finding a well-behaved function that is bounded and has a limit as $\tau \to \infty$.

In the past, many analysts would use a cubic spline with carefully chosen knot points, constructed so as to ensure continuity in the function and often in the first derivative, in the hope of obtaining smoothness.

But cubic splines often have proven less than ideal for this purpose, as the performance of the resulting function can be sensitive to the number and placement of knot points.

As a result, we prefer to specify a series of *anchor points*, through which our function must pass and then interpolate nonlinearly through these anchor points. In particular, the analyst chooses the horizontal coordinate of each anchor point. The vertical coordinates of the anchor points then can be considered parameters for manipulating the resulting function. Between anchor points, the values of the function are chosen to ensure that the function has maximum smoothness, defined here as the integral of the square of the second derivative of the function.

For our illustration, we choose to place anchors with maturities (in years) of: 0, 0.5, 1.0, 1.5, 2, 5, 7, 10, 12, 15, 20, 30, and 35.

The resulting regression residuals are shown in Figure 11.2.

Assessing the Quality of the Fit

The average absolute value of the residuals is 9 cents. When interpreting this figure, it's useful to note that there does appear to be some evidence of heteroscedasticity in the residual terms. In particular, the magnitudes of the residual terms appear to be relatively large for longer maturities. With this in mind, we plot the residuals in terms of basis point values for the bonds in Figure 11.3.

In this case, the average absolute value of the residuals is 0.9 bp, with only one residual term less than -2 bp and only two residual terms greater than

FIGURE 11.2 Bund regression residuals expressed in EUR.

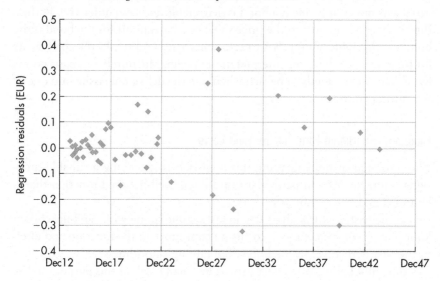

FIGURE 11.3 Bund regression residuals expressed in basis points.

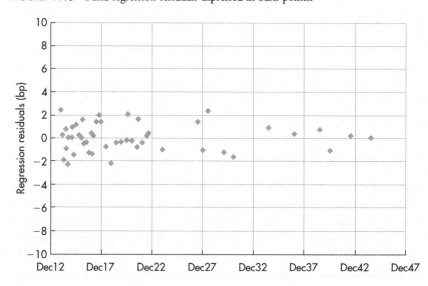

TABLE 11.2 Bund Regression Coefficients

Independent Variable	Coefficient Estimate
Amount outstanding (EUR bn)	EUR 0.025
Issue age (years)	0.027 years
Schatz deliverable? (bp)	3.6 bp
Bobl deliverable? (bp)	2.8 bp
Bund deliverable? (bp)	2.1 bp
Buxl deliverable? (bp)	2.4 bp

Source: Authors.

2 bp. The largest positive residual has a magnitude of only 2.3 bp, and the largest negative residual has a magnitude of only 2.2 bp. With these results in mind, the quality of the fit appears to be satisfactory.[2]

Interpreting the Regression Coefficients

The coefficients for the size, age, and deliverability variables are shown in Table 11.2.

The coefficient for the amount outstanding suggests that larger issues tend to be more expensive, which would be consistent with the existence of a benchmark effect in this market. In particular, an additional EUR 1 bn outstanding corresponds to an additional 2.5 cents in the value of the bond.

The coefficient for the age of the bond suggests that bonds tend to cheapen with age. This also is consistent with a benchmark effect, and it's perhaps consistent with a repo effect as well. In particular, in the German market, bonds tend to cheapen at a rate of 2.7 cents per year, all else being equal.

The results are broadly similar for the deliverability variables. In particular, issues that are deliverable into the Schatz, Bobl, Bund, and Buxl contracts tend to have yields that are lower by 2–4 bp than other bonds. The fact that the premium for the Schatz contract is the largest perhaps shouldn't be surprising, since the basis point values are so small for the bonds that are deliverable in the Schatz contract.

---

[2] Given that the residuals appear somewhat heteroscedastic when expressed in terms of price and less so when expressed in terms of basis points suggests further analysis may be warranted to assess the merits of WLS in this case.

Statistical Analysis of Rich/Cheap Figures

In our experience, the rich/cheap indicators for individual bonds generally tend to revert around a mean of zero, though this isn't always the case. For example, in some cases, bonds are structurally rich, and the rich/cheap indicator will revert around a number that reflects this structural richness.

In other cases, the rich/cheap indicator won't exhibit any particular mean reversion at all. While we would be reluctant to assume that the rich/cheap indicator is non-stationary, given the economic implications of this inference, the failure for a time series to exhibit clear mean reversion makes it difficult for us to estimate the speed of mean reversion, even if we have persuasive reasons a priori for assuming the indicator to revert around a mean.

Z-Scores and T-Stats

In our experience, many analysts model the mean reversion of rich/cheap indicators by calculating the number of standard deviations by which the indicator differs from its long-run mean. For example, if a bond currently appears 10 cents rich, and if its average degree of richness has been zero, and if the standard deviation of the rich/cheap indicator for that bond is 5.0, then a Z-score or T-stat[3] is calculated for the bond of 2.0, by subtracting the mean from the current value and dividing the result by the standard deviation of the rich/cheap indicator. In this case, $\frac{10-0}{5} = 2$.

The clear problem with this approach is that it ignores the information the data contain regarding the speed with which the rich/cheap indicator tends to revert toward its mean. For example, if the rich/cheap indicator for the bond in our example bond appears to be independently and identically distributed each day, then our expected value for the rich/cheap indicator the next time this bond is observed is zero, regardless of the current value of the indicator.

---

[3] The term *Z-score* typically refers to the case in which a demeaned normal random variable is standardized by a *known* standard deviation, in which case the resulting variable is also normal and can be compared to values in a standard normal table. The term *T-stat* refers to the case in which a demeaned normal random variable is standardized by a standard deviation that must be *estimated*. In this case, assuming the observations have been drawn from a normal distribution, the estimate of the variance will have a Chi-squared distribution. And the ratio of a normal variate to the square root of a Chi-square variate has a student-t distribution. In applications, we almost always need to estimate the standard deviation, in which case the student-t distribution is more appropriate.

On the other hand, if the rich/cheap indicator for our bond has exhibited slow mean reversion, say with a half-life of 200 days, then our expectation for tomorrow's rich/cheap indicator for the bond should be virtually identical to today's value for the indicator.

Knowing the Z-score is 2.0 in this example tells us almost nothing about the value we should expect for the rich/cheap indicator for this bond tomorrow.

Mean Reversion

In most cases, there are strong a priori reasons for believing that rich/cheap indicators for bonds tend to be mean reverting. And in our experience, the mean reversion of these indicators is confirmed as an empirical matter as well.

As a result, we suggest applying the mean reversion models of Chapter 2 to the rich/cheap indicators obtained in these curve-fitting exercises.

For example, we find it useful to report the half-lives of these rich/cheap indicators, assuming they follow stochastic differential equations with linear drift coefficients, as with the Ornstein–Uhlenbeck process. More generally, we find it useful to calculate the ex ante Sharpe ratios of the rich/cheap indicators on various horizons, such as two weeks.

Applications

Trading Bond Switches and Butterflies

One of the main reasons for a relative value analyst or trader to identify rich and cheap securities is to identify attractive relative value bond trades. For a hedge fund trader, this might mean establishing a short position in one bond against a long position in a nearby bond. For a portfolio manager at a pension fund, this might mean selling an existing long position in one bond and using the proceeds to purchase a nearby bond considered to offer greater value. We'll use the generic term *bond switch* for each of these trades. When a cheap (rich) bond is purchased (sold) against positions in two other bonds, one with a lesser maturity and one with a greater maturity, we use the generic term *bond butterfly*.[4]

---

[4] The intention is that these switches and butterflies will involve bonds within the same sector of the curve. Otherwise, a switch between bonds with significantly different maturities would result in a position with significant curve exposure.

The implicit assumption often made when conducting rich/cheap analysis is that bonds that are currently rich should be expected to cheapen and that bonds that are currently cheap should be expected to richen. However, this need not be the case, and the careful relative value analyst will try to identify the reasons that a bond is trading rich or cheap so as to form a reasonable expectation about the prospects for the bond in the future. For example, a bond that has begun to be squeezed in the repo market may have a spot price that appears expensive relative to other bonds, but it's quite possible that the squeeze will intensify before it weakens, to the detriment of a trader who has taken a short position. To protect against this and similar possibilities, we suggest taking care to understand changes in relative valuations rather than merely assuming that bonds will revert to fair value. It's not always possible to identify the reasons that a bond is rich or cheap, and to be honest it's not always necessary. But it's certainly prudent to make the effort.

Selecting Issues for Trade Expression

The rich/cheap analysis described here is also useful in identifying specific instruments for expressing views. For example, let's imagine that an analyst performed a principal component analysis of the yield curve, as per Chapter 3, and decided to implement a curve steepening trade between the two-year (2Y) and 10Y sectors. Further, let's imagine that he analyzed the term structure of swap spreads, as per Chapter 8 and Chapter 9, and concluded that bonds are likely to cheapen to swaps in the 10Y sector. As a result, he decides to express the 10Y leg of the trade by shorting a bond in the 10Y sector. At this point, he could use the rich/cheap analysis in this chapter, perhaps combined with the mean reversion analysis in Chapter 2, to identify the specific bond in the 10Y sector to short.

Predicting New Issue Pricing

It's sometimes useful to predict the pricing of a new issue even before it's announced. For example, there have been times when newly issued German Schatze have been CTD into the Schatz futures contract. These typically would be issued according to a regular schedule, so the yet-to-be-announced bonds could affect the pricing of the futures contracts.

To take a view on the fair value of the futures contract even before the new issue is announced in this case, one could forecast the coupon and maturity date of the bond and forecast the extent to which the bond was likely to trade rich to the curve at the time it was issued. This would allow the analyst to assume a spot price and a coupon for the bond. From these, a conversion factor and a basis point value could be computed. By assuming a repo rate for the new issue, the analyst then could calculate the presumed converted forward price for the new issue, and the pricing of the futures contract could proceed along the lines discussed in Chapter 5.

Creating Generic Notional Benchmarks

There are times when a relative value analyst would like to track the price or yield of a notional benchmark (i.e. a bond that doesn't actually exist). For example, we may want to compare the constant-maturity yield of a 10Y bond trading at par against the 10Y swap rate. In that case, we'll need to create a synthetic or *notional* bond for this purpose.

Having a fitted curve of discount factors allows us to solve for the size of a coupon that will cause the price of our notional bond to be equal to par. This can be done numerically, but it also can be done algebraically via the discount function.

In particular, if Z_{10} is the price of a 10Y zero-coupon bond that pays one dollar at maturity, and if A_{10} is the value of an annuity that pays one dollar on each of the payment dates for the notional coupon bond in question, then the size of the coupon, C, that will cause our notional bond to have a fair or fitted price equal to par can be determined by the equation

$$100 = 100Z_{10} + CA_{10}$$

We can solve the equation for C to get

$$C = \frac{100(1-Z_{10})}{A_{10}}$$

Conclusions

Our main innovation in this chapter is to place the rich/cheap analysis in the context of a regression, which is the tool of choice when forming expectations conditional on a particular set of information. These days, computing speeds tend to be sufficient for performing nonlinear regressions numerically in a real-time trading environment, allowing us to use a set of models that provide better fits to the data than models of the past, many of which relied on linear equations and/or simplifications.

Having real-time fitted curves in the context of a regression allows us to use the resulting regression residuals as real-time rich/cheap indicators. In a cross-sectional context, these regression residuals are preferable as rich/cheap indicators to swap spreads, whose deficiencies were discussed in Chapter 10. But, in addition, regression residuals are preferable to swap spreads as rich/ cheap indicators in a time-series context as well.

For example, the means of our regression residuals are presumed to be zero. As a result, we can model the residual of each bond as a mean-reverting process over time, allowing us to characterize the speed with which bonds tend to return to their fitted values.

In contrast, the fair swap spread for a particular bond can change over time, for all the reasons cited in Chapter 8 and Chapter 9, which include unobservable factors, such as the cost of equity capital for banks. As a result, it's difficult, if not impossible, to quantify the speed with which misvaluations correct when these misvaluations are identified using swap spreads. This is yet another reason we suggest using fitted curves rather than swap spreads as relative value indicators for bonds.

Nevertheless, rich/cheap analysis can play a role in determining which swap spreads are likely to widen and which are more likely to narrow. And it's to the topic of swap spread trading that we briefly turn our attention in the next chapter.

CHAPTER 12

A Brief Comment on Interpolated Swap Spreads

In recent years, interpolated swap spreads have been far and away the most popular structure for trading bonds against swaps, particularly given concerns about collateral and credit charges when trading par asset swap spreads or full asset swap spreads in an environment with so many bonds trading well above par. But while the interpolated swap spread appears relatively clean and simple, there are some issues with which analysts and traders should be familiar.

When the government market rallies relative to the swaps market, the investor long the bond and paying fixed in an interpolated swap spread will make money, and this investor will lose money when the government market underperforms the swap market.

But unlike an asset swap, the cash flows in an interpolated swap are not exactly matched. Of course, the maturity of the swap is chosen to match the maturity of the bond and the notional size of the swap is chosen so that the basis point value (BPV) of the swap matches the BPV of the bond. As a result, the combined position should be insensitive to small parallel shifts in the bond and swap curves.

However, as the market moves, the BPVs of the swap and the bond will change at different rates, so the combined position will not remain BPV-neutral. In other words, the position is not hedged against large parallel shifts and will need to be rebalanced periodically to maintain a neutral position.

Further, there is no guarantee that the curve changes will be parallel shifts. Because the cash flows of the bond and swap are not exactly matched, the combined position will be sensitive to non-parallel changes in the curves.

The lack of cash flow matching may seem like a small problem, but it can be quite serious. In particular, it will be a significant issue for bonds trading at significant discounts or premiums.

To see this, consider a swap spread trade involving DBR 6.25% Jan-24, priced at 147.52 to yield 1.595%, with a BPV of 13.01. The fixed rate for a swap with an end date equal to the bond's maturity date is 1.912%. The notional amount for this swap in order to match the BPVs of the two trades would be 120.2 MM notional amount in the swap for every 100 MM par amount of the bonds.

The cash flows for the bond and the swap are shown in Figure 12.1, and the net cash flows in the swap are shown in Figure 12.2.

FIGURE 12.1   Cash flows of DBR 6.25% Jan-24 and matching swap.

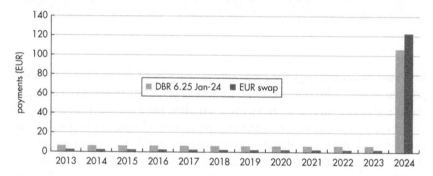

Source: Bloomberg.

FIGURE 12.2   Net cash flows of DBR 6.25% Jan-24 swap spread.

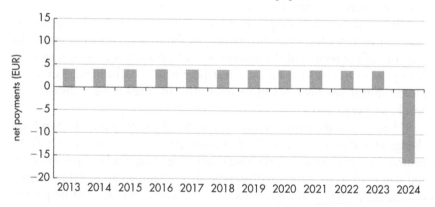

Source: Bloomberg.

We see clearly that the cash flow mismatch is considerable in this case. The cash flow mismatch in this example means that someone who buys the bond against swaps will have a curve steepening position embedded within the trade, while someone who sells the bond against swaps will have a curve flattening position embedded within the trade.

This example is somewhat extreme, given the considerable difference between the coupon of the bond and the fixed rate of the swap. But the point made here is an important one. Using duration and/or basis point values to calculate the hedge ratios can introduce other, presumably unintended, risk exposures into trades. At a minimum, analysts and traders should be aware of these additional risk exposures and decide explicitly whether and how these risks are to be managed.

CHAPTER 13

Cross-Currency Basis Swaps

Introduction

The discussion of swap spreads in Chapter 8 and Chapter 9 was limited to the special case of a single currency and the absence of credit risk. In the following, these conditions are relaxed.

In this chapter, we introduce the cross-currency basis swap (CCBS), and in the subsequent chapter we discuss the ways in which the CCBS can extend our analysis to include relative value comparisons between bonds denominated in multiple currencies.

In Chapter 15, we discuss the features and potential pitfalls of credit default swaps (CDS). And then in Chapter 16, we discuss the ways in which CDS can extend our analysis further, to include bonds that are subject to default risk.

Chapter 14 and Chapter 16 perform two functions. First, they allow us to extend our analysis to bonds denominated in different currencies and/or subject to default risk. Second, they extend the range of relative value trades.

For example, opportunities exist to apply principal component analysis (PCA) to the term structures of CCBS and CDS in order to identify attractive relative value trading opportunities. And then there are also opportunities to combine CCBS and CDS to form new relative value trades between instruments, such as trading the steepness of the CDS curve against the steepness of the bond curve.

In line with this general structure, the task of this chapter is to introduce the CCBS and to discuss its recent behavior.

Definitions

FX Swap

In a spot FX transaction, two parties exchange two currencies immediately upon agreement of the exchange rate.

In a forward FX transaction, two parties agree on an exchange rate and on a date in the future on which the two currencies will be exchanged.

The relation between the spot exchange rate and the forward exchange rate typically precludes arbitrage opportunities, in accordance with the standard equation:

$$F_{\frac{USD}{EUR}} = \frac{1 + R_{USD}}{1 + R_{EUR}} S_{\frac{USD}{EUR}} \qquad (13.1)$$

Where

$S_{\frac{USD}{EUR}}$ is the number of US dollars that can be exchanged for one euro in the spot market;

$F_{\frac{USD}{EUR}}$ is the number of US dollars that can be exchanged for one euro three months forward;

R_{USD} is the *non-annualized* rate at which a bank could lend US dollars on an unsecured basis for three months;

R_{EUR} is the *non-annualized* rate at which a bank could borrow euros on an unsecured basis for three months.

For example, at the time of writing, one euro would purchase 1.2712 USD in the spot market. The three-month USD LIBOR rate is 0.31%, and the three-month EURIBOR rate is 0.193%. As a result, the no-arbitrage forward exchange rate is 1.2716.

If this condition were not satisfied, one could make arbitrage profits by borrowing euros, buying dollars in the spot market, lending the dollars, and selling the dollars forward – or by doing the opposite, depending on whether the forward rate was higher or lower than the forward exchange rate implied by this no-arbitrage equation.

The FX swap is a combination of the spot and forward transactions discussed above. In other words, the FX swap consists of the spot and forward transactions by which one would attempt to exploit the arbitrage in the event that Equation 13.1 was not satisfied.

It's important to note the difference between an FX swap and an FX forward. In an FX forward, the two currencies are exchanged only on the forward date. In an FX swap, currencies are exchanged on both the spot date and on the forward date. As we'll see later in the chapter, the distinction is important for understanding the economic function of the FX swap, as it eliminates the FX exposure.

An FX swap can be conceptualized as consisting of three components:

1. an initial exchange of principal in two currencies;
2. a return at the swap end date of the principal exchanged at the start date;
3. a payment of interest in each currency at the swap end date, added to the principal returned.

Because the interest payments in step (3) typically differ in value, the exchanges of principal and interest payments at the end date of the swap constitute an effective forward rate that typically is different from the spot exchange rate.

FX swaps typically have tenors of up to one year. When the principal is to be exchanged for a period greater than a year, a CCBS is more typical.

In fact, the CCBS can be thought of as an extension of the forward FX market to longer maturities – just as we have thought of the asset swap spread to extend the repo market to longer maturities.

Cross-Currency Basis Swaps

A CCBS is very similar to an FX swap in that it involves:

- an initial exchange of principal in two currencies;
- the return of this principal at the end date of the swap;
- interest payments in each currency to reflect the time value of the funds borrowed by each counterparty in the swap.

Where an FX swap involves payment of a single interest payment in each of the two currencies, a CCBS involves a stream of interest payments in each of the two currencies.

Typically, when we refer to a CCBS, we have in mind a swap in which the stream of interest payments in each currency is floating. For example, a five-year (5Y) EUR/USD CCBS might involve quarterly payments of three-month (3M) USD LIBOR in exchange for quarterly payments of 3M EURIBOR. Or it might involve quarterly payments of the 3M USD OIS rate in exchange for quarterly payments of the 3M EONIA rate.

As an alternative, the stream of interest payments in a CCBS could involve fixed rates. For example, a 5Y EUR/USD CCBS could involve quarterly fixed payments in USD in exchange for quarterly fixed payments in EUR.

As yet another alternative, we could also have a mixed CCBS, in which a stream of floating rate interest payments in one currency was exchanged for a stream of fixed rate interest payments in another currency. For example a EUR/USD CCBS could involve quarterly payments of 3M EURIBOR in exchange for quarterly fixed payments in USD.

The key to understanding the CCBS is to keep in mind the three components of the swap:

1. an initial exchange of principal in each currency;
2. the return of principal in each currency at the end of the swap;
3. the interest rate payments during the swap paid to each counterparty to reflect the time value of money in that currency.

In these examples, we've discussed fixed and floating payments without reference to any spreads, while in practice CCBS typically are traded with an attached spread to reflect changes in pricing. For example, one swap counterparty might agree to pay USD LIBOR in exchange for EURIBOR less a spread in order to provide sufficient motivation for a counterparty to engage in the swap. Usually, the "CCBS spread" is referred to simply by the name for the instrument and is called "CCBS" as well.

As a practical matter, the spread could be attached to either leg of the swap. For example, the same counterparty might agree to pay USD LIBOR plus a spread in exchange for EURIBOR.

By convention, CCBS spreads tend to be quoted with reference to the non-dollar leg when the swap involves USD. For example, a 5Y CCBS quote of −38/−37 would mean that an investor could exchange dollars for euros by agreeing to pay 3M EURIBOR less 37 basis points (bp) and to receive 3M USD LIBOR for five years – or the investor could choose to receive 3M EURIBOR less 38 bp in exchange for 3M USD LIBOR for five years.

Economic Functions

The textbook function of a CCBS is to allow someone to engage in a transaction in a currency other than his domestic currency without taking FX risk. For example, an Italian issuer might issue bonds in USD and swap them into EUR via a CCBS in order to take advantage of a relatively large demand for his bonds among US investors. In so doing, he may be able to achieve a lower borrowing cost than he could achieve by issuing bonds in EUR.

In this example, there's nothing to prevent the issuer from simply selling bonds denominated in USD and then converting the proceeds to EUR, without engaging in any additional swaps. But in that case, the issuer is exposed to FX risk with respect to making payments of principal and interest in USD. To eliminate this FX risk, the issuer can engage in a CCBS immediately after issuing the bonds. The issuer receives EUR at the start of the swap, pays EUR at the end of the swap (equal to the maturity date of the bonds), and makes ongoing payments of EUR between the start and end dates.

Through the CCBS, issuers of debt can choose the currency in which they fund, independent of the denomination of their debt. For example, if an A-rated company funds in USD at LIBOR + 250 bp and in JPY at LIBOR + 150 bp, it has an incentive to issue Samurai bonds and to exchange its JPY into USD funding via the CCBS. If the CCBS were zero, it would realize about 100 bp funding advantage. Of course, the activity of Samurai issuers seeking to profit from this opportunity would be expected to pressure CCBS spreads and/or to widen JPY credit spreads so as to reduce the attractiveness of the opportunity.

On the other side of the supply/demand balance, buyers of bonds can also choose the currency in which they invest, through the CCBS. For example, if a US Treasury bond trades at USD LIBOR −50 bp and a Bund at EUR LIBOR −20 bp (and both issuers are considered risk-free),[1] a USD based investor might want to use the CCBS to obtain access to the EUR bond market without FX exposure. If the BSW were equal to zero, he would realize a return of roughly USD LIBOR −20 bp, thus about 30 bp pick-up versus the US Treasury investment. Now, the activity of investors seeking to take advantage of that opportunity will drive the CCBS up and/or Bund swap spreads wider (more negative) relative to US Treasury swap spreads.

The CCBS level observed in the market reflects the sum of global capital flows chasing the currency which offers superior funding and investment opportunities. For example, high credit spreads in USD relative to JPY could lead to an increase in Samurai issuance, driving the CCBS negative. This in turn might make basis swapped JGBs attractive on a USD LIBOR spread basis, generating flows that push the CCBS up again. Consequently, the pricing of the CCBS reflects the complex mixture of global funding and investment flows and can serve as a useful and quantitative indicator for these activities, which are often hidden from direct observation. Stated otherwise,

---

[1] For the moment, we ignore the local funding differences discussed in Chapter 10. The impact of those funding differences on the ASW difference will be analyzed in Chapter 14 (Figure 14.12).

the CCBS condenses the multitude of all cross-currency funding and investment flows into one easily observable and tradable number.

In abstract terms, basis swaps link global funding rates and therefore allow investors and borrowers to exploit global credit spread differences. And in a similar manner, global credit spread differences impact the level of the CCBS via global credit spread arbitrage.

Further impacts on the CCBS can arise from:

- Differences in yield curve steepness (carry) in different currencies. For example, a high carry difference between the Treasury and JGB yield curve typically prompts Japanese investors to increase their foreign bond holdings and to roll the FX hedge on a short-term (e.g. 1Y) basis. This mismatch between the maturity of the bond and of the CCBS results in a synthetic carry position along the US yield curve. Thus, whenever these carry positions are particularly attractive, demand for the short end of the CCBS curve tends to be affected.
- Hedging flows from structured products. Many structured products involve several currencies, and hence dealers require CCBS positions to hedge them. For example, the hedging flows of power reverse dual callables (PRDCs) introduce a link between the CCBS and the FX markets. When the FX rate moves, in particular through certain levels used in PRDCs, PRDC hedges need to be adjusted. Since most PRDCs are ultralong issues, this tends to affect 20Y and 30Y CCBS in particular.

A typical illustration of the impact of the textbook function of the CCBS on its pricing is given by the behavior of the 2Y JPY CCBS in 2002 and 2003. As depicted in Figure 13.1, when the swap spreads of US Treasuries narrowed relative to those of JGBs (i.e. when investing in US bonds became more attractive relative to investing in Japanese bonds), the demand for generating returns in USD increased and the CCBS became more negative. The R^2 of 0.34 in the regression of 2Y JPY CCBS on the asset swap spread difference between US Treasuries and JGBs suggests that this effect could be responsible for about one-third of the movements in the CCBS, with the remaining two-thirds being a function of other driving forces. This is in line with the CCBS reflecting the result of a multitude of different global funding and investment flows.

While this textbook example is illustrative, in practice it only works when the pricing action in the CCBS reflects the flows of capital freely chasing the best global returns. In case of a banking crisis (or of capital controls), however, other considerations can have an overwhelming impact on the CCBS.

FIGURE 13.1 The 2Y JPY CCBS in 2002 and 2003 as a function of the ASW difference in different currencies.[2]

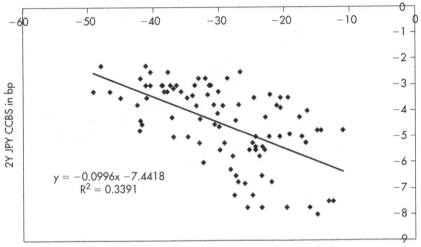

ASW difference between 2Y USTs and JGBs in bp

Sources: data – Bloomberg; chart – Authors.
Data period: 1 Jan 2002 to 7 Oct 2003, weekly data.

This is the reason that the textbook example hasn't addressed the actual dynamics in the CCBS market in recent years.

To illustrate the impact of a banking crisis on the CCBS, we regress the level of JPY CCBS on a proxy for risk aversion since 2010. In particular, we use the first factor from a PCA of the CCBS curve as the dependent variable. And as the independent variable, we use the realized volatility of the 5Y JPY swap rate. The results shown in the following figure underscore the point that in the presence of a banking crisis there is little room for global funding and investment flows to impact the level of the CCBS. Correspondingly, rather than a multitude of driving forces (e.g. Figure 13.1 with an R^2 of 0.34), there is now a single determining variable of the CCBS curve only (e.g. Figure 13.2 with an R^2 of 0.86).

Also note the difference in magnitude. While global funding flows usually cause the CCBS to move by a couple of basis points, a banking crisis can have an impact as much as 10 times larger.

---

[2] In the 10Y sector, the UST ASW in 2002 and 2003 was largely influenced by (waning) expectations about Fed buying at the long end of the curve. Thus, we use 2Y rather than 10Y (or factor 1 of the PCA on the CCBS curve), where results could be misleading.

FIGURE 13.2 Factor 1 of a PCA on the JPY CCBS since 2010 as a function of the 5Y realized swap volatility.

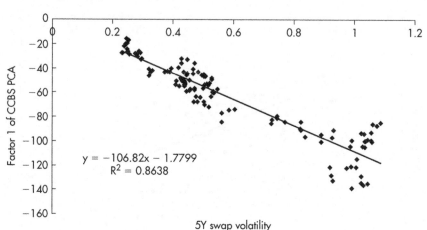

Sources: data – Bloomberg; chart – Authors.
Data period: 4 Jan 2010 to 4 Jun 2012, weekly data.

CCBS and the Subprime Crisis

With the advent of the subprime crisis beginning in 2008, European banks experienced increasing difficulties funding many of their USD-denominated assets, particularly mortgage-related bonds that had been financed in the US repo market.

One alternative option available to these banks was to sell these mortgage-related assets. But this alternative was considered relatively unattractive, as these assets were selling for relatively low prices.

Another alternative available to European banks was to sell euros to buy dollars in the spot FX market and then to use those dollars to fund their USD mortgage-related assets. But this alternative would involve considerable exchange rate risk.[3]

A third alternative, and the one chosen by many European banks, was to engage in CCBS with US banks, in which the European bank would:

- receive dollars in exchange for euros at the start of the swap;
- return the EUR and USD principal at the end of the swap;

---

[3] The observant reader might ask whether these European banks could have hedged this FX risk in the forward market. But, of course, combining a spot FX transaction with a forward FX transaction results in an FX swap or in a CCBS (depending on the term of the swap). So from a practical perspective, this is what the European banks did.

FIGURE 13.3 5Y basis swaps: EUR/USD and JPY/USD.

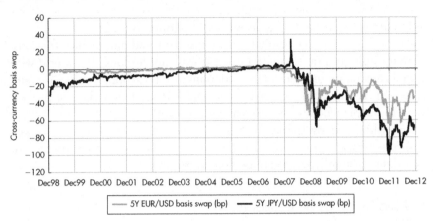

Source: Bloomberg.

- exchange ongoing interest payments – plus or minus a basis swap spread – during the life of the swap.

The European banks then used the dollars received in the CCBS to fund their USD mortgage-related investments.

Figure 13.3 shows the way in which the 5Y EUR/USD CCBS reacted to these events. The 5Y JPY/USD CCBS is shown as well, for reference.[4]

A couple of points worth noting:

- The basis swap spread was within a few basis points of zero until the start of the subprime crisis, at which time it began increasing (i.e. becoming increasingly negative, favoring the counterparty providing USD in the swap).
- Since the start of the subprime crisis, the 5Y CCBS spread has widened during periods of particular stress for European banks and has narrowed when those stresses have lessened.

Pricing the CCBS

Consider first the case of the FX swap, which is essentially a shorter version of the CCBS.

---

[4] In 1998, Japanese banks were in a situation similar to the one described above and used the CCBS to fund their extensive US operations.

The no-arbitrage relation between the spot and forward rates is determined by the borrowing and lending costs in the two currencies. And yet FX swap rates can and do change in ways that permit arbitrage.

In a world without capital constraints and without market frictions, arbitrage opportunities shouldn't exist, at least not for long. In a world with capital constraints and with market frictions, arbitrage opportunities can and do persist, acting as an incentive for people who are long dollars to provide them to people who are short dollars in this case.

So while, strictly speaking, these FX and CCBS swaps can be viewed from the perspective of arbitrage, this isn't the most useful perspective for providing economic insight about these spreads.

US Dollars "Going Special" as Collateral

In our view, the most insightful way to think about FX swaps and CCBS is from the perspective of collateralized loans, similar to the repo market for government bonds.

Recall that government bonds sometimes trade in the repo market at rates lower than the "general collateral" (GC) rates, as an incentive for people who are long the bond to provide it to people who are short the bond. The demand for the bond, the specific collateral in the loan, is the factor that drives the repo rate for the bond below the GC repo rate.

Likewise, in an FX swap or a CCBS, we can think of one currency as having particularly strong demand that increases its value as specific collateral.

For example, if the 5Y EUR/USD CCBS is −37 bp, the market is willing to provide an incentive of 37 bp per year to motivate people with dollars to provide them as collateral in a loan of euros. In this case, we can think of dollars as having "gone special" as collateral, similar to the way bonds go special in the repo market.

Seen from this perspective, the arbitrage that is available for providing dollars in exchange for euros for a fixed period is the incentive provided to people who are long dollars to lend them to people who are short dollars, against a loan of euros.

In contrast, consider the situation in which a comparable loan of euros is securitized not with US dollars but rather with some more GC, say gold or generic German Bunds. In this case, the interest rate paid by the person borrowing euros would be the generic rate for loans secured by GC (i.e. the GC repo rate). But when the euro loan is secured by US dollars, which are in short supply among European banks, the party borrowing euros enjoys a special borrowing rate as an incentive for providing the dollars for a fixed period.

From this perspective, the magnitude of the basis swap spread isn't determined by no-arbitrage considerations. Rather, it's determined via simple supply and demand considerations. If the spread is −35 bp and European banks still need more dollars, the spread is likely to widen still further, to −40, −45, or beyond. There are no pricing models of which we're aware to help us assess the valuation of basis swap spreads relative to other spreads.

As a result, in this book, we take the FX swap rates and the CCBS spreads as a given.

CCBS Spreads and Spot FX Rates

When a bond becomes special in the repo market, it assumes a value to its owner beyond the mere right to the intrinsic payments of principal and interest. The bond also allows its owner to borrow in the secured lending market at an interest rate lower than he could borrow with GC. In fact, by combining the resulting low-rate borrowing with collateralized lending at the higher rate prevailing for GC, the owner of the special collateral can monetize the specialness of his valuable collateral without incurring interest rate risk.

Since the bond trading special in the repo market offers its owner this additional economic value, its price in the spot market tends to be higher than it would be were it not special in the repo market. In other words, the spot price of a bond tends to increase relative to other bonds when it goes special in the repo market.

Likewise, our perspective that CCBS spreads widen when dollars "go special" in the repo market implies that US dollars should richen to euros in the spot market above the rate they otherwise would be were the dollars not special (i.e. were the basis swap not so wide).

Of course, the CCBS is by no means the only factor that would be expected to affect the price of US dollars vs. euros in the spot FX market, so a failure to observe the predicted relationship may not warrant a rejection of our hypothesized perspective. On the other hand, if we were to observe the hypothesized relationship, it should lend credence to our analogy between repo specialness and CCBS spreads.

Figure 13.4 shows the relation between the 5Y EUR/USD CCBS and the EUR/USD spot exchange rate over time since January of 2005.

Prior to the start of the subprime crisis, there was no correlation between the basis swap spread and the spot value of the EUR, particularly as the value of the basis swap spread always was within a few basis points of zero.

After the start of the subprime crisis, the correlation between the CCBS spread and the FX rate increased significantly. For example, in 2009, 2010, and

FIGURE 13.4   5Y EUR/USD CCBS versus the EUR/USD spot FX rate.

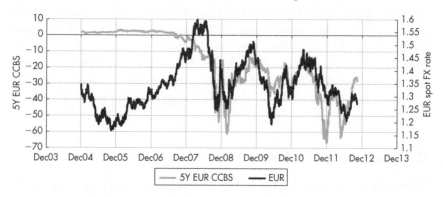

Sources: data – Bloomberg; chart – Authors.

2011 the correlations between the two series were 0.84, 0.80, and 0.78 respectively. In our view, the relation between the CCBS spread and the value of the dollar relative to the euro is consistent with our perspective that the CCBS spread can be viewed as the extent to which one currency has become more valuable as collateral against a loan in the other currency.

As the dollar tends to richen in the spot market, the other currency tends to appear relatively rich in the forward FX market. Correspondingly, the deviation of the forward FX rate traded in the market from the arbitrage relationship described by Equation 13.1 above is often referred to as the "richness" of the other currency (e.g. EUR) in the forward FX market.

With this in mind, our view is that the main economic function of the FX swap and CCBS markets is to provide an opportunity for people to borrow in one currency using another currency as collateral. As a result, many of the results we have developed for collateralized lending can be applied in this setting as well, the only complication being that the currency in which the collateral is denominated in this case is other than the currency in which the borrowed funds are denominated.

Conclusion

By treating FX swaps and CCBS as special cases of the collateralized lending markets, we can apply the approaches we've introduced already for comparing the relative values of swaps, futures, and default-free bonds in a single currency to the case of bonds denominated in multiple currencies.

We take up this discussion in the next chapter.

Relative Values of Bonds Denominated in Different Currencies

Introduction

Up to this point in the book, we've discussed relative value comparisons:

- among default-free bonds in the same currency;
- between bonds and bond futures contracts in the same currency;
- between default-free bonds and swaps in the same currency.

Our next task is to discuss ways in which analysts and traders can assess the relative values of default-free bonds issued in different currencies.

In combination with cross-currency basis swaps (CCBS), every bond can be expressed in USD terms (e.g. as a spread versus USD LIBOR or as a fixed rate). After describing the math leading to that expression, we investigate its applications and consequences:

- By combining the fitted curves techniques from Chapter 11 with the CCBS, the reach of the rich/cheap analysis can be extended from one specific bond market to all bonds globally. This gives a basis for assessing the relative value between global bond markets, irrespective of the currency of denomination.
- By combining the asset swap model from Chapter 8 and Chapter 9 with the CCBS, one can analyze the mutual influences.

The first part of this chapter describes in some detail the way to implement the comparison of bonds issued in different currencies. In the second part, we investigate the way this link between bonds in different currencies through the CCBS can affect their pricing in their local currencies.

Calculating USD LIBOR Swap Spreads for Foreign Bonds

Recall that a CCBS allows a USD-based institution to invest into any product independent of its currency without FX risk. For example, it could enter a JPY CCBS, use the JPY principal it initially receives, buy a JGB, asset swap it, and thereby create JPY LIBOR + ASW cash flows. With these cash flows, it can serve the running CCBS payments, receiving USD LIBOR (plus a spread). If the maturity of the CCBS equals the maturity of the JGB, it will receive JPY principal repayment from the bond, which the final principal exchange in the CCBS will convert into its original USD principal. Note that, though it has created its cash flows by means of a JGB investment, through the CCBS it deals in the end only with USD cash flows. Of course, any other currency could be used as a basis for comparison as well, and a EUR-based investor is able to express and evaluate all bonds globally as a spread versus EURIBOR.[1]

The importance of this statement (apart from the convenience it offers to USD-based investors) is that, through combining asset and basis swaps, all bonds can be reduced into a single number and can therefore be compared relative to the same benchmark. The mathematics of this expression is straightforward. The cash flow in foreign currency is the foreign LIBOR + foreign asset swap spread. Thus, after payment of foreign LIBOR + CCBS in the CCBS, one receives USD LIBOR (from the CCBS) and has the foreign swap spread minus the CCBS premium left in foreign currency. This then needs to be converted into USD by adjusting for the difference in basis point value (BPV).

Thus, the USD–LIBOR spread[2] is: $\frac{Swapspread_{foreign} - CCBS}{CF}$, where CF denotes the conversion factor (CF), that is $\frac{BPV_{USD}}{BPV_{foreign}}$ (with the BPV of the swap rates of the relevant maturity).

---

[1] Other floating or fixed rates can be used as a basis as well, for example all bonds could be expressed in fixed USD terms (see below) or as a spread versus EONIA.

[2] As a convention, when we speak of a "swap spread" or a "spread to LIBOR", we refer to the asset swap margin (ASW) and include the sign in it. For example, if the swap rate is at 1.5% and the bond yield at 1%, the bond quotes at about LIBOR −50 bp and its swap spread is close to −50 bp (including the minus).

FIGURE 14.1   USD swap spreads of US Treasuries, Bunds, and JGBs as of 23 Sep 2012.

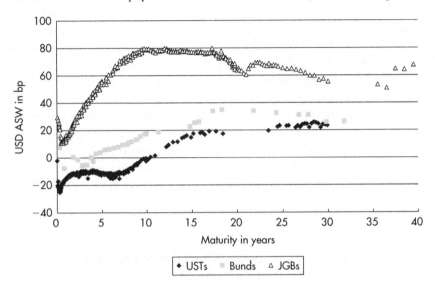

Sources: data – Bloomberg; chart – Authors.
Data period: "Current" market data as of 23 Sep 2012.

Note that in this equation the foreign swap spread needs to match the frequency of the CCBS (usually three-month, or 3M). If the foreign swap spread is quoted on another basis (e.g. 6M), it must be translated into 3M terms before applying the calculation above (e.g. by adding a 3M/6M intra-currency basis swap (ICBS)).

For example, at the time of writing, the 10-year (10Y) JGB benchmark was priced to have a 6M JPY ASW of −1 bp. Adding the 3M/6M JPY ICBS of 12 bp gives a 3M JPY ASW of 11 bp. With the CCBS at −64.5 bp and a CF of 0.95,[3] the equation above returns a spread of 79 bp above USD LIBOR for the 10Y JGB. That number is also called the USD asset swap spread (USD ASW) of the JGB.

A useful graphical representation of the way global bonds compare rel-ative to the universal yardstick of USD LIBOR is to display the USD swap spreads of the relevant bonds as a function of their maturities. Figure 14.1 shows the USD swap spreads for US Treasuries, basis swapped Bunds, and basis swapped JGBs. It can be seen that, while Bunds track the US Treasury curve (on a USD LIBOR basis) at a rather constant and low spread, JGBs are priced at a significantly higher USD ASW and follow an independent path.

---

[3] Calculated by dividing the BPV of a 10Y USD swap by the BPV of a 10Y JPY swap.

The equation above offers a mathematical explanation for the high USD ASW of JGBs. While the JPY ASW of JGBs has not moved significantly, the banking crisis resulted both in a higher 3M/6M ICBS and in a more negative JPY CCBS. Moreover, while the declining yield in the US has led to a narrowing of the BPV difference between 10Y JPY and 10Y USD swaps, it is still higher in Japan, and therefore the CF is smaller than one, magnifying the USD ASW of JGBs.

While calculating the USD ASW is straightforward, we outlined in Chapter 10 that swap spreads are a problematic way of assessing the relative value among bonds and suggested using fitted curves instead. We will now go on to describe the way fitted bond curve techniques from Chapter 11 can be combined with the basis swap in order to assess relative value among global bond markets.

Rich/Cheap Analysis through Fitted Curves for Bonds Denominated in Different Currencies

The general approach is straightforward, consisting of three main steps:

1. Express all bonds as fixed rate cash flows in the same currency, using IRS, ICBS, and CCBS as needed.
2. Fit a benchmark yield curve.
3. Calculate the extent to which bonds are rich or cheap relative to this benchmark fitted yield curve.

In this example, we'll assess the relative values between German Bunds and US Treasuries.

The first step in the analysis is to choose the currency in which the relative value comparisons are to be made. In this case, we choose US dollars, though the decision in this case is essentially arbitrary, as there's no clear advantage in choosing US dollars over euros.

Separate Yield Curves in Respective Currencies

Figure 14.2 shows yields as a function of maturity for the 59 German Bunds used in this analysis as of the close of trading on Friday, 16 Nov 2012. Also shown are the yields of the 86 US Treasuries used in this example.

FIGURE 14.2 Yields of German Bunds and US Treasuries in domestic currency.

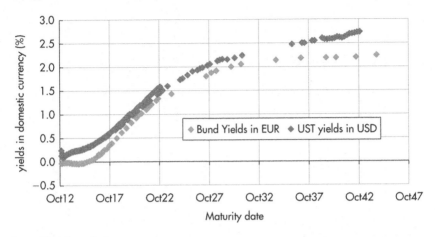

Source: Bloomberg, Authors.

Note that Bund yields are uniformly lower than Treasury yields and are particularly low for Bunds with maturities of less than three years and for Bunds with maturities greater than 20 years.

Swapping German Bunds into USD

The second step is to decide upon the series of swaps that will be used to convert annual fixed cash flows in EUR to semi-annual fixed cash flows in USD. For example, it is possible to swap fixed cash flows in one currency into fixed cash flows in another currency directly using a fixed-fixed CCBS, but these are less liquid than floating rate basis swaps. And most dealers who provide fixed-fixed CCBS will be pricing and hedging the swap using the underlying floating-floating CCBS. So for illustrative purposes, it's best to use the floating-floating swaps in our example.

Table 14.1 shows a list of the pay and receive flows in the transaction. The pay column is divided into two sub-columns: a "one time" column for cash flows that occur only once and a "recurring" column for cash flows that take place on a recurring basis. The cash flows that net to zero are shown in gray, while the remaining cash flows are shown in black. We'll follow these cash flows carefully as we work through this illustration.

Step 1: Buy the Bund. In this case, DBR 15% 4-Sep-22 has a clean price of EUR 101.555000 and accrued interest of EUR 0.320548, for a total

TABLE 14.1 Transactions Involved in a Cross-Currency Basis Swapped Bund

Step	Pay		Receive	
	One time	Recurring	One time	Recurring
buy Bund	EUR P at settlement		EUR 100 at maturity	Ce in EUR
fixed-floating EUR IRS: fixed to floating		Ce in EUR		6M EURIBOR on EUR 100
fixed-floating EUR IRS: up-front payment	EUR 100 at settlement		EUR P at settlement	
fixed-floating EUR IRS: swap spread		6M ASWe on EUR 100		
ICBS: 6M to 3M		6M EURIBOR on EUR 100		3M EURIBOR on EUR 100
ICBS: ICBSe spread				3M ICBSe spread on EUR 100
ICBS: convert 6M ASWe margin to 3M ASWe spread		3M ASWe on EUR 100		6M ASWe on EUR 100
CCBS: USD leg	USD X0 at settlement		USD X0 at maturity	3M LIBOR on USD X0
CCBS: EUR leg	EUR 100 at maturity	3M EURIBOR on EUR 100	EUR 100 at settlement	
CCBS: 3M CCBSu spread on USD X0				3M CCBSu spread on USD X0
CCBS: convert ASWe margin to ASWu margin		3M ASWu on USD X0		3M ASWe on EUR 100
CCBS: Convert ICBSe spread to ICBSu spread		3M ICBSe spread on EUR 100		3M ICBSu spread on USD X0
fixed-floating USD IRS		3M USD LIBOR on X0		USD fixed swap rate on X0

Source: Authors.

Note: P is the invoice price of the Bund in euros at settlement. Ce is the coupon of the Bund in euros. ASWe is the asset swap spread of the Bund in euros. ASWu is the asset swap spread of the Bund in US dollars. ICBSe is the ICBS spread in euros. ICBSu is the ICBS spread in US dollars. CCBSu is the CCBS spread in US dollars. X0 is the FX rate between US dollars and euros at settlement.

invoice price of EUR 101.875548. You'll be paid EUR 100 at maturity on 4-Sep-22.

Step 2: Swap the Bund into floating. In this step, the dealer agrees to pay you:

- the 6M EURIBOR rate on 4-Mar-13 and on every subsequent 4 March and 4 September up to and including the maturity of the bond on 4-Sep-22;
- EUR 1.875548 (the difference between the invoice price and par) at settlement.

In exchange, you agree to pay the dealer:

- annual coupons of EUR 1.50 on 4-Sep-13 and on 4 September of every subsequent year up to and including the maturity of the bond on 4-Sep-22;
- the asset swap spread of 31.8 bp semiannually (i.e. EUR 0.159 on every 4 March and 4 September up to and including the maturity date of the bond on 4-Sep-22).

Step 3: Swap the 6M cash flows into 3M cash flows via an ICBS. In this step, the dealer agrees to pay you:

- the 3M EURIBOR rate on every 4 March, 4 June, 4 September, and 4 December up to and including the maturity of the bond on 4-Sep-22;[4]
- The ICBS of 11.81 bp quarterly (i.e. EUR 0.05905 every 4 March, 4 June, 4 September, and 4 December up to and including the maturity date of the bond on 4-Sep-22);
- the asset swap spread of 31.8 basis points semiannually (i.e. EUR 0.159 on every 4 March and 4 September up to and including the maturity date of the bond on 4-Sep-22).

In exchange, you agree to pay the dealer:

- the 6M EURIBOR rate on 4-Mar-13 and on every subsequent 4 March and 4 September up to and including the maturity of the bond on 4-Sep-22;
- the *converted* asset swap spread of 31.74 bp quarterly (i.e. EUR 0.1587 on every 4 March, 4 June, 4 September, and 4 December up to and including the maturity date of the bond on 4-Sep-22).

Figure 14.3 shows the term structure of EUR 3M to EUR 6M ICBS rates.

---

[4] Another common structure would be for the 3M EURIBOR payments to be paid semi-annually rather than quarterly.

FIGURE 14.3 Term structure of EUR 3M/EUR 6M ICBS spreads.

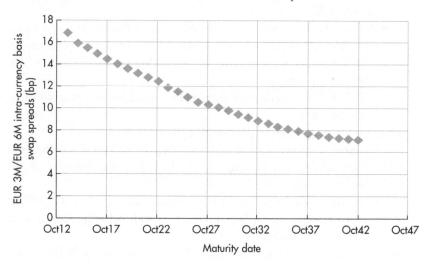

Source: Bloomberg, Authors.

At this point, you've bought the bond and effectively swapped it into 3M EURIBOR plus an intra-currency swap spread less a quarterly asset swap spread.

> Step 4: Swap the 3M EUR cash flows into 3M USD cash flows. In this step, the dealer agrees to pay you:
> - USD 127.43 at maturity;
> - EUR 100 at settlement;
> - 3M USD LIBOR on a notional of USD 127.43 quarterly (i.e. on every 4 March, 4 June, 4 September, and 4 December up to and including the maturity of the bond on 4-Sep-22);
> - a quarterly CCBS spread of 38.29 bp on a notional of USD 127.43 on every 4 March, 4 June, 4 September, and 4 December up to and including the maturity of the bond on 4-Sep-22;
> - the *converted* asset swap spread of 31.74 bp quarterly (i.e. EUR 0.1587 on every 4 March, 4 June, 4 September, and 4 December up to and including the maturity date of the bond on 4-Sep-22);
> - a *converted* ICBS spread of 12.07 bp on a notional of USD 127.43 quarterly (i.e. USD 0.038452 on every 4 March, 4 June, 4 September, and 4 December up to and including the maturity date of the bond on 4-Sep-22).

FIGURE 14.4   Term structure of EUR 3M/USD 3M CCBS spreads.

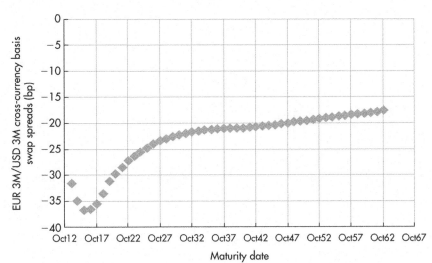

Source: Bloomberg, Authors.

In exchange, you agree to pay:

- USD 127.43 at settlement;
- EUR 100 at maturity;
- Quarterly payments of 3M EURIBOR on EUR 100 every 4 March, 4 June, 4 September, and 4 December up to and including maturity of the bond on 4-Sep-22;
- The 3M asset swap spread *converted* into USD of 32.41 bp quarterly, equal to USD 0.10325 paid on 4 March, 4 June, 4 September, and 4 December up to and including the maturity of the bond;
- The ICBS of 11.81 bp quarterly (i.e. EUR 0.05905 every 4 March, 4 June, 4 September, and 4 December up to and including the maturity date of the bond on 4-Sep-22).

Figure 14.4 shows the term structure of EUR 3M/USD 3M CCBS spreads.

Step 5: Swap quarterly USD payments into fixed USD payments. In this step, the dealer agrees to pay you:

- A quarterly fixed rate of 1.629% on a notional amount of USD 127.43 every 4 March, 4 June, 4 September, and 4 December up to and including the maturity date of the bond.

FIGURE 14.5 Yields of US Treasuries and German Bunds swapped into USD.

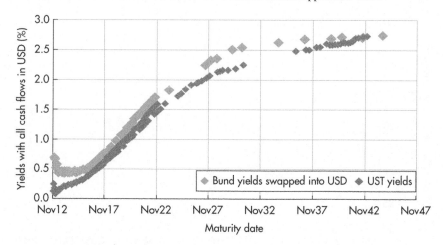

Source: Bloomberg, Authors.

In exchange, you agree to pay the dealer:
  • 3M USD LIBOR on a notional of USD 127.43 quarterly (i.e. on every 4 March, 4 June, 4 September, and 4 December up to and including the maturity of the bond on 4-Sep-22).

Separate Yield Curves in the Same Currency

Figure 14.5 shows the yields of German Bunds and US Treasuries once all the cash flows relating to the German Bunds have been swapped into US dollars.

Note that the yields of Bunds swapped into USD are now uniformly greater than US Treasury yields, particularly for Bunds with times to maturity less than three years and between 15 and 25 years.

Using Fitted Curves to Assess Relative Valuations

Now that we've swapped Bund cash flows into USD, we're in a position to compare the relative valuations of Bunds and Treasuries.

As we've outlined in Chapter 10 and Chapter 11, the proper way to compare the relative valuations between bonds denominated in the same currency is to fit a benchmark curve and to calculate the extent to which various bonds are rich or cheap to this benchmark curve. In this case, we'll fit a benchmark curve using US Treasury bonds and then calculate the extent to which German Bunds swapped into USD are rich or cheap relative to this benchmark curve.

FIGURE 14.6 Rich/cheap figures for US Treasuries relative to benchmark fitted curve.

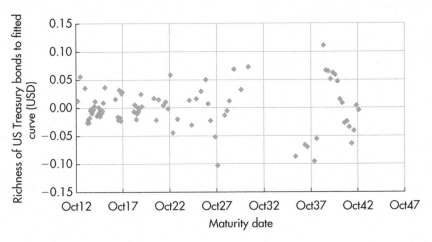

Source: Bloomberg, Authors.

FIGURE 14.7 Rich/cheap figures (in USD) for German Bunds relative to benchmark fitted curve.

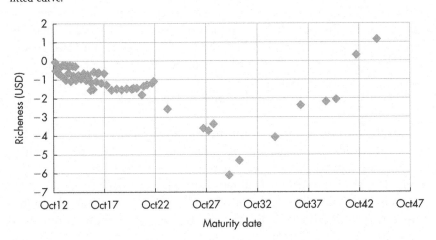

Source: Bloomberg, Authors.

To assess the quality of fit of our benchmark curve, the rich/cheap figures for the US Treasuries are shown graphically in Figure 14.6.

In general, we assess the quality of this fit as being very good, pricing almost every bond to within 10 cents and pricing the majority of bonds within 5 cents.

Figure 14.7 shows the rich/cheap figures for the German Bunds relative to our fitted yield curve.

FIGURE 14.8 Rich/cheap figures (in basis points) for German Bunds relative to benchmark fitted curve.

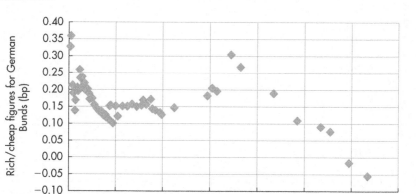

Source: Bloomberg, Authors.

Comparing the rich/cheap figures for Treasuries and Bunds in Figure 14.6 and Figure 14.7, we see that Bunds are cheap across almost the entire curve, particularly for Bunds with times to maturity between 15 and 25 years. The exception is the 30Y sector, in which the Bunds are rich to our fitted curve.

Figure 14.8 shows these rich/cheap figures converted to yields to maturity, expressed in basis points.

There are a few points worth noting in Figure 14.8:

• Virtually all Bunds appear cheap to our fitted curve, with actual USD-swapped yields greater than the yields the Bunds would be expected to have if they were priced in exact accordance with our fitted curve.
• Bunds with maturities under three years appear particularly cheap, as do Bunds with maturities between 15 and 25 years. For example, Bunds maturing in 2030 and 2031 offer yields that exceed those of our fitted curve for US Treasuries by 30 bp.
• Bunds in the 5Y to 10Y sector appear roughly 11–17 bp cheap.
• The two Bunds in the 30Y sector appear slightly rich to our fitted curve.

The Equilibrium between ASW and CCBS Markets

After describing the link between different bond markets through the CCBS, we focus in the second half of this chapter on the impact of these global relationships on the local swap spreads – and on our model for the local ASW. Conversely, applying the insights from the ASW model may help explain some of the structural richness and cheapness observed in Figure 14.8.

As the CCBS exists, there exists a USD ASW in addition to the local ASW and a relationship between the two. In particular, this relationship is given by the formula:

$$USDASW = \frac{EURASW}{CF} - \frac{CCBS}{CF} \qquad (14.1)$$

Hence, any change in one of the constituents affects all others, though there are different ways in which the equilibrium can be maintained. For example, a widening of EUR ASW of Bunds could be compensated either by a widening (more negative) of the EUR CCBS or by a richening of Bunds on a USD ASW basis.

As the equation does not determine the way a change in the USD ASW would be reflected by changes in the local ASW and CCBS, we need to leave the realm of pure mathematics and consider actual market data.

As a starting point for a brief empirical study of the way this equilibrium works in practice, we depict the evolution of the USD ASW of 5Y US Treasuries, 5Y Bunds, and 5Y JGBs in Figure 14.9. The USD ASW of 5Y Bunds followed the evolution of the USD ASW of 5Y US Treasuries at a

FIGURE 14.9 USD swap spread history of the 5Y US Treasury, Bund, and JGB.

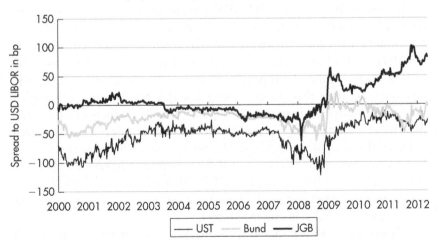

Sources: data – Bloomberg; chart – Authors.
Data period: 8 Feb 2000 to 12 Jun 2012, weekly data.

rather constant spread. Actually, the correlation between the two time series is 0.73. This means that, for Bunds, the existence of a global yardstick (the USD ASW) links the pricing of Bunds to the pricing of US Treasuries. Therefore, the USD ASW level of US Treasuries as well as the CCBS should have a significant impact on the pricing of Bunds denominated in euros.

On the other hand, the USD ASW of JGBs has appeared more independent. This could reflect the fact that JGBs are considered riskier than Bunds and hence are not as attractive alternatives for US Treasuries. As the influence of the global asset selection process illustrated in Figure 14.5 is greater if the bonds have a comparable credit standing, the USD ASW of US Treasuries has a significant impact on the pricing of low-risk bonds. Risky bonds, by contrast, have more scope to follow their own USD ASW pricing. This leads to the issue of the determinants of the USD ASW of JGBs. And as the USD ASW of JGBs is not tied strongly to the USD ASW of US Treasuries, it is conceivable that the existence of the USD ASW exerts less influence on the pricing of JGBs in yen.

From Figure 14.9 it is obvious that the same equation manifests itself differently in different markets. We therefore divide our empirical study into two parts: one for Bunds, representing low-risk bonds whose USD ASW is tied to US Treasuries, and one for JGBs, representing risky bonds whose USD ASW is not strongly tied to US Treasuries.

The Equilibrium for Bunds (Low-Risk Bonds)

In the case of Bunds, the USD ASW appears to be relatively stable. This observation is in line with the fact that Bunds are considered reasonably close substitutes for US Treasuries with about the same safe-haven status. Thus, if the USD ASW of Bunds become too high or too low, either against USD LIBOR on an absolute basis or relative to the USD ASW of US Treasuries, investors allocating their funds among low-risk bond markets through a process illustrated in Figure 14.1 or Figure 14.5 usually increase or decrease their Bund holdings. This keeps the USD ASW of Bunds at a comparatively stable level and a comparatively stable spread versus US Treasuries.

The mathematical consequence of the stability of USD ASW of Bunds is that Equation 14.1 links a volatile CCBS with a volatile local ASW. In other words, most of the moves on the right-hand side of the equation cancel out, leaving the left-hand side rather constant.

Figure 14.10 shows that this describes the actual market quite well. When Bunds richened considerably in the EUR funding market, a constant CCBS would have led to Bunds quoting through US Treasuries on a USD

FIGURE 14.10 Local and USD ASW of 5Y Bunds versus the 5Y EUR CCBS.

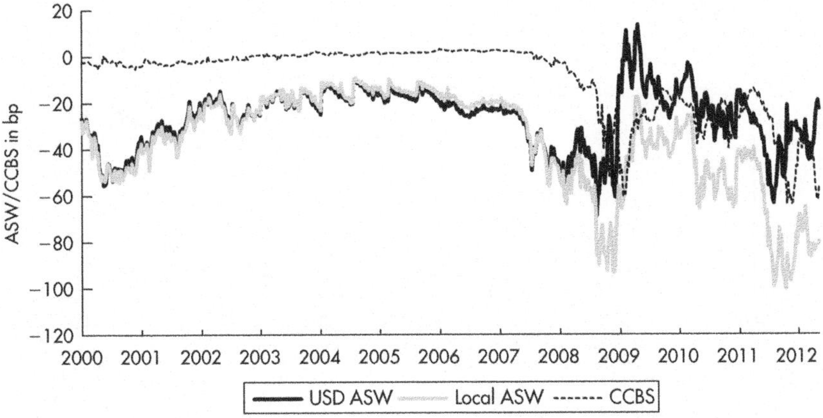

Sources: data – Bloomberg; chart – Authors.
Data period: 8 Feb 2000 to 12 Jun 2012, weekly data.

ASW basis (Figure 14.9). This situation prompts reallocation flows from Bunds into US Treasuries (in USD) and thus a widening (more negative) of the EUR CCBS. In other words, investors allocating their funds among low-risk bond markets through a process illustrated in Figure 14.1 or Figure 14.5 transfer some of the local funding moves away from the USD ASW to the CCBS. The result is that some of the richness of Bunds in the local funding market is absorbed by the CCBS. In terms of volatility, the CCBS therefore has a moderating impact on the USD ASW, as it absorbs some of the local funding volatility through global investment flows.

The ASW Model Revisited

Figure 14.10 suggests that the USD ASW level and spread over US Treasuries, as well as the CCBS, can have a major impact on the EUR ASW of Bunds. If the CCBS widens (becomes more negative), the EUR ASW is required to widen if the USD ASW is to remain constant. In Chapter 8 and Chapter 9, we have discussed the local ASW in isolation. Now that we observe external influences on the local ASW, we need to investigate the way this affects the ASW model.

The ASW model explains the local ASW as a function of the funding spread. Thus, if a widening of the CCBS results in a wider local ASW, the no-arbitrage model for local ASW predicts a higher 5Y LIBOR–repo basis swap. Figure 14.11 shows that this is precisely what has happened. In the

FIGURE 14.11 5Y EUR CCBS versus the EUR ASW of 5Y Bunds and their 3M funding spread.

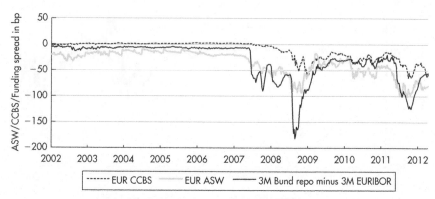

Sources: data – Bloomberg; chart – Authors.
Data period: 5 Mar 2002 to 12 Jun 2012, weekly data.

absence of a LIBOR–repo basis swap, we use the 3M EURIBOR–repo spread as a rough proxy and observe that the CCBS-related widening of EUR ASW of Bunds coincided with the widening of their funding spreads.

Moreover, the ASW model explains the LIBOR–repo basis swap by two main driving forces:

- The risk in LIBOR as measured by the LIBOR–OIS basis swap. And in fact, the widening of the EUR CCBS coincided with a widening of the LIBOR–OIS basis swap (in EUR).
- The cost of equity (CoE) of banks, driving the preference for collateralized loans. While we don't have a useful proxy for this variable, the data suggest that roughly half of the EUR ASW widening was due to LIBOR increasing relative to the OIS rate and the other half due to the increase in the CoE for banks.

The common background for this picture is the banking crisis, which caused a simultaneous increase in the CoE for banks, in the LIBOR–OIS basis swap in EUR (and hence in the EUR ASW of Bunds), and in the EUR CCBS.

As in this example, global impacts (such as the CCBS) interact with the input variables in the local ASW model, which illustrates the way the arbitrage relationship from the ASW model is maintained in the presence of moves in the CCBS. In brief, the link (CCBS) to USD ASW does not affect the *model* (and its no-arbitrage statements) but rather the *input variables* in that model.

Vice versa, the no-arbitrage principle which determines the local ASW as a function of the funding costs should also influence the USD ASW. Figure 14.12

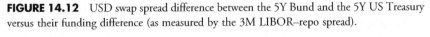

FIGURE 14.12   USD swap spread difference between the 5Y Bund and the 5Y US Treasury versus their funding difference (as measured by the 3M LIBOR–repo spread).

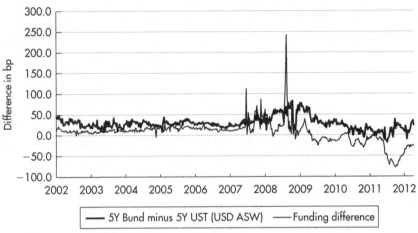

Sources: data – Bloomberg; chart – Authors.
Data period: 5 Mar 2002 to 12 Jun 2012, weekly data.

shows the evolution of the spread between the USD ASW of the 5Y Bund and the 5Y US Treasury (i.e. the difference between the lines of Figure 14.9) versus the evolution of the difference of both domestic funding costs.

It can be seen that, overall, the USD ASW follows the funding difference closely: an increase in the funding difference (i.e. the repo rates of US Treasuries versus USD LIBOR dropping relative to the repo rates of Bunds versus EUR LIBOR) is usually accompanied by an increase of the USD ASW difference between Bunds and US Treasuries. More specifically, before the Lehman crisis, the almost constant spread between Bunds and US Treasuries on a USD LIBOR basis (Figure 14.9) was matched by a rather constant funding spread. Note that the 3M funding difference used for Figure 14.12 is likely to underestimate the 5Y LIBOR–repo basis swap. Thus, it is possible that if 5Y LIBOR–repo basis swap data were available the two lines in Figure 14.12 would be even closer.

This provides empirical evidence for two statements made in earlier chapters:

- According to the swap spread model from Chapter 8 and Chapter 9, the swap spread of low-risk bonds is mainly a function of their expected funding spreads (the LIBOR–repo basis swap). Thus, the spread between the USD ASW of Bunds and US Treasuries should also depend on the difference of their expected (local) funding spreads. Figure 14.12 shows that this is indeed the case. Hence, the expected funding costs are not only the major driving force of individual ASW markets (Chapter 8), but these costs also are a major driving force of their USD ASW.

• Furthermore, Figure 14.12 provides empirical evidence for the statement at the end of Chapter 10 that the funding differences of bonds in domestic currencies have a major impact on the "relative value" between their USD ASW.

Finally, after the Lehman crisis, the volatility of the funding difference is significantly higher than the volatility of the USD ASW difference. This corresponds to the statement above that in case of low-risk bonds most of the volatility of local ASW (differences) is absorbed by the volatility of the CCBS, while the USD ASW difference is relatively stable. In particular, as the USD ASW difference is likely bounded by zero, the sharp drop in local EUR funding rates of Bunds relative to the USD funding rates of US Treasuries at the end of 2011 did not cause a move in the USD ASW difference of a similar size.

The Equilibrium in Case of JGBs (Risky Bonds)

Repeating the same analysis given in Figure 14.10 for Bunds with JGBs returns a completely different picture in Figure 14.13. Now the local ASW (rather than the USD ASW) is rather stable and the USD ASW is a mirror image of the JPY CCBS. Thus, the same mathematical equation (14.1) between the three elements local ASW, USD ASW, and CCBS works in two different ways:

• In the case of Bunds, the USD ASW has little volatility, shifting most of the volatility from the CCBS to the local ASW (and vice versa).
• In the case of JGBs, the local ASW has little volatility, shifting most of the volatility from the CCBS to the USD ASW (and vice versa).

In the case of Bunds, the USD ASW is driven by the USD ASW of US Treasuries (Figure 14.1 and Figure 14.9). By contrast, the USD ASW of JGBs follows a different path (Figure 14.9). It turns out that the USD ASW of JGBs is largely determined by the credit default swap (CDS) for Japan. As depicted in Figure 14.14, the correlation between the 5Y Japanese CDS and the USD ASW of 5Y JGBs since 2009 is 0.78. Thus, the same widening of the CCBS in EUR and JPY (Chapter 13, Figure 13.3) was accompanied by two different effects:

FIGURE 14.13 Local and USD ASW of 5Y JGBs versus the 5Y JPY CCBS.

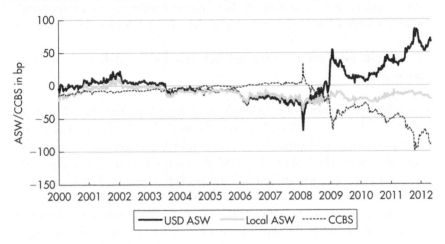

Sources: data – Bloomberg; chart – Authors.
Data period: 8 Feb 2000 to 12 Jun 2012, weekly data.

FIGURE 14.14 5Y JPY CCBS versus the USD ASW of 5Y JGBs and the 5Y Japanese CDS.

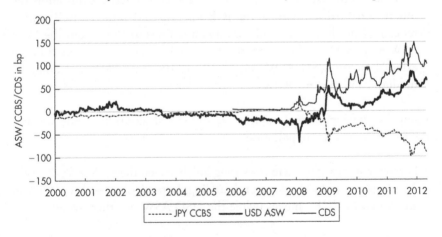

Sources: data – Bloomberg; chart – Authors.
Data period: 8 Feb 2000 to 12 Jun 2012, weekly data (CDS since 3 Jan 2006).

- In the case of Bunds, a wider (more negative) CCBS correlates with a wider local ASW (keeping the USD ASW stable) (Figure 14.10) and thus higher local funding spreads (Figure 14.11).
- In the case of JGBs, a wider (more negative) CCBS correlates with a wider USD ASW (keeping the local ASW stable) (Figure 14.13) and thus a higher CDS premium (Figure 14.14).

Note that these relationships are symmetric and imply no statement about causality. It is quite possible that a higher funding premium for Bunds caused the wide EUR CCBS and a higher Japanese CDS caused the wide JPY CCBS.

We can interpret the observed behavior by the difference in credit standing:

- Bunds offer a credit standing similar to that of US Treasuries. Therefore, there are large asset allocation flows between US Treasuries and Bunds along the lines of Figure 14.8. This results in a rather tight and stable spread between the USD ASW of Bunds and US Treasuries and in a strong international participation in the Bund market. Together, Bunds are priced versus US Treasuries on a USD ASW basis and the high share of international investors using Bunds as substitutes for US Treasuries ensures that this pricing impacts the domestic market, down to the local funding of Bunds.

- JGBs, on the other hand, are not considered substitutes for US Treasuries. First, this leads to the USD ASW reflecting mainly the credit risk as expressed in the Japanese CDS. Second, and closely related, this limits the international participation in the JGB market. And with the JGB market remaining firmly in the hands of domestic investors, for whom the USD ASW may well be of little importance, there is no significant impact of the external factors USD ASW and CCBS on the local ASW and domestic funding conditions of JGBs.[5]

Using these two markets as model cases for low-risk and risky bonds, we offer the following general hypotheses:

- For low-risk markets, there is a strong link between their USD ASW levels. This impacts the local pricing and funding. In particular, local ASW moves are related to CCBS moves (while the USD ASW is rather stable).

---

[5] This can also be expressed in terms of volatility. The absence of international US Treasury substitution flows for risky bonds (leading to their pricing against the CDS rather than US Treasuries) largely isolates the local funding market from global influences. Hence, the same reason which makes USD ASW volatile tends to make local funding costs rather stable. And with local funding rates tending to be stable, the volatility of the CDS-driven USD ASW is mainly absorbed by CCBS volatility. This is also in line with the relationship between the JPY CCBS and the USD ASW depicted in Figure 13.1 and Figure 13.2. (The variable "volatility" on the x-axis of Figure 13.2 is highly correlated to the CDS level and the USD ASW of JGBs.)

- For risky markets, the USD ASW level is mainly a function of the CDS, while the local ASW market is largely isolated from global influences such as the CCBS. In particular, moves in the CDS (and hence in the USD ASW) are related to the CCBS moves, while the local ASW is rather stable.

With regards to the ASW model, this means:

- For low-risk markets, foreign factors such as the CCBS can have a significant impact on the local funding situation (i.e. the input variables in our ASW model). While the no-arbitrage relationships of that model remain valid, its input variables can depend considerably on international events.
- For risky markets, there is a separation between the local ASW (as explained by an ASW model with input variables almost free from foreign impacts) and the USD ASW, which follows the CDS and the CCBS.

While the synthesis presented in this chapter finalizes our ASW analysis for low-risk bonds, for risky bonds, we can so far just address their local ASW. After outlining the CDS in the next chapter, we shall return to the question of ASW modeling for risky bonds in Chapter 16. We shall find that, while for low-risk bonds there are constant mutual influences between the global and local variables, the local ASW of risky bonds depends on their CDS-driven USD ASW only in specific circumstances.

Conclusion

In this chapter, we've seen the way the relative values of bonds can be compared when not all the bonds are denominated in the same currency. Namely:

- swap non-domestic cash flows into the domestic currency;
- fit a benchmark curve for the domestic currency;
- calculate the richness and cheapness of all bonds to the benchmark curve in the domestic currency.

We have then conducted a brief empirical study to illustrate the way these relationships between bonds in different currencies impact their pricing. The result led to a classification between those markets in which the spread to USD LIBOR is linked to the US Treasury curve and those markets in which it follows the CDS:

- The existence of a common yardstick has a major influence on the pricing of low-risk bonds. With their USD ASW being rather stable, the local ASW is partly driven by moves in the CCBS. Thus, the input variables in the ASW model need to consider external influences.
- For bonds with credit risk, in contrast, their local ASW is rather isolated from global impacts. On the other hand, their USD ASW (and CCBS) is largely driven by the CDS.

This discussion also clarifies that two of the main reasons bonds denominated in different currencies may exhibit systematically different relative values when compared in the same currency are different local funding rates and different credit risk.

CHAPTER 15

Credit Default Swaps

Introduction

So far, we've focused on deriving relative value relations between instruments relying mainly on the no-arbitrage principle, an approach that is possible based on the maintained assumption that the cash flows that define these instruments have been free from default risk.

In Chapter 14, however, we discussed empirical relations between US Treasuries, German Bunds, and JGBs that strongly suggested the need for incorporating credit risk in our analysis, particularly for JGBs. And as the pool of plausibly default-free issuers shrinks still further, incorporating credit risk into relative value analysis and trading becomes increasingly important.

There are two general approaches for incorporating credit risk into relative value analysis for the markets discussed in this book:

- fundamentally through credit analysis;
- via credit default swaps (CDS), the primary over-the-counter measure for credit risk.

While we recommend incorporating both approaches in a comprehensive assessment, fundamental credit analysis is outside the scope of this book.

CDS spreads offer the advantage of being quantitative and tradable measures of credit risk, allowing easy adjustments and comparisons:

- By using bond yields minus CDS rather than bond yields alone (i.e. by creating risk-free curves synthetically), the same analytical techniques for risk-free yield curves can be maintained in the presence of credit risk.

- By comparing the USD ASW with the CDS (i.e. by comparing credit risk reflected in the bond market *relative* to credit risk reflected in the CDS market), one can detect relative value opportunities, exploiting the *different assessment* of the same credit risk in bonds and in CDS, while being hedged against the absolute level of credit risk.

Unfortunately, however, sovereign CDS suffers from the disadvantage of being an imperfect measure for credit risk, expressing the information about credit quality in a deficient way (from the viewpoint of relative value analysis). While we make no attempt to rectify these deficiencies, we begin our treatment of the CDS with a brief overview of its pitfalls, of which we need to be constantly aware when incorporating the CDS into our analysis and trading strategies.

One can analyze and price the CDS:

- by a statistical model like principal component analysis (PCA) versus other CDS. This approach seems to be neglected by most market participants and therefore appears to offer correspondingly high rewards. In this chapter, we outline statistical pricing models for the CDS and their benefits.
- by the fundamental relationship of the CDS versus the bond it covers. This approach is based on the commonly applied valuation relation stating that the funding-adjusted asset swap spread should be approximately equal to the CDS spread. We shall discuss this relationship and the potential contributions of the funding rate discussion from Chapter 6 in the next chapter.

Structure of a CDS

A CDS contains information about a bond issuer's credit risk, but not in a clean form. Rather, a CDS presents the information about credit risk in connection with other elements, which arise from its structure and legal specifications. Here, we briefly discuss the specifications of the CDS as far as they are relevant for the potential distortion of the credit information. We shall find that the credit information in a CDS is given:

- together with information about the delivery option (DO);
- potentially in a different currency than the bond covered by the CDS.

Then, we address these two issues separately and investigate whether these two factors can be priced and thus whether the clean information about credit risk can be extracted simply from the CDS quotes observed in the market.

A CDS on a bond issuer exchanges floating payments (usually quarterly[1]) of the premium (which we shall also denote with the term "CDS") for the right to deliver a bond of the issuer for payment of its par value in case of a default of the issuer. We shall refer to paying the premium and enjoying the right to deliver the bond for payment of principal in case of a default as "buying" or "being long" the CDS.

The usual specifications of a CDS result in the following features, which overlay the credit information in a CDS with other elements:

- In most cases, the CDS terminates when an issuer defaults, even if the stated end date of the CDS is still in the future. For example, if we hold a 10-year (10Y) bond and hedge it with a 10Y CDS, and if the bond issuer defaults after five years, then we can deliver the bond into the CDS in exchange for the bond principal at the time of default rather than waiting until the maturity of the bond. In contrast, cash flows of other instruments traded in conjunction with the bond, such as asset swaps and basis swaps, would not end in the case of default by the issuer. In our example, if we hold a 10Y *asset-swapped* bond and hedge it with a 10Y CDS, and if the bond issuer defaults after five years, then we receive the principal from the CDS counterparty after five years, but we'll no longer receive the bond cash flows that we had matched against our open asset swap position. Thus, we would need to take our principal and reinvest it at the prevailing interest rate after five years in order to fulfill the remaining asset swap contract. Obviously, this introduces an interest rate risk in case of a default.
- A CDS usually[2] pays the principal of a defaulted bond *in USD*. We refer to the currency in which the principal of a defaulting bond is paid to the buyer of a CDS contract as the settlement currency or *denomination* of the CDS. As a consequence, a non-USD-denominated bond and a USD-denominated CDS assess the credit risk *in different currencies*.

  In the likely case of the currency of a defaulting country weakening this can result in overcompensation for the CDS buyer. The holder of a USD-denominated CDS will not only get his principal back but very likely receive the principal in a stronger currency. This results in an additional profit, which should be reflected in the pricing of the CDS. In fact, if CDS

---

[1] Since CDS are over-the-counter products, any terms can be agreed on. We focus on the most common terms.

[2] There are JPY-denominated CDS contracts on Japan and EUR-denominated CDS contracts on Italy trading, but liquidity is rather poor. The only exceptions are CDS contracts on the US, which are usually denominated in EUR.

denominated in local currencies trade at all, they tend to quote at a tighter premium than USD-denominated CDS on the same issuer.

Combining this point with the previous one leads to a specific issue when a 10Y asset *and basis swapped* bond in local currency is hedged with a 10Y *USD-denominated* CDS. A default after five years results in payment of the principal in USD, while the asset and basis swap contracts remain unaffected and require service of the cash flows in local currency. In this case, the default results not only in an open interest rate exposure but also in an open FX exposure, since we need to exchange our USD back into local currency in order to serve the payment obligations in the ASW and CCBS. If the local currency weakens in the event of a default, we can obtain an additional profit, since through the CCBS and CDS we are over-hedged against the weakening currency.

- CDS contracts usually do not specify which bond needs to be delivered in the event of default but rather allow any of the issuer's bonds to be delivered into the CDS contract. This results in a DO, similar to a bond futures contract, though in this case the buyer of CDS is long and the seller of CDS is short the DO. If we own a bond and a CDS on its issuer, in the event of default we can deliver our bond in exchange for our principal. But we also could sell our bond, buy another bond of the same issuer, and then deliver that bond into the CDS. If the other bond is cheaper than the one we originally held, we realize a profit.
- Other specifications with a potential impact on the pricing of a CDS include the treatment of coupons, margin and collateral requirements, consideration of the time value for the settlement process, and the potential difference between the frequency of coupon payments and CDS premium payments.

Trying to strip out the pure credit information from the CDS quotes observed in the market, we need at least to obtain a fair value for the DO and the impact of having the CDS and the bond denominated in different currencies. The next two sections address the issues involved in this task.

Delivery Option

When pricing the DO, we face two major hurdles:

- the absence of enough relevant precedents to estimate the price spread volatility between deliverables *in the event of default*;
- the changing settlement procedures.

With regards to the first issue, let us assume that only physical settlement takes place. Then, one could replicate the DO model for bond futures contracts from Chapter 5 for the delivery situation of a CDS. As discussed in Chapter 5 (Figure 5.4), this model requires the price spread volatility of deliverables as an input variable, and its results will largely depend on this input.

While the issues regarding modeling have been solved in Chapter 5, we need to estimate a realistic price spread volatility for deliverables in case of a default and face the basic problem that there are little to no precedents of *relevant* defaults. While the yield spread volatility between cheapest-to-deliver (CTD) candidates in the June Bund futures contract is likely to be similar to the yield spread volatility between CTD candidates in the March Bund futures contract, which historical precedents could we use to get an idea about the price spread volatility between Bunds in the event of a German default?

Using the price spread volatilities between the bonds of defaulting Latin American countries as inputs, our model returns an average DO value of 6 dollars per 100 dollar par CDS contract *in the event of default*. This might mean that about 6% of the CDS quote observed in the market could be due to the DO. However, the significant standard deviation of the DO in the case of Latin American defaults suggests that defaults and the DO value they produce are hardly comparable, even within the Latin American sovereign universe. And using the price spread volatility between a handful of Argentinean or Ecuadorian bonds as an estimate for the price spread volatility between German issues in case of a default is obviously even more problematic.[3]

Turning to the second issue, even if we had a reliable fair value for the DO in a physical settlement process, it remains unknown whether this DO value could be realized through cash settlement. And since the settlement process keeps evolving, we cannot be sure of the conditions under which a future settlement will take place.

In more detail, the earliest CDS documentations assume physical settlement of CDS contracts, with the defaulting bond being delivered to the seller of the CDS. With CDS becoming popular and their outstanding volume increasing relative to the size of outstanding bonds of the defaulting issuer, physical settlement has an increasingly distorting impact on bond

---

[3] The data situation is better in the US credit universe; but, again, would the default of a corporation be a relevant precedent to assess the expected price spread volatility in case of a bank defaulting, which involves completely different considerations (e.g. between senior and subordinated debt)?

prices, since it artificially increases demand for the bonds of defaulting issuers, just for them to be delivered into CDS contracts. Actually, in the case of more CDS contracts (net) than bonds being outstanding, the need to deliver a bond in order to receive payment from the CDS contract should theoretically result in the bonds of a defaulting issuer trading at par. Therefore, a cash settlement clause is now usually part of CDS contracts, whereby the price of bonds is determined through an auction process between the largest market participants. The idea is to obtain a "fair price" for the bonds of a defaulting issuer without disturbing the pricing of the bond market by the requirements of physical delivery into CDS contracts. Then, buyers of CDS are compensated with the difference between par and the price determined at auction, without the need to deliver a bond.

Changes to the settlement and auction details can affect the value of the DO. In the case of physical settlement, the buyer of a CDS can always deliver any bond of his choice, in particular the one he hedged with a CDS, or a cheaper one. Hence, the compensation he receives is always at least the par value of the bond he holds. And he may profit from delivering a cheaper bond. The same DO is hard to replicate through a cash settlement. Unlike in a physical delivery, it is possible that he is undercompensated and receives a cash payment, which may be less than the discount of his bond to par. This possibility increases as the auction settles closer to the price of the CTD.

All in all, quantitative statements about the DO in CDS contracts are fraught with difficulty, given precedents currently available and a settlement process still under construction. We shall therefore try to base our analysis on qualitative statements about the DO and apply the 6% rule of thumb from above only in cases when it is absolutely necessary to have numbers, keeping in mind that its use introduces a significant amount of imprecision (e.g. results in arbitrage "corridors" rather than arbitrage equations).

Difference in Settlement Currency

Similarly, when pricing the portion of the CDS due to currency effects, we face two issues:

- which pricing model to use;
- which parameters to use (e.g. which impact of credit risk on the FX rate should we assume?).

While we do not intend to participate in the ongoing academic discussion about the pricing model, we propose an original approach, modeled on the delta hedging of an option. The goal is not to present a solution but rather to gain a framework for illustrating the problems.

As starting point for the construction, we buy a USD-denominated CDS on Japan and sell a JPY-denominated CDS on Japan with the same end dates. Then, in case of a default, we can take the bond we are delivered and deliver it against receiving USD at a pre-defined FX rate. Assuming the yen weakens in the event of a default, we realize the difference between the pre- and post-default FX rate as profit. For example, if the JPY was to weaken from a pre-defined 80 to 160 in the event of default, our CDS spread position would be a binary option which pays us $50 in the event Japan defaults. Then, the fair difference between the CDS settling in USD and the CDS settling in JPY would be given as the annuity value of the fair value of that binary option.

Alternatively to pricing a binary option, we could replicate the delta hedging of the Black–Scholes framework, increasing a long JPY/short USD position as the credit risk of Japan (as measured by the CDS) increases. Then, in the event of no default, we have no FX position. But in the event of default (i.e. a default probability of one), our FX hedge covers the full long USD/short JPY position we get from settling the CDS spread. As in the case of delta hedging an option, this transfers the profit from the payoff at expiry to the profit from continuous adjustments of the hedge ratio. We can buy JPY when the default risk of Japan is high (and thus the JPY is expected to be cheap) and sell JPY when the default risk of Japan is low (and thus the JPY is expected to be rich). Consequently, the fair value for the CDS spread (i.e. for the overcompensation through USD-denominated CDS) is a function of the *default probability volatility*. In other words, the higher the volatility of the CDS, the higher the premium of USD-denominated versus JPY-denominated CDS should be.[4]

Given the current stage of modeling the CDS, to our knowledge, there remain significant hurdles on the way to a consistent pricing of the overcompensation through USD as settlement currency (which we also refer to as the "FX component"). In particular, as our delta-hedging approach does not seem to have entered the academic discussion, it remains unclear whether and how it can be reconciled with the binary option approach.

---

[4] As far as we are aware, this approach has not been discussed or formalized. Its implications for CDS pricing remain therefore unknown. However, our preliminary model based on this approach suggests that it could be a major driving force for CDS markets which exhibit a high volatility, such as Portugal.

An even bigger problem is posed by the estimation of the input variables in any model, just as in the case of the DO (where at least the model issue could be adequately addressed):

- How much should the currency of a defaulting country be expected to weaken?
- Does this weakening occur linearly as the credit risk increases, or are there jumps in the process?
- How can influences on the FX rate other than credit risk be excluded from the analysis?[5]
- What is the correlation between the default probability (and thus the FX rate) and the volatility of the default probability?

Again, one could look at historical precedents of sovereign defaults. But it is of no practical value to use the weakening of the Argentine peso as an estimate for the weakening of the JPY in case of a default, given the difference in foreign reserves, among others. Actually, if someone were to argue for the JPY to appreciate against the USD in case of Japan defaulting, due to Japan being forced to repatriate her large USD reserves, we could not refute this argument.

If it is possible to reasonably doubt even the *direction* of the currency movements of defaulting developed countries, there is little hope of achieving consensus about the *size* of the weakening of a currency in the event of default. Actually, one might even try the other way round. If quotes for the JPY-denominated CDS were available, one could translate the spread between the USD-denominated and the JPY-denominated CDS on Japan into the market-implied FX level in the event of default.[6]

We started the valuation exercise with the prospect of extracting the pure credit information from the CDS by adjusting for the fair value of its other elements. To achieve that goal, we would need to be able to price *both* the DO and the overcompensation from USD as settlement currency. The quick overview provided here reveals that there is little hope of pricing either of the two:

- For pricing the DO, we have a model, but no estimate for its parameters (and face the additional issue of changing settlement terms).
- For pricing the FX component, we have neither a model nor an estimate for its parameters.

---

[5] Imagine that in the CDS spread construction from above the Japanese credit risk does not change but that the USD weakens due to an unrelated factor (e.g. China selling her US Treasuries).

[6] Under some assumptions for the probability distribution of default.

Consequently, at the current stage of development, it is impossible to extract the clean credit information from the CDS quotes observed in the market. The advantage of the CDS (versus fundamental credit analysis) is that it is a *quantitative*, traded variable. The disadvantage is that it is a variable that combines credit information with other elements in an *unquantifiable* way. Hence, we face a situation in which an ideal CDS (from the viewpoint of relative value analysts) simply reflecting credit risk does not exist, and the actual CDS cannot be decomposed quantitatively in its components.

This leads to three consequences, which will accompany our analytical treatment of the CDS throughout the book:

- As the credit element in the CDS spread cannot be quantified, we shall restrict ourselves to qualitative statements about the CDS whenever possible.
- These qualitative statements often lead to inequalities. For example, while we cannot quantify the DO or the FX component, we can say that neither of the two should be negative and that thus the "pure" credit risk should not be higher than the CDS quote representing the combination of credit risk, DO, and FX component.
- Since quantifiable variables are a condition for hedging, the unknown impact of the DO and FX component on a trading strategy involving the CDS cannot be hedged. Therefore, any trading strategy involving the CDS should be subjected to a performance test for a set of different numbers for the DO and FX component.

Two Different Pricing Approaches toward CDS: Pricing of CDS versus Other CDS or versus Bonds

Conceptually, one can price any instrument either versus instruments of the same type or versus other instruments. In the first case, one evaluates the intrinsic, typically statistical, properties of the instrument; in the latter, one assesses how the same information is expressed through different instruments.

We can use this conceptual difference to classify CDS pricing models and trades (and shall use it later on to classify option pricing models and trades):

- Since both bond yields and CDS quotes are driven to some extent by the credit quality of the bond issuer, one can compare the way the information is expressed in both markets, derive the "fair" CDS quote by the bond yields (or, vice versa, the "fair" bond yields by the CDS quotes), and exploit potential mismatches by trading bonds against CDS. This is the approach of the commonly used models based on the link between the USD asset swap spread and the CDS spread. Turning this general concept into a trading strategy that works in practice requires taking into account the elements other than credit that also impact swap spreads and CDS. The following chapter will be devoted to this work, highlighting the way the insights in swap spreads from Chapter 6 can support improving the common pricing of the CDS relative to swap spreads denominated in USD.

• In this chapter, we analyze the CDS in isolation of its relationship to other markets. Thus, we are mainly concerned with the statistical properties between CDS quotes, for example with the factor structure of a CDS curve (different maturities of a CDS on the same issuer) and with the factor structure of the CDS market on euro sovereign issuers (same maturity of CDS on different euro governments). As far as we are aware, this approach is less commonly applied by market participants. Consequently, we often find more relative value opportunities in these "neglected" statistical relationships within the CDS market than in the well-analyzed link of the CDS to swap spreads.

When considering CDS in isolation from its relationship to bonds, it is easy to lose sight of the issues involved in the event of default. And in fact, sometimes the CDS market seems to trade *as if these issues did not exist.* For example, trading occurs without the two partners being concerned about the inability to price the DO. And as long as there is no default, this abstract treatment of CDS as a statistical time series without connection to bonds (thus also in abstraction from the problems of the connection between CDS and bonds) works well. A 5Y-10Y CDS curve trade, for example, can be assessed by its statistical properties and traded just like a yield curve position. And if mean reversion occurs before default, it is unlikely that this abstraction will cause any problems. However, in the event of a default, the abstract treatment of CDS can no longer be maintained; when faced with the physical delivery of a bond, at the latest, the relationship of a CDS to the bond market can no longer be ignored.

Accordingly, we shall begin our treatment of CDS on an abstract basis, using statistical methods to derive trading strategies within the CDS market. Then, we shall analyze the way those strategies are likely to fare in the event of a default and restrict our positions to those that can be expected to perform well in the event of no default (due to their statistical properties) and to be unaffected by potential problems in case of a default (e.g. by not being short the DO).

A PCA on the CDS Curve

Figure 15.1, Figure 15.2 and Figure 15.3 depict the results of a PCA of the Italian CDS curve (2Y, 5Y, and 10Y USD-denominated CDS quotes, weekly level data since January 2006).

It turns out that the first factor explains 99.5% of the overall variation across the CDS curve. This is a typical result for a PCA run on CDS curves (same issuer, different maturities) and indicates that CDS curves exhibit basically a single-factor structure. It means that the whole CDS curve contains in essence just one piece of information (factor 1, the overall CDS level), and that given one maturity on the CDS curve the whole maturity spectrum can be reconstructed with high accuracy (by the sensitivities of the first eigenvector). This statistical property is in line with anecdotal evidence about the pricing of CDS traders. They tend to focus on the most liquid maturity (usually 5Y) and to adjust their quotes for other maturities as a linear function of the moves in the most liquid one.

Like the example of Italy above, CDS curves typically display a single-factor structure, which is indicative of a market in an early stage of development.[7] The theoretical conclusion is that the credit risk element in bond yields cannot explain the three-factor structure observed in bond yield curves.

FIGURE 15.1 Scaled eigenvalues of a PCA on the Italian CDS curve.

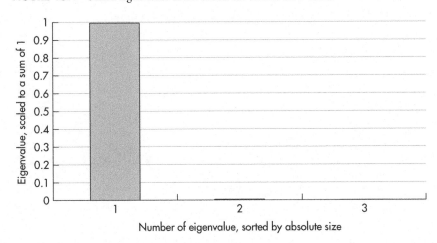

Sources: data – Authors, Bloomberg; chart – Authors.
Data period: 1 Jan 2006 to 26 Aug 2012, weekly data.

---

[7] See Chapter 3 for more details on PCA.

FIGURE 15.2 First three eigenvectors of a PCA on the Italian CDS curve.

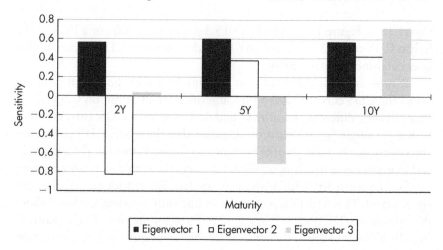

Sources: data – Authors, Bloomberg; chart – Authors.
Data period: 1 Jan 2006 to 26 Aug 2012, weekly data.

FIGURE 15.3 First three factors of a PCA on the Italian CDS curve.

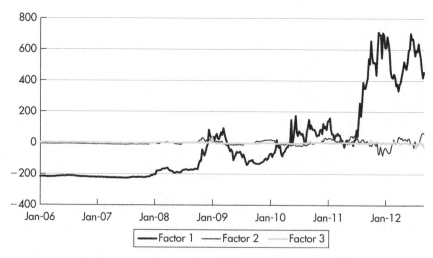

Sources: data – Authors, Bloomberg; chart – Authors.
Data period: 1 Jan 2006 to 26 Aug 2012, weekly data.

Thus, the three-factor structure of bond yield curves must arise from the risk-free yield curve (e.g. from inflation expectations) rather than from the default risk element.

The practical consequence for trading the CDS curve is that there is little scope for relative value trades across CDS curves. For example, a 5Y-10Y CDS curve trade *unaffected* by directional impacts on the CDS curve (i.e. a position on factor 2) faces the problem of a low range of factor 2 (since 99.5% of the variance across the CDS curve is already explained by directional impacts), which means that the potential profit from relative value trades on the CDS curve is usually too small to cover the relatively high bid–offer spreads. Hence, relative value considerations can only play a role in selecting the best maturities for expressing directional views on the CDS curve. In the example above, an investor who wants to position for a decrease of the Italian CDS in general (factor 1 decreasing) can enhance his profit by expressing his view through selling 5Y or 10Y rather than 2Y Italian CDS (given the shape of the second eigenvector and the fact that factor 2 is positive).

While a single-factor structure for the CDS curve as in the example above is typical, there are some exceptions when more than just one point on the CDS curve is actively and independently traded. In these instances, one can observe a richer factor structure and deploy the entire arsenal of statistical yield curve analysis outlined in Chapter 2 and Chapter 3 to the CDS curve as well.

Among relative value traders focusing on the CDS, it is common to strip out the implied default probabilities from CDS curves and scan the result for anomalies, in particular for negative implied default probabilities. While there is nothing wrong with this approach, we recommend complementing it with the additional perspective from a statistical analysis along the lines above.

A PCA on the EUR Sovereign CDS Universe

While CDS curves on different maturities of the same issuer usually display single-factor structures, a set of CDS of different issuers, with the same maturities, can exhibit a richer factor structure and thus allow a wider variety of trades, in particular also relative value trades, which are hedged against factor 1 (i.e. the overall level of CDS quotes) and exploit meaningful higher factors. A natural application for a PCA on CDS of the same maturity (here 5Y) covering different sovereign issuers is an analysis of the euro universe, with the results being shown in Figure 15.4 and Figure 15.5.

FIGURE 15.4   Scaled eigenvalues of a PCA on CDS quotes for EUR sovereigns.

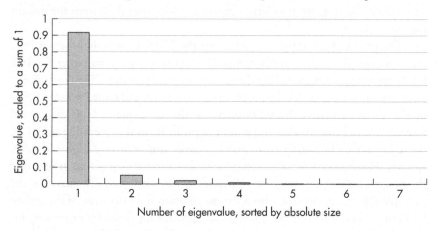

Sources: data – Bloomberg; chart – Authors.
Data period: 4 Mar 2009 to 26 Sep 2012, weekly data.

FIGURE 15.5   First three eigenvectors of a PCA on CDS quotes for EUR sovereigns.

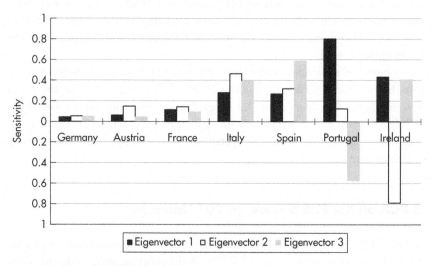

Sources: data – Bloomberg; chart – Authors.
Data period: 4 Mar 2009 to 26 Sep 2012, weekly data.

It turns out that the first factor, explaining 92% of overall variation in the EUR sovereign CDS market, represents the overall level of CDS in the Eurozone. Thus, factor 1 can serve as a measure of the market's perception of sovereign credit risk in the Eurozone in general. The sensitivities to factor 1, given by the first eigenvector, show the extent to which a specific country is affected by a general worsening (or improvement) of the euro crisis. The qualitative results are unsurprising, with Germany being less affected than Austria, Austria less than France etc. Figure 15.5 offers the additional insight into the quantitative relationships. An overall worsening of the crisis that leads to a 10 bp (basis point) widening of German CDS usually leads to a 26 bp widening of French CDS, a 64 bp widening of Italian CDS and so on, with the relationships being given by the quotients of the sensitivities to the first factor. It is interesting to note that the inclusion of non-European countries in the PCA does not change the results significantly; in particular, no "euro-block" is evident (i.e. there is no eigenvector grouping together all euro countries through positive sensitivities versus all non-euro countries through negative sensitivities). Thus, euro sovereigns seem to be priced in the CDS market as individual countries, not as part of a euro-block.

The higher eigenvectors have positive entries for all countries except one. Thus factors 2 and 3 are country-specific factors, measuring the differentiation of a particular country's CDS versus the overall CDS level given by factor 1. As it happens, a country has a specific factor (with some meaningful eigenvalue), if and only if it is a bailout country (Portugal and Ireland). Hence, the PCA decomposes the EUR sovereign CDS market into its general level, subject to the overall worsening and improvement of the crisis (factor 1), and into the pricing action subject to the bailouts of specific countries (factors 2 and 3). Using this framework, a particular move in the CDS market can thus be attributed to the different pricing mechanisms as expressed by the eigenvectors. For example, a narrowing of Irish CDS quotes can be decomposed into the part due to a general improvement of the euro crisis (factor 1) and into the part due to Ireland-specific developments (factor 2).

While this is a reasonable result, it also means that "pure" relative value trading on the whole EUR CDS universe is hardly possible. Factor 1 represents the overall crisis and factors 2 and 3 country-specific developments, both of which are highly influenced by political decisions. For example, European Central Bank support drives factor 1 lower, while bailout programs in Ireland cause factor 2 to increase, and civil unrest in Portugal results in a drop of factor 3. If the analyst has a view on political developments, the PCA can guide toward the best expression: 1-factor residuals show the best country with which to express a general expectation about the euro crisis worsening or improving. And the PCA hedge ratios allow expressing a view on country-specific developments cleanly, isolating a trade on factor 2 or 3 (e.g. a view that Ireland will improve *relative* to other EUR sovereigns) from the overall level of the euro crisis (factor 1).

If the analyst has no political view and is looking for "pure" relative value trading opportunities, he should exclude the bailout countries from the PCA input data. This allows factors 2 and 3 to reveal the relative value mechanisms across the EUR sovereign CDS market, irrespective of the political developments in a bailout country. Figure 15.6 and Figure 15.7 show the results of a PCA on the EUR sovereign CDS market, which has been restricted to the core countries Germany, France, the Netherlands, and Austria.

FIGURE 15.6   Scaled eigenvalues of a PCA on CDS quotes for core EUR sovereigns.

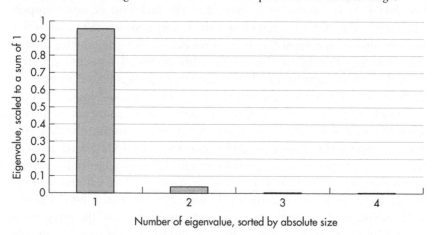

Sources: data – Bloomberg; chart – Authors.
Data period: 6 May 2009 to 26 Sep 2012, weekly data.

FIGURE 15.7   First three eigenvectors of a PCA on CDS quotes for core EUR sovereigns.

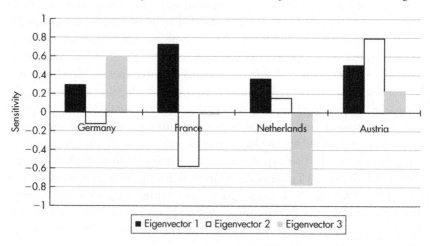

Sources: data – Bloomberg; chart – Authors.
Data period: 6 May 2009 to 26 Sep 2012, weekly data.

Like the PCA of the whole EUR sovereign CDS universe, the first factor represents the overall CDS level, producing a fever chart for the EUR crisis (Figure 15.8). Also, the relative sensitivity of individual countries as given by the first eigenvector is very similar to the first PCA. Unlike the first PCA, however, there are no country-specific factors anymore. Rather, factor 2 groups together Germany and France (negative sensitivities) and the Netherlands and Austria (positive sensitivities) and can thus be interpreted as "big versus small core country" factor. The scaled eigenvalues (Figure 15.6) suggest that the differentiation between big and small countries is in fact the only powerful mechanism (besides the overall CDS level represented by factor 1) in the core CDS market. And since the size of a country is independent of political influence, factor 2 of the core PCA can be considered a basis for "pure" relative value trades. This is further supported by the high speed of mean reversion of factor 2 (Figure 15.8). The differentiation between big and small core countries appears to be like statistical noise – unlike the differentiation of bailout versus non-bailout countries, which is subject to long-term (slow speed of mean reversion) political (little value of statistical models) decisions.

Thus, trades on factor 2 of the core PCA can be justifiably treated as "pure" relative value positions, exploiting the statistical properties like mean reversion and being hedged (through PCA hedge ratios) against factor 1 (i.e.

FIGURE 15.8   First three factors of a PCA on CDS quotes for core EUR sovereigns.

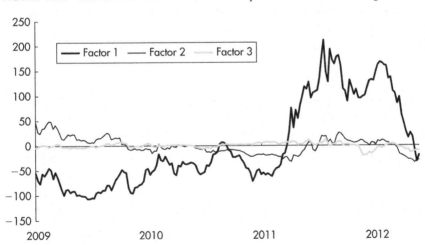

Sources: data – Bloomberg; chart – Authors.
Data period: 6 May 2009 to 26 Sep 2012, weekly data.

politically driven developments of the euro crisis and their impact on the CDS market). With factor 2 being currently considerably away from its mean, big core countries have CDS spreads that appear too high relative to small core countries. Figure 15.9 suggests that selling French versus buying Austrian CDS offers a 42 bp profit potential. The hedge ratio is given by the first eigenvector (buy 0.7 Austrian CDS for every French CDS sold) and should ensure that the performance of the trade is independent from political developments and their impact on the CDS market in general, which have caused the wild swings of factor 1 in Figure 15.8.

Of course, a risk to the position is that France drops out of the group of core countries and becomes a bailout country (with a country-specific factor like Ireland in the first PCA). However, given the high speed of mean reversion of factor 2, the trade is likely to perform before slow-moving macroeconomic events cause the market to reassess the status of France in the core group. Also, an investor concerned about France could still exploit the deviation of factor 2 from its mean by selling German or Dutch versus Austrian CDS, for an expected profit of 23 or 29 bp.

While a statistical analysis like the PCA above can provide interesting insights into the structure of CDS markets and lead to their exploitation through profitable relative value trades, we need to keep in mind that we are operating in an abstract world, assumed to be free from potential pitfalls. At the end of this chapter we shall describe ways to address these issues.

FIGURE 15.9   Current 1-factor residuals of a PCA on CDS quotes for core EUR sovereigns.

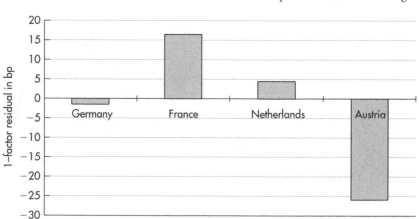

Sources: data – Bloomberg; chart – Authors.
Data period: 6 May 2009 to 26 Sep 2012, weekly data; "current" as of 26 Sep 2012.

Other applications worth investigating along the same lines include the CDS quotes of a set of corporations of the same sector, or of the same country, or over different sectors, or over different countries.

Overall, we consider the CDS market as an excellent field to apply PCA, since:

- PCA can structure the information from a multitude of different bond issuers (different country, different rating, different sector) in the form of a few relevant factors, at the same time revealing significant interpretations.
- PCA thereby gives the basis for relative value trades within the credit universe, that is for exploiting mismatches between different issuers while being hedged against overall moves in the CDS market.

A PCA on CDS-Adjusted Bond Yields

Subtracting the CDS quotes from bond yields (what we shall also call CDS-adjusted bond yields) gives a proxy for the risk-free yield curve. The bond yield can be considered a combination of the risk-free yield plus information about the market's assessment of its credit risk. Thus, subtracting the CDS quotes from the bond yield can be considered an expression of the risk-free yield level.[8]

The theoretical benefit of this exercise is that we become able to analyze the factor structure of risk-free yield curves. In addition, we shall find that the statistical properties of risk-free yield curves are superior to those of unadjusted yield curves. In particular, problems like correlation between factors of a PCA during subperiods tend to be much less pronounced when using CDS-adjusted yield levels as input data.

On the practical side, analyzing the risk-free yield curve (i.e. the difference between the yield and CDS curve) gives insights into the pricing mechanisms of the bond yield curve *relative* to the CDS curve. These insights can then be translated into relative value positions on the yield versus CDS curve, for example a steepening position on the JGB curve *relative* to the Japan CDS curve. What has been said above about applying PCA analysis to the CDS market is true for applications of PCA to CDS-adjusted bond yield curves as well: being among the first to gain insights into new types of relative

---

[8] More precisely, it is the risk-free yield level *in combination with* information about the expected repo value of the bond, the delivery option of the CDS, etc. Hence, these statements need to be understood in broad conceptual terms, not as an exact trading strategy.

value relationships, as in the shape of the bond yield curve *relative to* the CDS curve, suggests high returns from trading strategies based on these insights.

Figure 15.10, Figure 15.11, and Figure 15.12 display the results of a PCA on the CDS-adjusted BTP (Italian government bond) yield curve in comparison with the PCA on the unadjusted bond yield curve. Note that the data input starts in 2006, that is it covers both a period when CDS were close to zero and exhibited virtually no volatility (see Figure 15.3) and a period when CDS quotes became a major driving force of bond yields. These results are typical and appear in a similar form in the US Treasury and JGB markets (and hence the outcome is not limited to Eurozone sovereigns), though the quantitative impact of the adjustment is sometimes less than in the case of Italy.

Starting the discussion of the results from the theoretical side, the data period covers the pre-crisis situation (2006, 2007), when credit considerations had a negligible impact on BTP yields. Actually, before the crisis, market participants usually considered these government bonds as risk-free and thus there was little difference between the two PCAs until 2008. (See Figure 15.11.) Starting in 2008, however, this assumption was revised and credit quality became a major driving force of government bond yields. Consequently, the two PCAs show a distinctly different behavior from 2008 onwards. (See Figure 15.11 and Figure 15.12.)

Moreover, the PCA of CDS-adjusted bond yields always uses default-free data, both before and after the credit crisis started. On the other hand,

FIGURE 15.10 Scaled eigenvalues of a PCA on the CDS-adjusted BTP yield curve in comparison with those of a PCA on the BTP yield curve.

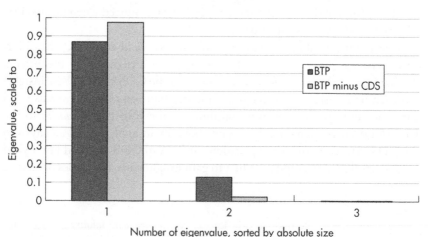

Sources: data – Authors, Bloomberg; chart – Authors.
Data period: 1 Jan 2006 to 26 Aug 2012, weekly data.

FIGURE 15.11 First factor of a PCA on the CDS-adjusted BTP yield curve in comparison with the first factor of a PCA on the BTP yield curve.

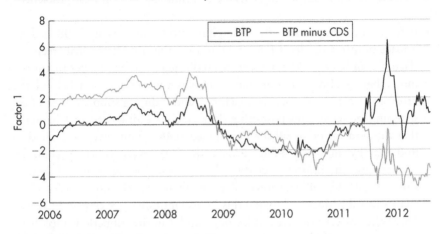

Sources: data – Authors, Bloomberg; chart – Authors.
Data period: 1 Jan 2006 to 26 Aug 2012, weekly data.

FIGURE 15.12 Second factor of a PCA on the CDS-adjusted BTP yield curve in comparison with the second factor of a PCA on the BTP yield curve.

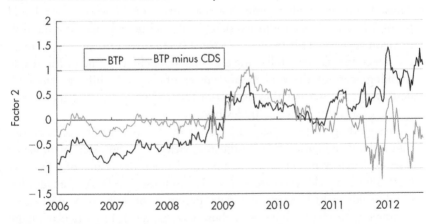

Sources: data – Authors, Bloomberg; chart – Authors.
Data period: 1 Jan 2006 to 26 Aug 2012, weekly data.

the benefit of excluding impacts from credit on the bond yield curve by subtracting CDS levels could introduce statistical noise if the CDS quotes were erratic. By contrast, the PCA of unadjusted bond yields covers both a period when government bonds were considered default-free and a period when credit concerns drove most of the price action along the bond yield curve.

This caused a break in the statistical properties of the bond yield curve when the credit crisis started, which is visible in a number of statistical problems.

• Perhaps most important, the emerging credit concerns in 2008 had an impact both on the level (factor 1) and on the non-directional steepness (factor 2) of bond yield curves, since credit quality affects longer maturities more than it affects shorter ones.[9] This is the main reason behind the problem of correlation between factors 1 and 2 during subperiods of PCAs spanning pre-crisis and post-crisis data. We have discussed in Chapter 3 that this is a major pitfall for PCA-based trades. Thus, we are excited to find that by adjusting bond yields with CDS levels we can exclude by construction the impact of credit on every factor of the PCA and thereby also get rid of a major source of problematic correlation between PCA factors in subperiods.[10] Proving this important point, we display in Figure 15.13 the correlation between factors 1 and 2 in the subperiod since 2010 of a PCA using BTP yields and of a PCA using CDS-adjusted BTP yields since 2006 as input. We observe that the problematic correlation between factors 1 and 2 of a PCA using BTP yields (Figure 15.13, top graph; compare also with Figure 3.23) is largely absent in a PCA using CDS-adjusted BTP yields (Figure 15.13, bottom graph).

• Thus, a shift in credit regime causes a correlation between factor 1 and factor 2 in a PCA of unadjusted data (in the subperiod following the shift in credit regime). This results in factor 2 being driven in large measure by the directional factor 1 following a change in credit assessment. Intuitively speaking, part of the explanatory power of factor 1 shifts to factor 2, destroying its interpretation as non-directional steepness and the performance of any relative value trades based on it.

• Correspondingly, the explanatory power of the first factor decreases significantly. (See Figure 15.10.) Adjusting yield levels, however, maintains a high explanatory power of the first factor. In fact, the results of a PCA on CDS-adjusted yield levels are very similar to those of a PCA of unadjusted bond yields, which uses only data pre-crisis or only data post-crisis. (Compare the charts above with those in Chapter 3, in particular Figure 15.10 with Figure 3.24.) In a manner of speaking, CDS adjustment

---

[9] This statement can be backed up with ratings transition matrices, which show that the yearly default probability increases with the length of exposure – unless the credit quality is very bad at the beginning, which was not the case for the sovereign examples used here.

[10] Of course, there can still be correlation between factors in subperiods for other reasons and we advise to check for it also when running a PCA on CDS-adjusted yields.

FIGURE 15.13 Correlation between factors 1 and 2 in the subperiod since 2010 of a PCA using BTP yields and of a PCA using CDS-adjusted BTP yields.

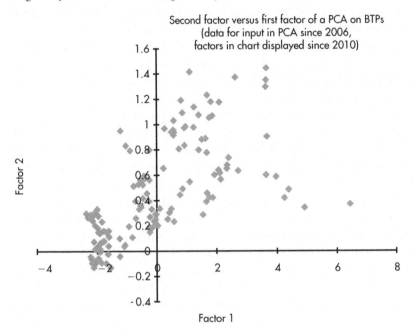

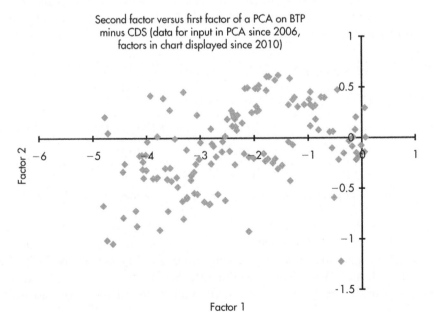

Sources: data – Authors, Bloomberg; chart – Authors.
Data period: 3 Jan 2010 to 26 Aug 2012, weekly data.

maintains the usual three-factor structure of bond yield curves *independent of credit impacts.* While we have seen above that the credit component does nothing to *explain* the three-factor structure of bond yield curves, adjusting for it can *maintain* the normal mechanisms of yield curves also in times of major shifts in the assessment of the credit quality of government bonds. The first factor loading of the CDS curve actually seems to have precisely the shape needed to correct the three factor loadings of the bond curve, so that they remain stable in changing credit regimes.

This is a crucial condition to conduct analysis in times of shifting credit assessments – and to construct trades which are hedged against their impacts on the bond yield curve. Imagine we had put on a 2Y-10Y BTP curve trade based on pre-crisis PCA hedge ratios (without any credit impact in the data). Our actual P&L would be a function of an unforeseen impact of credit quality on both the hedge ratios and the yield curve dynamics.

- Likewise, the explanatory power of the first factor of a PCA on unadjusted data not only decreases generally in times of a shift in credit quality but its impact also becomes unevenly distributed over the yield curve. The explanation can again be found in the correlation between factors 1 and 2 following a shift in credit regimes. Now factor 2 contains part of factor 1, but the second eigenvector differentiates across the yield curve, causing a decrease of the explanatory power of factor 1 in a specific sector of the curve. This effect is summarized in Table 15.1, which compares the correlation of factor 1 of an unadjusted and a CDS-adjusted PCA to different points on the yield curve.

TABLE 15.1 Correlation between Different Points on the Yield Curve and the First Factor of a PCA on BTP Yields and a PCA on CDS-Adjusted BTP Yields

	BTP	BTP minus CDS
2Y	0.95	0.99
5Y	0.98	1.00
10Y	0.79	0.96

It turns out that the first factor of a PCA on unadjusted data has only limited explanatory power at the long end of the BTP curve. The PCA of CDS-adjusted data returns significantly better results; the explanatory power of the first factor over the BTP minus CDS curve over the last five turbulent years is comparable with a traditional PCA before the crisis and as evenly distributed over the yield curve.

- Factor 2 exhibits a significantly higher speed of mean reversion in the CDS-adjusted PCA. Intuitively, this can be understood by the fact that in the case of the PCA on unadjusted data some of the directional moves (with low speed of mean reversion) usually explained by factor 1 become part of factor 2 due to the shift in credit regimes. By contrast, factor 2 of the CDS-adjusted PCA does not need to bear any elements of factor 1 (reflected in a lower-scaled second eigenvalue in Figure 15.10) and shows therefore a speed of mean reversion typical for a factor 2 of bond yield curves in the absence of credit regime shifts (compare, for example, Figure 15.12 with Figure 3.13).
- While CDS moves may sometimes on the surface appear to be irrational or erratic, the good PCA results suggest that they follow a rather stable, predictable pattern. This alleviates our concern regarding the use of CDS-adjusted data as inputs into statistical models.
- Bond yields usually have a lower boundary at 0%. Thus, when (short end) yields approach 0%, their volatility tends to decrease, leading to unstable eigenvectors at the short end (see Figure 3.24). This is a problem that can affect hedge ratios, for example. On the other hand, bond yields minus CDS are not bounded by zero and can therefore exhibit a higher volatility also in low-yield environments. This leads to a better stability of eigenvectors at the short end.

Turning from the theoretical benefits of adjusting bond yields with CDS levels to their practical exploitation, we observe that factor 2 of a PCA of CDS-adjusted BTP yields is away from its mean (Figure 15.14). This means that the BTP yield curve is too flat relative to the Italian CDS curve. In other words, steepening positions of the CDS-adjusted BTP yield curve (buying short end BTPs and short maturity Italy CDS versus selling long end BTPs and long maturity Italy CDS) are attractive. As always, one can choose the statistically most attractive expression for steepening positions on the BTP relative to the CDS curve by looking at the one-factor residuals.

One might therefore consider a 2Y-5Y steepener as a candidate for a trade idea. This would involve selling 5Y BTPs and 5Y CDS versus buying 2Y BTPs and 2Y CDS, with the hedge ratios being given by the first-factor sensitivities (resulting in a ratio of roughly 5:3 for the 2Y:5Y instruments).

Note that this trading opportunity does not show up in a PCA of the unadjusted BTP curve. Hence, it arises from the *relationship* between the

FIGURE 15.14 One-factor residuals of the PCA on CDS-adjusted BTP yields.

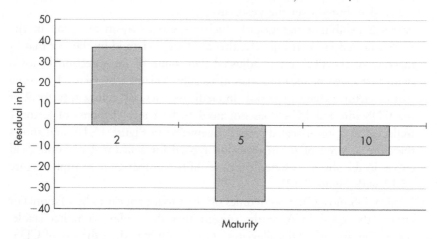

Sources: data – Authors, Bloomberg; chart – Authors.
Data period: 1 Jan 2006 to 26 Aug 2012,[11] weekly data; "current" as of 26 Aug 2012.

yield curve and the CDS curve, which is only visible through the CDS-adjusted PCA. The 2Y-5Y BTP curve is too flat *relative to the CDS curve*. The fact that few analysts consider the steepness of bond yield curves in relation to the CDS curve may help explain the unusually large profit potential of 73 bp for a relative value position on the yield curve.

Pitfalls

We can thus use the CDS to make statistical models work also in an environment of unstable credit risk. On the other hand, this introduces the particular features of the CDS, and we recommend checking any trading strategy derived by statistical models on the CDS market for the following problems:

- FX component. If the CDS is denominated in a different currency than the government bond it protects, the holder of a long CDS position profits from the currency of the defaulting government weakening in case of

---

[11] Note that the result is not materially affected by using shorter data periods (e.g. only post-crisis data). This is in line with the discussion above and a contrast to a PCA on unadjusted BTP yields.

default (and vice versa). For example, in the 2Y-5Y steepening trade discussed above, the notional weights (long 5:short 3) give us a net long position in the Italian CDS, thus in that case we seem to be on the profitable side of the FX exposure in case of default. Had the trading strategy resulted in a net short position of the CDS, on the other hand, we might have chosen to assess the profit potential and the expected holding horizon of the trade versus different estimates for the unquantifiable potential loss from the EUR weakening in case of an Italian default.

- Delivery option. Similarly, the net long or short position in the CDS decides about whether we are net long or short the DO in case of a default. Again, in our example we are net long the CDS, thus also the DO, and have passed this check. As a general rule, being net long the CDS usually results in being on the safe side of potential issues surfacing in case of a default.
- Repo. What is the expected value of the bonds involved in the repo market? When approaching default, repo markets may well become dysfunctional, driving the actual costs away from the estimation. How would this affect the overall position?
- In case of euro sovereign bonds being involved, the redenomination risk. While the CDS is and remains USD-denominated, BTPs might be repaid in lira. Thus, we face the problem that by construction of the bond versus CDS curve trades, if we are net long the CDS (which is the "safe side" concerning the FX component and DO), we are also net long the lira in case of BTP redenomination (without default). In the example above, if Italy does not default but redenominates in lira, the steepener with a notional ratio of long 5:short 3 is exposed to a lira weakening. An investor assigning a significant probability to this risk may therefore want to refrain from applying these trading strategies to euro sovereign bond curves. For example, he could also enter a 2Y-10Y flattener on the CDS-adjusted JGB yield curve for an expected profit of 47 bp and then assess whether the exclusion of redenomination risk was worth the loss of a 26 bp profit potential (and the bigger distance between the two points on the yield curve).

As a general note, given the high speed of mean reversion for most (good) relative value trades, chances are high that in reality they will not be subjected to these problems. In other words, if the expected holding horizon of a statistical trade involving the CDS market is shorter than the time period over which issues arising from default can reasonably be expected to occur, then one can justify ignoring the potential problems and analytically treating trades involving CDS as if those problems did not exist. As mentioned in Chapter 1, one then has a useful but not necessarily theoretically rigorous statistical model for CDS trades. Still, we would like trades involving CDS to work also in the event of default and therefore advise checking for the above points, even when a high speed of mean reversion makes it unlikely that a real default will test our performance in this task.

Conclusion

- CDS can be priced either against other CDS through a statistical model or against bonds through a relative value model, covered in the next chapter.
- The CDS curve over different maturities often exhibits a single-factor structure and thus permits little room for relative value trades.
- A PCA of the CDS of different issuers reveals the pricing mechanisms and potentially attractive relative value trading opportunities. For example, it segments the CDS of euro sovereigns into bailout and no-bailout countries, and the core group according to the size of the bond markets.
- A PCA of CDS-adjusted yield curves can alleviate some of the statistical deficiencies of a PCA of unadjusted yield curves. Moreover, at times it detects significant relative value opportunities between the shape of the yield curve and the shape of the CDS curve.
- Since the DO and FX component of a CDS are unquantifiable and therefore unhedgeable, every trading position involving the CDS should be assessed from the viewpoint of its performance in the event of default for a set of different values for the DO and the FX component.

CHAPTER 16

USD Asset Swap Spreads versus Credit Default Swaps

Introduction

While in Chapter 15 we ventured into the rather new territory of statistical CDS analysis, this chapter deals with the widely discussed fundamental link between the CDS and the bond it covers. At the beginning we shall briefly and intuitively deduct the common no-arbitrage relationship USD ASW = CDS. Since a comprehensive description of that relationship has been given already by several authors, we shall focus on the connection of the no-arbitrage condition to other topics of our book.

A principal problem of the no-arbitrage relationship USD ASW = CDS is that it assumes both sides of the equation to be *pure* reflections only of the credit risk. As we have shown in Chapter 15, both sides are in fact imperfect measures of credit risk. As a result, we investigate the way in which the conclusions from Chapter 6 can be used to adjust this equation so that it can be applied to the actual instruments trading in the market. This additional perspective from our funding spread analysis suggests that the no-arbitrage equality should actually be a no-arbitrage *inequality*: USD ASW ≤ CDS under some simplifying assumptions.

Then, we apply the no-arbitrage inequality to three topics:

- In the absence of a no-arbitrage equality, relative value positions between the CDS and USD ASW are only advisable when the USD ASW exceeds the CDS. We shall discuss the consequences for relative value trades between the two markets.

- Having obtained the no-arbitrage inequality from our funding analysis, we can integrate it into the swap spread model based on that funding analysis. In particular, we discuss in this chapter the way the link between the USD ASW of risky bonds and the CDS can have an impact on the local ASW. This fills in the last remaining puzzle piece in our treatment of swap spreads.

- By integrating funding considerations in the relationship between ASW and CDS, we can build an EMU model, which detects relative value opportunities among EMU sovereigns and quantifies the redenomination (EMU exit) probabilities.

General Concept of No-Arbitrage Models

In Chapter 14, we described the combination of asset and basis swaps[1] conceptually as a reduction of every bond to a spread over USD LIBOR. Credit default swaps (CDS) follow precisely the same concept. Every bond globally is evaluated by a CDS in the form of a spread (the CDS premium) over USD LIBOR.[2] Moreover, the source of that spread is in both cases to a large extent driven by the credit quality of the bond. The perception of poor credit quality results in a large USD ASW and in a large CDS.

Let us now assume that both the USD ASW of a bond and its CDS are driven by the credit quality of the bond not only *to a large extent* but *exclusively*. Of course, this is an artificial assumption, which allows us to outline the general concept of no-arbitrage models for CDS pricing in clean and easy terms. After the assumption has fulfilled this function, we shall describe the way the general concept needs to be modified in order to work in the real world, where both the USD ASW and the CDS provide the information about credit quality in different forms, overlying that information with other elements.

Under that assumption, *the combination of asset and basis swaps can be considered as a synthetic short position in a CDS on the bond issuer.*

---

[1] In this chapter, the term "basis swap" (BSW) refers to the cross-currency basis swap (CCBS), adjusted for the intra-currency basis swap (ICBS) where necessary.

[2] The choice of LIBOR as a basis for comparison is arbitrary. See below for a more detailed discussion.

- The risk in the combination asset&basis swap[3] as well as in a short CDS is the default of the bond issuer.
- For taking that risk, an investor is compensated with a spread above USD LIBOR, in case of asset&basis swaps with the USD swap spread of the bond, and in case of a short CDS with the default swap premium.

Since both the USD ASW of a bond and the CDS of the issuer of that bond reflect the credit risk in terms of a spread versus USD LIBOR, it is natural to compare the two. This comparison allows detection of relative value opportunities between the two markets, i.e. the investigation whether the credit risk is reflected in the bond and CDS markets *relative to each other* in a consistent way. If it is not, trades between the USD ASW and the CDS can exploit the different assessment of the same credit risk in both markets, without being exposed to the level of credit risk or to a default.

If the USD swap spread of a JGB was higher than its CDS, we could asset&basis swap the JGB and buy default protection on Japan, realizing the difference between the two spreads versus USD LIBOR, the USD ASW of the JGB minus the CDS, as risk-free arbitrage[4] profit: until a default occurs (and until the maturity of the bond if no default occurs), we obtain the difference as profit. And in a default, the CDS payment covers our losses from the bond.[5]

Put otherwise, by combining the three swaps (asset, basis, and default)[6], we have step by step reduced the risks involved into a bond investment, as illustrated in Table 16.1.

As the combination of all swaps results in a risk-free position, there should be no compensation for taking that position. Thus, as ASW&BSW&DSW = 0, the cash flow from asset&basis swapping a bond (its USD swap spread) should compensate for its default protection (i.e. the USD ASW should equal the CDS). This is an alternative way to reach the conclusion from above, that there is an arbitrage relationship between asset&basis swapped bonds and CDS. Also note that while analyzing the

---

[3] By the symbol "ASW&BSW", we refer both to the action of asset and basis swapping a bond and to its result (i.e. the USD swap spread of that bond). Note that while the actions and the symbol "&" are additive, the USD swap spread is given by the difference (ASW-BSW)/CF.

[4] This arbitrage requires the artificial assumption made above. Later, we will discuss how to apply that arbitrage concept also in the real market, where the assumption does not hold, which may require us to drop the term "risk-free arbitrage" in its strict sense.

[5] Issues like the remaining ASW and BSW after default will be considered later.

[6] In order to express the uniformity of the swaps involved symbolically, we refer to the CDS also as "DSW".

TABLE 16.1   Risk Exposure of a Bond Together with Different Combinations of Swaps

Position	Exposed to		
	Yield risk[7]	FX risk	Default risk
Bond	Yes	Yes	Yes
Bond&ASW	No	Yes	Yes
Bond&ASW&BSW	No	No	Yes
Bond&ASW&BSW&DSW	No	No	No

ASW, the BSW, and the CDS in isolation, there are many driving factors and complex relationships between them to consider, when putting them all together, one arrives at a simple arbitrage relationship that should hold independently of the specific issues and flows that drive the BSW.

Thus, we have intuitively derived the equation USD ASW = CDS of the no-arbitrage models for CDS pricing and trading (with the difference between CDS and USD ASW being called "basis"). In reality, however, this framework is just the starting point for further and deeper analysis. Since the derivation of the equation USD ASW = CDS required us to artificially exclude all other elements except credit information from both USD ASW and CDS, we need to investigate the way those other elements (which are a natural part of the actual market instruments) impact the "arbitrage relationship" USD ASW = CDS. On the USD ASW side of the investigation, we can apply the results from the funding discussion in Chapter 6. The aim is to find an expression of the general concept that is valid also in the actual market and to avoid the pitfalls of an overly naive approach (e.g. the dangers of reverse asset&basis swapping bonds and selling CDS protection when the USD ASW is slightly below the CDS).

Credit Information in the CDS

We have shown in Chapter 15 that the CDS combines information about the credit risk of the issuer with information about the value of the delivery option (DO). And for cases in which the settlement currency (which we also refer to as the "denomination") of the CDS is different from the

---

[7] This table should be understood in broad conceptual terms. In particular, as the duration of an asset-swapped bond position is very low, we enter "No" in the yield risk column, even though strictly speaking it has some P&L, depending on the level of short rates.

FIGURE 16.1 Cash flows in an investment into a 5Y asset&basis swapped and default protected JGB, with default after three years.

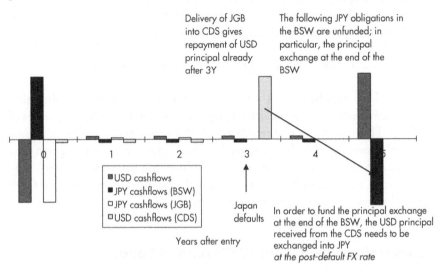

Delivery of JGB into CDS gives repayment of USD principal already after 3Y

The following JPY obligations in the BSW are unfunded; in particular, the principal exchange at the end of the BSW

■ USD cashflows
■ JPY cashflows (BSW)
□ JPY cashflows (JGB)
□ USD cashflows (CDS)

Japan defaults

Years after entry

In order to fund the principal exchange at the end of the BSW, the USD principal received from the CDS needs to be exchanged into JPY *at the post-default FX rate*

Source: Authors.

denomination of the bond, we've discussed the importance of the FX component (i.e. the overcompensation from receiving USD rather than the weakening currency of a defaulting country).

In order to illustrate the way the FX component affects arbitrage positions between asset&basis swapped bonds and the CDS, imagine we are long a five-year (5Y) asset&basis swapped JGB and a CDS on Japan, and after three years into the trade Japan defaults (Figure 16.1). We can deliver the JGB into the CDS and receive our initially invested USD principal back. However, we still need to serve all cash flows in the outstanding swap agreements. In particular, at maturity of the BSW, we need to pay the JPY principal, which we thought to match with the JGB principal repayment. Since we now lost our JGB (to receive USD ahead of time), we need to replicate the JPY cash flows by exchanging the USD we received from the CDS back into JPY and invest that capital again in JPY in order to generate the JPY cash flows needed to serve the remaining payments in the outstanding ASW and BSW. Thus, entering into an asset&basis swapped JGB and a CDS on Japan includes entering into an *exposure to a JPY weakening conditional on a Japan default.* If the JPY weakens, say from 80 to 160, following default, we can reproduce the JPY cash flows[8]

---

[8] Of course, we face the risk that we cannot generate JPY cash flows at the original yield level. However, the gain from a weakening currency in case of its issuing government defaulting is likely to be much bigger than any potential losses from moves on the yield side.

we need to serve the BSW with just half the USD we received from the CDS payment, keeping the remaining half as extra profit.

The credit information can theoretically be extracted from the actual CDS quotes observed in the market by the equation:

$$CreditInformation(CDS) = CDS - DO - FX\,component$$

We have highlighted in Chapter 15 the major hurdles in obtaining quantitative estimates for the delivery option (DO) and the FX component of a CDS. Thus, getting actual numbers out of this equation remains an elusive goal. However, as both the DO and the FX component are not less than zero (unless one expects the currency of a defaulting country to strengthen), one can obtain the qualitative statement that the credit information in a CDS should never exceed the actual CDS quote.

Credit Information in the (USD) ASW of Bonds

Just as the CDS contains the credit information in combination with other elements, so does the ASW express the credit information about a bond in combination with information about its funding. For example, the fact that Bunds quote at a negative spread to EURIBOR could be due to the better credit of Bunds relative to EURIBOR banks or to the funding advantage of Bunds (allowing to fund at repo rather than at EURIBOR). Actually, both statements are closely related: as outlined in Chapter 6, the repo rate tracks the OIS rate closely.

Hence, most of the funding of a bond (the LIBOR–repo spread) is intrinsically linked to its credit. Imagine that the credit quality of EURIBOR banks worsened relative to the credit quality of Bunds. Then we would expect the EURIBOR–repo spread to increase for credit reasons. But at the same time, the worsening of the credit quality of EURIBOR banks relative to Bunds should also result in a higher cost of equity (CoE) of the EURIBOR banks relative to the yield of Bunds. Thus, we would as well expect the EURIBOR–repo spread to increase for funding reasons, since the higher CoE results in a higher preference for secured lending with a lower capital charge. (See Chapter 6 for a detailed discussion.)

As in this example, we usually observe a strong relationship between the credit and the funding of bonds. The reason is that most of the driving forces of the (fair value) for the LIBOR–repo basis swap of a bond, in particular the ECB haircut, are directly linked to the credit quality of the bond, as discussed in Chapter 6. As a consequence for our current task, the strong link between credit and funding makes a decomposition of the information given by the ASW of a bond into pure credit and funding information difficult. While the example above suggests that credit information is about the same as funding information, we cannot prove that the two correspond exactly to each other. Hence, we cannot exclude the possibility that the worsening credit of EURIBOR banks versus Bunds would result in a credit-driven increase of the EURIBOR–repo spread by 20 bp and that, at the same time, the CoE would increase in such a way that the funding-driven increase of the EURIBOR–repo spread would become 30 bp. In that case, 10 bp of the increase in the EURIBOR–repo spread would be due to funding *unrelated* to credit.

In the absence of a measure for pure credit (and for the CoE), there is no way to quantify credit-driven versus funding-driven moves. The only exception, which is clearly only funding-driven (with no relationship to credit), is the expected specialness premium. The premium of a bond in the repo market, for example due to its chance of becoming cheapest-to-deliver (CTD) in a futures contract, is obviously not connected to its credit quality. Thus, we can decompose the LIBOR–repo basis swap into a LIBOR–GC (general collateral) basis swap and a GC–repo basis swap and summarize the discussion above as follows:

- The LIBOR–GC basis swap is driven both by credit and funding, most of which is closely related. While part of the GC funding might be unrelated to credit, it is impossible to quantify.
- The GC–repo basis swap is driven by funding unrelated to credit. By using historical data (e.g. by analyzing how special benchmarks and CTDs usually become in the repo market) the fair value of the GC–repo basis swap can be quantified. Figure 16.5 provides such an analysis for EMU issuers.

Now we apply this discussion to our task of extracting pure credit information from the ASW quotes observed in the market. For reasons of simplicity, we assume that all bonds trade at par, thereby avoiding the problems of coupon effects in the ASW (and the CDS). Starting with the local ASW (e.g. of JGBs versus JPY LIBOR), the ASW could underestimate the credit risk due to:

- GC funding effects (in local currency) *unrelated* to the credit, which we shall refer to as "net funding";
- the part of the ASW which reflects the GC–repo basis swap (i.e. the expected repo specialness).

Both effects lead to the quoted ASW being below the credit risk information in the ASW. Hence, we need to adjust the local ASW for the parts not related to credit before converting it into USD. The expression:

Local ASW + GC–repo basis swap + Local net funding

represents the ASW of an artificial bond, which always trades at GC (thus excludes repo specialness effects) and whose GC funding fully reflects credit only, and is therefore a clean representation of credit.

Then, applying the conversion into USD terms from Chapter 14, we obtain a USD ASW which only represents credit, that is:

$$\frac{\left(ASW(local) + GCrepoBSW + Netfunding(local) \right) - BSW}{CF}$$

This expression represents the USD ASW adjusted for parts other than credit, that is the compensation for taking the credit risk of investing into the bond *in terms of a spread over USD LIBOR*. In order to get the credit information in terms of a spread over risk-free bonds, assuming GC to be risk-free, we need to add the LIBOR–GC basis swap (with the GC rate now being the GC rate of US Treasuries in USD). However, we face again the issue that part of the GC rate might reflect funding effects unrelated to credit, now on the USD side. And we suggest the same solution of adjusting the LIBOR–GC basis swap for those GC funding effects (in USD), which have nothing to do with the credit difference between USD LIBOR and the GC rate.[9] This leads to the final expression of the credit risk contained in the ASW in USD terms:

$$CreditInformation(ASW) = \frac{\left(ASW(local) + GCrepoBSW + Netfunding(local) \right) - BSW}{CF}$$
$$+ \left(LIBORGCBSW(USD) - Netfunding(USD) \right)$$

Note that for a risk-free US Treasury assumed to be always GC, the credit information given by this equation is zero independent of the level of its ASW.

---

[9] Unlike in local currency, where we deal with a specific bond, there are no repo specialness effects to consider on the USD side.

As in case of the CDS, this equation contains unquantifiable variables (the "net funding" in local currency and USD). However, we are again able to make some qualitative statements:

- The local net funding is not less than zero.
- The GC–repo basis swap is not less than zero.
- The LIBOR–GC basis swap minus the net funding in USD is not less than zero.

Consequently, the credit information in the USD ASW of a bond is never below the actual USD ASW quote.

Figure 16.2 summarizes and connects the arguments of this and the preceding section. It can be seen, how the USD ASW tends to underestimate the credit information, while the CDS tends to overestimate the credit information.[10]

FIGURE 16.2   Schematic relationship of instruments in the no-arbitrage inequality (all on a USD basis).

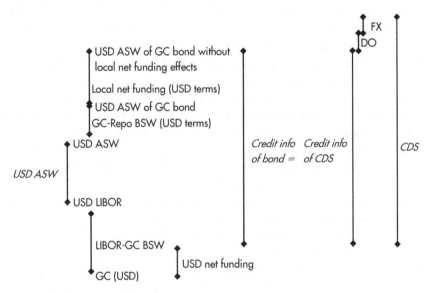

Source: Authors.

---

[10] While the CDS is quoted against LIBOR, this has no influence on its level. That is, a CDS quoted against GC (exchanging GC payments versus GC+CDS payments) would be identical. This is a difference to the USD ASW, which measures the compensation for credit exposure to a bond relative to the credit of USD LIBOR. In Figure 16.2, we can therefore apply the basis for the credit information in the bond (GC, adjusted for net funding) also as basis for the CDS.

The No-Arbitrage Relationship in Practice

The *credit information* in the USD ASW should equal the *credit information* in the CDS. However, as there is a discrepancy between the USD ASW and the credit information in the USD ASW as well as between the CDS and the credit information in the CDS, one cannot translate this statement into the equality USD ASW = CDS.

Rather, combining the conclusions of the preceding two sections, one can derive the following *inequality*:

$$\text{USD ASW} \leq \text{Credit information in USD ASW}$$

$$= \text{Credit information in CDS} \leq \text{CDS.}$$

Thus, USD ASW ≤ CDS.

The replacement of the no-arbitrage equality by a no-arbitrage inequality which works with the actual market instruments has the following consequences:

- Since all unquantifiable elements are bounded by zero and have the same sign in the equations above, we are able to maintain the no-arbitrage relationship between USD ASW and CDS, at least as an inequality.
- If any of the unquantifiable elements has a different sign than the others, the no-arbitrage inequality cannot be maintained. In particular, if one did not assume the currency of a defaulting country would weaken in the event of default, then the FX component in the CDS could become negative and the inequality "Credit information in CDS ≤ CDS" might be violated. Hence by extension the inequality "USD ASW ≤ CDS" would also be violated. Thus, *the precondition for every arbitrage position between USD ASW and CDS is the assumption that the currency of a defaulting country would weaken.* If that assumption cannot be made, one should refrain from any spread trade between USD ASW and CDS.
- The inequality allows arbitrage trades only if the USD ASW exceeds the CDS (i.e. only long asset&basis swapped bonds and long CDS positions).
- Being long an asset&basis swapped bond and long the CDS is also the more attractive side for a number of practical reasons. In particular, in the event that an issuer nears default, repo markets may well cease to function altogether, which could make it simply impracticable to maintain a short position in the reverse asset&basis swapped bond versus a short position in the CDS. Moreover, on this side of the trade we do not need to worry about the bond becoming special in repo, being short a delivery option, or the FX component.

- As Figure 16.2 illustrates, the inequality is rather weak. It is therefore probable that quite a number of violations of the sharp equality "*Credit information* in USD ASW = *Credit information* in CDS" do not show up as violations of the tradable weaker inequality "USD ASW ≤ CDS". As a result, some theoretical arbitrage opportunities cannot be executed in practice.

- One can obtain a somewhat sharper inequality by including a quantification for the GC–repo basis swap. Then, an arbitrage trade is already possible when the USD ASW exceeds the CDS *minus the GC–repo basis swap* (expressed in USD terms). We shall use this in the subsequent construction of an EMU model.

- Our intention was to show the way the incorporation of the additional perspective from our funding spread discussion in Chapter 6 can lead to a no-arbitrage relationship, which works with the actual market instruments. We do not claim to have given a comprehensive discussion of the CDS basis (CDS minus USD ASW), which is extensively covered elsewhere. In particular, we have excluded coupon effects (through our assumption of par bonds) and not even touched on technical issues (such as counterparty risk or liquidity). Thus, while the viewpoints of the funding discussion in Chapter 6 and from the CDS discussion in Chapter 15 combine to suggest that the basis should always be positive, it is possible that there are negative bases due to coupon or technical effects not covered here.

- Given the capital charge for holding bonds, sufficient availability of capital for arbitrage trades is a condition for the arbitrage inequality to be imposed on the market. The general scarcity of capital for arbitrage trades in the aftermath of the banking crisis has resulted in negative CDS bases persisting longer than usual. Thus, the discussion of Chapter 6 leads both to the arbitrage inequality and explains its potential violation in times of scarce capital.

In order to monitor the market for violations of the no-arbitrage inequality, we recommend comparing the two spreads graphically against USD LIBOR, from asset&basis swapped bonds and from CDS for every issuer. This could be done, for example, by adding the CDS (ask) quotes as a line to the USD ASW levels shown as a function of maturity, as in Figure 14.1. Figure 16.3 provides this picture for Japan.

Note how well the no-arbitrage inequality is observed by the market. The USD ASW of JGBs with short time to maturity follow the upper boundary given by the CDS ask level very closely, while JGBs with a longer time to maturity quote significantly below the CDS ask level. This means that there

FIGURE 16.3 USD ASW of JGBs versus the Japanese CDS of the same maturity as the bonds.

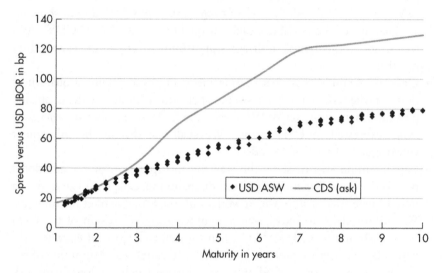

Sources: data – Bloomberg; chart – Authors.
Data period: "Current" market data as of 23 Sep 2012.

are currently no trading opportunities for asset&basis swapped JGBs versus the Japanese CDS.[11]

In our experience, most of the violations of the no-arbitrage inequality occur in practice due to strong volatility in the BSW, which can increase the USD ASW faster than the CDS (and faster than local ASW react). As a case study of the way trading opportunities from violations of the no-arbitrage inequality arise and how quickly they perform, we depict the history of the USD ASW of a 10Y Korean government bond versus the 10Y CDS ask level for Korea in Figure 16.4. Following the Lehman crisis, the KRW ASW of Korean government bonds widened, partly due to a general scarcity of risk capital forcing some investors to sell their bond holdings. At the same time, the KRW BSW became highly negative as Korean banks needed USD funding. On the other hand,

---

[11] Buying 2Y asset&basis swapped JGBs and 2Y CDS on Japan at a basis of zero could be considered as buying the delivery option and the position on JPY weakening in case of Japan defaulting for free and therefore to be a good idea. However, there is no way of quantifying the value of the option bought for free, which could thus be quite low. Also, very short JGBs with time to maturity of less than one year (not shown in the chart) could actually have a USD ASW in excess of the CDS (if it traded for such short maturities.) (See Figure 14.1.) However, there could be special influences from redemptions distorting the ASW level.

FIGURE 16.4 USD ASW of the Korean government bond 5.75% 09/18 versus the 10Y Korean CDS level.

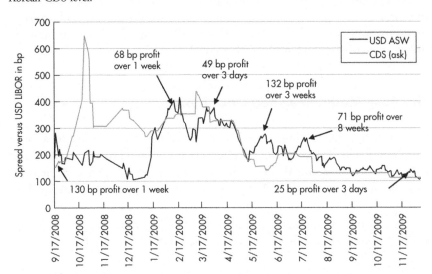

Sources: data – Bloomberg; chart – Authors.
Data period: 17 Sep 2008 to 9 Dec 2009, trading daily data.

while the Korean CDS also widened, it followed a different timing (probably because the credit quality of the Korean government was not directly linked to the trouble in the US banking system). As a result, the USD ASW of Korean government bonds at times greatly exceeded their CDS levels, presenting those investors with risk capital available with arbitrage profits in excess of 100 bp. These precedents illustrate that constant monitoring of USD ASW through charts like Figure 16.3 can be very rewarding.

Figure 16.4 illustrates the frequency and magnitude of these violations of our inequality, as well as the time over which these relative misvaluations have tended to correct. In quiet times, however, these opportunities tend to be much rarer and to offer less profit. The shift to quiet times is visible at the right-hand side of the chart, when the pricing of Korean bonds against USD LIBOR became closely linked to the Korean CDS level again.

Summarizing our experience, in comparison with the abundant relative value discovered by a principal component analysis on the CDS universe in Chapter 15, opportunities when the no-arbitrage inequality is violated arise infrequently. But when they do arise, they have so far never disappointed us. In contrast, bonds whose USD ASW spread is below the CDS are not necessarily candidates for similar trades. This side of the arbitrage would require both a way to quantify the necessary adjustments and an instrument to hedge against currency weakening post default. We have discussed above the difficulties involved. For the same reason, we do not generally recommend spread positions between two USD ASW versus CDS spreads between different maturities[12] or different issuers.[13]

The ASW Model Revisited Once More

Conceptually, the funding spread analysis from Chapter 6 led to a swap spread model in Chapter 8 and Chapter 9 that was then expanded in Chapter 14 to the case of bonds denominated in different currencies. It turned out that the pricing of the USD ASW depends on perceptions of credit quality:

- Low-risk bonds are mainly priced versus US Treasuries (Figure 14.9).
- Risky bonds are mainly priced versus the CDS (Figure 14.14).

In order to be able to finalize the swap spread analysis also for risky bonds, we therefore considered the CDS and the implications of the funding spread analysis from Chapter 6 on the relationship between USD ASW and CDS. Now, we integrate the result of incorporating the funding model from Chapter 6 in the CDS pricing (i.e. the no-arbitrage inequality USD ASW ≤ CDS) back into the swap spread model based on the same funding model and see the way the no-arbitrage inequality can help us better understand the behavior of the USD ASW of risky bonds.

At a very basic level, the mere existence of a relationship between the USD ASW and the CDS of risky bonds explains the correlation observed empirically in Figure 14.14. However, since the relationship is an inequality, its effect is one-sided and therefore depends on the proximity of the USD ASW to the upper boundary CDS.

- In the event that the USD ASW trades close to the CDS level, moves in the "global" variables (i.e. the closely related BSW, USD ASW, and CDS) can have an impact on the pricing of local ASW. For example, as the USD ASW of 2Y JGBs is at the 2Y CDS level of Japan, investors monitoring the

---

[12] For example, a "curve trade" long (asset&basis swapped) 2Y JGB/long 2Y Japan CDS against a short 7Y JGB (reverse asset&basis swapped)/short 7Y Japan CDS position (see Figure 16.3).

[13] For example, a long (asset&basis swapped) JGB/long Japan CDS against a short US Treasury (reverse asset swapped)/short US CDS position (see Figure 14.1).

market through charts like Figure 16.3 would translate a widening of the JPY BSW into demand for asset&basis swapped JGBs. In case of the CDS not moving (i.e. the widening of the BSW being a function of Japanese banks' credit worsening independent of the credit quality of Japan), we would expect the local JPY ASW of JGBs to widen. Thus, if the USD ASW is close to the arbitrage boundary CDS, moves in the global variables can have an impact on the local swap spreads – just as in the case of low-risk bonds. In fact, for risky bonds a stable CDS boundary has the same effect as the pricing of low-risk bonds versus US Treasuries: it can stabilize the USD ASW and transform BSW volatility into local swap spread volatility.

- For cases in which the USD ASW trades considerably below the CDS level, moves in the global variables may well have little impact on the local ASW. For example, with the USD ASW of 10Y JGBs (79 bp) being far below the 10Y CDS of Japan (130 bp), a widening of the JPY BSW could very well lead to just the USD ASW of 10Y JGBs increasing, while the local JPY ASW of 10Y JGBs might not be affected. Thus, *the one-sidedness of the no-arbitrage inequality explains the separation between local ASW and USD ASW observed for risky bonds, even when the CDS is relatively stable* (Figure 14.13).

The no-arbitrage inequality not only helps us to understand the observations from Chapter 14 but can also support the global asset selection process pictured in Figure 14.1 and Figure 14.8.

- For cases in which the USD ASW trades close to the CDS level, one can conclude that the credit risk (as priced in the CDS market) is fully reflected in the USD ASW level. Given the weakness of the inequality, the USD ASW could actually be too high relative to the CDS level, though it is hard to quantify by how much. Thus, incorporating Figure 16.3 back into the assessment of the USD ASW levels of JGBs from Figure 14.1, we can conclude that, unless the credit quality of Japan (as priced in the CDS market) deteriorates further, the USD ASW levels of 1Y and 2Y JGBs should not continue to increase.
- For cases in which the USD ASW trades considerably below the CDS level, on the other hand, the one-sidedness of the inequality prevents a firm conclusion. The USD ASW level of 79 bp for 10Y JGBs could be fair, too high, or too low compared to the 10Y CDS level of 130 bp.[14]

---

[14] While the relative value relationship provides little guidance, we could of course still consult fundamental credit analysis to address this issue.

It is unfortunate that the key investment decision of allocating money in global bond markets cannot be completely based on a quantitative and formal model, since both measures (for funding costs and credit risk) are imperfect. Thus, we need to rely on a one-sided no-arbitrage inequality rather than a sharp equality.

Nevertheless, this key decision needs to be made, and the informal assessment can at least be enhanced by incorporating these imperfect measures. Figure 14.12 has shown the way funding differences (discussed in Chapter 10) can be incorporated in the asset selection between low-risk bonds. And for risky bonds, Figure 16.3 can be added to the consideration of Figure 14.1. The no-arbitrage inequality does not allow universal precise quantifications, but it offers at least a firm upper boundary, which can support global asset selection.

In the example of Japan, Figure 16.3 reveals that the USD ASW of 10Y JGBs is still quite far below the CDS level. While we cannot say how far below the CDS level is "fair", we can say that the USD ASW could increase by another 51 bp before the no-arbitrage inequality is violated. By contrast, the credit risk of Japan (as priced into the CDS) is at least fully reflected in the USD ASW of 2Y JGBs. Thus, in the event of stable CDS levels, the downside of basis-swapped 2Y JGBs is significantly smaller than for 10Y JGBs.

Applying the General Concept to an EMU Model

While we have analyzed the pricing mechanisms within the euro sovereign CDS market in Chapter 15 through a statistical model, we now apply the insights into the fundamental relationship between bonds and CDS to develop a no-arbitrage model between the euro sovereign bond and CDS markets.

As a start, we can repeat the general concept of a relationship between ASW and CDS for the special case of *spreads* between EMU issuers. The relative credit standing of, for example, Italy versus Germany is assessed by the market in the form of an Italian government bond (BTP)–Bund yield spread and in the form of the difference in CDS quotes for Italy and Germany. It is therefore natural to compare the two and to ask, for example, whether a 5Y bond yield spread of 333 bp is consistent with a 5Y CDS difference of 282 bp. If it is not, this would mean that the bond market assesses the relative credit standing of Italy versus Germany differently than does the CDS market – and the obvious exploitation would be a relative value trade between the two, which just profits from the *difference* of the assessment in both markets, while being hedged against the credit spread of Italy versus Germany. For example, if we found the bond market to overstate the credit difference between Italy and Germany *relative* to the CDS market, we could buy BTPs and CDS on Italy versus selling

Bunds and CDS on Germany, only exploiting the relative mismatch without taking a view on the "fair" level of Italian versus German debt – and being (theoretically) hedged in the event that either Italy or Germany defaults. Likewise, a real money investor allocating his EUR holdings could use this information, replace his Bund holdings by BTPs, and enter into a long Italy/short Germany CDS spread position. In this way, he has the same risk exposure as before but receives a higher income.

Trying to translate the general concept into a model that works with the actual market instruments, we again face the issue of their imperfections, which led us to replace the no-arbitrage equality with an inequality. This inequality is sufficient for a one-sided assessment of BTPs, as in a chart like Figure 16.3, comparing the USD ASW of BTPs with Italian CDS levels. However, now we want to examine the spread between BTPs and Bunds versus the spread between Italian and German CDS levels, which requires a no-arbitrage *equality* working in both directions. Fortunately, as the currency is the same, in case of dealing with *spreads* between EMU sovereigns, most unquantifiable terms in the equations connected through Figure 16.2 cancel out. Using CDS contracts with euro as settlement currency,[15] we also exclude the problem of the FX-component in the CDS (and the need to basis swap everything into USD).[16] The result is the following equality (with all terms, including ASW, in EUR):

$$CreditInformation(BTP) - CreditInformation(Bund) =$$
$$(ASW(BTP) + GCrepoBSW(BTP) + Netfunding(BTP)) -$$
$$(ASW(Bund) + GCrepoBSW(Bund) + Netfunding(Bund))$$

---

[15] Currently, liquidity in these instruments is still poor. While they can be traded, getting reliable data for historical analysis is difficult.

[16] Using EUR-denominated CDS is a requirement not only for our analysis but also for obtaining a reasonable trading position. To illustrate that point, imagine first that we execute the example from above (short Bunds/short German CDS versus long BTPs/long Italy CDS) with EUR-denominated CDS contracts and Italy defaults. Then, we can deliver our BTP in the CDS and receive the EUR principal, with which we can cover our short Bund position (only exposing us to the comparatively small risk that we may not be able to replicate the coupon payments of the original BTP). Now imagine that we use the usual USD-denominated CDS contracts instead. Then, when Italy defaults, we get the principal in USD and need to exchange it back into EUR to cover our short Bund. If the EUR weakens after default of one of its constituents, we make an additional profit, which is potentially significant. This FX exposure biases the spread trade in favor of being short the CDS of the good credit and long the CDS of the bad credit.

The discussion in Chapter 6, in particular about the ECB haircut, suggests that the "net funding" (i.e. the funding effects which are unrelated to credit) is negligible. Thus, we drop that term from the equation and combine it with the credit information difference in EUR-denominated CDS, that is:

$$CreditInformation(CDSItaly) - CreditInformation(CDSGermany)$$
$$= (CDS(Italy) - DO(Italy)) - (CDS(Germany) - DO(Germany))$$

As the credit information difference in the ASW and CDS market should be the same, we get:

$$(ASW(BTP) + GCrepoBSW(BTP)) - (ASW(Bund) + GCrepoBSW(Bund))$$
$$= (CDS(Italy) - DO(Italy)) - (CDS(Germany) - DO(Germany))$$

The good news is that in the special case of spreads between EMU governments, the general concept only needs to be adjusted by the GC–repo BSW and the DO:

- The fair value of the GC–repo BSW (i.e. the expected specialness premium) can be calculated by using historical repo specialness data and assessing how special a bond of a certain issuer and with a certain maturity is expected to become over its life. The result, based on ABN Amro's database for repo rates, which was first published in the ABN Amro Research note "Many EUR sovereign default swaps are undervalued" from 17 April 2002 and is reproduced here with kind permission from RBS, is depicted in Figure 16.5. The effect of the Bobl and Bund futures contracts on the expected specialness is clearly discernible.
- In the absence of precedents for defaults by EMU members, the delivery option of the CDS is impossible to quantify equally precisely (see Chapter 15). As a rough approximation, we could assume that in line with Latin American defaults about 6% of the CDS value is due to its delivery option. To account for potential errors, we shall use a "no-arbitrage band" around the no-arbitrage level. Thus, we shall see a potential trading opportunity only in the event of the mismatch between the bond and CDS markets being larger than our no-arbitrage band.

We can now calculate the adjusted ASW (i.e. the ASW plus the fair value of the GC–repo basis swap) and the adjusted (EUR-denominated) CDS quotes (i.e. the CDS minus the DO) for every EMU sovereign issuer and

FIGURE 16.5   Historical average for the GC–repo BSW for different EUR sovereign issues.

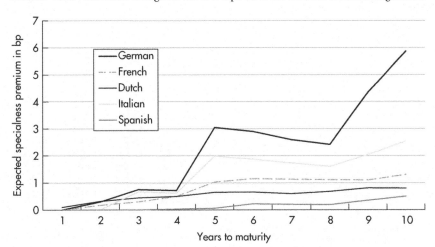

Source: ABN Amro, reproduced with permission from RBS.

every maturity. This allows us to state the general concept of the EMU model while accounting for the imperfections of the actual market instruments as:

$$\text{Adjusted ASW difference (e.g. between BTPs and Bunds)}$$
$$= \text{Adjusted CDS difference.}$$

Figure 16.6 and Figure 16.7 compare the adjusted ASW and adjusted CDS levels for 5Y and 10Y maturities.

It turns out that for the core countries the adjusted swap spreads are less than the adjusted CDS levels, while for the peripheral countries the adjusted swap spreads are greater than the adjusted CDS levels. Thus, *relative* to the CDS market, the bond market overestimates the risk difference between peripheral and core countries. Alternatively, *relative* to the bond market, the CDS market underestimates the risk difference between peripheral and core countries. This means that trades like the example above, replacing core with peripheral bonds and hedging the higher credit risk by an offsetting CDS spread position, generally seem attractive.[17]

Choosing Germany as a reference, we can calculate the pick-up from replacing Bunds with peripheral bonds and a long peripheral CDS/short

---

[17] For the moment, we ignore the risk of countries exiting the euro and redenominating their bonds. This risk will be incorporated into the analysis later on.

FIGURE 16.6 Adjusted ASW levels of EMU sovereign issues versus adjusted CDS levels of their issuers in the 5Y segment.

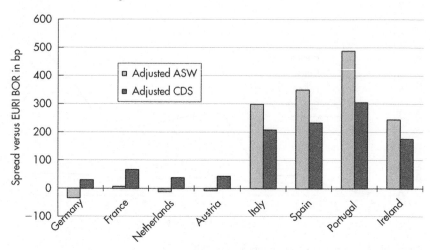

Sources: data – Bloomberg; chart – Authors.
Data period: "Current" market data as of 23 Sep 2012.

FIGURE 16.7 Adjusted ASW levels of EMU sovereign issues versus adjusted CDS levels of their issuers in the 10Y segment.

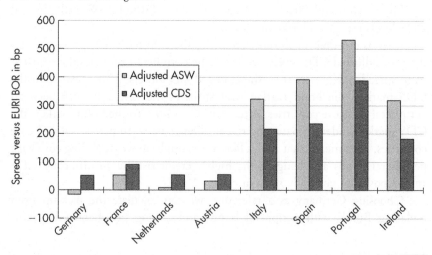

Sources: data – Bloomberg; chart – Authors.
Data period: "Current" market data as of 23 Sep 2012.

FIGURE 16.8 Pick-up from replacing Bunds with a portfolio of peripheral bonds, long peripheral CDS and short German CDS, adjusted for the expected loss of repo specialness advantage (and the delivery option of the CDS).

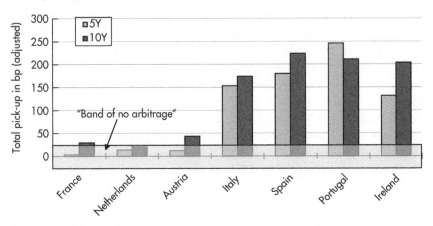

Sources: data – Bloomberg; chart – Authors.
Data period: "Current" market data as of 23 Sep 2012.

German CDS spread, both adjusted.[18] Since we have made a rough assumption about the delivery option of the CDS and face significant bid–ask spreads for EUR-denominated CDS, the arbitrage is practicable only outside the "no-arbitrage-band", which we set for the purpose of Figure 16.8 arbitrarily at 25 bp. Better information about the delivery option or tightening bid–offer spreads would result in a smaller no-arbitrage band. A point outside the no-arbitrage band suggests credit-neutral asset reallocation among EMU issuers. For example, if the adjusted 10Y BTP–Bund spread is 339 bp and the adjusted 10Y CDS spread between Italy and Germany is 165 bp, then we can conclude that the bond market assesses the Italian credit risk (relative to Germany) 174 bp higher than does the CDS market. While it is impossible to judge which of the two markets is "correct", investors can make use of the mismatch between the two by shifting their EMU bond portfolio from Bunds into BTPs and by hedging against the decrease in credit quality by the opposite spread position in the CDS market. In our example, an investor holding 10Y Bunds could sell them, buy 10Y BTPs, sell German default protection, and buy Italian

---

[18] Constructing a real arbitrage relationship would require the GC–repo BSW to trade. But even in the absence of that market, our ability to price it allows connecting bond and CDS markets and quantifying the mismatches between them (i.e. opportunities for EMU portfolio reallocations).

default protection. His credit exposure is the same (the one of Germany), and he has realized a 177 bp pick-up, 3 bp of which he is expected to lose due to missing more opportunities for his bond becoming special in repo.

In the following, we consider additionally the possibility of a country leaving the EMU and redenominating its bonds in a different currency. To our knowledge, whether redenomination following an EMU exit constitutes a credit event of the CDS depends on the specific CDS documentation, and potentially even on the specific country. In case an EMU exit triggers the CDS, the EMU model is complete with Figure 16.8. In this case, when Italy redenominates in lira, a BTP can be delivered for payment of euros in the Italian CDS, thus there is no risk from redenomination for long BTP/long Italian CDS versus short Bunds/short German CDS positions. On the other hand, if an EMU exit does not trigger the CDS, an investor executing the arbitrage from Figure 16.8 could be left with a BTP denominated in a currency depreciating versus the euro. We therefore need to investigate how our EMU model is affected by the redenomination risk and describe subsequently the necessary modifications in the case that a euro exit does not constitute a credit event of the CDS.

Actually, the risk of an EMU exit and redenomination of peripheral bonds is clearly visible in Figure 16.6 and Figure 16.7 and is probably the reason for the difference between core and peripheral countries. Core countries, whose currency might appreciate in case of an EMU exit, show a lower adjusted ASW for bonds (profiting from redenomination) than the adjusted CDS. Peripheral countries, whose currency is likely to depreciate in the event of an EMU exit, exhibit a higher adjusted ASW for bonds (suffering from redenomination) than for the adjusted CDS. Thus, as a final step in the construction of an EMU model, we need to incorporate the redenomination risk into our analytical framework.

If in the example above (short Bunds/short German CDS versus long BTPs/long Italy CDS) Italy does not default but redenominates in lira, we face again an FX exposure, since the BTP is repaid in lira. But we would need to cover the short Bund in EUR (or marks). Hence, we have excluded the FX exposure from the CDS in case of a default by choosing illiquid EUR-denominated CDS[19] but face another potential FX exposure, this time not from the CDS side of the trade but rather from the bonds involved.

Again, just as in case of the FX exposure coming from a CDS denominated in USD, the potential FX exposure from lira redenomination results in a

---

[19] Since we assume an EMU exit would not trigger the CDS, in case of Italy redenominating BTPs in lira *and* defaulting afterward, one could still deliver the BTPs into the CDS contract and receive EUR. Thus, the risk is that Italy redenominates and does not default.

no-arbitrage *inequality:* assuming that the currency of the exiting peripheral country would weaken relative to the currency Germany would use, we would always like to be long Bunds/long German CDS versus short peripheral bonds/ short peripheral CDS in the arbitrage positions described here. In terms of Figure 16.8, when taking the possibility of lira redenomination realistically into account, we see only a trading opportunity when the pick-up is sufficiently negative (i.e. below the no-arbitrage band), just as the no-arbitrage inequality derived in Figure 16.2 restricted trading ideas to points above the line in Figure 16.3. The fact that there is no negative pick-up in Figure 16.8 is a strong indication that the redenomination risk does indeed have a major influence on the relationship between EMU bond and CDS markets.[20]

On the other side, the only justifiable reason for a positive pick-up in Figure 16.8 is the risk of BTPs being redenominated in lira. Under the assumption of arbitrage-free pricing between the bond and CDS markets, one can actually translate the positive pick-up in Figure 16.8 into the market-implied probability of Italy leaving the EUR. Thus, points below the no-arbitrage band violate the no-arbitrage inequality and are candidates for trades, while points above may be interpreted as the market's price for the lira redenomination risk. In conceptual terms, we turn the problem of the no-arbitrage inequality into an insight, that is the market-implied EMU exit probability for peripheral countries.[21]

In order to perform this calculation, the first step is to adjust the pick-up from Figure 16.8 for the default risk, as only in the event of no default is the redenomination risk valid.[22] Then one needs to determine the devaluation a country leaving the EMU is likely to suffer relative to Germany, for example by applying macroeconomic estimates of changes in the relative costs of production. Under some reasonable assumptions, the result could be as shown in Figure 16.9.

For example, the EMU bond and CDS markets imply a 26% probability that Italy would leave the euro over the next five years (and redenominate its bonds in lira) assuming a 30% devaluation of the lira versus the currency used by Germany. Surprisingly, the implied exit probability for Austria over the next 10 years is 88%, which reflects the combination of an exceptionally low Austrian CDS (see discussion in Chapter 15, Figure 15.9) and a low

---

[20] Moreover, it also indicates that CDS contracts which are not triggered by an EMU exit seem to determine the pricing across the euro sovereign markets.

[21] This is similar to calculating the market-implied FX rate conditional on a default mentioned in Chapter 15.

[22] All under the assumption that an EMU exit does not trigger the CDS.

FIGURE 16.9 Market-implied EMU exit probability over the next five and 10 years.

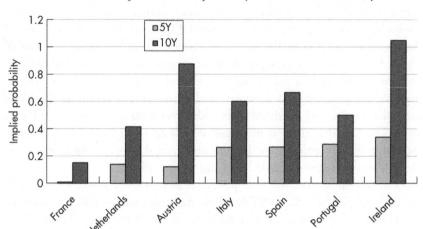

Sources: data – Bloomberg; chart – Authors.
Data period: "Current" market data as of 23 Sep 2012.

estimated devaluation (5%) of the schilling versus the currency Germany uses
in case of an Austrian EMU exit. As in this example, Figure 16.9 synthesizes
the information in the euro bond and CDS markets with the currency risk in
the event of EMU exits and can thereby detect imbalances.

This information may well be interesting in its own right, but it can also
be applied to our trading strategies. If one finds that the market-implied EMU
exit probability exceeds one, as in the case of Ireland over the next 10 years,
then at least part of the positive pick-up in Figure 16.8 cannot be justified by
the redenomination risk. In that case, entering into short Bunds/short
German CDS versus long Irish bonds/long Irish CDS positions should
profit even in the case of Ireland exiting EMU. That is, the mismatch between
the bond and CDS markets is so large that it covers even the expected losses
from a redenomination of Irish bonds in punts (assumed to devalue 20%
versus the currency Germany uses). Thus, we can translate the 100% market-
implied EMU exit probability back into a pick-up level (Figure 16.10).

Now, both negative pick-up levels (below the "no-arbitrage band") and
positive pick-up levels exceeding the ones corresponding to a 100% euro exit
probability[23] can be considered as trading opportunities. Negative pick-up

---

[23] An allowance for the rough estimate made for the DO value and the high bid–ask spreads
for EUR-denominated CDS should be added to the 100%-exit-probability boundaries as well.

levels are attractive because they will profit from the likely appreciation of the currency Germany uses against any other currency used in the former Eurozone in case of a euro break-up. Positive pick-up levels exceeding the 100%-exit-probability boundary are attractive because they can be expected to fully cover the losses from devaluation in case of a euro break-up. In the current example shown in Figure 16.10, switching 10Y Bunds into Irish bonds and buying Irish CDS versus selling German CDS yields a pick-up of 204 bp (adjusted, also in the following). If Ireland does not exit the euro, this pick-up will be realized as profit. If Ireland exits the euro, the devaluation of the punt is expected to cost 194 bp of that pick-up, still leaving 10 bp of profit. These trades are also attractive for countries with a small exit probability and/or a small expected devaluation even if the pick-up is somewhat below the 100%-exit-probability boundary. Switching 10Y Bunds into Austrian bonds and buying Austrian CDS versus selling German CDS gives a pick-up of 43 bp. If Austria were to leave the euro, the devaluation would be expected to be equal to 50 bp of that pick-up (i.e. result in a loss of 7 bp). Given the low likelihood of Austria leaving the EMU, the 7 bp loss in that scenario may still compare favorably with the 43 bp profit in the much more likely case of Germany and Austria still sharing a currency in 10 years' time.

FIGURE 16.10 Pick-up from replacing 10Y Bunds with a portfolio of peripheral bonds, long peripheral CDS and short German CDS, adjusted for the expected loss of repo specialness advantage (and the delivery option of the CDS) versus the pick-up level which corresponds to an implied EMU exit probability of one.

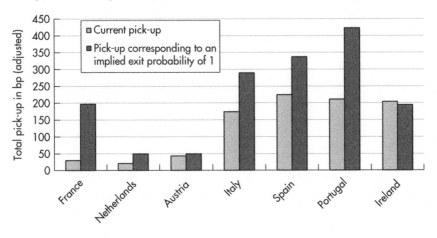

Sources: data – Bloomberg; chart – Authors.
Data period: "Current" market data as of 23 Sep 2012.

Conclusions

- Incorporating funding considerations into the commonly applied relationship between USD ASW and CDS leads to the no-arbitrage *inequality* USD ASW ≤ CDS (under some simplifying assumptions, excluding technical issues and in the presence of sufficient capital for arbitrage trades).
- As a consequence, arbitrage trades are only advisable in the relatively rare instances when the USD ASW exceeds the CDS.
- The no-arbitrage inequality explains the behavior of the USD ASW of risky bonds observed in Chapter 14. If the USD ASW is significantly away from the CDS boundary, isolation of local swap spreads from USD ASW (and the BSW) is possible.
- Incorporating the no-arbitrage inequality in the global asset selection process suggests preferring those bonds whose USD ASW is close to the CDS boundary.
- In cases of spreads between EMU issuers, a no-arbitrage *equality* can be derived, with the violations of that equality being a measure for the market-implied euro exit probability of a specific country.

CHAPTER 17

Options

Introduction

A fruitful application of the no-arbitrage principle mentioned in Chapter 1 is the approach of Black and Scholes to option pricing. As the payoff of an option can be replicated by a dynamic self-financing portfolio, the price of an option can be determined by the cost of that portfolio. We start this chapter with a brief sketch of that idea and its implications for option pricing.

However, for trading purposes, delta hedging is particularly important when the gamma of the option is large. This leads to a segmentation of the volatility surface into a sector with high gamma (short expiry), where frequent hedge rebalancing is an important trading strategy, and into a sector with low gamma (long expiry) for which it is not. After introducing this segmentation, we shall discuss the appropriate analysis tools and relative value trades for each of the sectors separately.

A Brief Review of Option Pricing Theory

Since a complete description of option pricing theory and models is outside of the scope of our trade-oriented book, we assume some familiarity of the reader with the basic ideas like the payoff profile of a call and put. In the following, we briefly highlight just those concepts of option pricing theory, which are of vital importance for finding and exploiting value in option markets.

Delta

The key for both pricing and hedging options is the relationship of the price of an option to the price of its *underlying* (the security the holder of a long

299

FIGURE 17.1 Delta of an option as a function of the difference between the price of the underlying and the strike price.

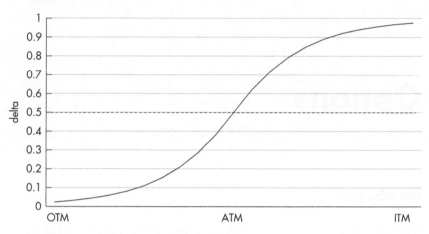

option has the right to buy or sell). (In the following examples, these securities will often be swaps on a yield curve.) That relationship is expressed by the number delta, defined as $\frac{\partial PriceOption}{\partial PriceUnderlying}$. As a first derivative of the option price with respect to the value of the underlying, delta tells us the number of units by which the option price would change for a given instantaneous change in the value of the underlying, holding the values of all other inputs constant.

The delta depends in part on the difference between the price of the underlying and the strike price of the option. Figure 17.1 shows schematically the way delta changes with the difference between the price of the underlying and the strike price. For far out-of-the-money (OTM) options, it is close to zero; for far in-the-money (ITM) options, it is close to one; for at-the-money (ATM) options, it is 0.5.[1] Also note that the change in delta (called gamma) is highest for ATM options.

This means that for far OTM options with a delta close to zero the option price varies only slightly as a result of changes in the price of the underlying. Intuitively, this makes sense, as an option with very little chance of ending ITM will quote close to zero and still quote close to zero even if the underlying changes a bit. Imagine the S&P500 index quotes at

---

[1] More precisely, for Black–Scholes $N(d_2) = 0.5$ while $N(d_1)$ could be slightly different.

1400 and we have a three-month (3M) option to buy it at 5000. Even if the S&P rises to 1500, our option will still be virtually worthless, hence the change of 100 in the underlying will have produced a negligible change in the option price, which translates into a delta of (almost) zero. On the other side, imagine we have a 3M option to buy the S&P index at 100. At the current price of 1400, this option will be worth about 1300 (plus a tiny premium). If the S&P rises to 1500, the option value will increase to about 1400. Thus, the change of 100 in the underlying induces a change of about 100 in the option price (i.e. the delta is almost one). Again, this makes sense intuitively, since far ITM options are basically the same as a position in the underlying security.

Delta Hedging

Moreover, delta gives the hedge ratio of an option versus the underlying security. In order to hedge one option, one needs to buy or sell delta of the underlying. For example, to hedge a long ATM call on the S&P500 index we need to sell 0.5 (delta of an ATM option) S&P indices. If the S&P500 index then increases from 1400 to 1500, the option will increase by 100 * delta (0.5) = 50, which is the same amount we lose from being short 0.5 of the underlying.

However, the strike of the option did not change and what was an ATM call at an S&P500 index of 1400 is now an ITM call at an index value of 1500. Consequently, as shown in Figure 17.2, the delta of the option has

FIGURE 17.2 Price of an option as a function of the difference between the price of the underlying and the strike price.

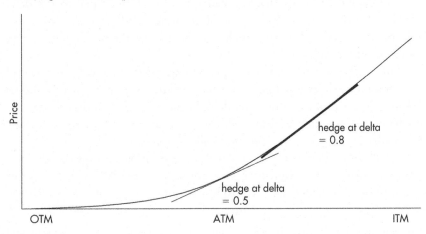

Source: Authors.

increased, perhaps to 0.8. This also means that the hedge ratio required has changed. We now need to be short 0.8 of the underlying (i.e. we need to sell an additional 0.3 units of the S&P index). Actually, since delta increased as soon as the S&P500 began to increase from 1400, we were underhedged during the entire move from 1400 to 1500 (with the amount of the underhedge becoming increasingly large as the S&P increased). As a result, we profited from being underhedged in a bull market.

Let's assume we adjust our hedge at an underlying of 1500 so as to be short 0.8 units of the S&P, and then subsequently the stock market declines again to 1400. Now the option is ATM again with a delta of 0.5, and we need to buy back 0.3 units of the underlying index in order to adjust our hedge ratio to the change in delta. We are back to where we started. The S&P index is again at 1400, we have a long ATM call (now with less time value, however), and we have a hedge versus the underlying by being short 0.5 units of the index. However, simply by adjusting our hedge ratio to the moves in delta as the market went up and down, we have sold an additional 0.3 of the underlying at 1500 (when delta went from 0.5 to 0.8) and bought back 0.3 of the underlying at 1400 (when the delta went from 0.8 to 0.5). Thus, we made a profit through our hedging operations, from selling the underlying stock market high and buying it back low. This is the same as saying that we were underhedged in an upward move and overhedged in a downward move of the market. At the end of the round trip, we have therefore pocketed a profit from adjusting the hedge ratio to the changes of the delta of the option (and lost some of its time value).

In general terms, the hedge ratio for an option changes with the price of the underlying. Ensuring that the hedge ratio is always equal to the delta of the option is called *delta hedging* of an option and requires continuous adjustment of the hedge ratio to changes in delta as the underlying market moves up and down.

Since delta changes when the underlying moves, our delta hedge will most always be a bit too much or a bit too little, such that market moves will result in a profit or loss from delta hedging. The key point is that the holder of a long option position will always profit from delta hedging, while the holder of a short option position will always lose.[2]

To illustrate that point, let's consider the example above from the perspective of an investor who is short a call on the S&P500 with a strike of 1400. In order to hedge, he needs to buy 0.5 of the index initially (at 1400).

---

[2] At this point, we're assuming that there are no changes in other variables, such as the implied volatility of the option.

When the index increases to 1500 (delta increases from 0.5 to 0.8), he needs to buy an additional 0.3 of the index at 1500, and after the index returns to 1400, he needs to sell 0.3 again at 1400. Thus, as a mirror image to the example of a long option holder above, the short option holder is forced to buy high and sell low. Or, in other words, delta hedging a short option forces a trader into the unfavorable position of being underhedged in a declining market and overhedged in an increasing one.

In theoretical terms, the option price is the cost of the dynamic self-financing portfolio that will replicate the payoff of the option, including the costs or benefits of delta hedging. And it's this sense in which Black–Scholes is said to be a no-arbitrage model.

From a trading perspective, exact dynamic replication of an option is impossible, so we can think of *the option premium as the market price for the right to be on the profitable side of delta hedging* (i.e. buying the underlying low and selling it high, and being underhedged in rising markets and overhedged in falling markets). As delta hedging means that the option is always hedged versus the underlying, there will be no profit and loss at expiry of the option. If the option expires ITM, it will be hedged with one underlying; if it expires OTM, it will be hedged with no underlying. In fact, delta hedging can be thought of as increasing the hedge ratio toward one as the option moves ITM and decreasing the hedge ratio toward zero as the option moves OTM, just as it is required for the option to yield no P&L at expiry. Hence, *delta hedging an option transfers all P&L of the option position from the expiry (difference of underlying versus strike) to the P&L of the delta hedging operations before expiry.* As a consequence, the market price of an option should depend on the cost of delta hedging that option. This was the key insight of Black and Scholes, which enabled them to determine the option price by the cost of a dynamically hedged, self-financing portfolio. While we shall not go into the mathematics and quantifications, we highlight some important consequences of that approach in qualitative terms:

- The option price is determined by profit from the dynamically hedged, self-financing portfolio that hedges a long position in the option. The profit from delta hedging a long option position increases with the volatility of the underlying market moves. In the example above, if the market had moved twice from 1400 to 1500 and back (in the same time period), we would have made twice the money from delta hedging (selling at 1500 and buying back at 1400 0.3 of the S&P500 index). And if the market had moved from 1400 to 1600 and back (with a delta of, say, 0.9 at 1600), we could have sold 0.4 at 1600 and bought 0.4 back at 1400.

Thus, the higher the volatility (number and scale of moves in the underlying market) until expiry, the higher the profit from delta hedging a long option position.

- From a trading perspective, the option price is determined by the expected profit from delta hedging, which in turn is determined by the anticipated volatility in the underlying market until the expiry of the option. Consequently, *the option price reflects the anticipated volatility in the underlying market until expiry*. In other words, the option market reflects the market consensus about anticipated future volatility. If overall market participants anticipate a period of high volatility ahead, they see considerable potential to profit from delta hedging long option positions and should thus be willing to pay a high price for the right to be on the profitable side of delta hedging (i.e. they'll pay a high option premium).

- The anticipated future volatility in the underlying market reflected in the option price is called the *implied* volatility of that option. And as we have seen above, in the framework of delta hedging (i.e. Black–Scholes option pricing theory), implied volatility is the main determinant of option premiums. Put otherwise, for a specific option, with given underlying, strike, and expiry etc., its price depends only on the implied volatility. Therefore, instead of quoting the premium of an option in terms of dollars and cents, it can be and often is quoted as well in terms of the implied volatility associated with that premium.

- While the *implied* volatility is the *anticipated future* volatility of the market, the *actual* volatility occurring in the market until the expiry of the option is called the *realized* volatility. The implied volatility determines the premium of the option, whereas the realized volatility determines the actual P&L from delta hedging the option until expiry. Thus, *the P&L of delta hedging an option is the difference between the implied volatility and the realized volatility*. Put otherwise, the implied volatility reflects the market consensus at the time of purchase about expected future volatility, which determines the price of the option. In contrast, the realized volatility indicates the volatility that actually has occurred prior to the expiry of the option, which determines the P&L realized by delta hedging the option. If implied and realized volatility turn out to be the same (i.e. the market consensus about anticipated future volatility is matched by the actual volatility), then the premium of the option and the P&L from delta hedging it would be equal. If, on the other hand, the realized volatility turns out to be less than the anticipated volatility, the option premium is higher than the P&L from delta hedging, and therefore the one who bought the option (and delta hedged it) loses and the one who sold the option (and delta hedged it) wins.[3]

- Therefore, trading in options and delta hedging them means taking views on the spread between implied and realized volatility. We buy options and delta hedge them if we believe that the realized volatility of the underlying will be greater than their implied volatility. Since option prices depend on the volatility anticipated by the market, their actual ending value at expiry can only be known after expiry, when the realized volatility and thereby the P&L from delta hedging is known. Before expiry, trading in options always involves assessing the market consensus about future anticipated volatility as reflected in the implied volatility of the option prices versus our own view about future volatility.

- The option value today is *not* determined by the price of the underlying at expiry. In the Black–Scholes approach, the option value today depends on the volatility of the price path of the underlying. Put in simple terms, for pricing options it does not matter *at which level* the underlying of the option will end, only *how* it gets there: in a volatile or a smooth fashion.

Note how a simple analysis of the delta of an option has naturally translated into a hedging (delta hedging), pricing (Black–Scholes), and trading (implied versus realized volatility) strategy.

Theta, Vega, and Gamma

Similarly to delta, which assesses the price of an option as a function of the underlying security, one can also analyze the way the option price would change in relation to changes in other determining variables. In particular:

- Theta is defined as $\frac{\partial PriceOption}{\partial Time}$ and indicates the changes in the value of the option as a function of time.

---

[3] Note that the calculation of delta should be based on the anticipated future volatility. Consider two traders who anticipate that future realized volatility will be 20%, while the current implied volatility is 30%. Both are motivated to gamma trade the difference between the implied volatility and the volatility they anticipate (i.e. to sell the option and delta hedge it). Trader A calculates all his hedge ratios using a volatility of 20% (i.e. the volatility he anticipates), while Trader B calculates all his hedge ratios using a volatility of 30% (i.e. the volatility currently implied by the pricing of the option). Let's say that the realized volatility actually does turn out to be 20%, as these two traders anticipated. While trader A will have realized a profit in line with the Black–Scholes model, the P&L of trader B, using a number for delta which is different from the Black–Scholes model, can be different (higher or lower than the profit of trader A).

- Vega[4] is defined as $\frac{\partial PriceOption}{\partial ImpliedVolatility}$ and shows the change in the value of the option as a function of changes in implied volatility.
- Gamma is defined as $\frac{\partial Delta}{\partial PriceUnderlying}$ and quantifies the change in delta as a function of the change in the price of the underlying (i.e. it's the second derivative of the option price with respect to the price of the underlying, i.e. the slope of the line in Figure 17.1). Thus, gamma is close to zero for far ITM and far OTM options and maximal for ATM options.

Given a certain realized volatility of the market, the P&L from delta hedging will be higher, if the (given) price changes of the underlying induce a higher change in delta (and thereby require a larger amount of the underlying to be bought or sold in order to maintain the delta hedge). Thus, the higher the gamma of an option, the larger the changes in delta and the larger the P&L from delta hedging, given a certain realized volatility. As a consequence, the trading strategy developed above of delta hedging an option and thereby exploiting the difference between implied and realized volatility requires options with a sufficiently large gamma. Both far ITM and far OTM options are not suitable for that strategy. And also ATM options which have a low gamma for different reasons, in particular because of a long time to expiry, require another trading strategy than delta hedging. Thus, this brief and purely qualitative review of option pricing yielded a hedging and trading strategy (delta hedging) for options with high gamma as well as a segmentation of the option market into those options for which this approach is suitable and into those for which is it not. Subsequently, we shall build on this result so as to classify the option market into different segments and to associate them with their respective suitable trading strategies.

Classification of Option Trades

Relationship between Gamma and Theta

Theta measures the time decay of the option. Figure 17.3 shows schematically that theta becomes increasingly negative as the option moves closer to expiry. That is, options with a long time to expiry have a small negative theta,

---

[4] For both systematic and philological reasons, we would like to suggest replacing "vega" with "sigma", but stick in the following to the conventional term.

FIGURE 17.3 Theta of an ATM option as a function of the time to expiry (schematic).

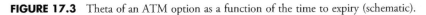

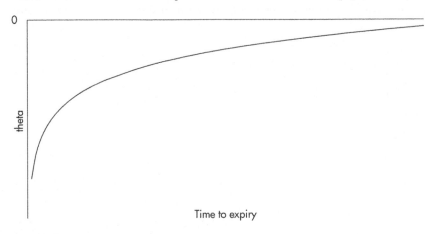

Source: Authors.

while options with a short time to expiry have a high negative theta (all else being equal).[5]

It can be deduced from the Black–Scholes formula that (all else being equal) a decrease of theta (i.e. theta becoming more negative) is linked to an increase of gamma. More precisely, an increase in gamma by one is equivalent to a decrease in theta by $\frac{2}{P^2\sigma^2}$ where P is the price of the underlying and σ is the implied volatility (again, with all other parameters assumed to remain unchanged).

Together, this results in options with a long time to expiry having a relatively high theta (small negative number), thus a relatively small gamma (small positive number). As the time to expiry decreases (and assuming that the ATM option remains ATM), theta decreases, from a number closer to zero to a larger negative number, while gamma increases, from a number closer to zero to a larger positive number. Consequently, the exposure of an ATM option to changes in delta becomes increasingly large as the expiry date approaches. This is depicted in Figure 17.4, which illustrates that the move of delta from 0 to 1 becomes more and more concentrated around the ATM point as the time to expiry decreases.

This mathematical result also makes sense intuitively: using the example above, imagine we had a 10-year (10Y), rather than a 3M, call to buy the S&P500 index at 5000. Given the very long time to expiry, that option will

---

[5] While it is possible for theta to be positive for ITM options, the chart depicts the usual situation for ATM options.

FIGURE 17.4 Delta of an option as a function of the difference between the price of the underlying and the strike price, as the time to expiry of the option becomes shorter and shorter.

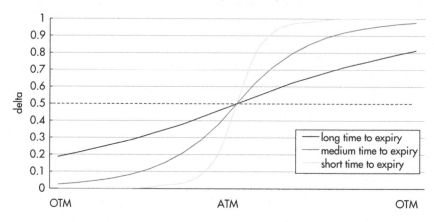

Source: Authors.

have some (time) value, which decreases every day only by a small amount (low negative theta), and will hardly change if the S&P index moves from 1400 to 1500 (low positive gamma, thus a flat delta curve in Figure 17.4 above). On the other side of the extreme, consider an ATM option that expires tomorrow. Like any ATM option, it has a delta of 0.5, but at expiry tomorrow it will either be ITM with a delta of 1 or OTM with a delta of 0. Tomorrow, it will have lost all time value (theta approaching negative infinity), and the slightest move of the index up or down will decide between a delta of 1 or 0. As illustrated in Figure 17.4, when the time to expiry decreases, the gamma of an ATM call option increases (approaching positive infinity). That is, the delta curve becomes steeper and steeper until at expiry it is a binary curve with a value of 0 below the strike and a value of 1 above the strike.

Segmentation of the Volatility Surface

Turning from option theory, from which we have picked only those parts which are needed for constructing the right trading strategies, to its practical application, we can summarize the result as follows:

- *The prices of ATM options with short times to expiry mainly depend on price moves in the underlying security.* Due to the high gamma of options with short times to expiry, delta changes significantly when the underlying moves. This means that price moves in the underlying security have a large impact on the P&L from delta hedging an option and therefore on its premium as well.

- *The price of ATM options with long times to expiry mainly depend on moves in the implied volatility.* In contrast to options with short times to expiry, for a low gamma option a move in the underlying does not result in a meaningful change of delta and thus has no significant impact on the P&L from delta hedging and therefore nor on the option price. In the limit of very long expiries, the slope of the delta line in Figure 17.4 approaches 0, which means that moves in the underlying security do not result in a change in the delta, and therefore they have no impact on the P&L from delta hedging and therefore neither on the option price. On the other hand, given the long time value of the option, even a small change in the implied volatility has a significant effect on the option price. This intuition is reflected in the mathematical fact that (excluding extremely long times to expiry) vega rises with increasing time to expiry,[6] while gamma declines.

The impact of delta hedging is a decreasing function of the time to expiry. For our practical approach this means that delta hedging is an appropriate trading strategy only for options with a short time to expiry. For swaptions, this usually covers a range of expiry times up until six months or in some cases one year. Swaptions with times to expiry of three years or more have values that are largely independent of changes in the value of the underlying and mainly influenced by changes in the implied volatility.

Thus, the swaption volatility surface (i.e. the two-dimensional grid of swaptions sorted by time to expiry of the option and by time to maturity of the underlying swap) should be divided into a gamma sector, where delta hedging is the appropriate trading strategy, and into a vega sector, where it is not (Figure 17.5). Usually, options with a time to expiry of roughly two years fall in a gray area between those two sectors, and the appropriate trading strategy must be determined on a case-by-case basis. The precise location of the border between the gamma and vega sectors differs for each option market, and often the gray area is somewhat tilted to the right (see Figure 17.20, where we provide more details for the case of JPY swaptions).

---

[6] Strictly speaking, vega depends on the time to expiry, t, in accordance with the term $\frac{\sqrt{t}}{e^t}$. As a result, vega first increases with t. For higher values of t, on the other hand, the exponential function increases at a faster rate than does the square root function and vega decreases with t. The specific point at which vega shifts from being an increasing function of time to a decreasing function of time also depends on additional parameters, including the implied volatility. However, for common values of implied volatility and times to expiry, it is relatively safe to assume that vega increases with time.

FIGURE 17.5 Classification of the volatility surface into a sector suitable for gamma trades and another suitable for vega trades.

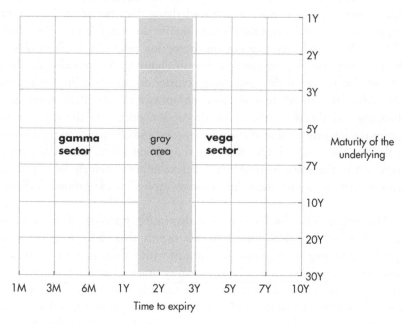

Source: Authors.

This segmentation of the volatility surface into a gamma and vega sector provides the most basic classification of option trades:

- Options with a short expiry horizon provide a strong link to the underlying and thus an exposure to changes in the realized volatility (i.e. the price moves of the underlying).
- Options with a long expiry horizon have less contact with the underlying and are therefore mainly exposed to changes in the implied volatility.

And consequently:

- Options in the gamma sector can be appropriately traded in the Black–Scholes framework of delta hedging.
- Options in the vega sector need an analysis and trading strategy different from delta hedging. We shall show below that a statistical analysis of the mechanisms of the implied volatility can provide appropriate trading strategies for the vega sector. For example, a principal component analysis (PCA)

is able to reveal the way implied volatility affects the volatility surface and how to exploit this knowledge. Hence, we shall not attempt to build an option pricing model for the vega sector, which is superior to Black–Scholes, but rather use statistical techniques to find value within that sector.

We restrict our discussion to the volatility surface of at-the-money-forward (ATMF) options (i.e. those with the strike of the swaption at the forward rate of the underlying swap). Including different strikes would expand the volatility surface to a volatility cube, with the additional dimension representing the skew. The discussion of skew in the gamma sector requires an option model, while in the vega sector it can be addressed through the same statistical methods (e.g. via expanding the dimensionality of the PCA).[7]

Classification of Option Trades in the Gamma Sector

Continuing with our classification within the gamma sector, one is free to choose the *type* of exposure to the realized volatility one wants:

① Without delta hedging, one is exposed to the overall realized volatility of the underlying until expiry of the option. This corresponds to choosing exposure to the payoff profile of an option at expiry. We refer to this strategy as option trade type ①.

② With delta hedging, one is exposed to the continuous realized volatility of the underlying until expiry of the option. This corresponds to choosing exposure to P&L from continuous adjustments to the hedge ratio (in the Black–Scholes framework). We refer to this strategy as option trade type ②.

While theoretically speaking, ① and ② only differ in the number of time periods, the exposure in market and trading terms is different:

① gives a *conditional* exposure to the overall move of the underlying, while being largely unaffected by continuous realized volatility;

---

[7] Indeed, a "skew factor" can be identified when running a PCA on the volatility cube in the vega sector. However, given limited liquidity in many of the OTM series, the input data often represent not actual price moves but constructed data. Correspondingly, the output of a PCA skew factor does not reveal the mechanisms of real market action but rather the assumptions of the model a trader used to construct the artificial data series. Thus, expanding the reach of a PCA from the volatility surface to the volatility cube will only be meaningful when liquidity across the volatility cube has increased and provides real market data as input.

② gives an exposure to the realized volatility of the underlying until
expiry, while being largely unaffected by the overall move of the
underlying and its price at expiry.

For these two types of option trades in the gamma sector, implied volatility
only matters at the beginning, as it determines the price to enter into these
strategies. Afterward, their performance only depends on realized volatility, not
on changes to the implied volatility (as the options are held until expiry). By
contrast, in the vega sector, only trading strategies involving changes in the
implied volatility are sensible (since the option price depends largely on implied
volatility) and practicable (since holding until expiry takes too much time).

In order to further minimize the impact from moves in the underlying
and thus the need for delta hedging, one should execute option trades in the
vega sector by using straddles. By having largely excluded realized volatility as
a driving factor, one obtains a pure exposure to implied volatility and can
now consider and trade the volatility surface *in abstraction* from the underlying swap rates, by statistical analysis and trading tools.

Option strategy type ③ is therefore constructed using straddles in the
vega sector, mainly exposed to changes in implied volatility, and unwound
well before expiry.

Different Exposure of Different Types of Option Trades

This abstract classification of option trades into three different types is
important in order to ensure clarity about the exposure and a correct
expression of the exposure desired. We stress this point because some analysts
tend to confuse the driving factors in option trades and therefore construct
option trades whose exposures do not match the ones outlined in their
reasoning. As an illustration, we show how similar three "2Y versus 10Y"
option trades provide very different exposures:

① Buy 6M2Y receivers,[8] sell 6M10Y receivers, and do not delta hedge.
Then you have a 2Y-10Y yield curve steepening position, *conditional
on a rally*, with no exposure to the continuous realized volatility[9] and
no exposure to changes in implied volatility after entering the trade.

---

[8] This notation refers to a receiver swaption on 2Y swaps with 6M time to expiry.
[9] Except from the part of continuous realized volatility that is reflected in the position of the
underlying at the end (i.e. the "1-period-realized volatility"). However, as in the example of
the S&P500 index above, it is possible that a high (continuous) volatility results in no change
of the underlying between entry and expiry of the option.

② Buy 6M2Y receivers, sell 6M10Y receivers, and delta hedge until expiry. Then you have a realized 2Y volatility minus a realized 10Y volatility position, with no exposure to the curve steepness at expiry[10] and no exposure to changes in implied volatility after entering the trade.

③ Buy 5Y2Y straddles, sell 5Y10Y straddles, and unwind after one month. Then, you have an implied 5Y2Y volatility minus an implied 5Y10Y volatility position (with very little exposure to the curve steepness and very little exposure to realized volatility).

Of course, it is possible to switch categories. For example, starting with ②, after three months of delta hedging, one could decide to stop delta hedging (i.e. to shift to ①) or to unwind the remaining 3M options (i.e. to shift to ③). However, within each category of trades, both the exposure and the corresponding expression/execution are defined and must not be confused with another category.

In the following, we shall discuss these three types of option trades separately. Given their different exposure and construction, they require different analysis tools, which we shall also develop below.

Option Trade Type ①: Single Underlying

Buying or selling any combination of options on the same underlying and not delta hedging gives an exposure to the payoff profile of that combination of options. Since the payoff of an option depends on the underlying *if it is above or below the strike*, this results in a *conditional* exposure to the yield of the underlying at expiry. For example, buying a 6M2Y receiver with a strike of 1% and not delta hedging it until expiry means entering into a long 2Y swap position *conditional* on the 2Y swap rate in six months' time being below 1%.

In the absence of delta hedging, there are only two driving forces of the P&L of such strategies: the option premium received or paid at entry and the loss or gain from exercising the option at expiry (if it ends ITM).[11] Depending on the payoff profile constructed and the implied volatility at entry, one receives or pays a premium. If one has received a premium at entry (e.g. by selling receiver swaptions), one has to pay at expiry in the event the option ends ITM.

---

[10] Except from the part of overall curve moves that is reflected in continuous realized volatility. A large move in one direction will be accompanied by some (continuous) volatility.

[11] We restrict this analysis to European options. However, similar analysis tools can be used for American options as well.

Thus, in order to assess value in option trades of type ①, one needs to compare the two driving forces of their profits and losses: premium at entry and potential payoff at expiry. The simplest way to do so is to calculate the breakeven value of the underlying at expiry (i.e. the value of the underlying at expiry at which the payoff of the option is equal to its initial premium). For example, if we sold an ATMF receiver swaption, we could calculate the decline in the underlying swap rate which would cause a loss at expiry that was equal to the premium we had received upfront. If the yield ended above that breakeven level, our overall P&L from that strategy would be positive; if it finished below the breakeven level, it would be negative.

By assessing the breakeven levels of these option strategies, an analyst can see:

- whether expressing a macro view on the yield curve with options (rather than with the underlying) is attractive at all;
- and, if it is, which option strategy (e.g. short receivers or short straddles?) is better;
- and then, once that is decided, which underlying and expiry provides the best expected return.

In order to support that analysis, the basic tools are charts depicting the spot yield curve, the forward yield curve, and the breakeven levels. Each expiry (1M, 3M, 6M, 1Y) and strategy (payers, receivers, straddles) requires

FIGURE 17.6 Breakeven curves for 1Y ATMF straddles on different maturities of the JPY yield curve.

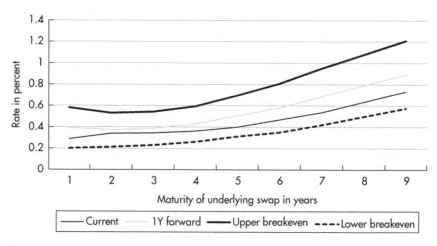

Sources: data – Bloomberg; chart – Authors.
Data period: "Current" market data as of 18 Jun 2012.

FIGURE 17.7 Breakeven curves for 1Y ATMF payer swaptions on different maturities of the JPY yield curve.

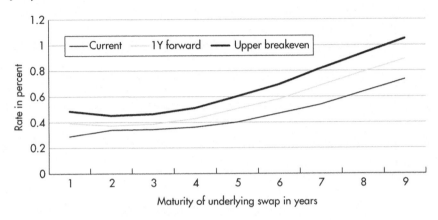

Sources: data – Bloomberg; chart – Authors.
Data period: "Current" market data as of 18 Jun 2012.

one of those charts. Figure 17.6, Figure 17.7, and Figure 17.8 show the example for 1Y expiry ATMF straddles, payer, and receiver swaptions on the JPY yield curve.

In this example, an analyst could answer the questions from above as follows:

- Looking at the straddle chart (Figure 17.6), the width of the breakeven band around the forward curve appears to be rather narrow. This corresponds to a relatively low implied volatility, thus a low option premium, which translates into a narrow breakeven band. The conclusion is that expressing a macro view on yield levels through long option positions is attractive in general.
- In the next step, one can assess the different strategies (straddles, payers, receivers) versus each other. In the current example, one may conclude that given the low likelihood of BoJ rate hike expectations changing over the next year, the forward yields may well converge toward the current spot yield levels. This would imply a bias for lower rates and thus for long receiver swaption trades. This conclusion is confirmed by the breakeven chart for receivers (Figure 17.8), which shows that for 1Y rates and at the long end of the curve the current yield level is below the breakeven level of a long ATMF receiver. Hence, if the yield curve remained unchanged over the next year, buying a 1Y1Y or 1Y7Y receiver swaption would return a small overall profit.

FIGURE 17.8 Breakeven curves for 1Y ATMF receiver swaptions on different maturities of the JPY yield curve.

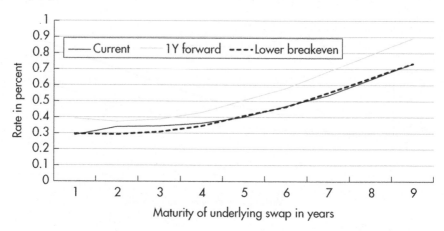

Sources: data – Bloomberg; chart – Authors.
Data period: "Current" market data as of 18 Jun 2012.

- Finally, since the distance between the breakeven line and the current yield level in Figure 17.8 is maximal for 1Y and 7Y underlying swap maturities, buying a 1Y1Y or 1Y7Y receiver swaption seems best from a breakeven point of view. As the yield outlook is usually more certain for shorter maturities, the best risk/reward balance could be found in 1Y1Y receivers.

Additionally, one may want to assess whether the current distance between breakeven levels and spot rates is a unique opportunity or rather close to the historical average. This could be done by plotting a time series of that difference. In the current example, it may reveal that the potential profit from being long 1Y1Y receivers is relatively small both on an absolute basis (Figure 17.8) and from a historical point of view. Thus, investors might be enticed to enter those trades at the current levels only in case they have a strong view that 1Y rates will decline further.

These simple breakeven charts already contain much of the information relevant for trading decisions: the roll-down (difference between forward and spot), the absolute level of implied volatility (width of breakeven bands around forward curve), and its relative distribution across the maturity spectrum. In the example above, this information could be combined to find (relatively small) value in long 1Y1Y receiver swaptions, offering a good roll-down even slightly below the breakeven band, which reflects low implied volatility in general and at the short end of the curve in particular.

On the other hand, we observed two shortcomings of this basic approach:

- It requires many breakeven charts, one for every expiry (e.g. 1M, 3M, 6M, 1Y) and for every strategy (at a minimum, straddles, receivers, and payers). This makes at least 12 charts, each of which features a yield curve of maybe 10 points. More than one hundred potential trades present a challenge to the oversight of the analyst and become hard to assess informally. In the example above, how does the greater distance between current yield and lower breakeven (Figure 17.8) in 7Y relative to 1Y compare with the greater sensitivity of 7Y relative to 1Y to potential rate hike expectations? It would therefore be desirable to have a uniform and quantitative criterion to assess all potential trading strategies.
- Every option trade of type ① with a single underlying is a macro position, as it takes a view on the level of the underlying at expiry. Thus, the approach of the breakeven analysis to compare the option premium (via translation into breakeven levels) with the level of the underlying at expiry in essence links the option market through breakeven levels to the macroeconomic expectations of the analyst. In the charts, the comparison of the option market as expressed in breakeven levels to macroeconomic scenarios is done *outside* of the analysis tool (breakeven charts) and thus informally. For example, we argued above verbally: "Given the BoJ is very unlikely to hike soon, it is also unlikely for 1Y rates in a year's time to exceed 0.3% [lower breakeven in Figure 17.8] and thus for a long 1Y1Y receiver swaption to lose money [from ending less ITM than its upfront premium requires to break even]".

The idea is therefore to solve both shortcomings together by linking the breakeven analysis to a uniform and quantifiable macroeconomic variable. This incorporates the informal macroeconomic assessment of breakeven levels into the framework of the analysis and allows us to compare different option strategies by their performance with regard to the relevant macroeconomic variable. The macroeconomic variable chosen depends on the goal of the analysis and on the views of the analyst. If he has a view on BoJ policy, he will choose the policy rate; if he has a view on CPI, he will choose CPI. For example, if a 1Y yield of 0.3% corresponds to a CPI level of −0.1, then he can argue that for the lower breakeven not to be reached CPI in Japan would need to rise to above −0.1 over the next year.[12]

---

[12] This is for illustration purposes only and does not intend to make statements about the link of interest rates to CPI, etc. Actually, the recent correlation between JPY swap rates and macro-economic variables such as CPI or seasonally adjusted GDP growth has been rather poor.

A formal analysis linking the option market through breakeven levels to macroeconomic variables and scenarios can be done in two directions:

- Either the breakeven levels are translated into corresponding macroeconomic variables. In the example above, we have calculated the "option implied" (i.e. breakeven level implied) CPI figure. This indicates the macroeconomic scenario to which the current pricing in the option market corresponds. Now that the analyst can assess the pricing in the option market in macroeconomic terms, he can express his macro views through options, if he sees that the pricing in the option market does not match his economic expectations.
- Or, the other way round (which is more practicable when the macro model of the yield curve involves more than a single variable), one could define macroeconomic scenarios (baseline, recession, recovery), translate them via a macro model (like a VAR model) into yield forecasts, and compare these forecasts with the breakeven levels. If one finds an option strategy that benefits under each scenario, one has found a good candidate for a trade idea. This comparison of yield forecasts in different economic scenarios with breakeven levels could be done, for example, by calculating the number of standard deviations by which the breakeven level exceeds the yield forecast. Displaying these *t*-stats for different options simultaneously (e.g. in the form of a heat map for each macroeconomic scenario) can facilitate the selection of the best strategy.[13]

In the following, we provide an example of the first approach, assuming that we have a view on the Japanese CPI and want to compare the pricing of the swaption market with our CPI forecast. Note that this is for illustrative purposes only, as the correlation between CPI and interest rates in Japan (0.5) would, in our view, be too weak to base trades on.

In the first step, the breakeven levels for long receiver swaptions are calculated for each expiry (3M, 6M, etc.) and for each time to maturity of the underlying swap (1Y, 2Y, etc.). Then, the difference between that breakeven level and the current yield level is expressed in terms of the corresponding change in factor 1 of a PCA on the JPY swap yield curve.[14] As described in Chapter 3, the change in factor 1 can then be associated with a change in the

---

[13] An example of this second approach can be found in "Front-End Payer Swaptions: Shorts Offer Value", published by ABN AMRO Research on 25 February 2005.

[14] By dividing the yield difference in a certain maturity with the entry in the first eigenvector for that maturity.

CPI. As a result, for each expiry and underlying maturity of the receiver swaption, we obtain the CPI at which a long receiver position is expected to break even. In other words, we have translated the prices in the option market into the corresponding CPI figures. And since we have several expiries, we have even obtained the *evolution* of the CPI as implied by breakeven levels of receivers. Every underlying swap maturity results in a different implied CPI evolution, all of which are depicted in Figure 17.9.

Thus we find that a view on a low CPI can best be expressed through long 6M1Y receiver swaptions. Note the way the formal comparison of all option strategies through the uniform macroeconomic variable "breakeven implied CPI" has confirmed the informal argument we made verbally when looking at the breakeven charts. If in six months' time the CPI is below −0.08, then the 1Y swap rate level is expected to be below the breakeven level of 30.4 bp (basis points), and hence the profit from a long 6M1Y receiver swaption at expiry is expected to be greater than the upfront premium payment required.

Likewise, a view on a high CPI can best be expressed though short 1Y2Y receiver swaptions. As long as the CPI in one year is above −0.17, the option

FIGURE 17.9 Option market-implied evolution of the CPI as calculated through the breakeven levels of long receiver swaptions.

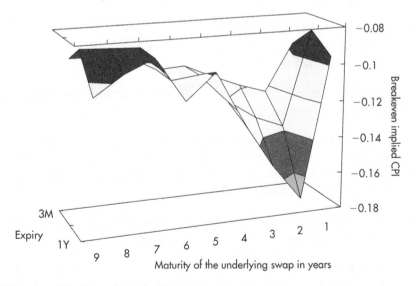

Sources: data – Bloomberg; chart – Authors.
Data period: "Current" market data as of 18 Jun 2012.

premium received upfront is expected to exceed the potential loss from the option being exercised at expiry.

Furthermore, in case a tradable instrument is selected as universal comparison for all breakeven levels (e.g. a commodity future rather than the CPI) this approach leads us to compare the volatility in the swaption market with the volatility in the option market on the tradable instrument (e.g. options on the commodity future). Thereby a relative value link between two option markets (and their implied macroeconomic scenarios) is established. This could be the basis for exploiting mismatches between the two (e.g. via long swaptions versus short options on the commodity future). These relative value trades are hedged against the macroeconomic scenario actually materializing, just exploiting the different anticipation of macroeconomic scenarios in the two option markets.

Option Trade Type ①: Two or More Underlyings

Option trade type ① on one single underlying gives a conditional expression of macro views (yield level), while option trade type ① on two or more underlyings gives a conditional expression of relative value views (e.g. yield curve steepness).

For example, we could express a 2Y-10Y curve flattening view via any of the three following alternatives:

- pay 2Y, receive 10Y (no options);
- sell a 2Y receiver, buy a 10Y receiver (swaption);
- buy a 2Y payer, sell a 10Y payer (swaption).

In comparison with the first alternative, the expression with options has the following specific features:

(1) It is conditional (i.e. it is exposed to the underlying curve steepness only under the condition that the options are ITM at expiry).
(2) It involves an option premium, which is determined by the difference in 2Y and 10Y implied volatility at entry.

And the two possibilities (via receivers or payers) to express the curve flattening through options are different in the way they offer (1) and (2):

(1) The expression with receivers gives a curve position conditional on a rally, while the expression with payers gives a curve position conditional on a selloff.

(2) The expression with receivers will return an upfront premium pick-up if implied 2Y volatility is higher than implied 10Y volatility (adjusted for hedge ratios); the expression with payers will return an upfront premium pick-up if implied 2Y volatility is lower than implied 10Y volatility.

The conditionality (1) allows selecting the directional environment that is favorable for the trade. For the following example, assume that the 2Y-10Y yield curve usually flattens in a selloff and steepens in a rally. Thus, we would prefer to express a curve flattening view with *payer* swaptions: only in the case of a selloff would these options expire ITM, hence giving us exposure to a curve flattening position, which is expected to perform well in a selloff. In the case of a rally (associated with curve steepening), both options expire OTM, thus preventing us from exposure to (underperforming) yield curve flattening. Illustrating this crucial point, Figure 17.10 depicts the way that conditionality of option trades of type ① can be used to select the favorable directional environment and to eliminate exposure to curve positions in unfavorable directional situations.

Note that for this purpose we want curve trades to be directional. Thus, we use here a basis point value (BPV) neutral weighting rather than a PCA-neutral weighting (see discussion of Figure 3.14). Put otherwise, when expressing curve trades with swaps (no options), we wanted to *solve* the problem of directionality (Figure 3.14); when expressing curve trades with swaptions, we want to *exploit* the directionality (Figure 17.10).

Technical point

The BPV of an option is calculated by multiplying the BPV of the underlying with the delta of the option. Thus, the BPV-neutral hedge ratio for a 2Y-10Y payer spread is given by $\frac{BPV_{10}\delta_{10}}{BPV_2\delta_2}$. If both options are ATMF (delta of 0.5), the hedge ratio of a conditional curve trade with options is the same as the hedge ratio of the underlying curve trade.

Having selected the right conditionality (1) (i.e. decided between receivers and payers), we now look at feature (2). In abstract terms, the expression of a yield curve position through options combines the yield curve with the volatility curve. In our example, the long 2Y payer versus short 10Y payer swaption position returns an upfront premium if the implied 2Y-10Y volatility curve (at entry) is upward sloping, and requires a premium payment if it is downward sloping.

FIGURE 17.10 P&L from a 2Y-10Y curve flattening position with swaps and with payer swaptions.

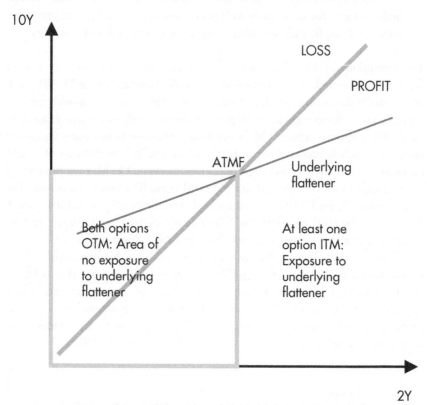

Together, we look for conditional curve trades with options that combine the advantages of (1) and (2) (i.e. that have the right conditionality *and* provide an upfront premium payment). If we get paid a premium to execute our 2Y-10Y payer spread, we can expect to win in either directional environment: if yields increase, options are ITM, putting us into the underlying flattening trade, which should perform well in a selloff. If yields decrease, options are OTM, and we keep the initial upfront premium payment as profit (of course, we also do in the event yields increase).

As an example for a conditional butterfly trade, assume that 5Y tends to underperform versus 2Y and 10Y in the event of a selloff. Thus, we can exploit the directionality by going long 5Y payers versus short 2Y and 10Y payers and by going long 5Y receivers versus short 2Y and 10Y receivers (or by combining both by going long 5Y straddles versus short 2Y and 10Y straddles). In each case, the options are ITM only in the case of a directional move that is favorable for the underlying butterfly position. In the next step, we need to calculate whether we get paid for entering those trades (i.e. whether the curvature of the 2Y-5Y-10Y implied volatility curve is negative).

Unfortunately, as a sign of the efficiency of option markets, these opportunities are rare. The 2Y-10Y yield curve flattening in a selloff means that realized volatility in 2Y is higher than in 10Y, and if this is reflected in the implied volatility (option prices), 2Y payers will be more expensive than 10Y payers. Likewise in the butterfly example: 5Y underperforming 2Y and 10Y in a selloff is another way of saying that realized volatility in 5Y is higher than in 2Y and 10Y. Most of the time this is reflected in the option prices (i.e. in a positive curvature of the 2Y-5Y-10Y implied volatility curve). Therefore, usually strategies with the right conditionality (1) require a premium payment (2).

However, sometimes these opportunities arise and provide good candidates for trade ideas when they do. In order to screen the market for these chances, we recommend calculating for every curve steepness and butterfly trade:

(1) its directionality and the strength of that relationship (e.g. the R^2 from a regression, as in Figure 3.14);
(2) for the "right" conditionality (i.e. payers or receivers) the premium pick-up or payment involved in expressing that curve trade through options.

Good candidates should have (1) a strong correlation to the direction (were the directionality to change, the conditional curve trade could lose) and (2) at least zero cost. Nhan Ngoc Le had the idea of simultaneously displaying both features of all candidates as a scatter plot chart (Figure 17.11) and looking for points in the upper-right corner. This can be a useful tool for screening the option market for trading opportunities with conditional yield curve trades. In the chart, one finds that among all possible strategies only a conditional 7Y-10Y-20Y butterfly provides stable directionality *and* a (small) premium pick-up for the right conditionality.

Similarly, one can construct conditional swap spread positions through a combination of bond options and swaptions. We have shown in Chapter 9 that before the Lehman crisis swap spreads widened (became more negative) in a selloff. Thus, if one believes that this directionality will hold true in the future, one would want to have swap spread widening positions

FIGURE 17.11 Premium pick-up/payment versus stability of directionality for conditional curve trades with options.

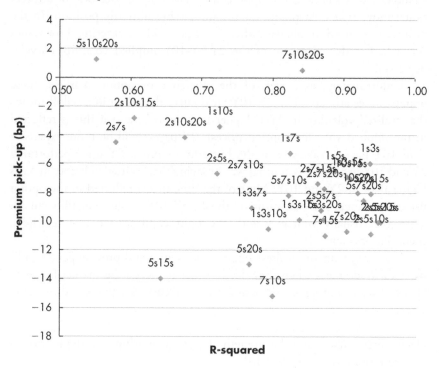

Source: Nhan Ngoc Le.

conditional on a selloff and swap spread narrowing positions conditional on a rally, that is:

- long payer swaptions versus short bond puts;
- long receiver swaptions versus short bond calls.

Again, swap spreads widening in a selloff means that the realized volatility in swaps is greater than in bonds. Thus, the right conditionality (1) is to be always long swaptions versus short bond options. How is that realized volatility relationship reflected in the option markets? In particular, do swaptions usually trade at a premium versus bond options (2)? Do we need to pay a premium for the right conditionality? Figure 17.12 answers these questions for the US market. For reasons of liquidity and comparability, we have used futures options rather than bond options. Due to future specific flows, the volatility of implied futures options is at times

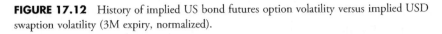

FIGURE 17.12 History of implied US bond futures option volatility versus implied USD swaption volatility (3M expiry, normalized).

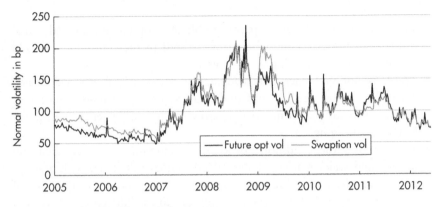

Sources: data – Bloomberg; chart – Authors.
Data period: 11 May 2005 to 3 Oct 2012, weekly data.

higher than that of implied swaptions or implied bond options (and shows up as spikes in the chart).

It appears that the directionality of swap spreads is very well reflected in the relationship between implied swaption volatility and implied futures option volatility. Before the Lehman crisis, when swap spreads tended to widen as yields increased, swaptions normally traded at a premium versus bond options. As the Lehman crisis caused both the cost of equity for banks and thus swap spreads to widen (see Chapter 6), and the yield level to decrease, the directionality of swap spreads broke down. Correspondingly, since the Lehman crisis the premium for swaption volatility has disappeared, and it currently trades close to implied futures volatility.

An investor believing that the directionality of swap spreads will return to pre-crisis levels may see this as an opportunity to enter into long swaption versus short bond option positions.

Option Trade Type ②: Single Underlying

Not delta hedging an option gives exposure to the overall realized volatility of the one period from entry to expiry, hence to the overall move of the underlying security.

Delta hedging an option (as continuous as practicable) restores the Black–Scholes framework (which assumes continuous delta hedging) outlined at the beginning of this chapter and results in the following changes versus trade type ①:

- The exposure shifts from the payoff profile of an option at expiry (the total realized volatility over the whole time period) to the continuous realized volatility of the underlying until expiry.
- The long option holder delta hedging his position is always overhedged when the market declines and underhedged when the market increases. Thus, the size of market moves (realized volatility) will determine his profit from delta hedging.
- This removes the conditionality: only the amount of moves (their frequency and scale) matters. Their direction does not. Even with a single underlying, there is no directional exposure – at least not to the direction of the underlying. (However, there is exposure to the "direction" of realized volatility.)
- The option premium (implied volatility) can be considered the market price for the right to be on the profitable side of delta hedging.

Thus, the P&L of option trade type ② is the difference between the implied volatility at entry point and the realized volatility of the underlying between entry and expiry. Put otherwise, it is the difference between the market price for the right to be on the profitable side of delta hedging and the actual profit one will realize by making use of this right. If realized volatility will exceed the current implied volatility, then the profit from delta hedging will exceed the initial option premium (i.e. the price for the right to generate profits from delta hedging).

The basic approach to the analysis of option trades of type ② is therefore to compare the two driving factors of their P&L, that is:

- the *current* implied volatility, which is a known variable;
- the *future* realized volatility (between entry and expiry), which is an unknown variable.

As the current implied volatility should reflect the market consensus about the future realized volatility, one will see value in option trades of type ② only if:

- the analyst's expectation of future realized volatility is different from the market consensus; or
- flows in the option market prevent implied volatility from reflecting the "true" market consensus about future realized volatility.

FIGURE 17.13 5Y JPY swaption volatility (normal): History of realized versus current implied volatility.

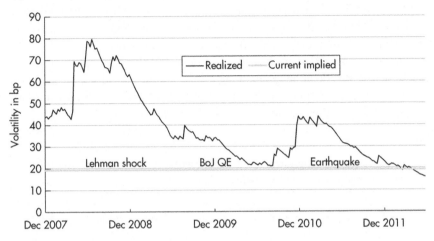

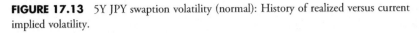

Sources: data – Bloomberg; chart – Authors.
Data period: 24 Dec 2007 to 18 Jun 2012, weekly data; "current" market data as of 18 Jun 2012.

A tool to support that basic analysis could be a chart that compares the current implied volatility level with the *historical* realized volatility in different scenarios. Figure 17.13 provides an example of such a comparison for Japan.

Of course, *historical* realized volatility over the last few months can be very different from the *future* realized volatility over the next few months, which will determine the P&L. Still, the historical perspective from Figure 17.13 allows one to assess those macroeconomic environments that have in the past led to realized volatility levels that were similar to the current implied volatility. Using Figure 17.13 as an example, we conclude that the current implied volatility level was realized during 2010, when quantitative easing (expectations) removed all uncertainty (= volatility) about BoJ policy. Any shock, whether caused by nature or mankind, has resulted in a realized volatility which exceeded the current implied volatility level, at times quite significantly.

Currently, the implied volatility (19 bp) is slightly higher than the most recent realized volatility (16 bp). However, the historical perspective of Figure 17.13 reveals that realized volatility has usually been much higher not only than the current realized volatility but also than the current implied volatility.

Based on this tool, an analyst can now judge whether the market consensus is in line with his forecast. If he anticipates the next few months to look similar to 2010, he will find no opportunity for an option trade of type ② with a single underlying. If, on the other hand, he sees the potential for another shock, for example a European banking crisis repeating the impact of Lehman on realized volatility, he will find value in buying options at 19 bp implied volatility. Actually, since the current level of 19 bp implied volatility seems to be close to the minimum of historical realized volatility, one could even think of long delta hedged options as a low-cost, low-risk way to position for potential shocks: If the dull period of 2010 is replicated in the next few months, delta hedging a long option should produce a profit that is about the same as the premium paid. On the other hand, any shock can result in a significantly higher realized volatility and thus profit.

Technical points: Lognormal and normal volatility, annualized volatility, time horizon for realized volatility calculation

---

In order to provide a clean analysis of realized volatility, two technical points need to be considered.

First of all, Black–Scholes assumes a (constant) lognormal distribution of yields. We do not intend to enter into a theoretical argument about the validity of this assumption[15] but instead to consider its practical pitfalls. Since lognormality assumes constant percentage changes independent of the level, the same lognormal move (percentage change) means a different absolute move (bp change) when the yield level is different. This makes comparisons of volatility on a lognormal basis meaningless in the event the yield level is different, for example when volatilities in different parts of the yield curve (with different yield levels) are compared or the historical evolution of volatility is displayed (as the yield level typically fluctuates over time as well). Moreover, as yields approach zero, the same yield change in basis-point terms results in increasing lognormal changes. This issue is of particular relevance in the current environment of globally low interest rates.

Since lognormality cannot deal appropriately with low interest rates (and with negative yields at all), we prefer to use normal volatility. Realized normal volatility can be easily derived by calculating the standard deviation over daily basis-point changes (rather than percentage changes). This result represents the realized volatility over the time period used in the input data (e.g. trading-daily realized volatility if the input data series consists of trading-daily data). Usually, volatility is expressed in annual terms and can be obtained by multiplying the volatility for a certain time period with the square root of the number of those time units in a year. For example, trading-daily volatility can be annualized by multiplying by the square root of 252; weekly volatility can be annualized

---

[15] Both the assumption of a *constant* lognormal volatility and of a constant *lognormal* volatility can be subjected to criticism. We deal here with the latter issue.

by multiplying by the square root of 52. Of course, this also works the other way round: an annual volatility can be translated into weekly and daily volatility.

If we prefer to calculate normal realized volatility, we also need to express the implied volatility in normal terms, for example for a comparison like in Figure 17.13. However, implied volatility is usually quoted through a Black–Scholes pricing formula (i.e. in lognormal terms). The cleanest way to "normalize" it is to translate the implied lognormal volatility through the Black–Scholes formula into an option price (in dollars and cents) and then to calibrate a normal option model so that the normal volatility input into the normal model replicates that option price. A faster, though less reliable method (in particular when yields are low and there is a chance of negative yields) consists in multiplying the implied lognormal volatility with the forward rate of the underlying security (with the forward horizon being given by the expiry of the option).

Second, the time window used for calculating historical realized volatility can become an issue. Commonly, analysts use a rolling window with a fixed time length (e.g. three or six months). Then, the realized volatility of a certain date is calculated as the standard deviation of the yield changes that occurred in the 3M or 6M time window prior to that date. The problem is that the result depends on the arbitrary choice of the rolling window. Imagine a time series with an average change of 1 bp per day, which contains one very volatile point with a change of 10 bp. When that volatile point enters the rolling time window, the realized volatility series spikes up. This is how it should be, since on that day there was indeed a high volatility. However, when that volatile point falls out of the rolling time window, the realized volatility series suddenly drops back to the average level. This is a problem since on the day when the sudden drop in the realized volatility occurs nothing special has happened at all. The only thing that occurred and caused that sudden drop was that the day with an extraordinarily high 10 bp volatility happened to be precisely three or six months earlier. And depending on the arbitrary choice of the time window, the sudden drop in volatility occurs after three or after six months. This effect can be seen in Figure 17.14. What was the realized volatility in Mar 2009: 24 bp or 45 bp? When using rolling time windows the answer depends on the arbitrary choice of 3M or 6M for the length of that window.

Consequently, using rolling time windows produces realized volatility series whose spikes higher in volatility correctly reflect market action, but whose spikes lower in volatility are the result of the arbitrary definition of the length of the time window. These can occur at different points in time and have little to do with the actual volatility on the day they occur. This problem is illustrated in Figure 17.15, which shows the realized volatility of 10Y JPY swap rates, calculated with a rolling 3M time window. The arrows indicate days on which the time series dropped sharply, not because something happened in the market but simply because the volatile day that caused the spike three months earlier rolled out of the window.

FIGURE 17.14   Realized 10Y JPY swap volatility, calculated with a 3M and a 6M rolling window.

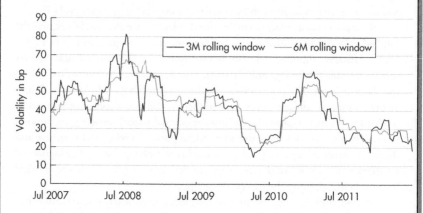

Sources: data – Bloomberg; chart – Authors.
Data period: 2 Jul 2007 to 18 Jun 2012, weekly data.

FIGURE 17.15   Realized 10Y JPY swap volatility, calculated with a 3M rolling window.

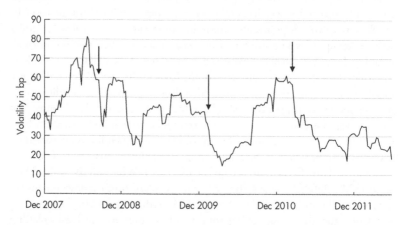

Sources: data – Bloomberg; chart – Authors.
Data period: 24 Dec 2007 to 18 Jun 2012, weekly data.

In order to mitigate this problem, we recommend replacing the fixed time window with weighting the data points with an exponentially decreasing function. For example, the latest point could have a weighting of 1, the point before that of 0.97, the point before that of 0.95, etc. The exponential weighting function assigns maximal weight to the latest data point. Thus, if this point turns out to be volatile, there will be a spike higher in the realized volatility series on that day, just as is the case with a rolling time window. On the other hand, a volatile data point will not drop out at a specific date but rather lose weight slowly and incrementally, day after day. In other words, a 3M rolling time window assigns a weighting of 1 to all points less than three months ago and of 0 to all points more than three months ago, which causes the sudden drop when a volatile point becomes more than three months old. Exponentially decreasing weightings, by contrast, assign every day a bit less importance to the volatile data point, so that its impact on the realized volatility fades away slowly. This fits the intuition of a gradually declining importance of older points for the current realized volatility quite well. Of course, there are still arbitrary decisions to be made, like the use of an exponentially decreasing weighting function (rather than a linear or quadratic one) and the choice of a decay parameter for that function. However, these choices affect the end result much less than the sudden drops in a realized volatility series calculated with a rolling time window. To demonstrate that advantage, we have calculated the same realized 10Y JPY swap volatility history from Figure 17.14 and Figure 17.15 with exponentially decreasing weightings and depict the series in Figure 17.16. We see that upward spikes to the realized volatility series are captured as well with the exponential smoothing as they are with the rolling window. But by using exponentially decreasing weightings, we can eliminate the sharp, meaningless drops that were produced by the rolling window, replacing them with a more accurate, smoother decline.

FIGURE 17.16 Realized 10Y JPY swap volatility, calculated with exponentially decreasing weightings.

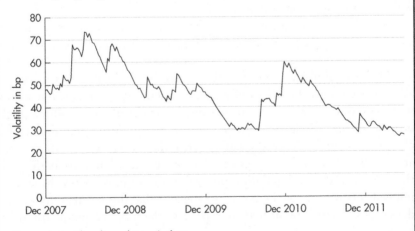

Sources: data – Bloomberg; chart – Authors.
Data period: 24 Dec 2007 to 18 Jun 2012, weekly data.

Option Trade Type ②: Two or More Underlyings

The risk in the trade described above is that the volatility actually realized may be greater or less than the volatility we anticipated. As a result, option trades of type ② with a single underlying can be seen as fundamental bets on whether particular macroeconomic scenarios materialize. As shown in Table 3.1, macroeconomic events tend to impact both the direction of the underlying swap rates and the realized volatility level, resulting in a significant correlation between them. Though option trades of type ② have no direct exposure to the underlying due to delta hedging, their exposure to the level of realized volatility does link them to the corresponding macroeconomic environment of high or low uncertainty (as caused by such events as central bank action, banking crises, etc.).

In order to reduce the macroeconomic exposure, the idea is to combine two of those trades, a long and a short option (both delta hedged), thus to hedge against the *overall* level of future realized volatility and to leave exposure just to the *relative* realized volatility distribution across the yield curve. This leads to relative value positions exploiting structural mismatches along the implied and realized volatility curves.

For example, buying 2Y straddles, selling 10Y straddles, and delta hedging both is a *box trade* between the current implied volatility curve and the future realized volatility curve, which will profit if the future realized volatility curve is flatter than the current implied volatility curve. If hedge ratios are constructed properly, the overall level of future realized volatility will have no impact on that position.

In order to screen the market for these trading opportunities, an analyst could look at a graph comparing the current implied and realized volatility curves (Figure 17.17).

In this example, we can first observe that implied volatility is currently above the recent realized volatility for all underlying maturities, but with a minimum difference for 5Y. This means that trades of type ② with a single underlying (i.e. a long delta hedged option position exploiting the relative cheapness of current implied volatility versus the average realized volatility[16]) are best expressed in the 5Y segment. Of course, the risk to these positions is that the realized volatility until expiry will turn out to be below the current implied volatility. While Figure 17.13 suggests that this is rather unlikely, it does expose a long option trade of type ② to the macroeconomic risk of an

---

[16] Though current implied volatility is slightly rich versus *current* realized volatility (see Figure 17.13).

FIGURE 17.17   Current realized and implied volatility across the JPY curve.

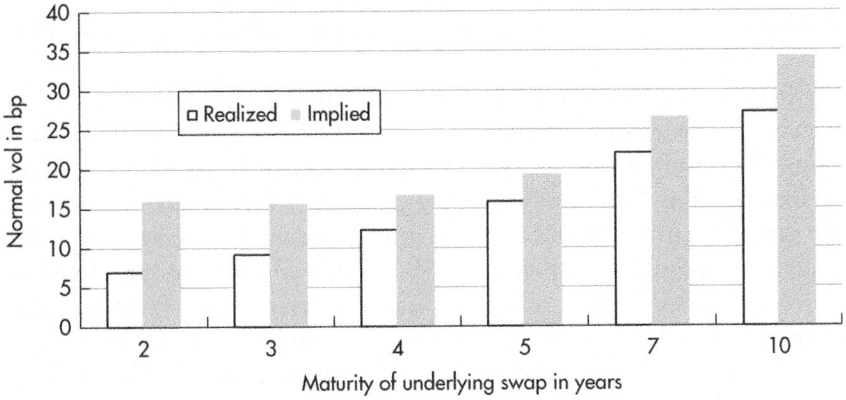

Sources: data – Bloomberg; chart – Authors.
Data period: "Current" market data as of 18 Jun 2012.

environment that produces extremely low realized volatility, such as BoJ announcements removing all uncertainty about future interest rates. Above, we have developed tools to assess the risk/return profiles of these positions.

Now we look at the same information displayed in Figure 17.17 differently, with the eyes of a relative value analyst who wants to be hedged against macroeconomic impacts as well as possible and just to exploit relative mismatches in the options market. Thus, our focus shifts from the *level* of implied versus realized volatility to their distribution over different maturities, to the *shape* of the implied volatility curve relative to the realized volatility curve. And it jumps out at the "relative value eye" immediately that the realized volatility curve is much steeper than the implied volatility curve between 2Y and 5Y. If we have reason to believe the realized volatility curve will remain steep in future as well, we could exploit the mismatch between the steepness of the implied curve relative to the realized volatility curve by buying 3M5Y straddles versus selling 3M2Y straddles and delta hedging both. Then, an increase in the overall level of realized volatility would cause the delta hedging of the long straddle position to win as much as the delta hedging of the short straddle position loses (if hedge ratios are appropriate). Thus, we are hedged against changes to the overall level of realized volatility. Instead, we are exposed to the difference between realized and implied volatility in 5Y *relative* to that difference in 2Y.

In order to assess that exposure, we recommend adjusting Figure 17.13 to two underlyings and thus depicting the history of the realized volatility *difference* between 5Y and 2Y versus the current implied volatility *difference* between 5Y and 2Y. Figure 17.18 shows the historical evolution of the 2Y-5Y realized volatility curve steepness versus the current 2Y-5Y implied volatility curve steepness.

In this case, the current implied volatility curve steepness was never matched by the realized volatility curve steepness during the past five years. Thus, if we had entered the long 5Y short 2Y straddle position at current implied volatility levels and delta hedged it until expiry at any point during the past five years, we would always have made money (on average 10 bp). Of course, it is possible that the future 5Y-2Y realized volatility spread will be below the current implied volatility spread. However, Figure 17.18 makes us confident that this is unlikely, given that the range of the 5Y-2Y realized volatility spread has over the tumultuous past five years been stably in a range between 6 bp and 27 bp, and even the lower end of that range is still away from the current implied volatility spread of 3 bp. Moreover, given recent BoJ announcements, we have no reason to expect realized volatility at the short end of the yield curve to increase relative to realized volatility in 5Y as much as is priced into the implied volatility curve. Thus, we have not only a statistical reason (history of Figure 17.18) but also a fundamental reason to believe that the steepness of the realized volatility curve will continue in the future and therefore for the current flatness of the implied volatility curve to be a trading opportunity.

FIGURE 17.18   History of 2Y-5Y JPY realized volatility curve steepness versus current 2Y-5Y JPY implied volatility curve steepness.

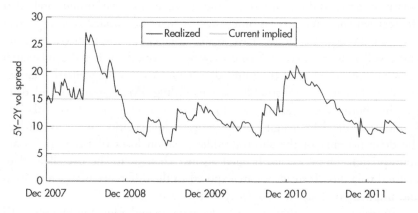

Sources: data – Bloomberg; chart – Authors.
Data period: 24 Dec 2007 to 18 Jun 2012, weekly data; "current" market data as of 18 Jun 2012.

As always, relative value considerations can also be used for asset selection purposes when expressing fundamental views. In this case, an analyst wanting to position for the overall future realized volatility level to be above the current implied volatility level (see Figure 17.13) could find best value in choosing long 5Y straddles to express his view (by looking at Figure 17.17).

Comparing Figure 17.13 and Figure 17.18, we observe significant correlation (0.71) between the level of realized volatility and the slope of the 2Y-5Y realized volatility curve: when overall volatility increases, the volatility curve tends to steepen. Depending on the goal, one can react to that observation in two ways:

- If we want to express the fundamental view of a high future realized volatility, we could do so via a 2Y-5Y straddle spread rather than a long 5Y straddle (trade type ② with two rather than one underlyings). If our fundamental view is correct, both the 5Y straddle and the 2Y-5Y straddle spread should perform well, as the two positions are highly correlated with one another. But the 2Y-5Y straddle spread is preferred, as it has a much better risk/return profile. While the 2Y-5Y straddle spread offers a 5 bp cushion against the volatility curve flattening associated with lower overall realized volatility (Figure 17.18), a long 5Y straddle will only win if realized volatility increases by at least 3 bp from its current level (Figure 17.13). Thus, for this goal we exploit the correlation between the "fundamental" and the "relative value" trade to improve the P&L from the same macroeconomic events.
- If, on the other hand, our goal is to hedge against the impacts of the overall realized volatility level, we can adjust the hedge ratio of the 2Y-5Y straddle spread in order to immunize against the exposure to the "direction" of realized volatility. Selling 1.23 2Y straddles for every 5Y straddle bought results in neutrality against the overall level of realized volatility. Figure 17.19 shows the history of the non-directional 2Y-5Y realized volatility curve steepness and illustrates the attractiveness of the pure relative value trade.

Note that option trade types ① and ② both depend on the difference between current implied volatility and future realized volatility. Therefore, both look for opportunities in where the current market pricing (implied volatility) is out of line with the expected realized volatility. However, since the way that the two types of option trades exploit these mismatches is different, we recommend displaying the same information (implied versus realized volatility) in two different ways: for type ① in terms of premium versus directionality (Figure 17.11) and for type ② in terms of implied versus realized volatility curves (Figure 17.17).

FIGURE 17.19   History of non-directional 2Y-5Y JPY realized volatility curve steepness versus current 2Y-5Y JPY implied volatility curve steepness.

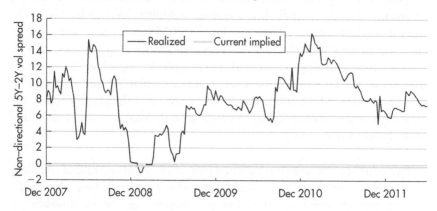

Sources: data – Bloomberg; chart – Authors.
Data period: 24 Dec 2007 to 18 Jun 2012, weekly data; "current" market data as of 18 Jun 2012.

Option Trade Type ③: Factor Model for the Vega Sector

By contrast, straddles in the vega sector of the volatility surface are almost unaffected by realized volatility in the underlying and purely exposed to changes in the implied volatility level. This allows analyzing implied volatility in abstraction from its link to external variables, focusing on the internal relationships between different points on the implied volatility surface by treating them as purely statistical time series (without making use of the knowledge that the time series represents option volatilities, which is a market consensus about future realized volatility). In brief, type ③ strategies are option positions that trade options not *as* options but as abstract time series, not linked via delta hedging to an external variable.

Consequently, while the analysis tools for type ① and ② were based on the structural link of options (*as* such, as an option *on something*) to the underlying (i.e. on the link between implied and realized volatility), analysis tools for type ③ need to consider options in abstraction from that link and focus on the statistical relationships between different points on the implied volatility surface. An equivalent statement is that option trades of type ② are analyzed within the Black–Scholes framework,[17] while type ③ is conceptually different and treats options in abstraction from their link through delta

---

[17] And trades of type ① can be considered in that framework as one-period (instead of continuous) delta hedging strategies.

hedging to the underlying. As in Chapter 15, where we have analyzed the statistical properties of credit default swaps (CDS) in abstraction from a default situation, we now consider the mechanisms in the vega sector of the volatility surface in abstraction from the connection (through delta hedging) to the realized volatility.

Thus, the vega sector of the volatility surface is the right place to apply a statistical tool like a PCA-based factor model. And conversely, the application of PCA on the volatility surface confirms empirically its differentiation into gamma and vega sectors. Running a PCA on the whole volatility surface reflects the break between the gamma and vega segments in different sensitivities to the first factor. As Figure 17.20 shows, sensitivity starts decreasing as the expiry increases – and even turns negative for very long expiries. The fact that the first eigenvector has entries with different signs is a clear indication for segmentation in the input variables and justifies empirically our approach to limit the statistical analysis to the vega sector.

FIGURE 17.20 First eigenvector of a PCA on the whole JPY volatility surface.

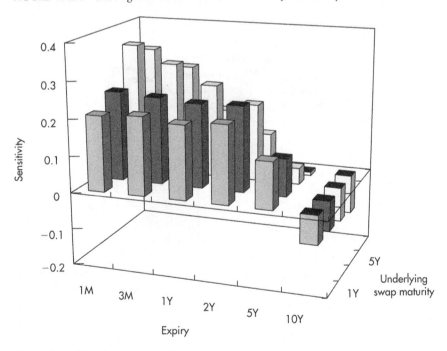

Sources: data – Bloomberg; chart – Authors.
Data period: 5 Jan 2009 to 19 Sep 2011, weekly data.

Restricting the data input to options with at least 2Y to expiry indeed solves the problem and returns a first eigenvector which has only negative entries (Figure 17.21). That is, this first factor can be interpreted as the overall implied volatility level, which affects all instruments in the same direction, though to a different extent. Figure 17.21 also reveals the location of the break between the gamma and vega sectors in the JPY swaption market. For the 2Y expiry, only underlyings of more than 5Y are clearly in the vega segment, while, for a 5Y expiry, all options can be considered to be in the vega sector, independent of the maturity of the underlying swap. In terms of Figure 17.5, this means that in the case of Japan the borderline between the two segments is somewhat tilted to the right. That is, the longer the maturity of the underlying swap, the shorter the expiry needs to be in order for an option to be part of the vega sector (e.g. four years for an option on 1Y swaps, three years for an option on 2Y swaps, and two years for an option on 5Y swaps).

FIGURE 17.21   First eigenvector of a PCA on the vega sector of the JPY volatility surface.

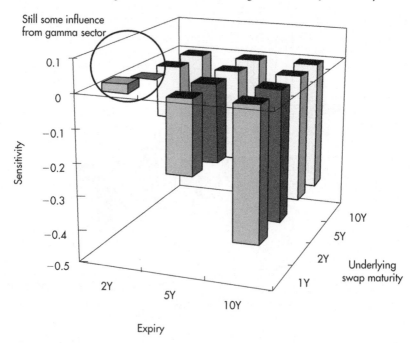

Sources: data – Bloomberg; chart – Authors.
Data period: 5 Jan 2009 to 19 Sep 2011, weekly data.

Now that PCA has revealed the sector of the volatility surface on which it is applicable, we can run through the usual analytical process, whose results are depicted in Figure 17.22, Figure 17.23, and Figure 17.24.

Factor 1 can be interpreted as the overall level of implied volatility, with the shape of the first eigenvector showing the way changes in overall volatility impact the volatility surface. Factor 2 represents the steepness of volatility curves (same underlying, different expiries). If factor 2 increases, options with a long expiry increase relative to those with a short expiry, almost independent of the underlying swap maturity. Factor 3 represents the steepness of volatility curves (same expiry, different underlyings). If factor 3 increases, options with a long underlying swap maturity increase relative to those with a short underlying swap maturity, almost independent of the expiry.

Thus, PCA can be considered a decomposition of the volatility surface into its two dimensions, with the second and third factors quantifying the variation that occurs in a specific dimension. Factor 1 represents the *overall* implied volatility level and correspondingly affects *both* dimensions. Factors 2 and 3 explain that part of implied volatility which occurs in a specific dimension of the volatility surface and is not already explained by the overall volatility level unspecific to a certain dimension. The result is an appealing breakdown of the pricing action among the multitude of options into three factors and two dimensions, with one overall factor (1) and one dimension-specific factor (2 and 3) for each of the two dimensions. This result can also

FIGURE 17.22 Scaled eigenvalues of a PCA on the vega sector of the JPY volatility surface.

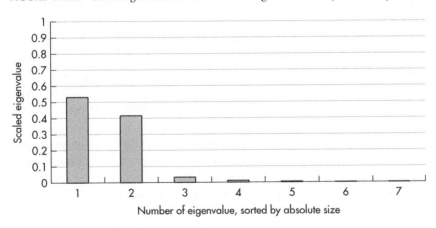

Sources: data – Bloomberg; chart – Authors.
Data period: 5 Jan 2009 to 19 Sep 2011, weekly data.

FIGURE 17.23   Second eigenvector of a PCA on the vega sector of the JPY volatility surface.

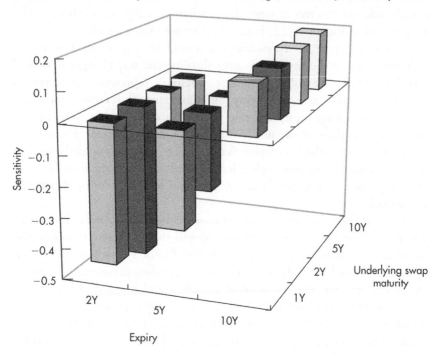

Sources: data – Bloomberg; chart – Authors.
Data period: 5 Jan 2009 to 19 Sep 2011, weekly data.

serve as a basis for trades on both implied volatility curves (those with variation across expiry and those with variation across underlying swap maturity). As explained above, trades on factor 2 (i.e. over different expiries) are only reasonable in the vega part of the volatility surface.[18] In that segment, however, the high scaled second eigenvalue (Figure 17.22) suggests that they have a significant impact on the shape of the volatility surface. PCA provides the right framework to approach those important trading strategies, and we shall give an example subsequently.

These results can vary for other option markets, and it is possible that factors 2 and 3 change place, that is that the variation across the dimension of same-expiry volatility curves is more important (has a higher scaled eigenvalue) than the variation across the dimension of same-underlying-swap-maturity

---

[18] Correspondingly, trades in the gamma sector always used options of the same expiry and considered only relative value across the volatility curve over different underlying swap maturities.

FIGURE 17.24   Third eigenvector of a PCA on the vega sector of the JPY volatility surface.

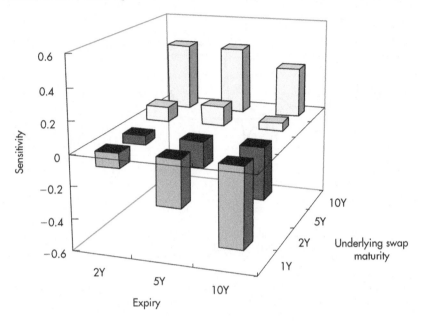

Sources: data – Bloomberg; chart – Authors.
Data period: 5 Jan 2009 to 19 Sep 2011, weekly data.

volatility curves. If the second and third eigenvalues are close (unlike in Japan), it is even possible that in the same option market such a switch takes place (i.e. that the two dimensions have different relative importance at different points in time). This is a problem for PCA-based trades on the volatility surface, which we shall discuss in the next section.

The statistical properties of the first three factors displayed in Figure 17.25 classify trades both on factors 1 and 2 as rather long-term (slow speed of mean reversion) macroeconomic strategies. Also note the significant correlation between factors 1 and 2 during subperiods, which can be a problem for relative value trades on factor 2. (See Chapter 3.) Thus in Japan, factor 3 is the only source for good relative value trades on the volatility surface, exhibiting a high speed of mean reversion and little correlation to factor 1 or 2 during subperiods. A trade on factor 3 is a position on the volatility *curve* (same expiry, different underlying swap maturities), which requires *three* instruments, a fact that may seem a bit puzzling at first. Again, the situation is different in other markets, where both factors 2 and 3 could offer relative value trades on the volatility surface with a high speed of mean reversion.

FIGURE 17.25 First three factors of a PCA on the vega sector of the JPY volatility surface.

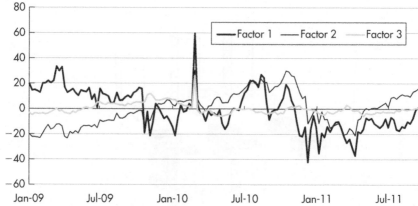

Sources: data – Bloomberg; chart – Authors.
Data period: 5 Jan 2009 to 19 Sep 2011, weekly data.

TABLE 17.1 Correlation of the First Three Factors of a PCA on the Vega Sector of the JPY Volatility Surface versus some Candidates for Explaining Variables

	SPX	VIX	Oil	BSW	5Y swap rate	Vol of vol
Factor 1	**−0.73**	0.52	−0.70	0.06	0.39	0.07
Factor 2	0.37	−0.34	0.34	−0.16	**−0.75**	−0.44
Factor 3	−0.11	−0.14	−0.02	0.15	0.21	−0.36

As always, one can link the PCA factors to external explaining variables (Table 17.1). While types ① and ② directly link options to the underlying as an external explaining variable, the approach of type ③ first analyses the *internal* relationships and might then also additionally consider external variables. These external explaining variables could of course include the underlying, and in the case of Japan it turns out that the yield level is in fact significantly correlated to factor 2 (confirming the impression from the statistical analysis that it is a rather macroeconomic strategy). Factor 1 shows a high degree of correlation to "risk" variables such as stock and commodity prices. Together, this means that demand for risk assets determines the overall level of volatility, affecting both dimensions of the volatility surface (factor 1). The overall level of underlying swap rates affects the differentiation between expiries (i.e. the dimension of factor 2). The differentiation between underlying swap maturities (i.e. the dimension of factor 3), on the other hand, seems to be largely uncorrelated to external macroeconomic variables, which is in line with its statistical properties as a rather "pure" relative value factor.

Again, the picture is different for other currencies. For example, at times factor 2 can be linked to the volatility of volatility, a result which might be used to replace the variable "volatility of volatility", which is of importance in many pricing models (SABR in particular) but does not trade, with the tradable and hedgeable variable "factor 2".

Given the statistical results and their economic interpretation, we would see no compelling relative value trade in the vega sector of the JPY volatility surface at the moment. The relative value factor 3 is close to its mean, and factors 1 and 2 represent macroeconomic events. In order to illustrate the way to construct a PCA trade on the vega part of the volatility surface, however, let's assume that we believe that factor 2 is too high (Figure 17.25) and will decrease in the future, perhaps because we expect interest rates to increase. Let's also assume that we have some good reason to expect the correlation with factor 1 will no longer continue.

In this case, we can look at the 1-factor residuals shown in Figure 17.26 and conclude that a short 2Y5Y versus long 10Y5Y straddle offers the best (though still rather small) profit potential. Hedge ratios are calculated according to the general PCA concept. The result is a position on the implied volatility curve (in the dimension of different expiries), hedged against changes to the overall level of implied volatility and its impact on the volatility surface (as given by the first eigenvector). If a hedge against factor 3 is desired as well (e.g. in case of the third eigenvalue being relatively high), expressing the position on factor 2 requires three instruments.

In conceptual terms, option trades of type ③ are hedged against the first factor (i.e. against changes to the overall level of implied volatility and its impact on the volatility surface). In contrast, types ① and ② hedge options against the underlying (delta hedging instead of vega hedging). Thus, the general approach of type ③ to treat implied volatility as an abstract statistical time series is correctly reflected in the choice of both the analytical tool and the hedge ratios of the trade execution. Note again that the low exposure of straddles in the vega sector to changes in the underlying is the basis that allows us to treat that part of the volatility surface conceptually by PCA statistics and to hedge against the implied volatility level rather than delta hedging.

Given the link of factor 2 to macroeconomic variables, a relative value analyst could be tempted to trade factor 2 *versus* the swap rate, thereby solving a number of problems. He obtains a relative value position hedged against the level of the macro variable "swap rate" (and against the level of the macro

FIGURE 17.26   1-factor residuals of a PCA on the vega sector of the JPY volatility surface.

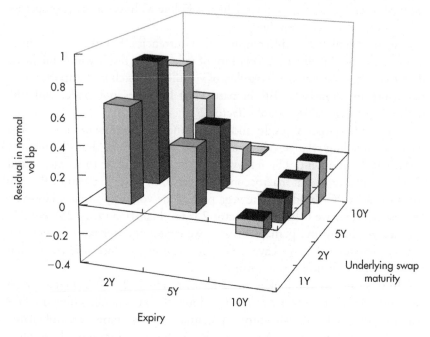

Sources: data – Bloomberg; chart – Authors.
Data period: "Current" market data as of 19 Sep 2011.

variable "factor 2"), which could well have a much better speed of mean reversion than factor 2. The basis for this trade is shown in Figure 17.27.

Unfortunately, the current point is close to the regression line and the relative value trade between factor 2 and the 5Y swap rate offers little profit potential (just as the "relative value factor" 3 in Figure 17.25). Moreover, there seems to be a break in the relationship, with the points in Figure 17.27 lying on two separate regression lines. All in all, we have run the right tools and tried hard, but the vega sector of the JPY option market simply does not provide a good relative value opportunity at the moment. As we have used throughout the book mainly examples that illustrate profitable trading strategies revealed through relative value analysis, we found it fair to finish with one example in which a proper relative value analysis leads to the correct conclusion that there are no good relative value trades. This is the more frequent experience relative value analysts will encounter, but which will in turn keep them on the lookout for the few really exceptional opportunities.

FIGURE 17.27 Factor 2 as a function of the 5Y swap rate.

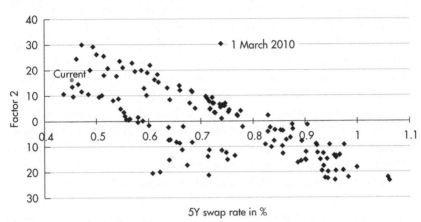

Sources: data – Bloomberg; chart – Authors.
Data period: 5 Jan 2009 to 19 Sep 2011, weekly data; "current" market data as of 19 Sep 2011.

Imagine an analyst who had set up the models developed here and run them on a daily basis. After many disappointing days, on 1 March 2010 a glance at Figure 17.27 would have given him an excellent relative value trade, returning a high profit within less than a week.

Pitfalls of Option Trades of Type ③

Treating options in the vega sector through a statistical model like PCA can be justified conceptually, as above, but involves a number of potential problems:

- While a one-dimensional yield curve usually has a clear factor structure, with the second eigenvalue being much larger than the third (Figure 3.4 and Figure 3.24), the two-dimensional volatility surface leads to the second and third eigenvalue being often of similar magnitude (unlike in Figure 17.22, which depicts the specific situation for Japan). The reason is that both the second and third factors of a PCA on the volatility surface represent curve steepness, just in two different dimensions. By contrast, a PCA on the one-dimensional yield *curve* contains all steepness information in the second factor only, with the third factor representing the (much less influential) curvature information in the same dimension. Therefore, higher-order eigenvectors tend to be less stable on the volatility surface than on yield curves. Moreover, the second and third factors can change their relative importance, which is a problem for PCA-hedged volatility curve trades.

- The ability to hedge against the first factor (i.e. the implied volatility level rather than delta hedging against the underlying) is based on the precondition that no delta hedging is required due to the low exposure of straddles in the vega sector to changes in the underlying. Over long periods of time, however, large moves in the underlying could violate that precondition and introduce an additional, unhedged P&L component.
- While theta is low in the vega sector, it could start to matter when holding horizons become very long. This is particularly the case when the thetas of the options involved are significantly different (e.g. in trades on a volatility curve with the same underlying and different expiries).

In general, it is important for any trade based on statistical tools to compare the time horizon over which mean reversion is expected to occur with the stability of statistical relationships. Just as in the case of statistical trades on the CDS curve, it is acceptable to ignore potential problems if the speed of mean reversion is significantly faster than the time horizon over which the assumed statistical relationships could break down. Applying these techniques can also mitigate the potential problems involved in the statistical analysis for option trades of type ③ (such as different thetas in the case of a factor 2 trade), since all three pitfalls are rather long-term issues that are less likely to affect trades with a short holding horizon. We therefore recommend restricting option trades of type ③ to such positions, whose speed of mean reversion suggests performance well before the problems described above are expected to become relevant.

Conclusion: Summary of Option Trade Types and Their Different Exposure

In general, we can summarize the exposure of the different types of option trades as follows. With only one underlying, all three types are rather fundamental positions, though exposed to a different fundamental variable:

- Type ① with a single underlying is exposed to the absolute level (direction) of the underlying.
- Type ② with a single underlying is exposed to the absolute level (direction) of the realized volatility.

- Type ③ with a single underlying is exposed to the absolute level (direction) of the implied volatility.

Adding at least a second underlying allows hedging against that fundamental exposure to the absolute level (direction) of a variable highly influenced by macroeconomic events and thereby constructing relative value positions. In particular:

- Type ② with (at least) two underlyings is hedged against the absolute level of *realized* volatility (and not exposed to changes in the level of implied volatility by nature).
- Type ③ with (at least) two underlyings is hedged against the absolute level of *implied* volatility (and essentially not exposed to the level of realized volatility).

Thus,

- Type ② with (at least) two underlyings is a relative value trade on the *realized* volatility curve.
- Type ③ with (at least) two underlyings is a relative value trade on the *implied* volatility curve.

CHAPTER 18

Relative Value in a Broader Perspective

Introduction

After focusing on the technical aspects of relative value analysis and trading, we conclude our discussion by taking a broader perspective on the macro-economic functions of relative value analysis in society. At a time when professionals in the financial services industry increasingly need to justify their role in society, we believe it's useful to offer a few thoughts about the role of arbitrage in society.

The Macroeconomic Role of Relative Value Analysis and Trading

The term *standard of living* means different things to different people. A macroeconomist might think of GDP per person when he hears this term. Parents might think of the infant mortality rate, while retirees might think of expected longevity. Teachers might think of literacy rates, and doctors might think of rates of disease, such as tuberculosis, cholera, and malaria.

But whatever one thinks about when one hears this term, one thing stands out when comparing standards of living across societies and over time: societies that rely on free markets to organize economic activity tend to have higher standards of living than societies that rely on central planning to allocate scarce resources.

Skeptics might raise the examples of Denmark or Sweden, with their generous social models and expansive public sectors. Or they may cite the

349

example of China, with her rapid growth rates under state capitalism. But China didn't see living standards increase until Deng made it acceptable to harness the market economy in China, and the examples of East and West Germany and of North and South Korea are usually sufficient to persuade all but the most ideological skeptics.

Market economies tend to deliver higher standards of living because prices determined in free markets act as reliable signals with which market participants can identify the best opportunities for scarce capital to improve productivity, which in the end is responsible for increases in standards of living.

For prices to act as reliable signals, they need to be efficient, in the sense that they need to reflect information that is available and relevant, particularly information pertaining to the supply and demand of the item in question. Much has been written about whether financial markets *are* informationally efficient – but there's little disagreement that financial markets *should be* informationally efficient if we want an effective allocation of capital. If a financial market was informationally inefficient, we would expect capital to be allocated in a way that resulted in few improvements in productivity.

The need for market efficiency brings us to the role of the arbitrageur, who makes a living by identifying and exploiting misvaluations among tradable instruments. As we noted in the introduction, a market characterized by too little arbitrage capital and too few arbitrageurs is a market that is likely to be plagued by market inefficiency, mispriced instruments, and ultimately an allocation of capital that does little to improve living standards in society.

While it might be an exaggeration to claim that arbitrageurs are responsible for improvements in living standards directly, arbitrageurs do play an important role in improving market efficiency and in reducing the incidence of mispriced securities – functions that are critical if capital in society is to be allocated efficiently.

Critics argue that many arbitrageurs are uninterested in living standards in society and act only in their own self-interest. To this, we have two retorts. First, the prevalence of charitable giving among hedge fund managers calls into question whether this characterization is accurate.

But second is the observation of Adam Smith: "It is not from the benevolence of the butcher, the brewer, or the baker, that we expect our dinner, but from their regard to their own interest".[1] Idealists may wish the world were other than Smith observed it in 1776, but until they find a better

---

[1] From Chapter 2 of *An Inquiry into the Nature and Causes of the Wealth of Nations*, by Adam Smith, published in 1776.

way to enlighten the masses than did Mao and Lenin, we should consider ourselves fortunate to have an economic system that marshals self-interest toward pursuits that provide others with meat, bread, beer – and greater efficiency in capital markets.

In a capitalist society, the economic benefit of an individual is linked to the economic benefit that individual's actions provide for society. The profit of arbitrageurs can therefore be considered as the fee for their service of supporting optimal capital allocation across the productive purposes of a society.

Arbitrageurs and Politicians

We acknowledge that there is a role for government intervention to ensure the functioning of free markets *in general* (e.g. preventing market failures or monopolies on natural resources) and limit our discussion to *excessive* interventions pursuing *particular* political objectives.

One result of excessive government intervention is very likely to be a market mispricing, potentially even an arbitrage opportunity. And the economic cost of this mispricing is likely to be a less optimal allocation of capital, with implications for productivity, growth, and living standards.

The market mispricing caused by excessive government intervention, like all mispricings in the market, is likely to be identified and exploited by arbitrageurs. And if there are enough arbitrageurs with sufficient arbitrage capital, the mispricing is likely to be mitigated and perhaps even eliminated, resulting in an undistorted set of prices that leads to improved capital allocation and ultimately to higher living standards.

The good news in this case is that society avoids the permanently higher costs associated with inefficient capital markets. But the bad news is that the government has created a mispricing in the market that has led to even greater profits for arbitrageurs. Of course the source of the profit in this case is the government. And in most societies, this means that the source is taxpayers. The result is that the government has transferred capital from society in general to arbitrageurs in particular. In fact, the mispricing as expressed by relative value relationships (i.e. the difference between the politically desired market equilibrium and the natural market equilibrium) is a measure of the ultimate cost of the interventionist strategy in the presence of arbitrage.

Arbitrage transforms the economic cost of excessive intervention from an inefficient capital allocation permanently affecting the whole society to a one-off cost to taxpayers from being on the losing side of arbitrage trades. Thus, in the presence of state intervention, the benefit of arbitrage to society is that it maintains functioning capital markets at a relatively low cost.

Let's consider some of the repercussions of excessive government intervention in greater detail:

(1) The mispricing is backed by taxpayers and central banks and can thus become larger and last longer than usual.
(2) The beneficial function of arbitrage for society appears now to be in opposition to political goals.
(3) Politicians have an incentive to blame their losses on arbitrageurs, concealing their beneficial function for society.

With regards to (1), it may be helpful to recall Mises' argument, that *partial* political impacts on the market (like keeping yields artificially below their natural level or suppressing prices) will not work.[2] If the intervention spiral does not lead to the abolition of free markets altogether, it will sooner or later come to an end. This means that at some point the government's influence on the market will disappear (if the market does not disappear instead). And consequently, relative value analysis would be correct in treating political intervention just like statistical noise, creating trading opportunities via disruptions of the natural market equilibrium that cannot last forever. However, given the large firepower of governments and the political will to pursue the intervention spiral, political impacts on the market can cause unusually large and long-lasting mispricings. In other words, governments have the ability to create a lot of noise in the markets. From a practical point of view, it is therefore essential to adjust the threshold for entering into arbitrage positions upwards now that the government is on the other side of the trade.[3] Conversely, the profit potential from eventually correcting imbalances is nowadays also especially large.

With regards to (2), the high profits of arbitrage trades when governments intervene in markets is a clear indication that the improvement in capital allocation and therefore of living standards resulting from the actions of arbitrageurs are of considerable value to society. In our view, one implication is that government intervention involves paying unnecessarily high fees to arbitrageurs.

---

[2] Ludwig von Mises, *Theorie des Geldes und der Umlaufsmittel*, 2nd edition, p. 232.
[3] Or alternatively to concentrate on those relative value relationships likely to be unaffected by political market interventions, for example those expressed in the higher factors of a PCA.

Taking just the last trade described in Chapter 16 as an example, the political decision to create the euro has caused significant imbalances in the distribution of capital among European economies, most recently the concentration of capital in the Bund market. This comes at an economic cost to Germany, which may suffer from trying to invest too much capital, and to the periphery, which suffers now from having too little capital to invest. This imbalance shows up in Figure 16.10 and prompted us to enter into the arbitrage position short Bunds/long Irish government bonds versus short German CDS/long Irish CDS. That trade helps correct the misallocation of capital among Eurozone bond markets by shifting funds from the Bund market into the Irish economy. If politicians reacted by stepping further down the intervention spiral and outlawing the use of CDS, this arbitrage would become impossible and society would have to bear the economic cost of permanently misallocated capital across Eurozone economies.

In summary, a democratic and capitalist society choosing excessive market intervention is contradicting itself. The intervention leads to lower living standards, so that the superficial political goals threaten the capitalistic foundation of that society. Choosing market intervention means choosing to pay an unnecessarily high price to arbitrageurs in order to maintain functioning capital allocation *despite* the intervention. Transferring taxpayer funds to arbitrageurs is an act of free will on the part of politicians.

That contradiction within society manifests itself as opposition between arbitrageurs and politicians. It leads to politicians considering the actions of arbitrageurs as being opposed to their goals and to ignoring the crucial service of arbitrage to society. The less a capitalist society understands its own foundations, the less it and its politicians understand the benefits of arbitrage.

The Misrepresentation of Arbitrage by Politicians

A fair representation of the function of arbitrageurs in a market suffering from political intervention would be something like this. The government decides to create a market imbalance, which arbitrageurs correct, continuing to provide the service of a functioning free market to society *and* profiting from the correcting imbalance. Focusing only on their interventionist goals, politicians tend to ignore the *benefits* of the actions of arbitrageurs and simply see them *profiting* from *opposing* the intentions of the government.

The narrow, interventionist perspective of governments explains the common misrepresentation of the function of arbitrage as "profit from opposing the state".

- **It isolates the fee from the service:** Arbitrageurs profit *because* they reestablish market efficiency, despite government intervention disturbing rational capital allocation. They transform the immense cost of suboptimal capital allocation into the small cost of their arbitrage profit. For a very modest fee, they maintain for society the invaluable benefit of free markets.
- **It confuses cause and effect:** The free decision of governments to disturb market equilibriums is the cause of the cost to society. The opposition between arbitrageurs and politicians is only the superficial manifestation of the contradiction in the heart of a capitalist society which has chosen to intervene in the free markets it requires. And it is the government and not the arbitrageurs who have caused that contradiction.

Arbitrageurs provide a service to society. Unfortunately, they also provide a convenient scapegoat for governments frustrated by the results of their interventions. In this case, governments confuse cause and effect. Governments point to arbitrageurs as the cause of the costs borne by society, motivating government intervention. They cite the profits of arbitrageurs as an unjustifiable cost for society, failing to link the profits arbitrageurs earn with the benefits they provide by promoting more efficient markets, more effective capital allocation, greater productivity, and higher standards of living.

What can a relative value analyst reply? All these "arguments" painting arbitrage as being opposed to society can easily be refuted by pointing out that the arbitrageurs are acting in line with the well-understood interests of a capitalist society, while its politicians, lacking that understanding in pursuing excessive interventionism, are not. The fact that arbitrageurs are able to profit from government intervention, at the cost of governments, is consistent with arbitrageurs acting to protect an essential element of capitalism, which is being attacked by governments, to the detriment of society.

Conclusion: Political Implications of Relative Value

Relative value analysis is founded on the presumption of free markets populated by rational actors. As a result, taking relative value positions requires faith that government intervention is ephemeral and not the first steps on the slippery slope leading to the abolition of free markets.

In recent years, however, that faith has been tested, as interventionist politics have become a more prominent feature of the market, working against the interests of efficient capital allocation. In contrast, the economic function of relative value analysis continues to support the efficient allocation of capital, via the improved informational efficiency that results when self-interested arbitrageurs identify and exploit pricing anomalies in the capital markets.

As part of the campaign to justify increased market intervention, governments and their apologists have found it useful to demonize speculators, branding them "locusts" and characterizing the foundation of neoclassical economics as "market fundamentalism", a pejorative designed to impugn the motives of those who advocate market mechanisms for allocating resources. But the vast majority of speculators also happen to be citizens of democracies and as such understand the roles played by the implementation and enforcement of regulations, including those that constrain the space of possible outcomes within otherwise free markets.

However, governments no longer seem content merely to constrain the space of possible economic outcomes. Instead, they intervene with increasing force and frequency in an attempt to engineer specific economic outcomes. As a result, capital is being allocated increasingly on the basis of political processes and government intervention rather than on the basis of productivity enhancement and economic return. We agree that even free markets can be subject to bouts of irrational exuberance, resulting in capital allocations that at times produce poor results. But we don't believe history supports the notion that increased government intervention results in more effective capital allocation. In fact, we believe a fair reading of history supports precisely the opposite view that improvements in living standards over time tend to vary inversely with the level of government intervention in the markets.

If the demonization and demagoguery are left unanswered, the risk is that societies will restrict speculative activities to the point that the informational efficiency of the markets is diminished, reducing the effectiveness of informed capital allocation. Therefore, it's important that we remind ourselves of the important role played by arbitrageurs.

Arbitrageurs are no more motivated by self-interest than were the butchers, brewers, and bakers of whom Adam Smith wrote in 1776, nor is the informational efficiency contributed by arbitrageurs any less praiseworthy than the meat, beer, and bread in Smith's examples. But because market efficiency is a more abstract contribution, and because arbitrage at times has generated significant returns for its practitioners, arbitrageurs and speculators, they appear as attractive scapegoats for politicians presiding over financial crises. But scapegoating is a poor substitute for sound public policy, and we're proud to advocate for a strong, effective and continuing role for arbitrageurs in helping to ensure efficient markets, productive capital allocation, and higher living standards for all.

Bibliography

Arrow, K. J., Debreu, G. (July 1954) Existence of an equilibrium for a competitive economy. *Econometrica,* **22**(3): 265–90.

Black, F., Scholes, M. (May/June 1973) The pricing of options and corporate liabilities. *Journal of Political Economy* **81**(3): 637–54.

Burghardt, G., Belton, T. (2005) *The Treasury Bond Basis: An In-Depth Analysis for Hedgers, Speculators, and Arbitrageurs.* New York: McGraw-Hill.

Burghardt, G. (2003) *The Eurodollar Futures and Options Handbook.* New York: McGraw-Hill.

Choudhry, M. (2006) *The Credit Default Swap Basis.* New York: Bloomberg Press.

Duffie, D. (June 1996) Special repo rates. *Journal of Finance* **51**(2): 493–526.

Einstein, A. (April 1934) On the method of theoretical physics. *Philosophy of Science* **1**(2): 163–9.

Friedman, M. (1953) "The methodology of positive economics." In: *Essays in Positive Economics.* Chicago: University of Chicago Press.

Huberman, G. (October 1982) Arbitrage pricing theory: A simple approach. *Journal of Economic Theory* **28**(1): 183–98.

Huggins, D. (April 2000) "Convexity and the upcoming 2032 gilt." *Deutsche Bank Fixed Income Weekly.*

Huggins, D. (1997) *Estimation of a Diffusion Process for the U.S. Short Interest Rate Using a Semigroup Pseudo Likelihood.* Unpublished doctoral dissertation. University of Chicago Graduate School of Business.

Ilmanen, A. (September 1996) Market rate expectations and forward rates. *Journal of Fixed Income* **6**(2): 8–22.

Ilmanen, A. (2011) *Expected Returns: An Investor's Guide to Harvesting Market Rewards.* Chichester: John Wiley & Sons, Ltd.

Ilmanen, A. (April 2011). *Expected Returns: An Investor's Guide to Harvesting Market Rewards* (Wiley Finance). Kindle edition (Kindle Locations 12474–12475). John Wiley & Sons, Ltd.

Merton, R. C. (1973) Theory or rational option pricing. *Bell Journal of Economics and Management Science* **4**(1): 141–83.

Moulton, P. C. (June 2004) Relative repo specialness in U.S. Treasuries. *Journal of Fixed Income* **14**(1): 40–47.

Ross, S. A. (December 1976). The arbitrage theory of capital asset pricing. *Journal of Economic Theory* **13**(3): 341–60.

Schaller, C. (February 2002) Exploiting the ignored delivery option in JGB contracts. *ABN Amro Research note*.

Stanton, R. H. (September 1995) *A Nonparametric Model of Term Structure Dynamics and the Market Price of Interest Rate Risk*. Available at SSRN: http://ssrn.com/abstract=6751.

Stigum, M., Crescenzi, A. (2007) *Stigum's Money Market*. New York: McGraw-Hill.

Tuckman, B., Serrat, A. (2011) *Fixed Income Securities: Tools for Today's Markets*. Chichester: John Wiley & Sons, Ltd.

Index

Note: Italic page numbers denote figures.